Advance Praise for

The Slave Master of Trinidad

"An original work that will appeal to academics, university students, and general readers studying Trinidad and Caribbean history in the late slavery and emancipation periods."
—Bridget Brereton, author of
A History of Modern Trinidad, 1783–1962

"*The Slave Master of Trinidad* is an unbelievably bold book that retells the story of slavery, emancipation, and indentured labor through an account of Burnley's life and work."
—Nicholas Draper, author of *The Price of Emancipation: Slave-Ownership, Compensation, and British Society at the End of Slavery*

The
Slave Master
of Trinidad

The
Slave Master
of Trinidad

WILLIAM HARDIN BURNLEY AND THE
NINETEENTH-CENTURY ATLANTIC WORLD

SELWYN R. CUDJOE

University of Massachusetts Press
Amherst and Boston

Copyright © 2018 by University of Massachusetts Press
All rights reserved
Printed in the United States of America

ISBN 978-1-62534-370-3 (paper); 369-7 (hardcover)

Designed by Sally Nichols
Set in Adobe Minion Pro and Dear Sarah
Printed and bound by Maple Press, Inc.

Cover design by Milenda Nan Ok Lee
Cover art: *Portrait of William Hardin Burnley,* colorized photograph of
black and white daguerreotype found in *From Colonial to Republic: One
Hundred and Fifty Years of Business and Banking in Trinidad
and Tobago, 1837–1987* (Port of Spain: Paria Publishing, 1987).

Library of Congress Cataloging-in-Publication Data

Names: Cudjoe, Selwyn R. (Selwyn Reginald), author.
Title: The slave master of Trinidad : William Hardin Burnley and the
nineteenth-century Atlantic world / selwyn R. Cudjoe.
Description: Amherst : University of Massachusetts Press, [2018] |
Includes bibliographical references and index. |
Identifiers: LCCN 2018019142 (print) | LCCN 2018045985 (ebook) | ISBN
9781613766163 (e-book) | ISBN 9781613766170 (e-book) | ISBN
9781625343703 | ISBN 9781625343703?(pbk.) | ISBN 9781625343697?(hardcover)
Subjects: LCSH: Burnley, William Hardin, 1780–1850. |
Slaveholders—Trinidad
and Tobago—Trinidad—Biography. | Slavery—Trinidad and
Tobago—Trinidad—History—19th century.
Classification: LCC F2120 (ebook) | LCC F2120 .C83 2018 (print) | DDC
306.3/62097298309034—dc23
LC record available at https://lccn.loc.gov/2018019142

British Library Cataloguing-in-Publication Data
A catalog record for this book is available from the British Library.

For my grandsons: William, Joshua, and Christopher

Contents

Abbreviations

The following primary sources, works by Burnley and selected other works, are abbreviated in the text.

AM   *Anti-Slavery Monthly Reporter.* London: 1825, 1827. British Newspaper Archive at the British Library.

AR   *Anti-Slavery Reporter.* London: 1841, 1842. British Newspaper Archive at the British Library.

C   *Colonial Gazette.* London: 1842. British Newspaper Archive at the British Library.

CO   Records of the Colonial Office, Commonwealth and Foreign and Commonwealth Offices, Empire Marketing Board, and related bodies. National Archives, Richmond, United Kingdom.

D   Burnley, William Hardin. *Description of the Island of Trinidad and of the Advantages to be derived from Emigration to that Colony.* New York: James van Norden, 1839.

DL   Parliamentary Papers (House of Commons). *Report from the Select Committee on the Disposal of Lands in the British Colonies.* August 1836.

G   *Glasgow Courier.* Glasgow: 1842. British Newspaper Archive at the British Library.

GE   *Gazette Extraordinary.* London: 1832. British Newspaper Archive at the British Library.

H   Fraser, Lionel Mordaunt. *History of Trinidad: From 1814 to 1839*, vol. 2. Port of Spain: Government Printing Office, 1891.

HT   Fraser, Lionel Mordaunt. *History of Trinidad: From 1781 to 1813*, vol. 1. Port of Spain: Government Printing Office, 1891.

L   *London Times.* London: 1842. British Newspaper Archive at the British Library.

M   *The Morning Herald.* London: 1842. British Newspaper Archive at the British Library.

N   *Naval and Military Gazette*. London: 1842. British Newspaper Archive
     at the British Library.

O   Burnley, William Hardin. *Observations on the Present Condition of
     the Island of Trinidad; and the Actual State of the Experiment of Negro
     Emancipation*. London: Longman, Brown, Green and Longmans, 1842;
     also, *Abolition de l'esclavage dans les colonies anglais. Observations sur
     la situation actuel de lile de la Trinite*. Paris: imprimerie royal, 1842.
     National Archives of Trinidad and Tobago, Port of Spain.

OG   Lamont, Norman. *Burnley of Orange Grove*. Port of Spain: Port of
     Spain Gazette, 1947.

OS   Burnley, William Hardin. *Opinions on Slavery and Emancipation in
     1823: referred to in a recent debate in the House Commons, by Thomas
     Fowell Buxton, Esq., with Additional Observations, applicable to the
     Right Hon. E. G. Stanley's Plan for the Extinction of Slavery*. London:
     James Ridgway, Piccadilly, 1833.

PG   *Port of Spain Gazette*. Port of Spain: 1832, 1835, 1842–44, 1846–51, 1887.
     National Archives of Trinidad and Tobago and Newspaper Archive at
     the British Library.

PO   *Public Opinion*. Port of Spain: 1887, 1888. National Archives of Trinidad
     and Tobago.

SC   *Report from the Select Committee on West India Colonies*. Port of Spain:
     House of Commons, July 25, 1842. National Archives of Trinidad and
     Tobago.

SF   *San Fernando Gazette*. San Fernando: 1850. National Archives of Trini-
     dad and Tobago.

TC   *Trinidad Colonist*. Port of Spain: 1863. National Archives of Trinidad
     and Tobago.

TG   *Trinidad Guardian*. Port of Spain: 1921. National Archives of Trinidad
     and Tobago.

TN   *Trinidad Negroes: Extracts from the Minutes take by the Committee of
     the Council for Trinidad, for enquiring into the Negroe Character*. Con-
     ducted by W. H. Burnley. London: House of Commons, June 14, 1827.

TR   *Trinidadian*. Port of Spain: 1839–40, 1848–51. National Archives of
     Trinidad and Tobago.

TRG *Trinidad Royal Gazette*. Port of Spain: 1833, 1846, 1921. National Archives
     of Trinidad and Tobago.

TS   *Trinidad Standard*. Port of Spain: 1839, 1842. National Archives of Trinidad
     and Tobago.

Prologue

Burnley at Orange Grove

Biographies have the ability to ease us into deep conceptual waters with quirky details and engaging stories . . . . Biographies give us more than just a sugar-laced kind of history. At their best, they show us a facet of history that history itself cannot.

—Christopher Caldwell, "No Sense of History without a Good Biography"

In the last week of 1850 William Burnley died. Although American-born, he was a founding father of British Trinidad and had been deeply involved in every controversy. . . . Burnley had been the largest slave-owner and the most powerful and eloquent advocate of immigrants to replace them. . . . No one else had so long an experience in the hurly-burly of public matters nor was there anyone else to speak with such authority for the conservative planting interest.

—Donald Wood, *Trinidad in Transition*

WILLIAM HARDIN BURNLEY, an American who was born of English parents, arrived in Trinidad, via England, in 1798. In 1802 he took up permanent residence on the island where he lived until he died in 1850. During the first half of the nineteenth century, he was considered one of the most learned and influential men on the island and a prominent personality in the discussion of colonial affairs. While he lived in Trinidad he had the good fortune to know and work with the first twelve British governors personally, beginning with Thomas Picton, the first governor, to Lord Harris, the twelfth governor of the island. During his time he dominated the islands' economic and political life in much the same way that Eric Williams, the late prime minister of Trinidad and Tobago,[1] dominated the island's national life during much of the second half of the twentieth century. He was not only the most important political figure in Trinidad but was also a central presence in British policy in these new colonial

territories. Donald Wood described him as "a founding father of British Trinidad [who] had been deeply involved in every controversy [in the colony]."[2]

As a planter and a member of the Council of Government (as the Legislative
Council was named at the time), his voice was also present in England during
the slavery, emancipation, and apprenticeship debates that took place between
1823 and 1838. His fight to maintain slavery, between 1832 and 1833; his opposition to the ending of apprenticeship; his search for new laborers for the colony
between 1834 and 1845; his attempt to stop the establishment of a railroad on
the island in 1847; his involvement in the laborers' rebellion in 1849; and his
opposition to the establishment of a postal system on the island in 1850 spoke
to his involvement in all the major events on the island during the first fifty
years of its existence.

When Hardin Burnley, William's father, died in 1823, he left an estate worth
£120,000, which placed him among the richest two dozen individuals dying in
Britain that year.[3] When William died in 1850 he was one of the largest *resident*
slave owners in the Caribbean. Although there were individuals who owned
more slaves or had mortgages over more enslaved people than Burnley, they
tended to be absentee landowners who lived in Britain. He left a net estate of
£122,697 and £94,296 in American securities, which were bequeathed to his
widow Charlotte, his sons, and his nieces and nephews, the children of his sister Maria and Joseph Hume. He even provided for his mistress, Mary Augusta
Farquhar; his "godson," William Burnley Farquhar; and Mary's daughter, Elizabeth Curson Farquhar. He owned three estates outright: Orange Grove, Providence, and Cedar Hill. He held mortgages on St. Clair, Sevilia, Washington
and Wilderness, Golden Grove, and La Soledad. He possessed some interest in
Carolina, Union Hall, and Mon Plaisir.[4] His son, William Frederick, owned five
estates for which he received approximately £12,112 in compensation.

Burnley's story is also intertwined with my family's history. We grew up
on the Orange Grove estate on land rented from William Burnley. My great-
grandfather, Jonathan Cudjoe, was born in Tacarigua on April 19, 1833, a year
before slavery was abolished formally. According to historian Bridget Brereton,
this made him "one of the so-called 'Free Children' [because] the Emancipation
Act stated that children who were under the age of six on August 1, 1834, would
not be forced into the apprenticeship scheme imposed on everyone else."[5] He
died on May 14, 1909. My great-grandmother, Amelia Cudjoe, was born on
August 1, 1837, one year before apprenticeship ended, and died on June 8, 1891.[6]

My grandfather, Robert James Cudjoe, son of Jonathan and Amelia, was
born on December 5, 1869. He married Delcina Moriah Bonas, who was born

in Barbados in 1875 but immigrated with her family to Trinidad. My great-great-grandfather was one of the enslaved Africans who squatted on the Orange Grove lands after slavery ended and continued to cultivate his provision grounds at the foothills of the Northern Range. He was one of the many squatters whom Burnley railed against after slavery ended. So while Burnley was castigating the newly freed people for squatting and planting their provision grounds, my great-great-grandfather was trying to make a life for himself and to establish himself as a Trinidadian in a new land amidst new social conditions.

Burnley was an important presence in Trinidad and abroad. His relationship with Joseph Hume, his brother-in-law and member of the British Parliament, gave him instant access to the Colonial Office, members of Parliament, and introductions to some of the major leaders of his time, including John Quincy Adams of the United States. Meanwhile, some of the family members he left in Virginia became very prominent in state affairs. Burnley described them as being among "the first people in Virginia" (*OG*, 8). When his uncle Zachariah Burnley died in 1800, he was considered "a man of prominence and wealth and ranked among the most patriotic citizens of the state."[7] Zachariah and James Madison, president of the United States, served as census enumerators in Orange County, Virginia, and enjoyed a close relationship. Emma Dicken observed: "The families of President James Madison, the Taylors and the Burnleys seemed to be intimate."[8] Zachariah was also the godfather of Elizabeth, the sister of President Monroe.

William Hardin Burnley belonged to an international company of scholars and activists that included Nassau W. Senior, professor of political economy at Oxford University and a member of the "Poor Law Commission,"[9] and Alexis de Tocqueville, author of *On Democracy in America* whom he met in America and in Paris. Between 1833 and 1839 he corresponded with William Gladstone, secretary of state for the colonies and later prime minister of Britain. Burnley was aware of Edward Gibbon Wakefield's theories of colonization of the new British colonies having testified with him on the parliamentary hearing that examined the disposal of new lands in the British Commonwealth. He was also familiar with the works of Adam Smith, David Ricardo (the best friend of his brother-in-law), and Jean-Baptiste Say, suggesting an acute knowledge of the political economy of the time.

Burnley harbored the prejudices that most white men of his time possessed. He believed that Europeans were superior to the Amerindians they encountered on the island when they arrived. He considered the South American peons who came to Trinidad to look for work as existing in a savage state. He saw Africans as children. He believed that "negroes were things far short of human," who were not yet ready for freedom and who had yet to evolve out of their half-savage state of existence. He believed that slavery was a divinely inspired institution from which many desirable benefits were derived. It was a necessary phase of human development out of which "a better and more improved system would ultimately rise."[10]

In spite of these shortcomings, Burnley was one of the most remarkable West Indians (albeit adopted) of the first half of the nineteenth century. He was an active observer of his time, navigating in a world of slavery, emancipation, apprenticeship, and the beginning of colonialism. Although he always looked out for himself, he also sought the interest of the island's planters to which he belonged. With the exception of Eric Williams, no one enjoyed a similar status on the island. Burnley was a slaveholder, but he was also a man of letters who studied the history of the region and possessed a philosophical view of the races in the society. One can say of Burnley what Christopher Hitchens said of Thomas Jefferson: "He was a man of practice as well as ideas and delighted in the composition of exhaustive reports [and letters]."[11] Each played a prominent part in shaping the political and social destinies of their respective societies, even though they held repulsive views of black people.[12] These views kept him yearning for a past that had ended.

Burnley left an enormous volume of writings—some published and some unpublished—all of which demonstrated his views on slavery, emancipation, and apprenticeship, the most pressing social and political issues of the time. On November 29, 1946, Sir Norman Lamont, the grandnephew of John Lamont (one of Burnley's dearest friends), drew on Burnley's letters, notebooks, and accounts when he offered "Burnley of Orange Grove," a lecture he delivered under the auspices of the Historical Society of Trinidad and Tobago in which he tried to piece together a connected story of Burnley's life.[13] Lamont acknowledged that during the first half of the nineteenth century Burnley was widely known as "Trinidad's richest man, the owner of its premier estate, and the most prominent figure in its political life" (OG, 1). Thus, "when an opportunity was given to me of exploring a boxful of his letters, note-books and accounts, I felt that they might contain material of interest to the Historical Society" (OG, 1).

In 1813 when Governor Ralph Woodford appointed Burnley to the Council of Government, he referred to Burnley as English-American. I argue that his importance must be understood within the context of his response to slavery, his relations with the enslaved Africans in his society, his fights with the various governors and the Colonial Office, and his conception of himself as a European

American, a sugar planter, and a man of letters. Franklin Kane reminds us that "the course of history depends on the daring of individuals who act in terms of goals that are historically viable."[14] Burnley's story is a narrative of a strong-willed person caught up in the traumatic changes of his time, bent on securing the best for himself and his family.

In his review of Robert Caro's fourth volume on the life of Lyndon Johnson, Christopher Caldwell observed that biography has the ability "to ease us into deep conceptual waters with quirky details and engaging stories." He continues, "At their best, they show us a facet of history that history itself cannot."[15] In this context, a well-told biography of William Hardin Burnley can ease the reader into the deeper currents of Trinidad and Tobago's early history and the titanic forces that shaped the Atlantic world of the nineteenth century without all the benumbing historical paraphernalia that sometimes obscures the richness of the period, place, and individual achievement. Focusing on the life and work of Burnley can add considerably to our understanding of the growth and development of Trinidad, Tobago, the Caribbean, the Americas, and even British colonial history.

Although it was not planned this way, *The Slave Master of Trinidad* can be seen as the front end of a Trinidad and Tobago journey, the back end of which was chronicled in Selwyn Ryan's *Eric Williams: The Myth and the Man*.[16] While Eric Williams stood center stage and virtually monopolized the last fifty years of twentieth-century Trinidad and Tobago's history, Burnley was at the center of the first fifty years of Trinidad and Tobago's development, shaping, in many ways, the country that Williams set out to change. Both were indefatigable workers; each wrote prodigiously; each fought strenuously to shape the direction of their society; and each was at the center of momentous transformations of their society: Burnley directing the changes from slavery to post-apprenticeship and Williams orchestrating the changes from colonialism to independence. Although he was born in the United States, Burnley played a seminal role in the early history of Trinidad and Tobago, serving as the founding father.

Acknowledgments

FOR MANY YEARS I wondered why I had commenced this long, arduous task of writing a book on William Hardin Burnley—I had first written about him in *Movement of the People* in 1983—until I had a discussion with Nathan Richards, a graduate assistant at London University School of Oriental and African Studies, at a Starbucks in Kew Gardens, London. Today, Nathan is a doctoral researcher at the University of Sussex. On that fateful evening after discussing my project at length and sharing the frustration at how long this project was taking, Nathan said to me, "You are not just writing a book. You have undertaken a spiritual journey into yourself and your own people." I had not thought of my project in this way, but Nathan's assessment gave me more focus and allowed me to see the value in what I was doing. And it was Nathan who discovered Burnley's connection to Joseph Hume, Burnley's brother-in-law, which opened up a world of insights into this study. I am grateful to Nathan for all his assistance. It made the trek into Burnley's life easier to undertake.

This book would not have been possible without the series of faculty grants and the conferral of the Margaret E. Deffenbaugh and LeRoy T. Carlson Professor in Comparative Literature that made it possible for me to spend a considerable amount of time at several archives and institutions across the world. They included the Public Record Office at the National Archives (UK) at Kew, Richmond, which holds the most information on Burnley; the Watson Collection at the University of Oxford; the British Library, London; the Harrow School for Boys, Harrow, London; Glasgow City Archives, The Mitchell Library, Glasgow; the National Library of Scotland in Edinburgh; the Library of Congress, Washington, D.C., the Trinidad and Tobago National Archives in Port of Spain, Trinidad; and the West India Collection at the University of the

West Indies at St. Augustine, Trinidad. I also want to thank Dr. Stephen Mullen, postdoctoral researcher in history, and Dr. Rachel Douglas, lecturer in French, both at the University of Glasgow, for their assistance and friendship during the many trips I made to Scotland. I also wish to thank Sharmin and Trevor Farrell of Maryland, who were so helpful when I visited Washington, D.C.

Special thanks are due to Robin Blackburn, professor of sociology and Leverhulme research fellow (Essex University) and Arnold Rampersad, the Sara Hart Kimball Professor in the Humanities, Emeritus (Stanford University) for their support. Their recommendations to the Institute of the Americas, University College of London, resulted in my being granted a professorial fellowship that allowed me to spend the spring of 2013 there, where I delivered several lectures on my research and had enlightening discussions with scholars and students alike. While at UCL, Maxine Molyneaux, professor of sociology and director of the UCL Institute of the Americas (until 2014) and Katherine Quinn, senior lecturer in Caribbean history at UCL, provided enormous assistance.

I offer a special thank you to Nicholas Draper, director of the Centre for the Study of the Legacies of British Slave-Ownership (University College London), and his wife Lalli, who took me into their home and made me feel especially welcomed. Nick's explanations of the compensation that Burnley and other planters received from the British government and the other nuances of that history were helpful to me. I also profited from Nick's reading of my first draft and his many helpful comments. I am especially grateful to Gerard Besson for alerting me to the correspondences of the Colonial Bank, to Judith Wright for her expert guidance at the West India Collection, and to Geoffrey MacLean for granting permission to use the Cazabon paintings in this book.

I also want to thank the myriad of research assistants and friends who helped to make this project possible: Dr. Shantelle George, at the State University of New York, College of Oneonta, for helping me transcribe the almost indecipherable handwriting on some of the documents I encountered at the National Archives at Kew; Dr. Louisa Egbunike, lecturer in English, City University of London, who was never too tired to discuss any point I raised or to find a document for me; Judith Raymond, who led me to Burnley's tombstone; the late Dr. John Campbell, senior lecturer in the History Department and Heather Cateau, the dean of the Faculty of Humanities and Education, for inviting me speak on Burnley at UWI, St. Augustine (Heather Smith and Victoria Lee of Wellesley College who provided the technical assistance on that occasion); and Olivia Funderburg, who acted as my research assistant over the last two years.

I also wish to thank Andrew Shennan, provost of Wellesley College, who has always supported my work; William Cain, Lawrence Rosenwald, Terry Tyler, Timothy Peltason, and others in the English Department who helped me in various ways; and my colleagues in the Africana Studies Department who provided spiritual and intellectual support. I also wish to thank Vicki Mutascio at Wellesley's copy center; Frances Adams at the college post office; the staff at Wellesley's Clapp Library; and Susan Lange, Africana's administrative assistant, who helped me tirelessly in seeing this project through. I also thank Betty Ann Tyson, my editor, who assisted me over the eight years that it took to write this book.

I want to thank Yashica Olden, for making her home available me while I studied and researched this project in London; Brother Kwadwo Osie-Nyame, Joshua Ballantyne, Ini Dele-Adedeji, and my niece Tracey Reyes also made me feel at home while I was in London. They listened willingly as I talked about my project. I wish to thank my cousins and friends in the United States for the support they gave me: Margaret Cudjoe, Marva Cudjoe, Rhonda Cudjoe-County, Lystra and Junior Boyce, Michelle Collins, Ronald and Judith Thomas, Anthony County, and all my nephews and nieces. There is always a special place for my daughters Frances and Kwamena and my sons-in-law James and Andrew.

My Trinidad family and friends were also important in my completing this book. I refer to Rianella, my other daughter, Ewart Williams, Jerome Lewis, Oscar Gooding, Louis Lee Sing, Maxie Cuffie, Bernard and Mavis Bailey, Judith Reyes, and all my nieces and nephews there: Dianne, Dana, Deisha, Gregory, and Jason.

I dedicate this work to my daughters and especially my grandsons to give them a sense of where they came from. They may not treasure the place as much as I do, but I hope I can pass along the love that I feel for Tacarigua, my little village in Trinidad, West Indies.

Finally, I wish to thank Wellesley College for the subsidy it granted to the University of Massachusetts Press to support the publication of this book. It testifies to the commitment of the college to ensure that the research and scholarship of the college's faculty members can reach the larger world.

The Slave Master of Trinidad

CHAPTER 1

Burnley's Emergence

If lions could paint, in the room of those pictures which exhibit
men vanquishing lions, we should see lions feeding upon men.
—Jean-Baptiste Philippe, *Free Mulatto*

IN 1796 AFTER Spain declared war against England, Sir Ralph Abercromby was instructed by His Majesty's government to sail to the West Indies to capture Trinidad and Puerto Rico that were in Spanish hands. It was a time when Spanish fortunes were declining, British supremacy in the Atlantic was rising, and the relationship between Spain and her colonies was at a low ebb. Abercromby arrived in Martinique in January 1797. Finding that the troops there were overcome with yellow fever, he sailed for Trinidad, where he arrived in the middle of February. After war broke out the English began to attack shipping in the Trinidad harbor. Six vessels bound for Grenada and St. Vincent were captured. Among the ships captured was the Spanish brigantine corvette *Galgo*. This ship "was bound for Mexico to Port of Spain with over 80,000 dollars in cash and a cargo of provisions consigned to the Governor of Trinidad."[1] Such hostilities had made the Spanish forces more vulnerable. Their naval forces were composed of 4 ships-of-war, 1 frigate, 91 commissioned officers, 581 marines, and 1,032 seamen. The land forces consisted of 24 officers and 504 noncommissioned officers. The British forces under Abercromby consisted of 9 ships-of-war, 3 frigates, 5 corvettes, and 6,750 soldiers.[2] The Spanish troops had only a poorly fortified garrison with no buildings sturdy enough to withstand the might of a British onslaught. Don José María Chacón, the governor of the island, could not even keep his prisoners safe. He wrote to his superiors: "In a word, I am dependent on the goodwill of a public composed of other nations with but few of our own."[3] In 1796 a Spanish squadron under the command of Rear Admiral Sebastián Ruiz de Apadoca on its way to Spain anchored at Chaguaramas Bay. Seeing Chacón's helplessness he decided to stay a while. It was his undoing. He did not anticipate the might of Abercromby's forces.

Abercromby's ships approached the island and formed a semicircle around Chaguaramas Bay to prevent Apadoca from escaping. Chacón tried to rally his troops without success. The two hundred men he ordered to Chaguaramas to act as reinforcements disappeared into the woods. They never reached Chaguaramas. The officers of the militia companies presented themselves at Chaguaramas, but their men could not be found anywhere. Hearing of the commotion, anxious Trinidadians quickly gathered in Port of Spain to see the show. They were not disappointed. Early the next morning (February 17), about half past one, "the western sky was suddenly lighted up by the flames of a conflagration. . . . Explosion after explosion shook the still morning air, but the anxious listeners were ignorant of the exact nature and extent of the catastrophe." At nine o'clock that morning, Admiral Apadoca reported to Governor Chacón that his forces were overwhelmed, the forts were without water, and he was unable to defend the bay. Escape was not an option. Therefore, he assembled a council of war. They "unanimously agreed that the ships should be burned at their anchorage rather than . . . fall into the hands of the invaders."[4]

As the ships burned, the fire quickly reached the magazine causing the explosions heard throughout the night. Realizing that the enemy had been reduced to ineffectiveness, Abercromby and his men disembarked and headed for Port of Spain. Apadoca and his men used their boats to reach Port of Spain. Finding himself outnumbered and defenseless, Chacón retreated to St. Joseph, the old capital of the island, where he prepared to make his next move. At eight o'clock that evening Abercromby sent an officer to St. Joseph with a flag of truce, offering him an honorable capitulation. He welcomed it. The next morning (February 18) the terms of capitulation were agreed upon, the Spanish laid their arms down, and the war was over. That evening a treaty was signed at the home of Don José Mayan, the Teniente de Justicia Mayor, on a Valsayn estate, and Trinidad formally became a member of the British Empire.

Two months after he signed the capitulation Abercromby departed for future glories, leaving his aide-de-camp, Lieutenant Colonel Thomas Picton, in charge of the island. He offered him the following advice: "I have placed you in a trying and delicate position—nor to give you any chance of overcoming the difficulties opposed to you can I leave you a strong garrison. But I shall give you ample powers. Execute Spanish law as well as you can; do justice according to your conscience and that is all that can be expected of you. His Majesty's Government will be minutely informed of your situation, and no doubt will make all due allowance."⁵

After many deliberations, the Spanish forgave Chacón and Apadoca their transgressions. Twenty-five years later Jean-Baptiste Philippe, one of Trinidad's more accomplished sons, paid Chacón the ultimate compliment. He said Chacón's administration "was the golden age of Trinidad! Commerce flourished, justice poised an equal scale, and prejudice was driven to skulk in the dark abodes of a few illiberal earth-born breasts. His ear was open to every complaint; his arm extended for the support of every petitioner! He long since has mouldered in the dust, but if the fervent prayers of a grateful people can aught avail, the sod lies gently on him."⁶ Baptiste's exuberance was a reaction to Governor Ralph Woodford's oppression of his people—the people of color or, as they sometimes called themselves, "Persons of African Descent." The colored people admired Chacón and felt comfortable under Spanish rule.

In 1798 William Hardin Burnley, an American-born merchant, entered this tumultuous society that was breathing with violence and conflict and trying to reestablish itself. His great-grandfather, John Burnley, was born about 1670 in England and became an officer in the English army. He married Miss Hardin and settled in Hanover County, Virginia, where he died. According to Norman Lamont, "One may hazard the conjecture that his family had originated at, or near, the town of Burnley in Lancashire" (*OG*, 1).⁷ Hardin Burnley, John's son, a planter and merchant, was born in 1704. He was married twice. His second wife, Anne Buck, gave birth to three sons and a daughter, Mrs. Littlepage. At his death he bequeathed property, lands, and slaves to each of his sons. Hardin, his eldest son, received an estate not far from the James River. He used his inheritance well and became a wealthy man owning as much as seventy-six hundred acres in Hanover and Albermarle counties. He may even have cheated others out of their property. In his will dated in 1783, Francis Smithson of Hanover County mentioned that he possessed a "third part" interest in five Negroes that Burnley had controlled since 1757.⁸ Eventually eight children emerged from Hardin Burnley's marriage: Richard, John, Zachariah, Hardin Jr., Judith, Ann, Keziah, and Elizabeth.

When the Revolutionary War broke out in the United States in 1775, the Burnley family found itself in a quandary. Most of Burnley's children, with the exception of Hardin Jr., and John, supported the revolutionary cause. One of his sons even became a colonel in the American army (*OG*, 1). John and Hardin Jr., both of whom were engaged in extensive business dealings with England, remained loyal to England. In 1771 John left Virginia to live in England. Later, he died at sea in 1779. He left two wills when he died, one dated in 1771 and another in 1778 in which he directed his executors, Zachariah and Hardin, to invest £600, the interest of which should be paid annually to his sister Elizabeth Duke, the proceeds of which were to be equally divided among her surviving children after she died. He left a similar amount to Hardin, his brother. This arrangement would lead to legal problems for Hardin that followed him to his death.

Hardin Jr. became a merchant in Virginia. We first hear of his business activity in 1765 when, in partnership with George Brackenridge, he traded under the name Burnley and Brackenridge, exporting tobacco and other such items. However, the business contracted a lot of debt that resulted in many suits being brought against it. For example, on May 12, 1773, Joseph Thompson of Trinity Parish, Louisa County, Virginia, brought suit against merchants Hardin Burnley Jr. and George Brackenridge to secure payment of £198 17s 2d which they owed them.

Hardin married Catherine (1752/3–1827), the daughter of John Ditcher, an officer in the Royal Navy. As a result of his marriage and his business ties, Hardin "took the Royalist side, to the great indignation of his brothers, who were violent on the American side" (*OG*, 1). After the British were defeated, Hardin fled to New York although his wife and children remained on the estate in Virginia. As a Royalist, he couldn't live in southern territory. Therefore, he turned everything he had in Virginia into money "and in a small leather portmanteau brought with him about £14,000 in gold" to New York (*OG*, 1–2). He could not sell his estates in Virginia. "They were tobacco-plantations, worth about £150,000. They also grew corn and flax, and everything necessary for their supplies. All of the clothing for the negroes was spun and woven upon the estate. He left the power of selling the estates to his nephew, Edmund Littlepage, who failed to obtain payment" (*OG*, 2).

While he was in New York, Hardin made several attempts to return to Virginia but was not permitted to enter the state legally. George Norton, in a postscript of a letter he wrote to Francis Jordan in 1799, observed: "Mr. Burnley has returned to New York after making an unsuccessful attempt to land in Virginia, but was obliged to depart by order of the Legislature."[9] He also traveled to London to explore business opportunities and to wind up his brother's business there. Eventually, Hardin's wife joined him in New York, where William Hardin was born on April 21, 1780.

In moving to New York City, Burnley had not given up on Virginia entirely because he still owned tobacco plantations and other property there, including slaves. In 1782 in a note to the governor of the state, John Syme requested instructions as to "the case of Hardin Burnley who on previous occasions, was not allowed or 'to take the oath of the state' or to record certain papers offered at last court. During Patrick Henry's administration he was refused admittance here."[10] In 1785, in what seemed to be a parting gesture, Hardin and his wife donated several hundred acres of land to the county of Hanover. The next year Hardin Burnley moved his entire family to London to start a new life there.

Given his wealth and previous ties with London, it was not difficult for Hardin to make a new start there. Having acquired a reputation for "steadiness and integrity," he became a successful businessman, an underwriter for Lloyds of London, and a director of the East India Company, the biggest monopoly in India at the time. Established in 1600 as a cartel of merchants, the company took control of Bengal and ejected French interests there during the Seven Years' War (1757–1764). David Gange explained: "The organization pursued trade on the Indian subcontinent and in China. The commerce was initially in spices but later in opium, saltpeter, and other commodities. Its members became wealthy and powerful, establishing huge estates in Britain and a powerful lobby in Parliament."[11] By the time Hardin joined the company it was so powerful that "it functioned like a state within a state."[12]

In 1800 the London City Directory listed him as "Hardin Burnley, Merchant, #12 America Square." In 1802 he was listed as "Hardin Burnley & Son, Merchant, #8 Barking Church Yard," and from 1808 to 1820 he was listed as "Hardin Burnley, Merchant, #1 Brunswick Square." In the early 1800s this address "was a first-class residential district occupied by professional and business men of London."[13] Even in London, his ties to his family properties in Virginia haunted him when his sister Elizabeth Duke brought a suit against him and Zachariah for the fraudulent handling of the legacy that was left to her by her brother John. The suit ended in 1822 when the court of appeals in Virginia voted in favor of Elizabeth and awarded her close to £1,900 with an interest of 5 percent payable from December 31, 1817.[14] In 1823, one year after the suit was concluded, Hardin died in London leaving a fortune of £130,000. His wife Catherine died in 1827 and, like her husband, was buried at St. Pancras. Burnley used part of his father's fortune to pursue his interest in Trinidad.

CHAPTER 2

Burnley's Schooling

As much as Harrow [School for Boys] attracted aristocrats, aristocrats attracted Harrovians. . . . Harrow prepared its pupils in almost every respect for their adult futures.

—Christopher Tyerman, *A History of Harrow School, 1324–1991*

WHEN HARDIN BURNLEY returned to London in 1786 the city was just beginning to take off. As the city grew rich and expanded so did its areas of poverty and squalor that Charles Dickens immortalized in *Oliver Twist* (1838).[1] Hardin Burnley, a member of the East India Company, enjoyed substantial wealth. Although Hardin Burnley was not a member of the aristocracy, he had attained professional status within the society and wished to enhance his family's social status.

Three years after the Burnleys arrived in London, the French Revolution broke out and upended many traditional values of the country. Thomas Hughes, in *Tom Brown's Schooldays*, acknowledged the social and economic upheaval caused "by the great war, when there was much distress and crime in the Vale."[2] In January 1793 Hardin enrolled his son William, age twelve and a half, in Harrow School for Boys (or more precisely Harrow Free Grammar School), one of the best public schools in England at the time that was dedicated to raising "a gentleman." It was founded in 1572 by John Lyon, a farmer in Preston, to provide a classical education for thirty poor children of that village. When William entered Harrow it had changed its mission. It was catering to

6

the "upper and upper-middle-classes"[3] and was a boarding establishment. At the beginning of 1660 children from other parishes ("foreigners") were allowed to attend, so long as they could afford to pay for their education.[4] Burnley, who lived outside the five-mile radius of Harrow, entered as a paying student at a cost of about £220 (or about U.S. $31,000 in 2016 currency) per year.

Harrow was located about ten miles outside of London where Burnley lived. Burnley lived with a local family as a "PG" or paying guest. At Harrow, the homes of many prominent people served as boarding houses for students. Joseph Drury, the headmaster of the school from 1785 to 1805, and his family owned five boarding houses from which they earned a handsome income.[5] Christopher Tyerman noted that almost "all the masters were involved in this commercial enterprise by taking in a few boarders."[6]

When William entered Harrow at what the school called "the half-year" there were 120 boys; some as young as six and a half years old; the oldest were about eighteen. Students between the ages of six and a half through ten years lived at the dames' houses for their own protection. The "School Dames" were appointed to teach the boys to read and some of the classes may have been conducted in their own homes.[7] Although William may have spent his earlier years at a small reading school, entering Harrow was a frightful experience. He may have felt very much like J. G. Cotton Minchin, a student, and Bosworth Smith, a master, who entered Harrow in 1864. Minchin said: "When my dear old tutor and I first looked at each other, like two strange dogs in surroundings that were equally strange to both of us, it was difficult to say which was the most afraid of the other."[8] William adjusted to the Harrow experience. He left Harrow in July 1795 after having completed the fifth form.

Lyon laid down a rigorous curriculum for Harrow that was based entirely on the classical subjects. Since Latin was the prevailing language of church services, legal documents, academic treatises, and communications between merchants of different countries, one could not be considered learned if one did not possess knowledge of Latin.[9] Harrow followed the Lyon curriculum for the first 150 years of its existence, as did most of the other public schools at the time. The memorization of facts and regurgitation of information were the chief methods of pedagogy. Following the example of Winchester College, the earliest of these public schools, students were obliged to speak Latin only during school hours.

The school consisted of five forms (a sixth was added in 1775). In the first year, each student studied Latin grammar. In their second year they translated Aesop, Cato, and Erasmus into Latin. In their third year "they were taught to write connected prose" and study Cicero and Ovid. In the fourth form they studied Greek and the works of Virgil, Caesar, Cicero, and Livy. In their fifth year they studied the work of Greek thinkers such as Demosthenes, Hesiod, and Dionysius.[10] The student's day began at six and lasted until eleven o'clock in the morning. The afternoon school started at one and ended at six. Tuesdays were a whole holiday as were the other semireligious holidays, such as May 29, January 30, and November 5. The monarchs' birthdays and Ascension Day were also holidays.

Crowded into one room, the fourth form, in the Old Schools, the students (or scholars as they were called) got to know one another well. It was divided into four different areas that consisted of benches that were known as forms. Each class was separated by a curtain. Each boy brought his candle to see what he was reading and a slate and chalk to do his writing. The teachers taught from a headmaster seat that resembled a pulpit and was erected in front of the room. To the immediate left of the headmaster's seat there was a birching cupboard. In front of the birching cupboard was a birching stool where the boys bent over to be birched. An original birch is still kept in the birching cupboard. The school even utilized the services of the porters to assist in the flogging of the students. Minchin noted: "Mr. Oxenham was the last [ostiarius] to draw a special salary in addition to other dues, and to enjoy the privilege of birching the boys, now the exclusive privilege of the head master."[11]

There was a close connection between the school and the parish church, St. Mary's Anglican, that was consecrated in AD 1094. On Sundays, the Harrow boys attended the church "to hear Divine service and the scripture read or interpreted with attention and reverence"[12] as the statutes of Lyon demanded. Two galleries were added to accommodate the students while the masters sat in the pews. Being at church provided a space from the harrowing happenings of the week. Minchin testified: "If there were one spot at Harrow where the bullied and the weak could, for a few moments at least, forget their troubles and imagine themselves at home, that was the chapel."[13] There can be little doubt that Burnley's association with the church prompted him to adopt St. Mary's Anglican Church in Tacarigua, for which he provided the land, when he arrived in Trinidad some years later.

Hardin Burnley did not choose Harrow lightly. Most of its masters were trained at Cambridge University, with which the school had an early connection. The masters had a huge impact upon the boys who judged them "as social figures, models of behavior and tone rather than as intellectuals."[14] Social breeding was as important (sometimes more important) as the acquisition of a classical education. It was a necessary prerequisite for whatever career a student wished to follow in his adult life. Athletics, particularly games such as cricket, was an important way to inculcate social values into the boys. Minchin observed: "The cricketer in his flannels was our hero, not the student immersed in his books. Can there be any question as to which is the more picturesque figure? Was there ever a race more intellectual than the ancient Greeks, and did they not worship the human form divine?"[15]

Sending William to Harrow was one way to connect with some of the most important citizens of the country. Most of the boys who attended Harrow came from wealthy families. David Turner notes that in the late seventeenth century Harrow "became a school for the sons of barristers, doctors, academics, vicars and landowners, a mixture of the upper classes and what were then called 'the learned professions' but are known today as the upper middle classes."[16] In 1796 over 15 percent of the boys came from families of peers. Between 1785 and 1805 Harrow produced five of the seven Harrovians who became prime ministers of England. By the time Christopher Wordsworth, brother of the poet William Wordsworth, became the headmaster of Harrow school (1836–1845), it had emerged as a "fashionable school for the aristocracy."[17]

Students made connections at Harrow. It was one of the most important functions of public schools in England. Tyerman has indicated that the basis of eighteenth-century success was the ability to form these connections. Joseph Drury, William's headmaster, was not known for his academic brilliance although his teaching staff was academically sound. He recognized that an educator of the aristocracy had to be "more accomplished socially than academically" which led him "to cultivate the great, the good and potentially useful."[18] The reverend Charles Vaughan, headmaster from 1845 to 1859, preferred the influence he wielded at Harrow to positions of power that other institutions offered. This led him to decline bishoprics that were offered to him.

All was not sweetness and light at Harrow. There was much bullying and fagging (younger students doing minor chores for senior students). Floggings were a regular part of the school day as the presence of the "birching stool" in the Fourth Form Room attested. Massive cruelty was inflicted upon the younger boys by the older boys. Some students were kicked and beaten. In 1808 there was a major uprising by the prefects "who were peeved that they were not allowed to flog their charges."[19] Sir Robert Peel, Harrovian and former British Prime Minister, wrote later in life, "I would not send my boys [to Harrow] . . . unless it is better conducted now than it was when I misspent my time there."[20]

Architecturally, Harrow remained the same since the first building was erected in 1615. In the nineteenth century many additions were made, beginning in 1819 with construction of a new wing to the old school at a cost of £5,000. It contained a speech-room, classrooms, and a school library. "William Burnley of Trinidad" is listed in the school's register as a subscriber "to the erection of the East Wing to the Old Schools."[21] In spite of the changes made to the Old Schools, one thing remained constant: the original condition and furnishing of the Fourth Floor Room in the East Wing. Edmund W. Howson and George Townsend Warner note:

> This room remained unchanged. The seats in which successive headmasters and ushers have, since the beginning of the seventeenth century, sat and taught; the cupboard in which the instrument of punishment were kept; the benches upon which succeeding generations of scholars have received their tuition and punishment, are all still preserved. On its panels have been carved, with their own hands, the name of many of the most honored and famous of the sons of Harrow; while above the panels are enrolled the names of later Harrovians.[22]

Burnley's name is carved into the panels of the Fourth Floor Room in the East Wing of Harrow School.

Harrow was important to Burnley's social and intellectual development. His education at Harrow and his association with fellow Harrovians cultivated an esprit de corps that remained with him long after he left the school. When Burnley left Harrow he accepted the ruling class notion that "a half-witted public schoolboy is better for command than an intelligent mechanic."[23] The school had given him a sense of privilege and laid the moral framework for his future behavior. Andrew Sanders wrote: "Public schools were 'miniature Englands', models on which future patterns of justice and social order could be based."[24] At Harrow, William adopted all the biases and prejudices of an English gentleman of the Victorian age and made them a part of his behavior. Most of all, he remained a Harrovian with all of the complicated loyalties that such an association entailed.

CHAPTER 3

Burnley's Entrance to Trinidad

The seed of Empire has been sown by the strong arms and watered by the blood of our Public School boys.

—J. G. Cotton Minchin, *Old Harrow Days*, 1898

WILLIAM BURNLEY LEFT Harrow before he reached the sixth form, which suggests he was not interested in proceeding either to Cambridge or Oxford universities. Like so many of the boys who left school after the fifth year, William did not want to follow a career in law, the army, the clergy, or become a gentleman farmer. A member of an old Harrrovian family explained: "If you were an older son in Britain and your family had an estate which you would inherit one day, that is where your work lay. A younger son would probably be expected to go into the army, or law or the Church. If you didn't go into any of those professions, then one went where one's career took one."[1] Burnley's career took him to Trinidad. He knew that if he made enough money he could return to England to join the ranks of the English aristocracy and attain a social status equal to many of the boys with whom he had shared so many hours at Harrow. The parents of many of his schoolmates had made their fortunes in the West Indies.

Three years after he left Harrow, Burnley sailed to Trinidad in search of his life's work. He might have been encouraged to do so by his schoolmates and family friends who had connections with the island. Ashton Warner, one of his schoolmates, may have played an important role in his desire to see what Trinidad had to offer. The Warners were big plantation owners in the West Indies. Many generations of that family had studied at Harrow. Ashton entered Harrow in April 1788 at the age of seven and a half and left between 1795 and 1798. Unlike Burnley, Ashton proceeded to Cambridge University in June 1798 to study for a degree. On October 28, 1800, he was admitted to Lincoln's Inn. On February 7, 1806, he became a barrister. Thereafter he went to Trinidad where he practiced law before being appointed the chief justice of the island in 1818, a post he held until his sudden death in 1830. He was described as having "combined a handsome person, graceful manners and an easy address with all the qualities of an English gentleman."[2] Like Burnley, in 1819, he also made a financial contribution to the erection of the new wing of the Old Schools building at Harrow. In Trinidad, in spite of the regulations, Ashton owned slaves and enjoyed a close relation with Burnley.[3]

Burnley's family friends in Trinidad may also have urged him to try his luck in that frontier society. When Burnley arrived there were more than two hundred British-born subjects on the island, approximately one-sixth of the white population that had settled there prior to Abercromby's conquest of 1797. Some of the better known British families were Mr. John Black, Messrs. (John) Dawson and Barry, Robert Eccles, Dr. O'Meara, Dr. Alexander Williams, Mr. (Robert) Mitchell, and others, "besides those respectable merchants of the mother country who then had immense capital invested such as a Mr. Joseph Marryat to whom the whole value of the Marabella Estate owned by one Mr. Lewis was due."[4] The 1813 Trinidad Slave Register noted that John Black and Hilliare Begorrat were in possession of Union Estate, a sugar plantation, as attorneys for the estate that was owned by Lieutenant General Thomas Picton and the heirs of John McDonald, deceased.[5]

In 1815, there were ninety-one enslaved people on the estate. Robert Eccles, a merchant of Ireland, owned a sugar estate for which he received £2,858 when slavery ended. He owned fifty-four slaves and fathered an illegitimate daughter, Margaret Eccles, with a black woman for whom he left an annuity of £60. Anthony Cooke described Margaret as "a mixed race woman of around 50 living in Trinidad."[6] In exploring the economic possibilities of the island, Burnley must have spoken with some of these planters and merchants. That Burnley and William Eccles Jr. (1805–1859), Robert's nephew, worked closely together in the years that followed suggests that Robert may have had an input into Burnley's decision to try his hand in Trinidad. Because Eccles Jr. had earned so much of Burnley's confidence, he was made one of the four executors of Burnley's will.[7]

Burnley spent a short time in Trinidad before he returned to England. In 1802 he returned with money to invest and a desire to make his way on the island. There were about 28,000 people on the island, of which 2,261 were white (British, French, and Spanish), 5,275 were free people of color, 20,000 were enslaved Africans, and 1,000 were American Indians. It was a propitious moment for Burnley. The British "were keen to see agricultural and population expansion, particularly after 1802 when Trinidad was formally ceded to Britain by Spain as part of the Treaty of Amiens."[8] The 663 British citizens who were residing on the island must have especially welcomed this bright, enterprising young man to the colony.

In the summer of that year the British replaced Picton with a three-man commission, consisting of William Fullarton as first commissioner, Picton as second commissioner, and Samuel Hood as third commissioner. Hood arrived in 1803 to take up his duties. The commissioners, particularly Fullarton and Picton, did not get along at all. A year later, in 1803, Picton was taken to London to stand trial for torturing Luisa Calderon, a young girl of African descent.[9] During his trial, Sir Robert Dallas, Picton's lawyer, described Trinidad as being "a site of social chaos, having become a receptacle for every description of undesirable and dangerous refugee from other islands."[10] It was not a situation with which Burnley was unaccustomed. James Epstein notes that the island also "presented itself not merely as a site of practical opportunities, but as something grander and more utopian; here was a place to reconfirm one's reputation, to chart a future for self and empire, to bring improvement to the world."[11] This dimension of Trinidad may have appealed to Burnley's imagination.

Apart from the money Burnley brought to invest in the island in 1802, he possessed another advantage. He was one of the most educated of its new inhabitants. This served him in good stead and opened many doors for him. Writing some thirty years after his arrival and bewildered by the challenges Burnley was posing to British rule on the island, Lewis Grant, governor of the island, acknowledged that Burnley came to the island "with the advantage of birth, capital, and an education superior to probably any other colonist and certainly with his own objects in sight."[12] Years later, when the emancipation of the enslaved became obvious to all, Burnley declared that Trinidad was the place where he had spent his best days.

After living for five years in Trinidad, William Hardin traveled to St. George's Church in Bloomsbury, in the fashionable part of London, to marry Charlotte

Brown, the daughter of William Brown, a Trinidad merchant and "a member of an old family from Carnoustie in Scotland."[13] The marriage, which took place on January 5, 1807, produced two sons. When William Frederick, his first son, was born in London on May 14, 1810, Burnley was in Trinidad. In keeping with family tradition, William Frederick was baptized in Bloomsbury, at the St. Pancras Old Church, on August 1, 1810. Joseph Hume Burnley, Burnley's youngest son, was born on the island on May 14, 1821. He seemed to be his father's favored child. Fortunately or unfortunately, Charlotte loved the amenities of Paris and London. She quickly left the island after Joseph's birth. She refused to live in Trinidad although she visited the island occasionally after that.

Burnley used his educational and financial assets to his advantage. In 1810, the society was just taking shape. He had the good fortune to meet George Smith, the *chief oidor* (chief justice) of the island, with whom he became fast friends. Chief Justice Smith, a former chief justice of Grenada, was appointed to his post in 1809. He seemed to be contemptuous of the whites on the island. In 1810 he joined forces with Governor Henry Tolley to suppress public discussion about the introduction of a British constitution to the island and, in the process, imprisoned "the headstrong printer Matthew Gallagher for refusing to comply with his direction not to print articles on the constitutional question."[14] Although the control of the press was stricter in the French, Dutch, and Danish West Indies, "the worst repression came as a rule from the local legislative bodies and from the judiciary, many of whose members played a contemptible part in attempts at muzzling the press in the 1830s and 1840s."[15]

Within a year of his appointment, Smith was at odds with Thomas Hislop, the new governor of the island. Smith requested permission from the governor to leave the country so that he could present his grievance to the secretary of state before the governor was scheduled to leave the island also to meet with the secretary of state. Governor Hislop forbade Smith to leave the island during the governor's intended absence, since Smith was supposed to act as governor when Hislop was away. Burnley, however, helped Smith leave the island surreptitiously by disguising him as a sailor and getting him aboard a schooner at Macqueripe Bay. Subsequent events demonstrated why Burnley was so indebted to Smith.

Smith aided Burnley in his rise to wealth and prominence by allowing Burnley to act as his *depositario* general, whose function it was to protect the widows and orphans of the society. Although the office was vacant from 1797 to 1810, Smith allowed Burnley to serve in that capacity. Together they used the office to fleece the widows and orphans of the island. All the property that became the subject of any litigation was placed under Burnley's control, and he received the revenues that were paid on those properties. No account of these transactions was ever kept, and the rightful owners seldom received any payments. It was crucial that Smith was dispatched to London to tell his story before Hislop got there. On June 12, 1810, Mr. Black, a member of the ruling Council, sent a devastating letter to Mr. Marryat, Trinidad's agent in London, that contained the following charges:

> Our political horizon grows darker and darker and will explode in a hurricane. A complete schism has I fear taken place between the Governor and the Oidor [Smith], which however will not as in former times split us into parties, for we shall all be in favor of the former, and with great justice.
>
> The Governor has long seen, and with great regret and dissatisfaction, the *imperiousness* of this man, but he never expressed his feelings openly until now. An extraordinary meeting of the Cabildo is to be held this day at which the Governor will preside, and we are to have a full meeting of Council on Wednesday, both of which have for their object the illegal, arbitrary behavior of this man, and I too suppose to take some steps for arresting the evil. His ambition is now entirely absorbed by one object—to throw into the hands of Burnley all the property he can find an excuse for laying hold of in the country, either from the death of the proprietors or from claims of creditors, and that the revenues of these properties shall be by him (after having had good pickings out of them) remitted to his friend Mellish.
>
> Burnley you see has the office of Depositario General of his Court, a place of immense responsibility according to the Spanish law and for which the holder is obliged to give real security to a very large amount. But nothing of the kind has been done. Burnley is Depositario at large and it is computed that by *Bienes de defuntos* alone which he will be in possession of by the Judge's pleasure, in a short time he will have the amount of a million and-a-half dollars. (*H*, 347)

After Smith left, the cabildo named Samuel Span as the depositario general. He also went on to own several sugar estates. After he did the necessary inventory, he discovered what many believed to be true: little of the money that was taken in could be accounted for. At the end of the year he informed the governor that he could get no account of "judicial deposits" from Mr. Smith and therefore "humbly prays Your Excellency's interference to prevent any such departure of His Honour George Smith from this Island, or of his deputed Receivers, W. H. Burnley or J. B. Littlepage, Esqrs., or any other receivers of deposits whom His Honour George Smith may have appointed" (*HT*, 349). The governor immediately convened the cabildo to deal with this matter. They agreed that if Smith wished to leave the country, the governor should ask him to give a proper record of the monies he or any other parties had received in the pursuance of his duties. Smith responded promptly with all the necessary courtesies: "I beg to state to Your Excellency that at this moment there is not, I believe, a deposit of any kind in the hands of any one under my authority" (*HT*, 350).

The evidence suggests that the chief judge was engaging in "deliberate falsehoods." Several notices had appeared in the local papers that attested monies had flowed through the office. Other notices in the local papers indicated that hundreds of debtors had delivered thousands of dollars to Burnley in his capacity as depositario general. While Smith served as the chief judge, close to £180,000 had been lodged in the court. Approximately £4,000 were paid to the plaintiffs. The rest went straight into Burnley's pockets. The merchants believed that "the large sums of money which passed through the hands of Mr. Burnley were used by him in his own business. This was repeated and strenuously denied by Judge Smith, who officially declared that the moneys were from time to time lodged in the hands of a Receiver in London, who was instructed to invest them in Government securities for the benefit of those concerned. The fact still remained that the estates were managed by the Court, and that Mr. Burnley had the control of them and supplied them with all things needed" (*HT*, 350). Lionel Mordaunt Fraser noted that to anyone who was acquainted with the way in which the court did business in the West Indies, "It will not appear strange that under such circumstances [Burnley] was believed to be amassing a fortune" (*HT*, 350). He used his wealth to develop his international contacts that allowed him to consolidate this power.

From these early years we see a pattern in Burnley's behavior: a tendency to assert his authority, to clash with the governors of the country, and to look out for his interest. While the governors came and left, Burnley remained a regular fixture on the island. Such a consistent presence allowed him to build a solid base in the colony that enhanced his business and political stature on the island. When the society was in crisis, most of the proprietors turned to him for guidance. The longer he stayed on the island the more it became home and the more powerful he became. He played a leading part in the country's affairs and, in many ways, can be considered the prime minister of the country during the last twenty-five years of his life (*HT*, 347).[16]

CHAPTER 4

The Coming of Ralph Woodford

I am persuaded that if an angel from heaven was sent down to administer the government of Trinidad in its present form, he would find it impossible to give satisfaction; and this is a sufficient reason why it ought not to be continued.

—Joseph Marryat, "Commission of Inquiry," 1822

WHEN SIR RALPH Woodford arrived in Trinidad to serve as governor on June 13, 1813, the island was governed primarily by a Spanish constitution (under an illustrious cabildo), influenced by French culture, and a teeming body of enslaved Africans. More importantly, the free people of color outnumbered the white inhabitants. Rather than place the power of governance in the hands of a local legislature, the British government made Trinidad into a crown colony, "a type of colony unknown at the time, . . . in which the British Government retained complete control, and which the British government hoped to establish as model for the self-governing colonies of the West Indies, in respect of legislation governing the treatment of the slaves."[1] This form of government, with little modification, remained in effect until 1925 when the first local representatives were elected to the legislature.

Woodford seemed especially equipped to reconstruct a society that was so recently under Spanish rule. His remit was to bring the colony under his control, which is why the Colonial Office invested him with all the powers of the executive government. He had the same power that was exercised by the governors when Trinidad was under Spanish rule; the same powers vested in the courts of judicature; and the judicial powers that that were conferred upon the Spanish governors. "The most important part of his commission," according to Fraser, "was that which gave Sir Ralph Woodford all the powers of a Court Royal Audience" (*H*, 3). In addition to his judicial functions, he controlled the financial, legislative, and executive machinery of the island.

Coming from "a good old English family," Woodford had much to recommend him. Sir Alexander Woodford, his first cousin, "commanded a battalion of Guards at Waterloo . . . [and] married Charlotte, daughter of Charles Henry, son of William Fraser who was Secretary of State for Foreign Affairs in [David] Pitt's Ministry in 1783" (*H*, 2). He was well educated and determined to manage the affairs of island. In his first address to the cabildo, the governing body of the island, he made it clear that he "would not tolerate any interference with him as Chief of the Executive, and that he intended to intimate in civil but unmistakable terms, that so far as it claimed any power of control over him as Governor the Illustrious Board was defunct" (*H*, 5). Given Burnley's prominence in the colony, it was almost inevitable that they would come to blows. Later that year, when Lord Bathurst, the secretary of state for the colonies, dismissed His Majesty's Council of Trinidad that assisted the governor in conducting the affairs of the island, Woodford named Burnley, described as English-American, a member of that body. The other members of the council were Count Charles Joseph Comte Loppinot (a French Royalist who emigrated from Haiti), Lawrence Nihell (Irish), and Don Manuel Sorzano; all seemed to represent the principal elements of the community.

One year after Woodford arrived on the island, he asked each member of his council to come up with suggestions to induce free laborers to settle in the country. Mr. Bigge, the chief judge of the island, favored the importation of European settlers. Nihell suggested that Africans be brought to the island as indentures for a period of ten years. Burnley, on the other hand, rejected the introduction of African laborers to the island. He felt that "although robust and hardy, they were so grossly ignorant that they required to be taught everything they were to do." He suggested that settlement of Asians, "a docile and intelligent class of laborers, already accustomed to agriculture, to whom the climate would present no drawbacks and whose very prejudices of caste would keep them from combining with the slaves, who, so long as slavery should exist, would be always more or less disposed to revolt. . . . Asiatic immigration would not only suffice to bring the whole Island into cultivation but would eventually 'banish the baneful system of slavery'" (*H*, 16). Through this act Burnley became the first person to advocate the bringing of East Indians to the island. He was also the first person to suggest that the "prejudice of caste" would prevent the Indians, particularly the Hindus, from coming together with the Africans to transform the political landscape of the island.

In 1815 Trinidad was having a difficult time in regularizing its flourishing trade with Venezuela. As a result, the Colonial Office directed that a drawback be placed on all goods that were exported to Venezuela in launches and open boats. On receipt of this order, Woodford put together a committee that included Burnley to examine and to report to the council on the matter. After its hearings the council resolved that it could not carry out the instructions of the secretary of state. Therefore Woodford suspended the execution of the original order until he received further instructions from the Colonial Office. Fortunately for him the Colonial Office supported his position, and in November of the following year, the secretary of state informed him "that after careful consideration the Lords of the Treasury had approved of the suggestion that all *British* dry goods and hardware should be exempted from import duties" (*H*, 50). In other words restrictions on trade between Trinidad and Venezuela were removed because Trinidad received a large supply of its dry goods and provisions from Venezuela.

This same year, 1815, Burnley's sister Maria married Joseph Hume, a member of the House of Commons who became the self-appointed guardian of the public purse and a friend of the working people of England against their masters. But he reversed this position when it came to supporting his brother-in-law's economic interests as a plantation owner and master against the rights of his slaves. Ronald Huch and Paul Ziegler reported that Hume "was in the forefront of nearly every major reform endeavour in the first half of the nineteenth century; and, though he never held office, his name was a household word in England for over thirty years."[2] He was a friend of James Mill with whom he attended Montrose Academy, considered the best school in his region[3] and developed a strong personal friendship with David Ricardo, the famous English economist. Thomas Piketty called Ricardo and Karl Marx "the two most influential economists of the nineteenth century."[4]

As a young man Hume wanted to become a member of the British Parliament and a director of the East India Company. He achieved his first ambition in 1812 when, "for a consideration," he bought the seat of the sitting member of Weymouth, Sir John Lowther Johnstone, upon his death. Hume was a proprietor of the East India Company and thus was eligible to become a director, which was an elected office. In January 1813 the *Morning Chronicle* noted that he was "very active" at the court of the East India Company and in April of that year ran an advertisement to support his candidacy. It ended in the following manner: "I rest my claims on many years of active employment in your service, and a constant and laborious consideration of your affairs in this country."[5] He even sought Ricardo's assistance in his campaign to become a member of this powerful organization.

Hume also looked to Burnley's father, Hardin, who had four shares in the East India Company. Although Hardin hated being "pestered for his support,"[6] Hume managed to get an audience with Hardin at his home. While there, Hume met Hardin's daughter Maria, and was attracted to her. "During the course of these visits Hume's attention was often distracted by Burnley's daughter, Mary [*sic*]. A courtship developed and in 1815, at age thirty eight, Hume married this young woman."[7] Although Hume's marriage did not result in his gaining a directorship on the board of the East India Company, "it certainly increased his wealth. It was the sort of connection, wrote one opponent of the Scotsman, that might be expected from a man who put money before all else."[8] Hardin was a wealthy man. When he died in 1823 he left a considerable fortune.

Hume's marriage proved a blessing to him. It provided him with wider contacts in the city of London, and the couple's combined fortunes secured a firm base for a resurgent political career. In 1818 he was adopted as the candidate for the Scottish Burghs and by 1821 became a celebrity when "he made the most statistical of all his speeches in the House of Commons. It was immensely long occupying seventy-seven columns of *Hansard*."[9] He and Maria had six children and were seldom apart except when he was in the House of Commons. When Hume died in 1855, Joseph Burnley Hume, one of Hume's sons, published a memorial "of excruciating banality" that he composed to eulogize his father.[10] Valerie Chancellor remarks: "It was not clear whether this arose from inertia or distaste for the subject. Hume's weaknesses were probably only too well known to his son."[11] The memorial did not speak well of his father.

Maria's marriage to Hume was beneficial to her brother William in that it introduced him into the highest levels of British society and gave him direct access to members of the British Parliament including the secretaries of state for the colonies and prime ministers of England. Burnley also kept Hume *au courant* with the political ideas of one of the most important outposts in the world. Hume intervened on his behalf in Parliament, and the Trinidad planters gained a direct channel to voice their concerns in debates that examined the amelioration, the abolition of slavery, slave compensation, and other measures that were to be undertaken to alleviate the conditions of enslaved Africans in Trinidad and Tobago. Charlotte, Burnley's wife, visited Maria's London home at 6 Bryanston Square, and Burnley stayed there whenever he visited London. In fact, Burnley became so close with Hume that he named his second son, his favorite, Joseph Hume Burnley, after his brother-in-law.

Burnley's direct connection to the Colonial Office led inevitably to conflicts between Woodford and Burnley. Woodford was determined to do his duty. He sought to gain more knowledge about the society by corresponding "personally with all heads of departments and brought government under his direct control,"[12] tried to mitigate the conditions of the enslaved, and regulate the land issues with which he was faced. He even learned patios in order to speak with the enslaved.[13] His reputed highhandedness led to many conflicts that could have been avoided if he had engaged in greater consultation with the inhabitants. Burnley, having resided on the island for a longer period of time, knew the colony more intimately than Woodford and therefore resented his intrusion into matters he did not think Woodford understood. Although Burnley was concerned about other social and political issues of the day, his chief interest lay in increasing the profitability of his estates and remaining a viable planter. Eventually he became the senior member of the Board of Council and so gained even more power, respect, and responsibility in the society.

The conflict between these two men increased in intensity in 1822 when R. J. Wilmot brought forward a motion in the House of Commons that a royal commission be named "to inquire into the state of the Settlements of the Cape of Good Hope, the Mauritius and Ceylon, and, also into the administration of criminal justice in the Leeward Islands."[14] As far as Wilmot was concerned, governors such as Woodford possessed too much arbitrary power and that was not good for the society. Hume spoke in favor of the motion. He was "anxious" to have a similar commission sent to Trinidad "to inquire into and report upon the nature of the Spanish Laws, both criminal and civil, as there administered; the extent of the taxes and other burthens imposed upon the inhabitants; the powers exercised by the Governor; his Proclamations respecting Grants of Land; and other matters that affect the welfare and prosperity of the Colony" (*H*, 134). This amendment was aimed squarely at Woodford who was having his problems with Joseph Marryat, the agent of the colony in London, and the Committee of Landholders of Trinidad that was headquartered in London and led by Marryat. Burnley had communicated to Hume the problems of the planters in Trinidad. Hume in his turn was determined to use his office to assist his brother-in-law in Trinidad.

As soon as Hume finished his contribution, Marryat rose to support Hume's amendment. Hume said he hoped that his "local knowledge of that island, and the extensive and constant correspondence that I have long maintained with it will enable me to state such additional facts, as will satisfy the House of the expediency of agreeing to his amendment."[15] During the debate a long exposition of his and the Committee of Landholders' grievances against Woodford ensued. Hume called Woodford's attempts to improve the condition of the roads "objects of embellishments" since the new roads were built through sugar estates during crop time thereby denying planters the valuable labor of Negro workers. Other grievances included: imposing and raising taxes on the inhabitants, the use of arbitrary power ("intercepts and opens letters addressed to individuals, demands a sight of those they may have received, and searches houses and breaks open locks, to obtain possession of papers, at his own will and pleasure"), and Woodford's refusal to allow Venezuelan independents from Guiria who sought asylum to land on the island.

Marryat devoted much of his speech outlining the attempts that were made to introduce British laws to the island. Although Lord Hobart wrote to Governor Hislop in 1804 about his desire to see the laws of Great Britain introduced to the island, it was not until January 1, 1814, that the English language was introduced into the tribunals of the island. Arguing that British dominion and British law ought to go "hand in hand," he drew on the example of Jamaica to demonstrate, in the words of Edmund Burke: "From that moment, as by a charm, the tumult subsided, obedience was restored, peace, order, and civilization followed in the train of liberty. When the day-star of the English constitution had arisen in their hearts, all was harmony within and without."[16]

Fraser called Marryat's speech "an elaborate indictment of the administration of Sir Ralph Woodford," a continuation of a fight that began after Woodford fired him from acting as the agent of the colony (*H*, 134). Even some of Marryat's statements, such as Woodford's refusal to give asylum to Venezuelans, were contradicted by the Colonial Office. By this time Marryat, totally in the planters' camp, opposed the views of Wilberforce and the abolitionists. Surprisingly, Henry Goulburn—representative of West Looe (1818–1826), chancellor of the Exchequer (1841–1846), and also a slave owner in Jamaica—came to Woodford's defense. He denied the accuracy of Marryat's statements and countered:

> In our Slave Colonies, the effect of the British constitution, as it was called, wherever it prevailed, is to throw the whole power into the hands of the white oligarchy, to the exclusion of every other class from the enjoyment of the advantages of that Constitution so that its boasted benefits are confined to a twentieth or thirtieth

part of the whole population, who are thus enabled to tyrannize over the rest. In Trinidad there are about 3,600 whites of all ages, and both sexes, but in the same island there are about 14,000 free persons of color, many of them persons of property; and nearly twice that number of slaves. Now, the Spanish laws secured certain privileges to the free people of color, and to the slaves, which they did not enjoy in colonies governed by what is termed the British Constitution and British Laws; so that, in giving the boon that is demanded to a fraction of the population we are inflicting a serious injury on the great mass of the community.[17]

Goulburn felt that imposing a British constitution or British law upon Trinidad at that time constituted placing power in the hands of a white oligarchy. He opposed this. He concluded by promising to give his "most determined resistance" to any proposition that Marryat brought forward on Trinidad because it was "fraught with cruelty and injustice."[18] Such determined resistance forced Hume to withdraw this amendment. Woodford responded two weeks after Marryat made his attack. However, the vehemence of Marryat's attack and Hume's amendment left no doubt that Woodford had three formidable enemies in Britain: Joseph Hume, Joseph Marryat, and the Committee of Landholders who were intent on making the concerns of the island "subservient to those of the sugar planters" (*H*, 132). Hume, however, was determined to support "the economic interests of his brother-in-law, William Hardin Burnley, a merchant and senior member of the council of Trinidad."[19] He would prove to be of tremendous assistance to Burnley in the British Parliament and was especially important when the question of compensation for slave owners was debated in the 1830s.[20]

If Woodford had his problems with Marryat, the Committee of Landholders, Burnley, and Hume, his relations with the free people of color were just as tortuous. When he returned to the island in February 1823 from a trip to England to defend himself against the onslaught of Hume and Marryat, he was greeted coldly by the people of color. While the white officials greeted him on his return with great pomp and ceremony, "the face of every colored man, woman and child, bore the unequivocal expression of discontent, sorrow, or fear."[21] The colored people of the island felt that Woodford, as a civilian governor, would have treated them better than the military governors who had ruled prior to his coming. They were disappointed by his supercilious attitudes toward them and his attempts to reduce the gains they had achieved, a case that Philippe made against him in *Free Mulatto*. While the coloreds were fighting for civil equality with the whites, the Africans were struggling for greater freedom on the island as the emancipation train was gaining much steam in Great Britain.

CHAPTER 5

Opposition to Emancipation from Tacarigua

≶

A black child is born today. Take him; do what you like with him; make him a brute, if it so pleases you: a brute in his labour, a brute in ignorance. Feed him like a brute; flog him like a brute. I say, how are we authorized, on a child that has done no wrong, to pronounce that sentence, to inflict that curse?

—Thomas Fowell Buxton, Abolition of Slavery Debate, 1823

B Y THE 1820s Burnley's influence and power on the island had grown considerably. Eventually he owned or controlled fourteen sugar estates of which Orange Grove was the largest. It consisted of twenty-six hundred acres and was serviced by over two hundred slaves. It was the largest grant of land to an individual on the island.[1] Only a few individuals possessed grants of land larger than six hundred acres. The size of the average Trinidad estate at the time was approximately three hundred acres. This credential alone made Burnley the natural leader of the planters on the island. His education and business savvy cemented that fact in the eyes of the local authorities and the colonial government. Moreover, his connection with Joseph Hume increased his political prominence and made him a more trenchant foe of Woodford.

In keeping with his new status, Burnley built a palatial mansion in 1821 at Orange Grove, in Tacarigua. It was equal in stature to the governor's residence in St. Ann's. Such a residence signified that Burnley had arrived at a position in the society where he could question the authority of the governor with impunity and without fear of retaliation. It was located in the Orange Grove Savannah, southward of the Royal Road (now the Eastern Main Road) not far from the St. Mary's Anglican Church that he assisted in building. L. A. A. de Verteuil declared: "A person visiting the island would meet with but very few neat, or even comfortable, residences in the country districts. . . . Several country residences can bear comparison with English and French villas—viz., that of the late Mr. Burnley, Tacarigua; of Mr. L. Agostini, Saint Ann; Zurcher; Dr. de Bossiere, and Cipriani, in the neighborhood of Port of Spain; and several others in the country."[2] This mansion was the subject of one of Michel-Jean Cazabon's paintings (*Orange Grove,* 1849) that Burnley commissioned. In 1960 the building was sold to Hati, an Indian gentleman from El Dorado, Trinidad, who broke it down and used the lumber to construct other buildings.[3]

Burnley set up court in this splendid residence while his wife shopped in Paris for furniture and cutlery for their mansion. It was here he entertained the white elite of the island. Like the Great House that Frederick Douglass described in his narrative,[4] Burnley's mansion was associated with greatness and elegance; the place from which he conducted his business. The planters of the island gathered there when they wished to protest the actions of the colonial government and the directives of the various governors who came and left the island as transient birds of flight. Orange Grove became an alternative seat of government, the fulcrum around which the local planters gravitated.

Life at Orange Grove was not immune from the tumultuous changes that were taking place in the slave world at the time. As the beginning of the century, enslaved Africans in the West Indies agitated for their freedom; chief among them were the Haitians under Toussaint L'Ouverture. Observing the example of the Haitians and the insurrections that were taking place in the British West Indian islands, on May 15, 1823, Thomas Fowell Buxton brought his first resolution against slavery, arguing that "the state of slavery is repugnant to the principles of the British Constitution and of the Christian Religion; and that it ought to be gradually abolished throughout the British Colonies with as much expedition as may be found consistent with a due regard to the well-being of the parties concerned."[5] He declaimed: "I have not a notion that slavery can endure investigation. It must perish when once brought under the public eye. And I feel confident that a few minutes ago, we commenced the process which will conclude, though not speedily, in the extinction of slavery throughout the whole of the British dominions." Buxton stuck to his position in spite of the opposition's insistence that the emancipation of enslaved Africans would lead to the insurrection of blacks, the murder of whites in the various islands, and the reversion of blacks "to their former habits of savage life."[6] A year later, Burnley used this argument when the Colonial Office issued instructions to ameliorate the conditions of enslaved Africans in the colony.

The planters in the West Indies were incensed when the news of these reforms reached the islands. They understood correctly that the advocates of African emancipation were gaining ground in Britain. The Trinidad planters had especial cause to worry since Trinidad was a new colony, and George Canning, foreign secretary, was determined to carry out this experiment on the island. Buxton notes that as the debate on his motion grew animated, "the discussion grew warmest when Mr. Canning brought forward his plan, that the proposed amelioration should be suggested to the colonial legislatures, but should be enforced in the island of Trinidad, which being one of the crown colonies had no legislature of its own, with the further condition, however, that any unexpected resistance should be met by authority."[7]

On April 18, 1790, Lord Henry Bathurst voted to repeal "the slave trade in the first such vote on abolition."[8] On June 26, 1823, Woodford sent Lord Bathurst's dispatch to the members of the council. When his dispatch came up at the council for discussion on July 9, Burnley and his fellow planters objected strongly to the measures proposed. Burnley took the position that the planters who lived on the island were better acquainted with the conditions under which the enslaved labored and so were better able to respond to the regulations that were proposed by His Majesty's government. He believed that these regulations arose primarily from "the great want of information [that] exists at the Colonial Office, as to the real state of this Island in particular" and an ignorance of "the customs, prejudices, and vices of the society for whom they are intended. Unless we supply that practical information, and decidedly oppose the adoption of every measure, not justified by reason and prudence, we are creating for ourselves a catastrophe similar to that which has recently hazarded the existence of a neighboring Colony."[9] The reference, no doubt, was an allusion to the rebellion that had taken place in Demerara.

Burnley was decidedly against any improvement in the conditions of the enslaved in spite of his protestations to the contrary. He believed that slave conditions in Trinidad were superior to those in the other islands and therefore it was better to leave well enough alone. He felt that the supporters of emancipation in the House of Commons were misguided. In his estimation, enslaved Africans had not arrived at a state of civilization where they would appreciate the blessing of freedom. It was "not by the application of restrictive laws, but by a gradual improvement in the feeling, temper, and judgment of the owners of Slaves, that this desirable object can ever be accomplished; and this is not fanciful theory which I am recommending. Gentlemen, our own experience, and our observation of what passes around us, fully bear me out in this assertion."[10]

Trinidad planters identified THE WHIP with slavery. They asserted: "We did, and do declare the WHIP to be ESSENTIAL to West Indian discipline; aye, as essential, my Lord Calthrope as the freedom of the press, and the trial by jury to the liberty of the subject, in England, and to be justified on equally legitimate grounds. The comfort, welfare, and happiness of our laboring classes cannot subsist without it" (*AM*, June 30, 1825, 19). It was part of the doctrine of the time. Burnley believed in it implicitly. "Negroes," he declaimed, "are children of a larger growth, and the fear of punishment has now the effect which, under the regulation proposed, will require the application of it" (*OS*, 38). To refrain from whipping them was tantamount to allowing them to retain their savage ways. He insisted that the planters needed to exercise their "Domestic Jurisdiction" by which a master is authorized to punish his slave without the intervention of a Magistrate. "This power," he wrote, "is essential to the system. If taken away totally, or even partially repealed by the enactment of regulations prohibiting all corporal punishments, from that moment the fabric of Slavery is virtually destroyed, and the Negro, though not free, will cease to be of any value to his master."[11]

The suggestion that the planters had to cease whipping their female slaves brought a violent response from Burnley. Such a regulation, he argued, was "so monstrous and extraordinary, that I hardly know how to approach the subject. . . . The intention of such an order, we are told, is to elevate the females in the scale of society, whilst the men are to be left as they were before, establishing, in fact, a decided superiority in favor of the former" (*OS*, 41). To him, the only question was whether females should be whipped decently (that is, with their scanty clothing on) or indecently (that is, naked.) Burnley believed that women were subordinate to men. It was "the fixed and natural state of women." To treat them differently from men "would bestow on our female Slaves prerogatives never to be aspired to, or enjoyed by their free sisters in Africa, and to attempt to arrest an unvarying law of nature by a British Order in Council" (*OS*, 41–42). Apart from subverting the unchanging laws of nature, this undesirable regulation had the potential of degrading men and "subverting discipline first, and then Slavery itself" (*OS*, 42).

In Burnley's mind there was another moral argument to be made against discontinuing the punishment of female slaves. He felt it led to the subversion of societal values in a slave culture. Without the whip, the master would be unable to control his female slaves. "Women," he said, "are as notoriously addicted as the men to lying, theft, broils, and every immoral dissipation" (OS, 42). In Europe there were many social constraints (such as the loss of character, the contempt of society, and so on) whereas there were fewer such constraints in a slave society where everything was turned upside down and values were distorted. Thus, he argues, "Even that ancient proverb, 'Honesty is the best policy,' the truth of which goes home to the feelings of every individual in a land of freedom, is false, as applied to a society of Slaves. The greatest rogue upon an estate may be, and is frequently the most valuable Slave upon it, and enjoys a corresponding superiority of comforts over his less artful associates" (OS, 43).

The members of council agreed in principle with the resolution of the House of Commons although they were disinclined to agree with three of the eleven articles that were proposed. The governor alerted the council that he would send the resolution to Lord Bathurst (H, 151–52).[12] Burnley was not appeased. Although he did not vote against the resolution, he asserted there were other ways to do things. At the council meeting on September 4 he proposed that complaints against the masters or those the masters made against the slaves should be published monthly in the Colonial Gazette "with full particulars as to the names of parties, nature of complaint and decision of the judge" (H, 152).

Burnley's proposal was discussed at length since he was the only resident proprietor of an estate sitting on the council. Finally, it was resolved that the monthly statements for which Burnley called should be laid before the council. Burnley seemed to be satisfied with this resolution. However, a few days later, the planters came together at Burnley's mansion to voice their displeasure and to plan further strategy. To Burnley and his friends, any thoughts of loosening the bonds of slavery or any movement toward emancipation would ruin them. They were sharply critical of Lord Bathurst's dispatch and Woodford's response to it. Burnley was more direct in his criticism of the draft order-in-council at the next meeting of the council. He expressed his frustration in trying to make amendments to orders-in-council, and argued that the enactment of the present order-in-council "will be productive of cruel injustice to them." He expostulated:

> Under the present system the whole of the youth and energy of a slave is devoted to the service of the master, but the latter in his turn is bound to take care of his slave when ill, and to protect him from want when no longer able to work; but under the system now proposed, this equitable arrangement will no longer exist. The slave will be allowed more time to himself, to his master's prejudice, who will

also be the loser if the slave over exerts himself and suffers in health when working for himself, and yet the law proposes still to saddle the owner with the care of the sick and aged slave. . . . (*H*, 152)

Burnley had asked that Woodford publish the proposed order-in-council so that the inhabitants could express their opinions on it. Woodford was not impressed. Trinidad was a crown colony. He had no intention of consulting the inhabitants about the measures. He had heard about the planters' meeting that took place in Tacarigua; was aware of Burnley's harsh condemnation of the measures; and expressed his displeasure about Burnley's behavior. Although Burnley apologized for his conduct, his whole demeanor toward the governor had changed. He was showing his displeasure of the governor's prerogatives openly and, in the process, began to assert his propriety rights over his fellow countrymen. Fraser observed: "The day had not arrived, although it was not very remote, for open opposition to a Government measure, either at the Council table or out of doors, to be safely undertaken. Burnley's tone on this occasion was much changed from what it had been a few years before, but it was still respectful though remonstrant" (*H*, 152). It would not take long before Burnley displayed his recalcitrance more openly.

CHAPTER 6

Toward Planter Control of the Colony

I am not conscious of having taken any steps out of doors which I am not prepared to repeat within. I should have done nothing out of doors had I met with any encouragement to act within, and if even now, I am permitted at this Board to use my best efforts to have the Order in Council annulled, revised or amended, I shall not be disposed to do so elsewhere.

—William Hardin Burnley, 1824

THE ORDER-IN-COUNCIL OF March 1823 that was introduced into the colony to improve the conditions of the enslaved with a view to their eventual emancipation had a profound impact upon the society. It rattled the planters' confidence and stirred them into action while the enslaved masses intuited that freedom was just around the corner. The planters would have hoped that these measures be stayed. However, the colonial government was adamant. George Canning informed the British Parliament that the government "was determined to compel amelioration in Trinidad, but to apply for the present no measure more stringent than 'admonition' to the contumacious colonies."[1] It helped that the enslaved assumed an emboldened position and challenged their masters' authority at every turn.

On March 16, 1824, an order-in-council for the general regulation of slavery in Trinidad was laid before the British Parliament. It called upon the colonial legislatures to adopt the reforms that were set out in Lord Bathurst's dispatches, primarily the appointment of a "Protector of Slaves" who was given the responsibility of caring for the welfare of the enslaved people. This dispatch called for "the registration of certificated slave witnesses, the non separation of families in cases of judicial sale, voluntary manumission, savings banks, and the Sunday market, which last was to be abolished as soon as adequate provision had been made for religious teaching. . . . The slave was to be entitled to purchase his own freedom and that of any member of his family; and if the price could not be settled by mutual consent, it was to be determined either by joint appraisers or, in default of their agreement, by an umpire."[2]

Amidst the planters' anger with the order-in-council of 1823, members of the West Indian Commission—Messrs. Fortunatus Dwarris, a slave owner in Jamaica, and Henry Maddock—were appointed by the Colonial Office in 1822 "to inquire into the administration of justice in the West Indies."[3] They arrived in Trinidad on January 19, 1824. They also "inquired into and reported on the titles of lands and the state therein."[4] This visit provided Burnley and his colleagues with a unique opportunity to express their indignation against the governor and what they saw as the tyrannous nature of the orders-in-council. It also allowed them to articulate their desire to make Trinidad a British colony with a British Constitution in spite of the limitations their crown colony status imposed upon them.

Sensing an opening, Burnley and his colleagues quickly called together a public meeting to express their views to the visiting commissioners. James Cadett, the chairman of the committee, was convinced that too much power was placed in the hands of the executive (meaning Woodford). He argued that the time had come to replace the Spanish laws that dated from the colony's founding. He reasoned: "However necessary it may have been at the time to arm the Executive with extraordinary powers when revolutionary fury, desolating St. Domingo, agitated every colony of this hemisphere with just apprehension, it must now be apparent to every reflecting mind that the time has at last arrived when more liberal institutions can safely be conceded" (*H*, 165). Like his colleagues, he felt that the planters should have a greater say in how the country was governed and how their taxes were being spent.

Having lived on the island for twenty-one years, Burnley was convinced that the island would "never enjoy the prosperity to which it is fairly entitled by its natural advantages until the inhabitants have a system of Law and Government founded upon British principles" (*H*, 166). He noted that the principal objective of every government is the protection of person and property. He did not believe that a government could achieve that objective if the powers in the executive's (meaning the governor's) hands were undefined and arbitrary. Taking direct aim at Woodford, he declared:

> I hope, therefore, that in any future scheme of Government the power of the Executive will be fairly limited, for the possession of undefined power as at present, answers no purpose but to render the Executive undeservedly the object of popular dread and hatred. It is most desirable that the taxpayers of the Colony should have some voice in the taxation and some control over the expenditure of the Revenue, without which the first would never be reduced nor the second kept within due bounds. With respect to the probability of obtaining a Legislative House of Assembly I agree with what has fallen from the Chair. We must rely upon His Majesty's Ministers, and even if we are offered the Law without the Constitution, my advice is that we should accept the offer, for that would give us trial by Jury and a free Press, and the rest would follow as a matter of course. (*H*, 166)

This was a call for devolution of powers and placing greater control of the government into the hands of the British (read *white*) segment of the population. It was a continuation of a call for some form of representative government that the Englishmen on the island were asking for since the British occupied the island in 1797.[5] The other inhabitants of the island interpreted the actions of Burnley and his party as a grab for power at their expense, which they believed would result in the lowering of their status on the island. To make matters worse, the free blacks and the people of color owned at least half of the property in the colony, which gave them as many rights at the whites. Such British nationalism alarmed them. This change, "under the guise of patriotism, was intended to strike a double blow, at their religion and at their social position" (*H*, 167).

The planters pleaded with Woodford to postpone the publication of the order-in-council but he would have none of it. They met again on April 29 and took "the unprecedented step" of asking the governor to lay before the council all the official correspondences that had transpired between him and the Colonial Office since July 9, 1823, "relative to the whipping of the female slaves and the subject of compensation to the owners; and also to the treatment of the slaves generally, as connected to the Order in Council" (*H*, 171). Burnley knew that Woodford would not accede to this request, but it indicated how far Burnley was prepared to go to assert his newfound authority.

Alarmed by their increasing demands, Woodford relayed his fears to Lord Bathurst in a letter he sent on May 1, 1824. He observed: "Notwithstanding the many and urgent applications that have been made to me to postpone the publication of and suspend the enforcement of the Order, I have not felt myself warranted in assuming so great a responsibility and therefore in compliance with the last clause of the Order, I issued the Proclamation of which copies are inclosed [*sic*], declaring the Order take force in one calendar month from the 24th instant, the date of that instrument."[6] On May 7 he informed Lord Bathurst that the order-in-council "had caused great alarm amongst all the slave proprietors, who were apprehensive that it would be followed by other and more direct demands" (*H*, 177). He also agreed that chaos would follow if the masters were not allowed to whip their female slaves and were prevented from using the cat o' nine tails to punish the male slaves.

No matter how he felt personally, Woodford had to carry out the instructions of his superiors at the Colonial Office. Unable to convince Woodford to yield to their imputations, Burnley, his fellow planters, and some of the leading inhabitants of the island decided to meet in Port of Spain on May 14, to prepare "a petition to the Sovereign, which they trust will meet with His Excellency's approbation."[7] Woodford responded the same day (May 1) he received their letter expressing "his very great concern that Gentlemen of their influence, should have determined upon a measure that the Governor cannot but consider as disadvantageous to the interests of the colony, and calculated to produce an unfavorable impression upon the minds of the slaves." Therefore, he deemed it his duty "to discourage such a meeting and to express his regret that he cannot sanction it with his approbation."[8]

Whether Woodford wanted it or not, "the Free Inhabitants of this Colony," as they called themselves, went ahead and held their meeting on the appointed day. They sought to go over his head by declaring their intention to take their concerns directly to the Crown. With Cadett serving as chair, they objected to an order they alleged, "inevitably [will] prove ruinous to the property of the master; injurious and demoralizing to the slave; peculiarly hazardous to the lives of the free colored inhabitants under the part of the 36 clauses of that order, and totally subversive to our gracious sovereign's benign intentions." They felt the governor should refrain from implementing the order until "a true representation of its effects may be made to His Majesty's ministers, to be laid at the foot of the Throne for His Majesty's gracious consideration."[9]

Woodford did not take the intransigence of these inhabitants lightly nor did he interpret it as a friendly gesture. He refused to dignify their correspondence by not responding to them in person. The next day—through his assistant secretary, Frederick Hammet (who was also his nephew)—Woodford expressed his "disapprobation" with the contents of the inhabitants' letter and refused to meet with their representatives. He did, however, assure them that he was ready, at any time, "to receive any applications of the Inhabitants or to reply to the same when transmitted in the usual manner to His Secretary for the purpose of being laid before Him."[10]

On May 17, 1824, the inhabitants responded to Hammet. They regretted His Excellency's refusal to meet their delegation to discuss "a subject so intimately connected with the vital interests of the whole population of every class and color." They had hoped that "a numerous and respectable deputation would have carried with the assurance that the petition conveyed the unanimous sentiments of the colony, a knowledge which might have been so easily collected from the signatures alone of those planters who were unable to quit their estates and attend the meeting in Port of Spain." In seeking to impress the governor about the popular nature of their concerns, Cadett informed him through Hammet that "similar instruments are in the course of signature in the different quarters which shall be handed to you when received, and which the committee respectfully request may be considered and accepted as the same petition now presented."[11]

A day later the governor responded to Cadett's letter. He expressed his indignation at having been sent such a petition from persons "styling themselves the free Inhabitants of the Colony" when he had noted "his concern that the assembly at which it has been adopted, should have taken place, notwithstanding the disapprobation which His Excellency had in the first instance expressed of a meeting being called for the purpose for which it was understood to be convened." His Excellency was pleased that they had reiterated the obedience they "owe to the Order of the King in Council" and was happy to learn of the petitioners' determination to improve the conditions of the slaves. He reminded them that the proclamation was comprised of recommendations to His Majesty's government "by the whole body of West India planters and merchants in London, as fit concessions on the part of the slave proprietors." He was not prepared to suspend any aspect of the proclamation since it received "the unqualified approbation of both Houses of Parliament and that of the country in general."[12] Moreover, he was not inclined to accept a deputation from the petitioners since he had disapproved of their meeting in the first place. The Trinidad planters could not know that the absentee owners in Britain were also losing faith in the efficacy of slavery.

On May 20 Burnley and his colleagues struck from another angle. Together with two members of His Majesty's council (Alexander Duncanson and Francis Pescheir), Burnley attacked the order-in-council from the standpoint of the impact it would have on the moral character of the slaves. They informed the governor they had examined the clauses in the order-in-council and concluded that "it can, in no way, tend to the improvement of the condition of the slaves, but on the contrary by the relaxation of discipline, which it will unavoidably occasion, must oppose serious obstacles to the acquirement of habits of industry, and to the improvement of their moral character." These members of His Majesty's council could foresee only the insurrection of the slaves, the eventual ruin of the planters, and the disruption of life in the country as they had known it. They reiterated the ambiguity of several clauses of the order and insisted that if the order was framed in Trinidad "this evil may have been remedied but under our present form of government, the proper construction or legal effect of a law can never be known until its meaning has been contested in the tribunals of first instance, and of appeal in the colony; and finally determined by the Lords of Appeal in England."[13]

The forty-second clause of the order caused the most grief to the planters. It provided that any master who had been convicted twice of "any cruel and unlawful punishment" should not only be fined or imprisoned "but should forfeit all slave and property and be incapacitated for owning or managing it in future."[14] Even Woodford asked that this clause be reconsidered on the ground that the female slaves were most prone to give offense and that a planter who succumbed to the temptation of striking them "might ruin not only himself but his family and creditors." Lord Bathurst however was insistent. He refused to change the clause but directed that the penalty should not be enforced "until it had been referred to the Home Government."[15] Having no choice in the matter, Woodford formally proclaimed the order, which came to be known as the "Trinidad Order," on May 24, 1824, and which came into force on June 24, 1824.

Burnley and his colleagues raised their objections again at the council meeting of October 7, 1824. Burnley noted that the colonists resisted the order from the time it was proclaimed on the specific ground that it would not improve the conditions of the slave population. He agreed with the leaders of the abolitionists "that slavery was in principle indefensible, in its consequences debasing and degrading and that strict moral justice required that its abolition should be deferred no longer than might appear to be advantageous to the real interests of the slaves themselves." To achieve the desired results, he felt the British government should be aware of what was taking place on the ground, the ignorance of which was manifest in the dispatches it sent to the colonies and the reportage that appeared in the London press. He believed that "until this mist of error was dispelled, it was impossible to expect beneficial results, from any representations which might be made by His Excellency and the Board, to His Majesty Ministers. Where parties argue from different premises, it would be impossible to arrive at similar conclusions, and the misunderstanding could be interminable."[16]

Burnley believed firmly that no practical scheme for the improvement of the slave condition could be advanced without a clear picture of the slave character. The whipping of the slaves was indispensable for order and discipline on the plantation since "without a firm government and rigid discipline, no measure or regulations, however, beneficial, could be carried into execution." He believed that if the British authorities were aware of "the habits and morals of the slave population, they would never have sanctioned that fatal error: the abolition of the whip, which, if not speedily remedied, would disappoint forever, the hopes of those who anxiously looked forward to a progressive improvement in the moral of the slaves. Instead of weakening the power, previously placed in the hands of the master, it ought rather to have been strengthened."[17] Interestingly enough, when this issue came up in Jamaica, one Mr. Barrett declared that he had abolished both the cart whip and the cat and would not allow the former to be used even on his cattle.[18]

Burnley also brought up the subject of compensation since he owned the most slaves on the island. He wanted to accumulate more accurate information "of the Negro character . . . both in a state of slavery and of freedom" hence his resolution that Sir Ralph Woodford appoint a committee "with powers to take evidence, call for papers, and generally under the authority of His Excellency to perform whatever may be necessary to the attainment of the information required."[19] Burnley had raised the question before at the April meeting of the Board of Council. Woodford was not inclined to appoint such a committee then. This time the entire council, with the exception of Lieutenant Colonel Young, voted for the measure. This put Woodford on the spot. He promised to take the vote under advisement and get back to the council to let the members know his decision.

On November 4 Woodford authorized the formation of the committee "provided it were limited to the objects expressed in said resolution."[20] On December 7 he sent a letter to Lord Bathurst informing him that he had agreed to form the committee but with an added proviso that it also "inspects the settlements of the free [Negro] settlers."[21] Woodford retained his reservation about the propriety of the committee in spite of his having agreed to its formation. However, he was devastated when Burnley insisted that he forward his [Burnley's] address to Lord Bathurst. On February 9, 1825, Woodford wrote to Lord Bathurst asking for guidance on the matter since "there are no regulations to guide me in such a case and W. Burnley insisted on it as a right inherent in his seat in Council. I did not think it desirable to oppose the measure, but I request Your Lordship's order for the future. It is only upon the particular subject of the slaves and with W. Burnley individually that this has occurred and it is not likely that a similar question would arise on any other topic."[22]

Flush with victory, Burnley and his committee began to work furiously to gather information on the character of the slaves and the freedmen. Ultimately, he wanted to prove the slaves in Trinidad were treated better than the slaves on the other islands, hence the undesirability of implementing measures that he and his fellow planters felt were detrimental to the well-being of the island. Burnley wanted his findings to reach the secretary of state as quickly as possible, which accounted for the haste with which he undertook his task. Initially, his committee met once a week but quickly increased its pace of work to expedite their assignment. The intensity of its activities only exacerbated Burnley's relations with Woodford as the former sought to establish who was boss of the island. Sir Norman Lamont observed that from this point on "Burnley's great political activity, both in Council, and out of doors, show him more and more in the role of a Leader of the Opposition. . . . He carried his opposition so that it almost became a duel between him and the Governor, Sir Ralph Woodford; and however much we may now differ from Burnley's opinions, we must admit that he carried on his fight with great ability, eloquence and resource" (*OG*, 4). The antagonism between these two men would be carried on until Woodford's death in 1828.

CHAPTER 7

Life on the Plantation

The economic superiority of free hired labor over slave is obvious even
to the slave owner. Slave labor is given reluctantly, it is unskillful, it lacks
versatility. Other things being equal, free men would be preferred. But in
the early stages of colonial development, other things were not equal.

—Eric Williams, *Capitalism and Slavery*

BURNLEY BEGAN HIS hearings on December 9, 1824, and ended them on
April 9, 1825. Twenty hearings were held in various parts of the country.
He examined thirty-one witnesses, all of whom were white except for one free
man of color, Jose Antonio Adia. These hearings were published as *Trinidad
Negroes* by the House of Commons on June 14, 1827.[1] Although the hearings
were designed ostensibly to obtain a more correct knowledge of the Negro
character in the state of slavery and freedom, the practical objective was to
demonstrate that slavery was not as bad as it was advertised to be and that
the enslaved fared much better than the disbanded soldiers, the American
refugees, the free laboring classes, and the peons in the colony. Burnley also
wanted to establish that the negative consequences of the institution of slavery
had more to do with the dissipation of the enslaved than the malevolence and
cruelty of the masters. In fact, the whole point of the exercise was to depict
the enslaved as having no human feelings at all, incapable of taking care of
themselves, willing only to gratify their animal needs, and having little consideration for their fellow blacks.

In spite of these biases, the hearings turned out to be an important exercise in adumbrating the conditions under which the enslaved lived. One scholar has described them as being conducted merely "to discredit the amelioration programme by 'proving' how vicious and unreliable was free black labor."[2] This was true. However, those four months of hearings threw much light on the plantation system in Trinidad, the manner in which the enslaved and the other laboring groups were treated, and the condition of the peons on the island. Although the Protector of Slaves report also described how the enslaved were treated, Burnley's report was the first to do so in a systematic fashion. It can be considered the first study of practical sociology on the island.[3]

Plantation slavery in Trinidad, as the hearings established, was a relatively recent phenomenon. Between 1784 and 1797 when Abercromby captured the island, the slave population grew from less than one thousand to ten thousand enslaved Africans. By 1802, that population had grown to twenty thousand. St. Hilaire Begorrat, a sugar planter and adviser of Governor Picton, testified that when he arrived in 1784, one year after the Cedula of Population was enacted, there were only two establishments in the country that could be termed sugar estates. During this early period Trinidad did not produce enough sugar for its own consumption. It relied on the other West Indian islands and the Spanish Main for the sugar it consumed.

Between 1784 and 1797 when Abercromby captured the island, most of the black population came from St. Vincent, Grenada, and Martinique. Few blacks came directly from Africa, but as Begorrat recalled, "Several Spanish vessels from the Havannah [*sic*] came here to take slaves away which had been imported by Barry and Black [English merchants], and some from Laguira for slaves for Caraccas [*sic*]" (*TN*, 51). Begorrat who began his sojourn in Trinidad as a merchant became a sugar planter on the island in 1795. As noted earlier, by 1813, Begorrat was running Picton's sugar estate in Point-a-Pierre.

Burnley began his hearings by examining Robert Mitchell, the chief superintendent of the African American refugees who had come to the island between 1815 and 1821 as a result of the Anglo-American War of 1812. They consisted of Africans born in Africa and those born in America. Arriving in the country in 1797, Mitchell spent his first five years as a merchant and the remaining twenty years as a planter and superintendent of the refugees. When the first batch of fifty-seven refugees arrived in November 1815, they were placed in four thatched buildings, each sixty feet long and twenty feet wide, that were set up to accommodate them. The overflow was handled by the Indian villages and "no individual suffered from want of shelter." (*TN*, 2).

Upon arrival each African American refugee received a hoe, a cutlass, an axe, an iron pot for cooking, and sixteen acres of land. The refugees were placed in eight villages under the superintendence of a sergeant and a corporal "whose duty it was to keep the peace" (*TN*, 3). They also had the authority to confine them to the stocks for twenty-four hours and to inflict twelve lashes for any disturbances of the peace.

They made their living by planting and cutting canes, cutting cords of wood that they sold, and felling the high woods to cut back the wilderness of the land. They planted provisions (corn, rice, and plantains) and occasionally cultivated a few coffee trees on their lands. Mitchell noted that the rice they produced was "well cleaned [and], fit for the London market. It is much broken for want of mills but is sweet and good for use" (*TN*, 5). Even as late as 1833, the disbanded soldiers of the 3rd West India Regiment continued "to raise a considerable quantity of rice" as Governor Lewis Grant observed.[4]

This is not surprising because Africans around the bulge of the West African coastline (that is, around Sierra Leone) were "long experienced in cultivating rice in the coastal swampland [and] fetched good prices from landowners establishing rice plantations in the American South."[5] When the African American refugees (later called the Merikins) arrived in Trinidad they brought their rice-growing skills, which Kim Severson called "the rice of their ancestors, sustaining slaves and, later, generations of Southern cooks both black and white."[6]

In 2018 B. J. Dennis, a Gullah chef from Charleston, "was stunned to find the rice [Moruga Hill rice] growing in a field in Trinidad, tended by a farmer descended from slaves who once lived in Georgia." Discovering this strain of rice in Trinidad, Dennis observed: "It is hard to overstate how shocked the people who study rice were to learn that the long-lost American hill rice was alive and growing in the Caribbean. Horticulturalists at the Smithsonian Institution want to grow it, rice geneticists at New York University are testing it and the United States Department of Agriculture is reviewing it."[7]

Mitchell also testified that the African American refugees were "generally observant of the marriage tie . . . and live decently together" (*TN*, 3). Sadly, these refugees were compelled to turn in runaway slaves as part of their agreement with the government. They were also rewarded financially for apprehending local blacks who passed through their settlements without passes. The British must have adopted this practice from their 1739 treaty with the Maroons of Jamaica who were forced to turn in runaway slaves. Such behavior led to much resentment among the various African groupings on the island toward the refugees. The only redeeming feature of this behavior (stopping and apprehending

Africans who passed through their settlements) was that the apprehension of Africans was infrequent.

Another witness, Alexander Williams, confirmed much of what Begorrat said about how the Africans came to the island and the source of sugar prior to the conquest of the island by Abercromby. He revealed that prior to the British conquest, not one ship had brought any Africans directly from the African coast to the country. Williams was a physician appointed as "the inspecting officer" by Picton in 1797 and was responsible for inspecting Africans who arrived in the island between 1797 and 1807. He testified that "the great influx of African slaves [to Trinidad] took place after the capture of the island by the British" (*TN*, 9). This did not mean that Africans were not arriving at the island before this as the case of Cudjoe and his wife demonstrated.[8] There was a high mortality rate among the new African arrivals from *mal d'estomac* [or dirt-eating] and dysentery which Williams ascribed to "chagrin [a form of sorrow], added to change of diet and a new course of habits" (*TN*, 9). In fact, it was thought that the French and Spanish planters were more successful in preserving Africans because they fed them with home-grown provisions that were "better adapted to the African constitution" than the rice, corn, and flour which the English brought from America (*TN*, 9).

Apart from seeking to convince the British authorities that the treatment of the enslaved in Trinidad was more benevolent than it was on the other islands, Burnley wanted to find out why the slave population was dwindling, whether it was attributable to diseases or to the behavior of the slaves.[9] Asked by Burnley if the majority of cases in the hospital could be ascribed to the nature or quantity of work performed by the slaves, Williams responded that their presence in the hospitals arose more frequently "from intemperance and impudent conduct; from exposure to night air, and over exertion in dancing. . . . The number of cases in the hospitals are invariably greater on the Monday than on any other day" (*TN*, 10). Williams also reported that the slaves would travel any distance at night to attend a dance regardless of the consequences. The same was true in Jamaica. Dancing, however, was not as innocent as it appeared. James Epstein reminds us that such "rituals of conviviality might shelter designs of resistance. This was why 'Negro' dances in Port of Spain either were officially banned or required permission, and the beating of drums was prohibited after nine in the evening."[10]

Burnley was intent on showing that slave labor was superior to free labor, a proposition that Eric Williams contradicted about one hundred years later when he noted that the "economic superiority of free hired labor over slave is obvious. Slave labor is given reluctantly, it is unskillful, it lacks versatility."[11] In his examination of Antoine Victoire St. Bresson, a former officer in the Royal Foreign Artillery who became a planter, Burnley asked why he had given up the habit of hiring free laborers, to which St. Bresson responded: "Because they cannot be depended upon. They only work as they please." When asked if he felt his estate could be conducted profitably by free labor, he responded that he did not believe that "an estate can be conducted at all by free labour, which I assert from my practical knowledge, as I never would have purchased additional negroes could I have managed without them" (*TN*, 12–13.) This theme is repeated throughout the hearings. After slavery ended, Burnley reversed himself and began to argue for the glories of free labor.

The sexual behavior (or morality) of the slaves, particularly the women, came under close scrutiny. Asked by Burnley if he considered chastity to be a virtue among the slaves, St. Bresson responded: "Not in the least." Asked further if any female slave upon his estate had confined her affections to one man, St. Bresson replied: "I have some who have lived regularly with the same man, but who have certainly not been faithful to him during that period" (*TN*, 13). Burnley even asked St. Bresson if he ever punished the slaves "for changing their wives or husbands" (*TN*, 13). Elegantly perceptive in his response, St. Bresson said: "I have occasionally punished some of the younger ones, but it had very little effect. The elder generally allege such plausible reason for a change that I have considered that I should render them miserable by obliging them to remain together. Whenever I find a man with two wives, I endeavor to persuade him to give up one; but their general customs admit it. The women themselves do not object to it; and it is so well understood, that they have a particular appellation for two women living with the same man: they call each other '*combosse*'" (*TN*, 13).[12]

Intent on depicting the women as being more difficult to manage than men, and certainly more loose sexually, Burnley elicited the following observations from Argent F. Blackwell, superintendent of the Royal Gaol where the prisoners were kept:

Amongst the slaves do you observe any difference in the conduct and behavior of the sexes? Yes. I find the men easier managed than the women. The latter are more insolent, use worse language, and are more quarrelsome amongst themselves. I am rarely obliged to go into the men's ward at night, but am frequently called into the women's ward to keep them in peace and order. I have generally observed less of decency and propriety of behavior amongst the most intelligent of the female slaves who reside in and about Port of Spain, than those who come in from the country.

What are we to understand by less of decency in the behavior? I mean that those who reside in and about the town are more bold and daring than the others in their indecent behavior. There seems to be very little sense of shame amongst any of them. Whenever a heavy shower of rain suddenly falls, it is the regular duty of a person under me to prevent their stripping themselves stark naked, and standing under the waterspouts; and at the time appropriated for the men to bathe, if a vigilant look out is not kept, they will slip in and mingle with the naked men, which has frequently occurred. (*TN*, 39)

Both Burnley and St. Bresson concluded that enslaved Africans were unable to be faithful to each other. They displayed lax moral standards and needed to be married to prevent unfaithful tendencies and practices. Asked if it would be in the interest of the master for the enslaved Africans "to be married together, and remain faithful to each other," St. Bresson responded: "They have invariably objected, and claim the right to consulting their own inclinations" (*TN*, 13). A new conception of marriage arose among enslaved Africans on the plantations of America. Basil Matthews notes: "The West Indian slave, with few exceptions, bluntly refused to be bound by matrimonial tie. All but two slaves on a Trinidad estate preferred death to marriage. . . . If 'Massa King George' ordered them to marry white wives they would marry as many of them as he wished. Meanwhile the utmost they were willing to do was to 'try to live wid 'em first a little bit for trial.'"[13]

W. E. B. Du Bois observed similar tendencies among the Philadelphia Negroes, which may help to explain the conjugal phenomenon that Burnley and St. Bresson were trying to understand. He noted: "In the slum districts there are many such families, which remain together years and are in effect common law marriages. Some of these connections are broken by whim or desire, although in many cases they are permanent unions."[14] Du Bois also noted that the great weakness of the Negro family "is still the lack of respect for the marriage bond, inconsiderate entrance into it, and bad household economy and family government. Sexual looseness then arises as a secondary consequence, bringing adultery and prostitution in its train."[15] The evidence of slave life as recorded in the Trinidad Slave Register of 1813 shows a more ordered sense of family life and little dependence on the slave master.

These hearings also provided Burnley with an interesting though biased description of the Spanish peons who came to the island to work. One person testified: "You never can depend upon them; they work only when they please, have a great repugnance to it, and what they do is done in a more slovenly indifferent way than by the slaves" (*TN*, 23). And the testimony continues, claiming that although the mothers were attached to their offspring, they love to fish, follow their husbands on their hunting expeditions, and the children are usually neglected. When they are home, they "work the provisions for their families, and wash their clothes when they have a change, which is not often. The greater part cannot sew but employ those who can to make up the garments for them. They spend the greater part of the day in smoking and sleeping" (*TN*, 24). The men are good at felling trees and work when they need the money. They exist mainly on salt fish, plantains, corn, salt pork, and the game they catch.

This pernicious view was contradicted by an insightful report on the life of the peons by James Hamilton who noted that the Spanish peons were a free people. The sugar planters wanted to enslave them. Like other human beings in history, the peons went to Trinidad because they got better wages there. Hamilton—who had employed peons both on the Spanish Main and in Trinidad (in villages such as Erin, Icacos, and Cedros) for fourteen years—called them an industrious people with "a considerable tinge of pride in [their] comportment which hardly ever leaves [them] under the most trying circumstances." He also offered a persuasive reason why the peons refused to work on the sugar plantations: "Too frequently, there have been scandalous abuses in the treatment of the Spanish peons [by the sugar estates]; their wages have been detained for the most frivolous pretexts; the conduct of one has been made responsible for that of the others; they have been given [sold] to excess in rum and charged four times its current rates in payment of their labor; and goods have been thrust on them at exorbitant prices."[16] Knowing that they were free men, the peons were unwilling to accept such condescending and dishonest behavior on the part of the Europeans. Eleven years later, Mr. Ward, chairman of the Select Committee on the Disposal of Lands, rebuffed Burnley strongly when he advanced an argument about the laziness and shiftlessness of the peons (*DL*, 163).

The committee also touched on the condition of the Amerindians, particularly those who resided in Arima, who were thought to be the most quiet and manageable of the subjugated persons. Just to be sure it had covered the subject comprehensively, the committee contrasted slavery as it existed in Venezuela, Tortola, Barbados, and Cuba with that of Trinidad. It even examined how manumission functioned in the other territories. They were especially interested in how the *coartado* functioned in the Spanish-speaking countries and how the manumitted slaves behaved after they were freed.[17] The differences between field slaves and domestic slaves and the Africans and Creoles were also given some attention.

Burnley's committee ended its hearing on what it might have considered a high note when it compared the wages paid to domestic servants in England with those paid to domestic servants in Trinidad. The planters were convinced that the slaves in Trinidad were better off than the working people of England. Reverend David Evans, the last witness called, observed: "I think one servant in England would do as much as three here, and with much more comfort to the master and mistress of the family, who must in this colony attend to everything. . . . Nothing can be worse than the morals of the domestics here. They seem to have no idea of chastity. They are generally so dishonest that it is useless to discharge them on that account, as you cannot expect to find one better than another. They are not sober and rarely tell the truth" (*TN*, 57).

On May 21, about a month and a half after the hearings, Burnley turned in his findings to Governor Woodford with a request that they be transmitted to the secretary of state for the colonies. On May 25, Woodford notified Burnley that he had consented to the formation of the committee on the condition that it limited its examination to the objects expressed in the resolution and confine its investigation to the state of the servant classes of free laborers in the colony. Before going further "the committee should have reported their proceeding [findings] and have awaited his further instructions."[18] Since Burnley and his committee did not comply with his instructions of December 7 and exceeded "the limits of their authority," Governor Woodford was not prepared to accept their report or transmit it to the secretary of state unless the objectionable parts were omitted.

Burnley was not inclined to back down. On June 1, he responded to the governor's letter saying he regretted that their proceedings did not meet with the governor's approbation. He informed the governor that although the resolution confined them to an investigation "of whatever may be necessary to the attainment of the information and perfection of the measures necessary to be adopted, for the future melioration of the condition of the slave population," he felt it was left to the discretion of the committee "to adopt such line of inquiry as might appear to them necessary for the attainment of the information required." Given the line of inquiry proposed by the board, and in the absence of any "expressed directions" from His Excellency, the committee felt that it had to investigate any matter that would throw light on its charge. After giving serious thought to Woodford's concern, they concluded that "the character of a slave is only to be ascertained by reference to his conduct in all possible situations, and circumstances or measures be suggested for the improvement of his condition but by an enquiry into the character, conduct and condition of those whom he is dependent, as well as into any object by which his welfare may be directly or remotely affected."[19]

Burnley hoped that his reasoning was persuasive and reminded the governor that his committee acted in good faith and with the sole purpose of obtaining information that was requested of them. No matter how "irrelevant" the governor considered the information that they had gathered, Burnley felt that ultimately it would be "beneficial in some shape or other, to the colony and to His Majesty's Government. Under either views of the case, they respectfully hope, that His Excellency will be pleased to transmit the Evidence, as taken by them, entire to His Majesty's Secretary of State."[20]

When the official findings of Burnley's committee were published by order of the House of Commons in June 1827, the evidence given by Reverend William Le Goff, George Fitzwilliams, Henry Gloster, Samuel Ely, and Robert Neilson were excluded. It was not published in its entirety as Burnley requested. The subtitle of the published document read "Extracts from the Minutes of Evidence taken by the Committee of the Council of Trinidad, for enquiring into the Negroe [sic] Character." One can only deduce that Woodford did not transmit the evidence of the full hearings to the secretary of state, leaving out the evidence from those areas that in which he had asked Burnley not to meddle.

Whatever may be said of the hearings, they gave its readers the first comprehensive view of how the enslaved and others lived their lives. It anticipated Du Bois's *The Philadelphia Negro* (1899), a study that was undertaken to enquire "into the history and social conditions of the transplanted Africans"[21] in the United States and which resulted in what Herbert Aptheker called "the first scientific study in African American sociology and the pioneering study in urban sociology in the United States."[22] These hearings drove a further wedge between Burnley and Woodford. The acrimonious exchanges between them did not bode well for their future relations. These two men were each determined to shape the destiny of the island. While Woodford remained governor, the rift between them continued to widen.

CHAPTER 8

Burnley's Ascendancy

〜

On the eve of my departure for the north, I am too much employed to interfere with your time, but I am too anxious to have from you, to any of the public or literary men in the United States of America, a few letters of introduction for my brother in law, M' William Harden [*sic*] Burnley, a Merchant in Trinidad, who intends to pay a visit to the United States in August next.

—Joseph Hume to John Quincy Adams, June 9, 1826

I F THE ORDER-IN-COUNCIL of 1823 succeeded in ameliorating the conditions of enslaved Africans in Trinidad, it also left the masters feeling uncomfortable. It threatened their absolute authority over the enslaved. According to William Law Mathieson, "The planters lived in constant fear of revolt; and any proposal from outside to alleviate the condition of the slaves, no matter how harmless in itself, was regarded as breaking the spell of subjection."[1] The enslaved, aware of their rights, brought more complaints against their masters. To carry out these reforms new revenues were needed, which led ultimately to more conflicts between the home office and the Trinidad government.

Increasingly Burnley asserted his prerogatives and challenged Woodford's authority, which put the latter on the defensive. On July 1, 1825, Woodford wrote to Lord Bathurst requesting guidance as to how to respond Burnley's continuing challenges to his authority. He wrote: "It appears that Mr. Burnley on the 7th of October last proposed two resolutions for the adoption of the Council of Trinidad, prefacing them by reading a written speech on the minutes of the

47

council, upon the demand of Mr. Burnley, who insisted that, as a matter of positive right, he was entitled to have a record made of it on the Council's books." Although Woodford recognized the right of council members to have their views reported in the minutes, it was usually confined to those cases where one member dissented from the majority and had his own vindication to enter a protest against their decision. Such a procedure allowed His Majesty's government to familiarize itself with dissenting views and give the members of His Majesty's government a sense of the council's thinking.

There was no precedent for Burnley's challenge. Faithful to his oath of office, Woodford sought guidance from his superior. He wrote: "If Lord Bathurst should determine that the pretentions advanced by Mr. Burnley, His Lordship may either direct that the Minutes of Council shall be amended by striking out the speech, or that, for the future, the precedent shall not be followed." Although Burnley was the senior member of the council, he would have to play by the rules of the game. Woodford would not allow Burnley to use the council to undermine his authority and to promote his own agenda. He was in charge of the government. In spite of their growing estrangement, on July 2, 1826, Woodford granted Burnley six months' leave of absence from the council.

Burnley was not to be denied. He had bigger fish to fry and was certainly acting as an accomplished statesman of his day. Burnley planned to spend part of his leave in the United States to promote his agenda and to keep himself informed of what was taking place there. On June 9, 1826, Hume wrote to John Quincy Adams, the sixth president of the United States, asking him to provide letters of introduction "to any of the public or literary men in the United States of America . . . for my brother in law, M' William Harden [sic] Burnley, a Merchant in Trinidad, who intends to pay a visit to the United States in August next. M'Burnley is an able man, and as such as you would, I am confident, approve of; and if you can introduce him to any of the men of the day there, you will oblige me."[2]

On June 19, in furtherance of this effort, Jeremy Bentham, a good friend and colleague of Hume and Adams,[3] also wrote to Richard Rush, attorney general (1814–1817) and secretary of the Treasury (1825–1829) of the United States also asking him to accommodate Burnley's desire to meet and speak with the prominent literary and public figures in the United States. Rush had also served as the U.S. minister to England from 1817 to 1825, so Bentham had come to know him well. In his letter to Rush on June 19, Bentham in his own laconic manner, penned the following: "Not having had, in my almost hermetically sealed Hermitage, the advantage of any personal acquaintance with Mr. Burnley the intended Traveler spoken of, I inclose a Letter which will afford him a so much more advantageous introduction than any recommendation I could have presumed to trouble you with."[4] Not content with being a mere merchant and slave owner, Burnley wanted to widen his acquaintance with the leading public and literary figures in the English and American world and to play a more influential role in Anglo-American affairs. His was a global rather than a local ambition.

Woodford wanted a firsthand view of how measures contained in the order were affecting the enslaved. After visiting several estates on the island in 1826, he declared that "the Negroes in general were conducting themselves well and that he had received few complaints as to work from the masters and none from the slaves." Crime, coming to work late, insolence, indecent language, and fighting and quarreling decreased although the masters had to exert great patience "to bear with the provoking tongues and noise of the women." Many of the planters who were opposed to the new code "acknowledged that their apprehensions had been unfounded; and Woodford was not without hope that the planters in general, if nothing occurred in the home country, would 'gradually become less disposed to attribute to the operation of the Order in Council every inconvenience arising in the management of their properties.'"[5] It was during this period that task work was adopted on the island.[6]

The sweeping changes that were made in the colony's law regarding the status of the enslaved demanded more revenues to carry out their work. On August 2, 1827, the governor called a meeting of the members of council at Government House to discuss the adoption of a stamp duty to produce "sufficient revenue to meet the alteration in the establishment of the island." Although this measure had been brought up prior to the meeting (it was contained in the original order-in-council of 1823), the council did not consider its enactment since its members needed more information before they did so. With the promulgation of these new laws, the government needed to hire new officers to conduct the business of the judicial and ecclesiastical establishments. Although the governor assured them there were sufficient revenues for 1827, he anticipated a deficit at the end of 1828, hence the need to consider raising more revenues.

The governor offered alternatives. He informed the board that a stamp duty would go a long way "to meet the expenses of the judicial and ecclesiastical establishments to which they were already pledged, and therefore thought that it would be well to request His Majesty's Government to place cotton and linen goods upon the same footing as all other importations." He also thought that "a duty on the salt fish which had been exempt by an order of this Board previous to his administration should be restored." L. J. C. Johnston, a member of the council, offered a corrective. He felt that any tax on salt fish should be stayed since it was "an article of necessity and the chief food of the slaves." He advised that a tax on cotton and linen goods should be selected rather than one on salt fish.

Burnley objected to the issuance of stamps as a new source of revenue. He saw it as "productive of serious inconvenience if applied to the common transaction of life. He also objected to the duty on Linen Goods, as they are likely to reduce the rate of exchange and interfere with the Spanish Trade [that is, trade with the Spanish Main], as far as Trade might be concerned." Burnley was not entirely negative. He conceded that the use of stamps in lieu of fees—extended to deeds and promissory notes, above a moderate sum—would not be so objectionable. He was mindful that there was a reduction in English stamp duty and so the Governor may want to give consideration to the legal implications of same. He warned that "the expense of such an establishment and the distribution of stamps would be subjected to consideration."

At this meeting the governor also laid before the board a report from the commissioners of Parliament on the Liberated Africans upon which he solicited their thoughts. He requested that Burnley, Dr. Llanos, and Mr. Johnston join a committee that was studying the issue. Burnley felt the Negroes should be kept as a "task gang" to take the place of the free laborers whom he felt were not always dependable. The governor informed the board that he had submitted proposals to the secretary of state for funds for work upon the road from Port of Spain to St. Joseph. He was not averse to providing monetary advance provided the planters would look after it, and that the work could be done by contract. In this too Burnley had the last word. He did not think that contractors could be found to do this kind of work since it was with great difficulty that he could get sufficient persons to transact his business. These were the last public exchanges between Burnley and Woodford.

On February 26, 1828, Woodford sent off his last dispatch to the secretary of state for the colonies. One month later, on March 29, Woodford informed the council he would take a short cruise on HMS *Slaney* to restore his health. Most of his colleagues knew he was ailing. On April 1, he left the island and named Major J. V. Capadose, a senior military officer on the island, to administer the government in his absence, although he was superseded quickly thereafter by Sir Charles Smith. By the time Woodford reached Jamaica some weeks later, he had become very sick. His friends hoped that a change of climate would bring him back to full recovery. There was no such luck. On May 16, he passed away on the *Duke of York*, leaving Benjamin Coombs, his faithful servant who was at his side when he died, to announce the sorrowful news to Trinidadians.

News of Woodford's death reached Trinidad on July 23. On July 26, Sir Charles Smith summoned Burnley, Dr. Llanos, Francis Peschier, and Henry Fuller to announce the death of Woodford and asked that they swear him in as governor by virtue of what he called "His Majesty's Commission to His Excellency Sir Ralph Woodford." The members of the board were reluctant to do so since they had no such explicit orders and were not sure what Sir Charles meant by "His Majesty's Commission," which he said gave him the authority to be sworn in. Sir Charles made it explicit that he was not requesting the advice of the board. He was simply demanding that they perform their duty.

The members of council were in a quandary. Sir Charles's demand was unprecedented. Burnley went on the defensive. However, having been informed by Sir Charles that the council was not required to deliberate upon the subject, he obeyed the order that was given and administered the oaths the acting governor demanded. After the oaths were administered, Sir Charles thanked Burnley and other members of council for their advice and support although he was visibly upset by their reluctance to adhere unquestioningly to his demands. A few days after the oath was administered, Colonel James Alex Farquharson, Smith's senior officer, hurried from Guyana and assumed the acting governorship of the colony "in spite of Sir Charles Smith's vehement protests, which . . . were overruled at the Colonial Office" (*H*, 220).

One year after Woodford's death, Burnley's resentment of Woodford resurfaced when many of Woodford's former colleagues, in and out of the council, planned to erect a "gorgeous statue of bronze on the most frequented place in Port of Spain"[7] in memory of Woodford. Without consulting Burnley, they included his name among the subscribers. When Burnley heard of this, he asked that his name be removed from the list. He did not wish to associate his name with Woodford although he respected some of his accomplishments.

In August 1829 Burnley explained his position when accusations of libel were made against Francis D'Abadie for writing two stinging articles in the *Trinidad Guardian* on the 4 and 21 of August 1829 that "contained libelous matters against the public and private character of Sir Ralph" (*H*, 220). Frederick Hammett, one of Woodford's nephews who had come to work in Woodford's administration and who remained on the island after Woodford's death, objected strongly to D'Abadie's articles.[8] Called as a witness in the case, "H.H. the King vs D'Abadie," on September 16, 1829, Burnley outlined his relationship with Woodford: "I believe that the late governor had been activated by the best of feelings and intentions. I supported some of his pubic measures in Council; a number I opposed. I entertained the highest respect for his private worth and integrity, and would have been amongst the foremost to have assisted in commemorating these qualities by the erection of a monument or cenotaph, but declined lending my name to [any] public resolution eulogizing the general tenor of his administration which I, from conscientious motives, found myself obliged to oppose."[9]

Burnley's antagonism toward Woodford did not diminish upon his death. It was festered, no doubt, by Burnley's desire for greater independence among the planters and what he saw as Woodford's impingement upon his territory. Lamont saw in Burnley's political opposition to Woodford "a certain admixture of personal animosity" (OG, 4); something akin to the young knight in shining armor versus the bruised and battle-scarred soldier. At this point, the bitter fight for power between the British government and the planter class intensified, which Governor Grant identified when, on August 12, 1829, he informed the secretary of state George Murray that "the Council has a great desire to obtain a power to control, instead of being advisers. The more I become acquainted with the circumstances of the Island, the more is my opinion strengthened that for a considerable time to come, no power of control, beyond what attaches to their opinion, should be given."[10]

Simply put, the planters wanted to have a greater say in the affairs of their country and how their taxes were being disbursed. The Colonial Office was adamant: as a crown colony, Trinidad had no choice but to follow the line of the Home Government. Although Burnley's outspokenness did not endear him to the British government in the colony, he was determined to carve his own path, utter his truths, and act on goals that benefitted him. As the richest man on the island and senior member of the council, he had the most to lose (even though he had gained the most financially from abolition) if the slaves were set free, which happened five years later. He represented the ruling class of his society and was troubled by the direction in which he saw the colony proceeding. His was a cause that he felt was worth fighting for.

CHAPTER 9

Declaration of Independence

Resolved: That the committee be directed to prepare an address to the Commons of Great Britain in Parliament assembled calling their attention to the peculiar grievances of the Inhabitants of Trinidad and praying for amelioration thereof, and specially praying that the Inhabitants of this colony should be empowered to exercise some effectual control over the enormous taxation and some examination into the extravagant expenditure of the public money under the influence whereof their properties are fast falling into decay, and the committee shall take all the required measures for procuring the said petition to be forwarded to England and presented to the House of Commons as soon as possible.

—Resolution of the Inhabitants of the Island of Trinidad, 1830

THE RISE OF the antislavery movement gave great impetus to the liberation struggle that was taking place in the Caribbean during the 1820s. The death of Reverend John Smith in Guyana and Reverend William Shrewsbury's banishment from Barbados in 1823 demonstrated that things were heating up in the Caribbean. Even the people of color were fighting for equality with the whites. On March 29, 1829, two weeks after Major General Sir Lewis Grant took up his appointment as governor of Trinidad, he issued an order-in-council that "removed all disabilities, civil or military, from all free persons of African birth or descent. This very natural and proper order was one which followed as a matter of course upon the previous measures taken to remove the disabilities of the free people of color" (*H*, 227). This change of policy resulted from representations the people of color had made to His Majesty's government against

Governor Woodford's curtailment of their freedoms, which they argued were "as contrary to the commands of His Gracious Majesty, as they are certainly are a direct violation of the meaning and intention of the Cedula of 24th November 1783."[1]

On May 15, 1830, the Anti-Slavery Society held one of its biggest meetings in London at which Buxton declared: "Slavery not having been ameliorated by the colonial legislatures in accordance with the resolutions passed by the House of Commons that day seven years ago, should as soon as possible be abolished." To the colonists, such sentiments seemed to be the beginning of the end of their cherished institution. One of their newspapers described the Anti-Slavery Society's meeting as "the last expiring effort of an exhausted faction." Lord Brougham, given the task of presenting the society's proposal to Parliament, declared "that man could have no property in his fellow creatures. 'Talk not to me of such monstrous pretentions being decreed by Acts of Parliament and recognized by treaties.'"[2] This sort of language put the fear of God into the hearts of the planters. They knew that things were coming to a head.

Burnley was acutely aware of what was taking place in London and the activities of the Anti-Slavery Society. During the early part of the year he had traveled to Paris to establish his wife's residence there. Charlotte was determined to live in Paris although she paid several visits to 6 Bryanston Square in London where Maria, Burnley's sister, lived. It was the place where Burnley resided while he was in London. Burnley's younger son, Joseph Hume, was named after his uncle-in-law and lived with his mother in Paris. In this same year (1830) William Frederick, Burnley's elder son was made a partner in the Glasgow firm Eccles, Burnley and Company, an association that brought him to financial ruin after his father died. By the end of June, Burnley had returned to Trinidad to attend to his legislative duties and to hone his response to the emancipation question.

As the year wore on, the planters intensified their efforts to have greater say in their affairs. Burnley was painfully aware that the members of the Board of Council were "selected by His Excellency the Governor, and not nominated by the free voice of the People; but I see in this only an additional motive to every liberal mind to guard with greater fidelity the interest committed to our charge" (OS, 25). Their only function was to advise the governor about any of the actions he was about to take. As early as 1823 he had affirmed that members of council had a responsibility "to recommend to His Excellency the rejection of every measure proposed, which may, on investigation, be found inconvenient to the Planters of this Island, without obvious benefit to their Slaves; injurious to their interests, if unaccompanied by fair and full compensation; and which may not clearly and manifestly appear to be in conformity with the unanimous Resolutions of the House of Commons, which my Lord Bathurst assures us, it is the earnest wish of His Majesty's Government to carry into effect" (*OS*, 26).

On November 30, 1830, the planters, merchants, and proprietors held an open meeting at the residence of Robert Neilson to advance their cause for greater representation of their interest in the local legislature. They called themselves the "Inhabitants of the Island" and formed a standing committee with Burnley as chairman and Reid as secretary.[3] They passed two resolutions. The first resolution, appointing Joseph Marryat as the agent of the colony, was in defiance of the secretary of state; the second directed the committee to prepare an address to the Parliament of Great Britain "calling on the peculiar grievances of the Inhabitants of Trinidad and praying for amelioration thereof"[4] and having control over their affairs. This was a bold move in the light of the political status of the colony.

In another petition to the British Parliament (to "the honorable the Commander of the United Kingdom of Great Britain and Ireland in Parliament assembled"), the petitioners complained that they were not being treated fairly by the British government after they had been induced to invest their capital in the island "with the promise which has long been held out to the Inhabitants of that colony [Trinidad] that the great principle of British independence, taxation by their representatives, should be extended to them." Dissatisfied that they had no say in their government or how their monies were being spent and disgusted with the arbitrary way in which the government conducted its affairs and the constantly changing and still unsettled state of the laws to which the colony has been subjected, they contended they were being "deprived of the advantages which they may otherwise (in common with the Inhabitants of the His Majesty's other colonies in the West Indies) have derived from the employment of British Capital in Trinidad and the credit of the colony amongst British merchants."[5]

One of the objects of George Canning's life, as they reminded His Majesty, was to make of Trinidad "the scene of an experiment in free labor" (*AM*, vol. 2, no. 6, November 1827, 132). They also argued that they were much injured by the privileges of British subjects that were being withheld from them. This resulted in their properties being systematically kept "for an indefinite period in a state of insecurity, which renders their industry unproductive and their economy useless."[6] To make matters worse, the West Indies was suffering from a general depression of trade, the price of muscovado sugar having fallen from thirty-seven shillings in 1828 to twenty-two shillings and eight pence in 1830.[7]

Challenges to Trinidad's special political status began to intensify after the planters' petition. On December 24, 1830, acting in his capacity as chairman of the "Inhabitants," Burnley informed Marryat of the committee's decision that he was selected to become the agent of the colony. Once Marryat received Burnley's letter and the resolutions adopted by the inhabitants he began his work on behalf of his clients in Trinidad. On March 3, 1831, he forwarded a copy of the inhabitants' resolution to Lord Viscount Goderich, secretary of state and student at Harrow from 1796 to 1799. On March 31, 1831, he informed Henry Short, the "authorized" agent of the colony, that the "Inhabitants of Trinidad" had appointed him to act as their agent. His experience told him that the Houses of Parliament were not likely to take kindly to the sentiments of the colonists. He asked Short to let him know any improvements being considered by His Majesty's government vis-à-vis the laws or political situation on the island that "will relieve me from the necessity of adopting a course which might be deemed hostile to His Majesty's Government."[8]

On May 19, Hume joined in the fray to assist his brother-in-law. Together with Marryat, he informed Goderich that the Inhabitants of Trinidad requested that he convene a general meeting with them to present an address to His Majesty. "We shall feel much obliged to Your Lordship," they said, if he could inform them "when it will be convenient for His Majesty to receive us." They appended the following request to their note: "It would be satisfactory to us if Your Lordship could fix some time to receive Mr. Marryat and myself before the presentation of this address to consider the second subject of Complaints which the Colonists in Trinidad may have to place before the House of Commons."[9]

On June 8, 1831, Hume and Marryat were granted an audience with Lord Goderich. He requested that they state "as distinctly as they could" what the Inhabitants of Trinidad wanted. The next day they responded to Lord Goderich's request. Referring to the inhabitants' petitions—which they had sent to him the previous month and which were presented to the House of Commons on June 8, 1831—Hume and Marryat made it clear that the inhabitants' principal grievance was "the arbitrary nature of the Government of Trinidad, and the heavy burden of taxation which they have so long borne." They argued that the planters in Trinidad had been subjected "to twice in most, and in some three times the amount of taxation that Grenada and other islands (their capabilities being considered) where the Inhabitants have control of their taxation and expenditure and the commissioner of legal enquiry, although instructed to enquire into their grievances, found it so great that they reported to His Majesty that no alteration in the Laws would give satisfaction, unless the Inhabitants were to have a control over the taxation, and expenditure of that Colony."[10]

The inhabitants contended that over the previous thirty years they had complained to His Majesty's government about their lack of representation, but their "requests and complaints have been but little attended to; and, particularly so, after the Commissioners [Dwarris, Maddock, and Henry] sent to the Island, had recommended certain alterations to be made, as the almost *unanimous* wish of the Colonists" (italics in the original). As a result of this lack of representation, and on behalf of the colonists, Hume and Marryat demanded that the Trinidad Council of Government should consist of "10 or 12 members, one half to be appointed by the King and the other half elected by the Inhabitants, to hold their situations from two or three years, re-eligible." They recommended that this council be given "power to lay on, or take off or to modify the taxes, the duties, fees, etc., by which the revenue of the island is raised, and also to examine and to regulate the salaries of all public officers, the expense of all establishments; and generally to control the expenditure of the colony, subject to such reference and approval by the King in Council as may be thought necessary."[11]

His Majesty's government was not persuaded by this request. Marryat and Hume needed to present more information to buttress their case. This task fell to Edward Jackson, the vice chairman of the committee, who, in his letter to Marryat on November 3, 1831, outlined the requests that were made to achieve such representation beginning as early as 1805 or 1806 when the Canadian constitution was proposed to the new subjects "as a basis to form a Representative [government] for themselves. [A] printed copy [was] sent by the Ministers was passed to the member of His Majesty's Council to be translated and circulated and the opinions of the *inhabitants* ascertained on the same."[12] Although the new subjects [the English], agreed with the formation of a legislature "with the powers of making Laws for the peace, prosperity and the good government for the island as in Canada . . . several of the *old* subjects who formed themselves into an assembly and a Committee and determined to send an envoy to England to ask for English Laws and constitution which . . . we were assured by Mr. Joseph Marryat's letters[13] we could not obtain from the obstinacy of the then Prime Minister Mr. Percival who was ready to allow the English laws immediately; but by no means a constitution."[14] Jackson recounted other failed attempts (up to and including those that were sent to Governor Woodford) to get a constitution in which the inhabitants could control some aspects of their affairs. Even as he corresponded with Lord Goderich, Marryat felt that His Majesty's government was not prepared to grant Trinidad subjects the relief they requested.

Britain, however, made some concession to the planters' grievances. On December 27, 1831, Governor Grant summoned the old Council of Advice to a meeting to tell them of "his" plans for the legislative future of the colony. He announced the establishment of a new Council of Government that consisted of six official members and six unofficial members with the governor having a casting vote. Rather than being a mere advisory group, the members of this new council would possess some legislative functions. Unfortunately, at this relatively peaceful time, Burnley showed his hand again. As the senior unofficial member (the other members were Andre Llanos, D. Murray, Robert Neilson, and Joseph and Francis Peschier), Burnley objected to Llanos's nomination to the council on the ground that he was an alien, which "incapacitated [him] from having a voice in the Legislation."[15] It did not matter that Llanos had served on the old council with Burnley since 1823. Burnley's objection was overruled on the ground that Llanos was "a person of superior education and in whom great confidence has long been placed, [and] might as an alien, have been expressly selected for the purpose of protecting the rights of the many other aliens who were in possession of property in Trinidad."[16]

Burnley's move did not help his relationship with the new governor or the non-British population in the country. He really cared little about the governor's reaction, since the governor had become very unpopular with the planter and mercantile classes on the island. It did not help that Trinidad, like the other British colonies, was undergoing a severe economic crisis. Burnley, however, had other things on his mind, the most important being the proposed changes to the island's constitution that would see the amelioration of the enslaved people of the island. The future of his business interests could not be very far from his mind.

CHAPTER 10

Brighter Horizons

I do hereby further Proclaim and Declare, That the Slave Population of this Island will forfeit all claim to the protection of His Majesty's Government if they shall fail to render entire submission to the Laws, as well as dutiful obedience to their Masters.

—from Governor Grant's Proclamation, May 26, 1832

THE YEAR 1832 was not a particularly good year for slave owners, but for the enslaved, the year brought hope for a better future. While the latter were looking toward brighter horizons, the slave owners could see that their kingdom on this earth was coming to an end. In England electoral reform was in the air as was the call for the immediate liberation of the enslaved. To transform and trespass upon a concept put forth by Eric Williams, "massa day" was coming to an end.[1] The fears that Burnley and his fellow planters had suppressed in their breasts would soon become manifest.

The principal source of their fear, an order-in-council of November 1831 that was proclaimed in January 1832, possessed 121 clauses. In the eyes of the planters and the merchants, this order had the potential to ruin their operations even as it eased the tremendous burdens under which the enslaved lived. On December 31, 1831, Edward Jackson, vice president of the "Inhabitants of the Island" and a barrister who had practiced on the island for eleven years prior to this proclamation, wrote to Governor Grant referring to the packet that he had just received, which was a "copy of the despatch addressed by Lord Goderich to the several governors of the Crown Colonies with which their Agents were furnished by the Colonial Office." He intimated that he had provided a short abstract of the prime provisions of the proposed order to several of the "respectable proprietors . . . informing them of your hope that they would voluntarily and immediately adopt and carry into operation the most material changes."[2]

Jackson noted that the planters' most strenuous objection to the new order "was the restriction on the hours of manufacturing labor," which he said "cannot be enforced without total and immediate ruin" to the planters. The words "ruin" and "ruinous" became new tropes of the planters' discourse. The new order reduced manufacturing labor from twelve to nine hours. Jackson argued that although twelve hours seemed long, it really constituted little exertion on the part of those who worked in factories such as the boilermen, the drivers of the cattlemill, and the firemen. From his observations, it was "clear that the Negroes employed in the manufacturing of sugar do not in fact undergo one half the labor required in the same period of field work." In other words, field work was more strenuous than factory work. To support this position, he spoke of the advantages of factory work and the joys the enslaved took in performing it.[3]

Even while yours truly was growing up on the estate in the 1950s, "crop time" dictated the rhythm of village life. In 1921, a correspondent from the *Trinidad Guardian* spoke of the excitement of crop time at Orange Grove Estate: "Situated in the Tacarigua district on a beautiful stretch of flat country of easy access and swept continually by most refreshing breezes, hundreds of people move about, each bent on his own particular duty. Hundreds of farmers' carts, laden with canes, line the route to the factory, and on every side one hears discussions as to the splendid results expected this year" (*TG*, "Tacarigua: Orange Grove Estate," April 5, 1921).

Jackson also acknowledged the effect the new order would have on the welfare of the Negroes although he claimed it was only a superficial consideration. He reminded the governor that "our Negroes" had been in the habit of receiving three and a half pounds of salt fish per week and would reject the "weekly dole of seven herrings or shads" that was being proposed in the new order. The planter who values "the health or the comfort of his Negroes would substitute the less plentiful, the less nutritive, and far more economical food provided by the law for the more expensive allowance which they now receive." Speaking for the few planters whom he had heard from, he also objected to giving the enslaved more time to work on their provision grounds, arguing that the colonial officials were ignorant of "local circumstances and practical details."[4]

The local whites even reached out for the support of their colored brethren whom they had ignored previously. On January 6, 1832, the white inhabitants held a public meeting in Port of Spain to organize their response to the order-in-council. The rhetoric of that day would have brought joy to the hearts of the most strident nationalists of the colonial era. In his address to this meeting, Jackson talked about the contempt the colonial officials had for the colonists. It is worth quoting his sentiments at length:

> His Lordship will have it that our pecuniary embarrassment, our want of literary leisure, of scientific attainment, and—will you believe it?—even of liberal recreations, unfit us for the tasks of attending to our own interests! And thus, because the blunders and negligence of the European statesmen have involved us in ruin—because we are not idle, do not read the new novels until some time after they are published—because our backs are not rubbed by Mr. St. John Long—because we do not go to Newmarket and Mousley Hurst—because we have private concerts instead of operas, and amateur concerts instead of the pantomimes at Drury-Lane and the melodramas of Covent Gardens—for these most excellent and unanswerable reasons, His Lordship contends that we are incapable of understanding our own affairs and taking care of our own interests, far less of embracing these comprehensive and enlightened views of general policies and justice by which it is tacitly understood the measures of government are so notably distinguished. Local knowledge and practical experience are held to be impediments to a wise system of legislature. The framers of the Order-in-Council are assumed to be possessed of unbounded sagacity in discerning premises, and unerring wisdom in drawing conclusions. . . . The intellectual powers of the colonists are assumed to be unequal to the task of comprehending, far less of engaging in logical discussion. (*PG*, January 14, 1832)

This was strong language indeed. Jackson, however, was merely reflecting the point of view of the white inhabitants. Yet one could not be but impressed with the vigor with which he articulated the planters' case. In fact, he was so blind to the needs of the enslaved that he even protested against the expense it would take to employ protectors and assistant protectors of slaves to ensure their rights were upheld. This was an expense he said that "the mother country had no right to saddle on us" (*PG*, January 14, 1832). Jackson, however, could not know that Lord Goderich had another view of the matter that read as follows:

> What property exists or has ever existed in the colonies is the direct product of the slave; that this labor has never received its due compensation is a matter of absolute certainty. Slaves still bear, and always have borne, a high price in the colonies. Why is it that any man finds it worthwhile to purchase a laborer? The answer is because his labor is worth more than the cost of maintenance he is to receive. The price paid is a fair criterion of the amount of wages which have been kept back and the loss sustained by the laborer. I cannot be a party to so gross an act of injustice as to refuse the slaves, from the property created at their expense, whatever may be required for their adequate protection. (*PG*, January 14, 1832)

At the public meeting Jackson repeated all the objections to the order that he had made to the governor. He was more spirited at this meeting than he was in the governor's presence, where he had to be more respectful. He was committed to, and certainly pledged to do, everything in his power "to promote any measure which he considered would ameliorate the condition of the Negro slave, that was not inconsistent with the just rights of the owners." He was not prepared to permit the protector and assistant protectors of slaves into our estates and "into our negro-houses [the masters owned everything, even the negro houses] at all hours of the day and night" (*PG*, January 14, 1832). He reminded the governor that when "we or our fathers paid the price of our slaves and of our land, either to the Government or to those who have acquired them from the Government, no such power were in existence; if they had been, no such purchases would have been made. Strangers from other colonies, allured by the promised advantages held out by His Majesty's proclamation of 1815, have removed their families and their slaves to this island; had the conditions of admitting these domiciliary visits been proposed to them, not one of them would have put foot in Trinidad."⁵

On January 13, 1832, Governor Grant responded to the questions raised by Jackson and the other colonists. He observed that "a few proprietors calling themselves members of a committee expressed a wish to have an interview with me on its subject. I objected to acknowledge them officially but received them as respectful proprietors." He conceded that with one or two exceptions, the language of the proprietors "was highly moderate and their conduct, throughout the occasion, perfectly unobjectionable." He reiterated his respect for members of the Cabildo but was not prepared to let them "claim any right whatsoever to interfere in matters connected with the general affairs of the colony or with His Majesty's commands regarding them."⁶

Meanwhile the enslaved were becoming restless. Although no one told them officially about the plans to ease their sufferings, they began to take their destinies into their own hands. On many of the estates, they withheld their labor. From January to June of that year they put down their tools on several estates to protest their treatment. Their actions seemed spontaneous as the estates on which the strikes occurred were far from one another and there was little opportunity for physical communications. Their actions troubled the governor. On January 13, he informed Lord Goderich that over two hundred slaves at the Palmiste estate in Naparima and others at the Felicity Hall estate in Carapichaima refused to work. They claimed they should have been free after having worked seven years on the plantation as was agreed upon with the owner. Ten years had elapsed and nothing was done to give them their freedom. Governor Grant wrote:

> Those in the Palmiste property have been tranquilized and have returned to their work. Those in Felicity Hall still hold out. I have commissioned the Commandant of Carapichima and the Protector of Slaves to allow three men and three women to come to Port D'Espagne [Port of Spain] to have the question of their pretensions to freedom tried in court. Whatever their impression may be, I little doubt no [he meant any] proof can be produced of their title to freedom, but it probably will be satisfactory to them that their claims are duly attended to and they will have an opportunity to see their claims are duly attended to and they will have an opportunity of being informed, by a case of this day's assurance that ill treatment to their class is seriously taken notice of.[7]

Such attempts of conciliation on the governor's part did not prevent the workers from continuing their strike action. Twice these "sinister discontents" made themselves manifest on a Cascade estate where all the workers decided not to work. The Palmiste workers continued to hold out for their freedom. Since the estate was about thirty miles from Port of Spain and could only be reached by "water conveyance," he informed Lord Goderich: "I intend to proceed thither immediately and having already restored to order the people on the Cascade and Felicity estate by reasoning with them. I trust I shall have equal success with those on the Palmiste property. . . . I have to intimate to Your Lordship that the discontents are in no way connected with the Order in Council of 2nd November 1831: the manager who was on Cascade estate when I visited it has been sent away, and a better description of provision grounds has been promised to the people. This, with an assurance of protection of their legal rights, so that they conduct themselves as they ought to do, appeared at the time to satisfy them."[8]

After his visit to Palmiste, he informed the secretary of state that most of the workers returned to work even though "all the discontent was not allayed but it seemed consistently to subside on my explaining to them that their real grievances where any existed would at times be resolved when made known to the proper authorities, and that, on the other hand, a corresponding conduct would be expected from them."[9] Interestingly enough, he had changed his approach to the workers. He had become less aggressive. That was not sufficient to calm the workers.

In an important number, the *Port of Spain Gazette* reported that innumerable fires were taking place in the colony. The slaves had a special code, embodied in the song "Fire in da Mountain," by which they called others to action. According to Alison Carmichael, a Scotswoman who lived on a Laurel Hill plantation, the mysterious words in "Fire in da Mountain" proved to be part of an insurrectionary song. It suggested that the fire in the mountain was that customarily lit by Negroes intending to burn their master's cane-fields. As "the Negroes had lit the fields, nobody would put the fire out. It was so hopeless that you might as well give the monkeys in the forests the planter's walking-stick and order them to beat out the flames."[10]

On Friday, March 23, some of the best canes of Madame Louis Philip were destroyed by fire. At the same time that Madame Philip's canes were being destroyed, another fire was being set on St. Andre's estate in Petit Bourg but "owing, we understand, to the very prompt and praiseworthy assistance afforded by the Military stationed there, . . . it was speedily got under" (*GE*, March 25, 1832). On the same day, the workers attempted to burn the canes on the nearby Retrench estate. Luckily the manager saw the fire that had just been set and was able to bring it under control by his own gang of workers.

What really scared the planters in that district was the general indifference of some of the workers to the destruction that was being wrought. The *Gazette Extraordinary* reported: "We learn, with much uneasiness and regret that the slaves on the Concord estate evinced by their conduct during the conflagration, a total want of any desire to save the property of their respectable and humane owner" (*GE*, March 25, 1832). Malcolm X would have called them the "field negroes" who were determined to get their freedom by any means necessary. Fortunately, the planters were saved by the heavy rains that "fell in the quarter on Thursday night, which probably, under God, saved the entire of that extensive district" (*GE*, March 25, 1832).

By May, the sabotaging of production extended to the Plein Palais estate in Carapichaima where many of the slaves abandoned the fields and went into the woods to protect themselves. Each slave wanted to work independently on his provision ground (the management wanted them to work "in gang") and more days to cultivate their grounds. In this strike, as in so many others, the women took the initiative. Once more the governor had to travel, via water conveyance, to the estate.[11] On this estate the women had taken the lead in the stoppage conducting themselves "with much violence, even to the extent of threatening the Commandant when they were called in from the field to be remonstrated with" (*GE*, March 25, 1832). This was not entirely unexpected. Female captives led many revolts aboard slave ships. Adam Hochschild reports: "In one famous case some female slaves on the Thomas bound for Barbados, seized muskets, overpowered the crew, and freed the male slaves. But they were unable to sail back to Africa, and a British warship eventually recaptured them."[12] However, the governor employed three magistrates to investigate the claims of the enslaved. The examination revealed that one of the drivers "had been the instigator of the others: he and two others of the most prominent were sentenced to corporal punishment, two of the most unruly of the women to the Tread-Mill, but it was concerted [*sic*] that the driver should be the only man severely punished, and one of the others slightly punished."[13]

While the pressure to end slavery originated a continent away, the slaves were not just passive actors in this struggle. In spite of what Burnley and the others thought about their circumstances, they expressed their feelings about the oppressive nature of their conditions through massive acts for self-assertion. As the planters watched their fields go up in flames, one could not but feel their contempt for "the villainous Order in Council of the 2nd November—that 121-pronged scourge, invented by the 'Saints' of Downing-street to goad to madness the oppressed, insulted and bitterly persecuted West India Planter. The die has at least been thrown—the work of devastation has commenced—Heaven only knows where it will stop" (*GE*, March 25, 1832). The Colonial Office was listening to all that was being said. They were forced to stay the course by the actions of the workers and the pressures of the antislavery movement.

CHAPTER 11

Monstrous Unnatural Results

The battle for colonial safety was not to be won by high sounding words, harsh epithets, or indignant vituperations; and in employing these arms they injured themselves by putting the just and the unjust cause on an equal footing.

—Edward Jackson, "General Meeting of Inhabitants," 1832

E VEN AS THE enslaved were making their wishes known the white inhabitants were intent on asserting the inviolable rights to their property (the slaves) and resisting the efforts of the Colonial Office to ameliorate the conditions of the enslaved. Facing the inevitable, the masters voiced their readiness to participate in the amelioration process. Yet, they fought unsparingly against the new order-in-council, particularly clauses 91 and 92, which caused the "Inhabitants" of the colony to meet on Monday, June 25, 1832, to select a deputy to represent their cause in England. At that meeting, it was proposed, and agreed to unanimously, that Burnley was "the fit person to represent the Inhabitants of Trinidad in England, and to act as their Deputy. Owing to talent, high character, and great practical experience of this gentleman, we may look forward to the best results to our just cause from his gratuitous exertions in our favor" (PG, June 27, 1832).

The atmosphere at this meeting was electric. It was like a nominating convention, and Burnley was their presumptive nominee. Resolutions were passed, actions were taken, and pledges were made—all with the intent of stopping (or certainly decelerating) the emancipation process. Burnley, it was agreed, would testify before the Committee of Enquiry of the House of Lords to get the British Parliament to modify some of the regulations in the order-in-council. It was felt that he was better able than anyone else to lay before His Majesty's ministers "the causes from which have originated the great distress so long prevailing in this island" (*PG*, June 27, 1832).

Burnley was the embodiment of humility as he accepted the nomination of his fellow inhabitants during this "important crisis of Colonial affairs" (their language). He felt that "no distinction could be more honorable than the spontaneous, unanimous declaration of his fellow colonists," and he was pleased that they "considered him worthy at so trying a period of their trust and confidence." Like a true politician, he pledged "to advocate to the best of his humble abilities the fair and just rights and expectations of every inhabitant in the colony, without distinction of color or condition for they were all well satisfied that the welfare of each particular class was intimately woven with the welfare of the whole, and that the comfort and moral improvement of the slave population constituted the best and securest basis on which to found the prosperity of the master" (*PG*, June 27, 1832). No one could have asked for more. His sentiments were synonymous with those of a progressive politician who was concerned about the interest of the entire community.

Burnley, very much a sociologist, had his own thoughts about how the relations between the whites and blacks, the master and the slave, ought to be conducted. He believed there was a distinction between savage and civilized groups and that slavery had its part to play in civilizing blacks. In his mind, Africans, American Indians, and the Peons of South America existed in a savage state of existence, which made it unwise for the British Parliament to put them on the same civilizational plane as the European. He was convinced that colonial officials only possessed a theoretical view of the slavery problem, which was distorted by a position that "strenuously maintained that all practical knowledge which we [the planters] do possess actually incapacitates us from giving a sound opinion on the subject." He believed the great masses of people in England were in favor of the emancipation of the blacks, which would make it difficult for him to establish the planters' case. Therefore, he affirmed that his best path "lay in a straight forward honest course, concealing nothing, blinking nothing, laying open the whole truth, without reservation, resting their cause upon the solid merits of their case. This course was not only their wisest, but their easiest plan" (*PG*, June 27, 1832).

Burnley believed that the crown colony system under which the colonists lived was unjust, dictatorial, and always ready to believe the worst about them. However, he was convinced that "if the whole [story] were fairly known, he was satisfied that the warmest and kindest sympathies of all the just and humane in Great Britain would be in favor of the Free Inhabitants of Trinidad, who were decidedly the greatest sufferers under this reprobated system—a system which His Majesty's Government might have suppressed with comparative facility and justice, at the capture of the Island, instead of encouraging and enforcing it, until millions of private capital, and the fortunes and prospects of thousands of individuals were irretrievably involved in its existence" (*PG*, June 27, 1832). Contrary to popular opinion, he believed that the putative cause of slavery remained with Great Britain for having encouraged "innocent" planters to invest in the slave system in the first place and over so many years.

The editors of the *Port of Spain Gazette* welcomed Burnley's selection, which they said offered "distinguished proof of the unlimited confidence reposed by the Colony in his talent, his zeal, and his integrity." They gave him the highest praise: "If great local knowledge, sound sense, uncompromising independence of character and an *identification of interest* with the proprietary and mercantile bodies of the community, are desirable qualifications in the man whom we would select to be our Representative at the present crisis of affairs, then we say the choice of the Colony could not have fallen upon a single other individual more competent to forward our objective in our newly appointed honorary and esteemed Deputy" (*PG*, June 27, 1832; italics in the original). The entire white community was in favor of his representing their cause in London. He had become the darling of his "constituents" as he called them on several occasions.[1]

In accepting the inhabitants' invitation, Burnley promised to undertake his mission immediately but demanded their unanimous support while he was abroad. On July 4, 1832, the governor granted him a twelve-month leave of absence from the Council of Government to proceed to Europe to represent the inhabitants.[2] Henry Fuller was selected to replace Burnley in the Council of Government. Burnley welcomed the change. In 1830 he had taken time out to establish his wife in Paris. She hated Trinidad and spent the rest of her life first at Rue de la Madeleine and after 1839 at Rue de Matignon, paying occasional visits to Burnley's sister, Maria, who lived at 6 Bryanstone Square in London. It is the place where Burnley stayed while he was in London. Between 1832 and 1837 Burnley spent most of his time in Europe.

The governor, however, had mixed feelings about Burnley's trip to London. He had become a thorn in the government's side; a position he shared with Lord Goderich when he corresponded with him on July 16. He wrote: "I am well aware that W. Burnley carries to home [England] the most hostile feeling to the Government established here. He openly has averred it and all of his proceedings in Council have a tendency to obstruct business and held out an example which has been followed by other members excepting some of the officials. Obstruction has been the study and I doubt not that as it has succeeded that the regulation of delay will succeed it." Although he professed an unwillingness to malign Burnley, he continued just as sharply:

> I wish not, My Lordship, to represent W. Burnley in any point of view to My Lordship that as a gentleman most strongly opposed to any interference with the colonies or which slavery and who has always shown himself against all the measures government has introduced relative to these topics ever since 1823. Burnley at that time did not, I believe, own all will of property in Trinidad. His declaration and those which he encouraged in others on that occasion spread such acrimony when the colony in respect to the safety and values of property that timid people sold at any price and W. Burnley soon became the principal proprietor in the island.
>
> Again My Lordship, I protest being understood to as alluding in any way to W. Burnley's private character. On the contrary he came here with the advantage of birth, capital, education superior to probably any other colonist, but he has his own object in view—much at stake and perhaps a desire to have more and it is but most natural to counsel and give information and render such representation as will but suit his private interest. I forward to Your Lordship two newspapers which are not so abusive as some others, but will show Your Lordship the main opposition which are encouraged here and which W. Burnley takes a prominent lead.[3]

Lord Goderich did not wholeheartedly agree with Governor Grant's depiction of Burnley. He wrote to one of his colleagues as follows: "It is not necessary to take any particular notice of what he [Grant] says respecting W. Burnley who however I dare say is sufficiently hostile and troublesome but I quite agree with you in thinking that L. Grant ought not to throw out general charges but should plainly state to whom he refers when he speaks of the conduct of some of the official members of the Council."[4] Burnley's meeting with Goderich later that year put a different spin on the matter. Gradually, these two men developed a genuinely respectful, if not fond, relationship with each other.

Meanwhile, cracks began to appear in the solidarity of the slave owners' camp. On October 9, the inhabitants of the island called a meeting in Port of Spain where, according to Fuller, the chairman of the meeting, "a larger number of the inhabitants has not, to my recollection, ever been assembled" for the purpose of "taking into consideration Mr. Marryat's letters of the 4th and 16th August, addressed to the Honorable William Hardin Burnley, Chairman of the 'Committee of Inhabitants' of this Colony." At their meeting they accused Joseph Marryat, their agent in London, of siding with the enemy and voting against their interest when a bill came up in the House of Commons on August 4, proposing financial relief for the planters in the crown colonies to compensate them "for the evils arising out of the Order in Council." Marryat was accused of saying that "the operations of the Order in Council had been satisfactory in Trinidad, that operations were beneficial, and that the objections to them were groundless" (*PG*, October 12, 1832).

Whether it was true or not, when the inhabitants heard what they thought Marryat had said they felt scandalized. Henry Murray, a member of the Council of Government, averred that from the point of view of someone who had lived on the island for the last thirty years, "he could confidently state that this Order has had a most pernicious effect, by causing an almost unconquerable feeling of dissatisfaction and discontent among the slaves, who cannot be dissuaded in any manner from imagining that the sole cause of their not being immediately emancipated, proceeds from the opposition given to that measure by their owners." By way of illustration, he said that "previous to the month of January last, whenever he met any of his own slaves, whether in the high road, or in the cane traces, coming from, or going to their houses, they universally met him with a cheerful countenance, and saluted him with the usual marks of courtesy, [and] asked him how he did. But since the above unfortunate period, not a single one of them, without any exception, had ever taken the slightest notice of him, *en passant*, but walked by as if he was their inferior, or not worthy of notice" (*PG*, October 12, 1832). It is difficult to know if these imagined bonds of courtesy and filial love ever existed among the master and his servants. However, by this time the enslaved were openly showing their hostility toward their owners. The year 1832 signaled a deep breach between them.

While this commotion was taking place in Trinidad, Burnley met (he called it an "interview") with Lord Goderich, the secretary of state, on October 18, to discuss the two modes for the sustenance of the enslaved envisaged by the November order-in-council: "Firstly, by the master supplying them wholly from his own store with fish and vegetable diet and secondly by the master applying them with a fixed quantity of land and forty days in each year to enable them, by the produce of their own labor, to purchase their necessaries."[5] Burnley objected to the first mode on the grounds that it would deprive every slave of procuring those luxuries to which he was already accustomed and might take away from the money he had been saving for his manumission.

Burnley's argument against the second mode raised an interesting question. It was this: "Allowance for fish under the new regulations will only be obtained in exchange for the produce of their gardens. Retaining profit in a community when the interest exacted on the loans of small sums is exorbitant, must under ordinary circumstances be great; but even these would be considerably enhanced to the slaves evident in their intentions from the difficulty of conveyance over roads frequently impassible, to any but pedestrians in the rainy season, and I have little doubt that in many cases, some insulated estates would be deprived of all regular supply." Even if this obstacle would have been overcome, the increased production, according to Burnley, "would only create a glut," which would not be in the interest of the enslaved but would "inevitably involve the whole of that portion of free-laboring population which subsists by the same occupations in pauperism and misery."[6] Burnley was mortally afraid of expanding the free-laboring population and allowing the slaves more time to work for themselves. The slave-sustaining plantations would not receive such a move positively.

Burnley's major concern, however, revolved around the hours of manufacturing labor prescribed by clauses 90 and 91 of the order-in-council that was to come into effect in the middle of December of that year. Although he could not assert what would happen in the other crown colonies where this order-in-council was promulgated, he was sure that "the necessities alone of paying for their extreme labor would immediately ruin the planter in Trinidad." The object of these clauses, as far as he was concerned, "appear to be to emancipate the slaves in the first instance for one fourth of the day only—this boom may then be extended until entire freedom be ultimately granted." If clauses 90 and 91 were enforced it would lead inevitably to the emancipation of the slaves. In this context Burnley referred to Lord Goderich's letter of May 13, 1832, which said that the introduction of such a system into the colony "might pave the way for more general substituting of hire service for free labor and a slave who during part of the year had been accustomed to work two or three hours daily for wages, would be rapidly preparing for the transition into the condition of a free laborer."[7]

Burnley felt that in such a plan, the "laboring class" would be assured "the comforts and necessaries of life with no other motive to labor but the desire of producing luxuries." Even if the cost was furnished, and the machinery worked, it would not fail to produce "monstrous unnatural results."[8] The only way to eradicate this social monstrosity was to suspend clauses 90 and 91 of the order-in-council as had happened in Mauritius. This position was endorsed by Robert Neilson, a member of the Council of Government and Marryat.[9] On December 12, Lord Goderich informed Burnley that His Majesty's government had suspended the clauses that he wanted suspended, allowing the governors of the various territories to fix the quantities of provision and clothing that were to be allotted to the slaves.

This was certainly a triumph for Burnley, but then again, like Lord Goderich, he was a Harrovian. What pleased him more was Lord Goderich's assurance that he would be happy at all times "to give his best attention to any communications which you may address to him; [and] feels it his duty [not] to decline to recognize the official character [of your claim as] a gentleman of property and consideration in the island of Trinidad."[10] Lord Howick, parliamentary undersecretary of the Colonial Office and the son of Earl Grey, the prime minister, conveyed this information to Burnley via a scribble on the letter that Lord Goderich sent to Burnley. No wonder then Lord Goderich was not inclined to accept Governor Grant's description of Burnley when he gave him leave to visit London to present the inhabitants' grievances.

Pleased by such a warm reply, Burnley wrote to Lord Howich on December 28 to ask him "to express to Lord Goderich my sincerest thanks for his promise to attend to any communications I may address to him." He also thanked Lord Goderich for suspending the clause that related to the issues of food and clothing. Burnley then informed Lord Goderich that he was appointed to the office of honorary agent of the colony: "This unexpected appointment—unlooked for by myself, unsolicited by my friends, and conferred upon me in my absence, affords another proof of the confidence reposed in me by the inhabitants, as well as an additional guarantee of their cheerful concurrence in such regulations as I trust may be successful in establishing."[11] After thirty years, in his own eyes and in those of Her Majesty's government, Burnley had arrived at a position of influence and respect. It was certainly another occasion in which his school ties had begun to pay off for him.

Even as he corresponded with Lord Howick, Burnley probably did not know that Howick was aware that the emancipation of the enslaved was just around the corner. In the summer of 1832 Lord Howick had written to the new governor of Jamaica to say that "the present state of things cannot go on much longer. . . . every hour that it does so, is full of the most appalling danger. . . . Emancipation alone will effectually avert the danger."[12] This was true for Trinidad as well. Trinidadians, too, believed that the king had sent their "freepaper" in the form of the order-in-council of November 2, 1831. No man had a right to withhold their freedom from them. It would only be a matter of time before freedom day would arrive.

CHAPTER 12

Opinions on Slavery and Emancipation

It is set down as an axiom, that whatever a slave can do, a freeman can do, and better *if he pleases*. But upon that contingency the whole question under consideration [slave labor versus free labor] depends. Wherever bountiful nature, or bountiful fortune, provides for all his wants, it will be his sovereign will and pleasure to do nothing. It cannot be otherwise: the Deity has so ordered it. Indolence is as necessary an element in the composition of society as industry: by it alone are accumulated heaps scattered, and properties in some degrees equalized, without which no wholesome state of society can exist.

—William H. Burnley, *Opinions on Slavery and Emancipation in 1823*

WHEN BURNLEY ARRIVED in England, the emancipation debate was in full swing with Thomas Fowell Buxton and the Anti-Slavery Society pressing for the immediate abolition of slavery. Whereas Buxton had supported the gradual emancipation of the slaves in 1823, by 1832 he had moved to advocating for the total emancipation of the slaves "with as little delay as honest necessity would allow."[1] In moving his resolution for the abolition of slavery on April 15, 1831, he averred that in the eight years since the House of Commons passed its motion to abolish slavery, the colonial assemblies "have not taken measures to carry the resolutions of the House into effect; that, deeply impressed with a sense of the impropriety, inhumanity, and injustice of colonial slavery, this House will proceed to consider and adopt the best means of effecting its abolition throughout the British dominions."[2]

On January 1, 1832, Buxton made his New Year's resolutions that reaffirmed his commitment to work toward freeing enslaved Africans. His greatest duty, he wrote, "is the deliverance of my brethren in the West Indies from slavery both body and soul."[3] On May 24, 1832, he moved that a select committee be appointed to consider measures "for the purpose of effecting the extinction of slavery throughout the British dominions at the earliest period compatible with the safety of all classes in the colonies."[4] By the beginning of 1833 Buxton was ready to carry out his plan to achieve the emancipation of the slaves. He was assured that his great determination to achieve this end would pay off.

While Burnley was in London, the Trinidad planters and Edward Jackson, the vice chairman of the inhabitants group, continued their battle to preserve slavery on the island. He published *Opinions on Slavery and Emancipation in 1823: referred to in a recent debate in the House of Commons*, which he wrote in 1823 immediately after the passage of George Canning's resolution respecting slavery. He added his "Preliminary Observations" in 1833 because of the fight for immediate emancipation and the introduction of the apprenticeship system. Drawing heavily on the findings in *Trinidad Negroes*, he set out to disprove the arguments advanced in the circulars and orders-in-council by the Colonial Office that challenged frontally the claims he and the Anti-Slavery Society made. Burnley insisted that their views should not be accepted as sacrosanct and reiterated the right of each colonial legislature to refute or challenge the positions taken by the Colonial Office. He believed that the colonial legislatures were acting in the best interest of their constituents (the planters and their slaves) and the British Empire and affirmed their right to have a say in their affairs. He owned that the circulars and orders-in-council from Downing Street "can never be considered as binding upon independent Legislatures; or their rejection, as meriting the charge of contumacy, if deliberately examined, and considered not to be in accordance with the manifest intentions of the Imperial Parliament" (*OS*, iii).

Burnley did not accept Buxton's contention that the planters were responsible for the conditions of the blacks or even the obstruction to the Colonial Office's attempt to ameliorate slavery. He also refuted Buxton's argument that the cruelty of slavery was having a devastating effect upon the slaves and used testimonies from *Trinidad Negroes* to support his position. In his testimony to the House on April 15, 1831, Buxton had affirmed that slavery, by its very nature, was harmful and destructive to the slaves. He noted, "In the last ten years the slave population in those fourteen colonies has decreased by the number of 45,800 persons."[5] In Tobago, within ten years, one sixth of the population had perished; in Trinidad by 6,000 persons within twelve years. "The fact is that in

Trinidad, as the late Mr. Marryat observed, 'the slaves die off like rotten sheep.'" Buxton believed that "*the forced labour in the sugar colonies*, and nothing else"[6] was responsible for the decreasing population of black slaves. "Where the blacks are free, they increase."[7] This was an unassailable truth in his mind.

Burnley did not accept this point of view. He asserted that the theory of population was the most difficult of all subjects to treat and argued: "No prudent man, therefore, would apply inferences, drawn from so uncertain a source, to the direction of practical affairs; still less would a charitable one urge them as decisive proof of the moral turpitude of whole communities. The Anti-Slavery Society had not hesitated to do both; they have fearlessly asserted, that this decrease is to be immediately and directly ascribed to the institution of Slavery, generating cruelty in the beast of the master, and, consequently, productive of ill treatment, over work, and premature death to the Slave" (*OS*, vii). While he believed that Buxton acted from the "purest motives," he also accused him of being preoccupied with one idea that "can admit only incidents in unison with it; and his eye unconsciously glances over every other important fact as valueless, or irrelevant" (*OS*, x). In the light of this bias, Burnley called upon Buxton to renounce his opinion that "the decrease in the Slave population in Trinidad must be ascribed to excessive labour in the cultivation of sugar estates, and that the increase in the population of Barbadoes [*sic*] is not altogether attributable to the comparative lightness of labour in that island" (*OS*, xxxvi).

Burnley believed that Buxton had arrived at his view without knowing all the facts and/or misreading the evidence at his disposal. He accused Buxton of "inaptitude to draw correct conclusions from the best evidence in his possession" and concluded: "If the same prepossessions in favor of his own pre-conceived ideas have governed all his inferences and deductions from other documents relative to other parts of the world, his evidence will prove a most dangerous guide by which to direct our present course" (*OS*, xxxvii, xliv). He objected most to the proposition that free labor was superior to slave labor, particularly in Trinidad. In his Trinidad hearings he garnered from Mitchell and Stuart, the superintendent and the assistant superintendent of the African refugees respectively, that "the reasonable rates of these free laborers were in fact less advantageous than the most extravagant description of Slave labor as furnished by hired gangs," or as Stuart put it: "I certainly expected assistance from these people in cutting wood, etc., but I think, a man would be mad to expect to carry on a Sugar Estate by any free labor, which I have had an opportunity of knowing" (*OS*, xlii).

Burnley saw that one of his major tasks was to inquire into "the nature and efficiency of 'free labor,' to enable us to form some idea of the cost of the process by which Slavery is to be extinguished" (*OS*, xviii–xix). To buttress his argument, Burnley turned to what he called a "philosophical view" of human nature that was predominant at the time and a point that even James Anthony Froude made use of when he visited the West Indies in 1887.[8] Burnley used a Malthusian argument to support his view when he suggested, "indolence is the most predominant of all human passions" (*OS*, xix). In Burnley's view, if indolence (habitual laziness) is the key to the Negro personality, then slavery was the corrective to that problem.

This mode of reasoning led Burnley to conclude that slavery or coercion is superior to free labor, which is why it was used in so many parts of the world. In fact, the United States, where he was born, provided a test case for him. He asks, "Why is labor cheaper in Britain, than in the northern section of the United States of America?" to which he answers: "Not on account of the generally supposed superiority of free labor . . . but from the difficulty of procuring subsistence; which circumstances alone obliges our laborers to work harder, longer, and cheaper, than the same class in any part of the world" (*OS*, xx–xxi). Since Americans are in close contact with both systems, they "understand well that the labour of Slaves is cheaper in America than that of freemen. The whole Union presents a practical example of this conviction" (*OS*, xxi). According to Burnley, this is true in other parts of the world, which led him to conclude: "It may, therefore, be set down as an axiom, that throughout the Western world, the labor of freemen is more expensive than that of Slaves; and that the difference, in favor of the latter, is always in proportion to the genial temperature of the climate, and the fertility of the soil" (*OS*, xxi–xxii).

Burnley was concerned about the economic implications of free labor and its likely cost to the planters. He argued that "the emancipation of our Slaves will be an immediate conversion of a cheap into an expensive system of labour throughout our West Indian Colonies; and it is, therefore, highly interesting to ascertain on whom this extra cost will fall. In an open and free trade, as in the case of the inhabitants of Venezuela, it falls invariably upon the cultivator: by the free labor of a month he is enabled only to procure the same articles which the Slave labor of a week could probably purchase" (*OS*, xxii–xxiii). In the event of emancipation, the cost of maintaining the African race in "luxurious idleness" will fall upon the planters of the West Indies and the consumers in Great Britain.

Burnley was also concerned about the implications of the apprenticeship system that was being proposed to prepare the enslaved for their new condition of existence. He felt that one could not evaluate such a system properly because it "never governed an entire community in any age or country" nor could it hope to be executed successfully if the master was not given the power of "reasonable correction" (*OS*, xxiv). Burnley had taken a similar position in 1823 when he informed Governor Woodford that the power of a master to punish his slave "without the intervention of the magistrate" was essential to the efficient functioning of slavery. He warned that "if taken away totally, or even partially repealed by the enactment of regulations prohibiting all corporal punishments, from that moment the fabric of Slavery is virtually destroyed, and the Negro, though not free, will cease to be of any value to his master" (*OS*, 4).[9] Apprenticeship, he believed, would involve "all that is most expensive in emancipation, and most demoralizing in Slavery." Furthermore, "it is not the harsh and despotic power of the master which renders Slavery demoralizing; on the contrary, it is by that power alone that the immoral tendencies, encouraged by the most charitable and humane parts of the system, are counteracted" (*OS*, xxv).

Burnley totally opposed apprenticeship. He was enamored with slavery's civilizing or humanizing virtues upon the African. He believed the freed African would be worse off in an apprenticeship system than he was in slavery and that the Colonial Office would face fierce resistance from West Indian planters if it tried to impose its plan on the colonists. Apart from the negative effects upon the Negro and the planters, apprenticeship would be equally bad for Britain's commercial interests since "the establishments in these islands, although termed Colonies, are factories only, supported by British Capitals" (*OS*, 11). He had an obligation to warn the Colonial Office about the disastrous consequences if such a plan were to be implemented. Such a position was self-serving on Burnley's part. It was in keeping with what he called "the first law of nature, the law of self-preservation" (*OS*, 19).

By 1833 most of England supported the abolishment of slavery. The debate on the slavery bill began on May 14 and dragged on until June 12. On July 5, Buxton introduced his Abolitionist Bill to the House of Commons. On August 7, the Bill for the Total Abolition of Colonial Slavery passed the Lower House of Commons. On August 28, the bill for the abolition of slavery received the royal assent and became law on August 29, 1833. The government had proposed that slavery be abolished throughout the British dominions but the slaves should be apprenticed to their former masters for a particular period and the former owners should be paid £20,000,000. There were other provisions in the bill, but on the whole Buxton was satisfied with the results. The main features of the plan were apprenticeship for the Negro and compensation to the planters.[10] Buxton voted to grant £20,000,000 sterling to the planters. It gave, as he said, "the best chance and the fairest prospect of a peaceful termination to slavery."[11]

At the end of his "Preliminary Observations," Burnley observed that "it seems by no means impossible, judging of the future by the past, that a Bill, embracing all these dangerous and unpopular principles, may be passed by majorities in both Houses." And it was. Yet he had warned that "if ever attempted to be carried forcibly into execution, in opposition to the remonstrances of the Colonists, it may be confidently predicted, that it will entail immediate destruction upon the whole of our dependencies in the West Indies, and shatter, to the foundations, one of the main supports of our maritime superiority, and national power" (OS, xxix). He was wrong in his predictions of doom.

William Law Mathieson, writing some years later, believed that if the planters had been more cooperative, things might have turned out differently. He observed that when Buxton met with his friends in 1823 to decide how to tackle the issue of emancipation their views wavered "all the way from the instant abolition of slavery without any compensation to its gradual extinction through the agency and with the cordial concurrence of the planters." But Burnley and his colleagues in the Caribbean would have none of it, which led Mathieson to wonder "if the Trinidad Order in Council had been established throughout the West Indies, the existence of slavery, in a form becoming less and less rigorous, might have been indefinitely prolonged?"[12] He averred that the British government had long kept that option open, but Burnley and the other planters were intent on defying the British Parliament and keeping their slaves, which led Mathieson to conclude that whatever difficulties "the planters had to now face were certainly of their own creation and it was magnanimous in Parliament, and especially the reformed Parliament, to break their fall by instituting apprenticeship and to endeavor, not only to satisfy their claim for compensation, but even to purchase their goodwill." In spite of his protestations, Burnley came out very well after slavery was abolished. As one who owned the most slaves in Trinidad, he received the largest share of the compensation.

After the announcement of emancipation on August 29, Burnley stayed in London to look after his business affairs. Trinidad received £1,039,119 of the 20 million sterling that the British government paid out as compensation to the slave owners. Burnley received £48,283 18s 5d for 980 people on the estates he owned (see table 1). John Lamont pointed out that even after slavery, Burnley kept on making money.[13]

The enslaved, on the other hand, gained their freedom, but they had to start out life anew with many challenges. Perhaps we can affirm with Mathieson that

TABLE 1. COMPENSATION AWARDED WHOLLY OR PARTLY TO THE BURNLEY FAMILY

AWARDEE	ESTATE	CLAIM NO.	AMOUNT	NO. OF ENSLAVED PEOPLE
Rosina Burnley		Trin. 1802	£3,827 5s 10d	57
W. F. Burnley		BG 2362	£1,275 8s 4d	27
W. F. Burnley		BG 2356	£8,627 3s 6d	62
W. F. Burnley	Palmira	Trin. 1754	£2,858 13s 7d	54
W. F. Burnley		Trin. 1802	£3,827 5s 10d	57
W. F. Burnley	Otaheit	Trin. 1924	£4,286 14s 7d	84
W. H. Burnley	St. Clair	Trin. 1183	£2,629 16s 4d	51
W. H. Burnley	Sevilla	Trin. 1337	£1,246 2s 3d	25
W. H. Burnley	Washington & Wilderness	Trin. 1416	£1,569 4s 11d	30
W. H. Burnley	La Soledad	Trin. 1468	£1,496 18s 9d	35
W. H. Burnley	Carolina	Trin. 1648	£3,048 17s 6d	59
W. H. Burnley	Providence	Trin. 1663	£12,064 17s 6d	234
W. H. Burnley	Cedar Hill	Trin. 1686	£8,147 16s 8d	170
W. H. Burnley	Union Hall	Trin. 1864	£3,746 15s 8d	73
W. H. Burnley	Mon Plaisir	Trin. 1959	£2,442 6s 9d	52
W. H. Burnley	Perseverance	Trin. 1960	£3,827 3s 9d	79
W. H. Burnley		Trin. 2066	£260 13s 11d	5
W. H. Burnley		Trin. 808	£217 7s 8d	4
W. H. Burnley	Orange Grove	Trin. 1460	£9,260 1s 8d	202
W. H. Burnley	Golden Grove	Trin. 1461	£2,088 5s 0d	39
W. H. Burnley	Aranjuez	Trin. 1234	£4,268 3s 5d	96
TOTAL				**1,495**

Data from: William Hardin Burnley, "Profiles and Legacies Summary," Legacies of British Slave-Ownership, Department of History, University College of London, 2018.

"it savors a paradox to say that the Act which abolished slavery did not emancipate the slaves; but this is only another way of saying that what Parliament took away with one hand it partially restored with the other." As a social institution slavery disappeared under what the preamble calls "'a general manumission' but it came back as a system of industry, the negroes, though they had acquired 'all rights and privileges of freedom,' having to work as slaves for so many hours a week, and for this purpose being so much the property of their masters that they could be seized and advertised as runaways and were liable to be bought and sold."[14] Whatever its shortcomings, the emancipation proclamation signified the end of a dark period of Trinidad and Tobago's history.

CHAPTER 13

The Politics of Compensation

≈

Numerous difficulties will inevitably present themselves under the new system not to be foreseen, which must be remedied upon the spot. This can only be effectually done by giving discretionary powers to the colonial authorities and decisive instructions that proprietors are no longer distrusted, and their advice and assistance rejected, solely because they possess the largest stake in the country.

The authorities must be distinctly informed that a new spirit is to pervade the administration of government; that strict impartiality is to be observed towards all classes; that the interests of the lowest are not to be preferred to the highest, nor that of the Black to the White.

—William H. Burnley to Secretary G. Stanley, 1833

THE EMANCIPATION OF the enslaved in Trinidad, a social revolution, involved a change in the relations between the former slave owners and the formerly enslaved. It increased the tension between the metropolitan government, bent on outlining in detail how the transformation ought to proceed, and the responsibility of the colonial government to carry out these reforms; the new regime of state power and the rule of law through a professional magistracy. Once it became clear that the British was intent on emancipating the enslaved, Burnley turned his attention to how best to implement those measures to suit his own interests. In this sense Burnley's anxieties in the immediate aftermath of emancipation were not only about "the economics of production but also about the distribution and exercise of power in this new dispensation."[1]

Once the emancipation bill had passed, Burnley changed his focus to deal with issues of compensation and apprenticeship, the new form of labor. Having spent much time in London, Burnley was better positioned to get his message through to the colonial authorities. Since Lord Goderich had responded to him in such a friendly manner, it paved the way for a more cordial relationship with the secretary of state (Goderich was forced out of the office in April to make way for Lord Stanley), with Lord Howick and John George Shaw-Lefevre serving as conduits. One indication of this new relationship can be gleaned from a letter Burnley sent to Lord Goderich, via Lord Howick, on January 16, 1833. After thanking him for making the Trinidad government live within its means, Burnley requested that His Lordship provide him with "copies of any instructions which may have been sent to the Colonial Government of Trinidad since 1st July last."[2]

Having failed to win any significant concessions for the inhabitants of the island and recognizing his changed relation with the Colonial Office, Burnley spent the second half of the year positioning the colony (and certainly himself) to get the best deal out of the proposed compensation that was to be awarded to the planters as a result of the abolition of slavery and to pave the way for an apprenticeship system they could live with. Nicholas Draper has observed that once the Slave Compensation Commission was established, the feeding frenzy began, and claimants who were close enough to the metropolitan centers had the best chance of shaping the new system and getting the most out of it.[3] This is one reason why Burnley remained in London for almost two years, although he found time to visit other European cities.

Meanwhile, the Committee of Inhabitants of Trinidad was holding the governor's heels to the fire. On July 18, Edward Jackson, installed as the president of the inhabitants' organization in Burnley's absence, wrote to Sir George Hill, the new governor of the colony, to inquire what measures he would undertake to carry out the resolution regarding the abolition of slavery and how they could assist in the process. On the following day the governor responded to the white inhabitants. He expressed the hope that they would accept the new social situation with "dispassionate seriousness; . . . deliberately estimate the progress and the present state of Public Opinion, as bearing on this subject, and as rendering the extinction of Slavery inevitable; [and] . . . unite in zealous prosecution of this great design to a successful issue." The governor suggested that they could make themselves more useful by preparing the apprentices for the intended change and to exert themselves "by friendly means, to dispel any illusions under which the Negroes may be found to labor as to what is to be the real nature of their new condition." He ended by warning that like all of His Majesty's subjects "they will be required and must earn the food they are to eat by industry, and entitle themselves to protection by subordination to the Laws. Let all classes of the Laity, and the Clergy of all the different persuasions, the Masters and the Magistrates, make due efforts to disabuse them of the mischievous suggestion that Freedom means 'No more work to be done'" (*TRG*, July 30, 1833).

On August 15, 1833, eight days after the emancipation bill passed in the House of Commons, Burnley wrote a sarcastic letter to Secretary Stanley in which he suggested that the new system that contemplated putting responsibility on the enslaved to support themselves and their families was a violation of a previous system of care and attention of the enslaved by owners, which one scholar suggests had been undertaken out of sense of noblesse oblige by a quasi-feudal class of benevolent owners. He acknowledged that this new system was quite a change from the old one in which the planters had administered the judicial system as it affected the laboring population; a system in which "differences have been satisfactorily terminated by a judge, always upon the spot, and intimately acquainted with the habits and character of the disputants. Redress has immediately followed the grievance; and punishment [for] the commission of offence, by a summary process, entailing no expense upon the parties in the community." To Burnley, slavery was "the most simple, economical and efficient [system] which could be devised. It was the offspring of no ingenious theory, but the results of the practical experience of generations."[4] This new artificial system that was being introduced would be costly to administer since, in proportion to the older colonies, a great number of special magistrates would have to be employed to ensure its success in Trinidad.

Trinidad presented other difficulties for the special magistrates and the administration of justice. According to Burnley, its many "intervening tracts of uncultivated land between detached portions of the scattered population" and "the peculiar severity and length of the wet season" made it difficult for citizens to get around the country and convey the goods from one part of the island to another. Since the special magistrates would need assistance in carrying out their duties on the estates the proprietors and their assistants would be better placed to assist them. Such an arrangement would have the "good effect of showing the Negro population that all power and authority has not been taken out of the hands of their former masters and that emancipation does not mean vagrancy and licentiousness."[5] According to this logic, the proprietors would always control the laboring population.

Anyone who was unaware of the situation would have thought that a great injustice had been done to the planters; at least, that is how they represented their situation to the world. Burnley asked the secretary of state to believe that he had "no further interest in opposing the views of its framers. If I am right in my unfortunate anticipations, nothing will more decidedly assist to prove their correctness than affording the measures of the proposed Bill full and fair play, so that the failure may be imputed only to the right cause; and, with the stakes I hold in the colony, it is hardly necessary for me to add, how happy I shall be to find myself ultimately in error."[6]

That evening Burnley informed Shaw-Lefevre, a member of the Colonial Office, that he had written to Secretary Stanley about "the increased number of magistrates which we shall require in Trinidad and other points in the [Abolition] Bill." He also informed him that "tomorrow morning I leave town to convey Mrs. Burnley to Paris but should be back in ten days, and will immediately on my return call on Downing Street."[7] This surely sounded like a man who was wired into the system. As promised, Burnley returned to Devonshire Place, London, where he stayed and quickly got back to the business that consumed him and involved his livelihood. Indeed, it seemed that Burnley took considerable pleasure in these exchanges and in acting the role of statesman or, as I have argued, the prime minister of the colony.

On September 4, he sent Secretary Stanley the long memorandum the Inhabitants of Trinidad had sent to him. In his cover letter he stated that he had little to add in support of so powerful an appeal to the justice and judgment to His Majesty's ministers: "They will recognize in it, I am persuaded, the language of men of sense and calm determination, moved by deep feelings naturally excited at a crisis when everything dear and valuable to them in life is apparently at stake." Although the inhabitants recognized why Great Britain had to dissolve the bond between her devoted subjects, "the great, the vital problem [remained]: how the cultivation of the colonies is for the future to be supplied, so as to preserve the white inhabitants and their families from destitution and beggary, [which] still remains unsolved."[8] This would become Burnley's major future concern.

The memorialists remained convinced that Great Britain still needed their assistance to make the new experiment work. Like Burnley, they proclaimed they had no objections to emancipation and held themselves ready to assist in "the promotion of the industry of the Negroes [which] must be to them an object of the most desirable importance, and reasonable compensation is all they ask for." To achieve these results, the order-in-council had to be framed in such a way to ensure that the Negroes continued to work in the fields or, as the memorialists put it, to frame the regulations in such a way that were "productive of industrial labor from the Negroes." He concluded his letter by suggesting that the provisions of the order-in-council be framed to "carry conviction to the breast of the colonists, that these results will in all human probability be secured, otherwise every hope of saving themselves by their own exertions will be immediately thrown in despair, and a general dissolution will cause all of the ties which connect and bind the society together which when once commenced not all the physical power of the British Empire can either stay or prevent."[9]

After Burnley sent the inhabitants' memorial to Secretary Stanley, he sent a note to Shaw-Lefevre telling him that he had done so and asked him to furnish him with him a copy of the proposed order-in-council that was being framed for the crown colonies. He asked that he "be favored with a sight of it as early as possible."[10] He also took the opportunity to inform Shaw-Lefevre that he would be leaving London to visit Edinburgh, Scotland, that evening but would be away for no more than three weeks. He also left an address in Edinburgh to which Shaw-Lefevre could send any correspondence to him. By that time his elder son, William Frederick, was living in Glasgow, Scotland.

After Edinburgh, Burnley went to Paris where his wife and younger son lived. By then, Shaw-Lefevre had sent him a copy of the order-in-council (Burnley thought it was a draft) for regulation of the apprentices that was being sent out to the crown colonies. As he sat in his room at the Hotel de Douvres on Rue de la Paix that autumn evening on October 19, he fixed all his thoughts on how he was going to make this new system work for his benefit and that of his "constituents." Contemplating the materials before him, he wrote to Shaw-Lefevre as follows:

> My principal task has been, not to extend, but to abridge them and to select from the mass of matter which presented itself that which was most worthy of attention, at the same time, I feel satisfied that innumerable other circumstances will arise when the new machinery is set in motion of which I presently cannot form any idea. Our safety therefore will depend upon the good sense and judgment of our local legislature.[11]

It took a dedicated, self-interested person such as Burnley to pore over that document and produce a written response of fifteen tightly hand-written pages (of approximately seventy-five hundred words) of corrections, suggestions, and comments to the regulations that were to control the apprenticeship system in the crown colony. Modesty demanded that he feint reluctance to offer suggestions for a state of society "with which I am unacquainted." However, he confessed: "It is only by an effort of imagination that I can figure to myself the wants and vices which may exhibit themselves under a regime in which the lower order will be secured by the fundamental laws of the state against most of the privations and miseries which invariably by attaching to idleness and misconduct in free society throughout the world." He concluded: "Because I have been long-acquainted with the classes to which the new system is to be applied I hope my observation may be found to contain something useful."[12] Whatever else may be said of him, no one could question his dedication to his cause.

On November 22, about one month after sending Secretary Stanley his comments on the draft of the order-in-council that was meant to govern the relations between the employers and apprentices, Burnley requested a meeting with Secretary Stanley to discuss "the functions and composition of our Legislative Council whose efficient aid will be so essentially necessary in smoothing the operation of the new system."[13] Burnley may not have known it, but the Colonial Office saw the regulations they had sent him as self-sufficient and required little or no room for improvement. They were transmitted to the colony in January 1834.

On January 4, 1834, Governor Hill informed Secretary Stanley that he had selected Jackson for a seat on the Council of Government that had been made vacant by the retirement of Francis Preschier, vice president of the council. This appointment was in response to a request Burnley had made to Secretary Stanley. Hill was effusive in his praise of Jackson whom he described as "barrister on a first rate practice, much esteemed for his acquirements, and [who] had already proved the propriety of my selection of him . . . by his diligent and useful services in our deliberations."[14] Jackson was an inspired choice. A few months later, he was working on the apprenticeship bill to which Burnley had offered his suggestions from his room in Paris.

CHAPTER 14

The New Society

The whole fabric of our previous jurisdiction—I mean that by which the great mass of the laboring classes was governed, has been destroyed by the Emancipation Bill, the want of which must be immediately supplied. . . . Every one of these laws must now be recast to meet the altered nature of our present situation, and that not to be with the aid of talented Spanish lawyers, but by a Board of Council in which the few professional members are British.

—William Burnley, on the draft of the abolition bill, 1833

INHERENT IN THE provisions of the abolition bill was the directive for how the apprentices, the manumitted slaves, were to be treated. On October 19, 1833, when Burnley offered his suggestions to Lord Stanley as to how the regulations for the apprentices ought to be structured, his major concern was to advance a formula that would give the planters every advantage over the employees. He envisioned a society in which the masters would be sufficiently rich and estates sufficiently profitable to keep the apprentices to distinct employments.

Before such a state could exist, Burnley and his fellow planters had to overcome many fears that were related to their future fortune. The first challenge, as he saw it, was to find "individuals disposed to submit to service and discipline."[1] The inability to do so would make it difficult for the colonists to cultivate their estates. The second difficulty lay in determining who would pay the proprietors for the loss of the apprentices' services when he or she was confined to prison; and third, how they would recoup losses that occurred when workers were found loitering, leading to lost time (ten to thirty minutes) before they started their day's work. The maintenance of private property was the most important consideration. All that mattered to him was the extraction of the most surpluses from his workers.

The next question revolved around the protection of the apprentices and providing a mechanism that would prevent the planters from abusing them. Previously, the planters acted as magistrates and possessed total control over their lives. To make the act work, the Colonial Office had to send special magistrates (stipendiary magistrates) to the colony to ensure the terms of the act were carried out, the disputes between the masters and the apprentices were adjudicated fairly, and sufficient control was kept over the new system through the submission of regular reports on its progress. In this next context, "the jurisdiction of the special magistrates replaced planter justice."[2] Burnley and his fellow proprietors did not take this development kindly. They argued that the colony needed efficient special magistrates to ensure that their privileges were not trespassed upon. Surveillance of the apprentices was their overriding concern.[3]

The planters argued that to make this system work, the special magistrates needed to be vigilant, particularly as it related to the apprentices' neglect of their work and persistent indolence. To accomplish their task, these magistrates had to act swiftly and be unafraid to use "a large proportion of punishments, particularly amongst the females." Such punishment should "consist of solitary confinement in their leisure, [at their] home on the estates to which they belong especially during the night." The proprietors feared the nights more than the days. It was the one space they could not control. As he did in *Trinidad Negroes*, Burnley attests once more to the nocturnal proclivities of the Africans:

> The night is to the Negroes the favorite portion of the 24 hours when the white man dares not encounter the slaves, and is obliged from the exhaustion of the day to seek repose. That period of time the African has always been accustomed to consider as preeminently his own. His principal journies [*sic*], and his principal amusements are carried on during the night; the loss of any portion of it will be felt more sensible than any other privations, and the apprehension of it will tend more to keep him to his duty than stripes or any other mode of punishment. These places of confinement must of course be so formed as to allow the culprit proper repose and be entirely free under the control and surveillance of the special justice.

Fines were also an important means of maintaining surveillance over the Negroes. It was the preferential mode of punishment. Therefore, the proprietors needed to have an input in the administration of same since they had a better understanding of how to use such fines to obtain the best results. These modes of punishment were important because they "may probably keep the majority of the apprentices to a fair performance of the 45 hours of weekly labor avoiding as much as possible stripes, and hard labor at the penal establishments, which can be reserved for grave offences."[4]

Paying for the introduction of this new service presented "the greatest difficulty" to the colony, which did not have enough money to absorb the cost of establishing this new system. It also required bringing in new talent and taking a new look at the constitution, which Burnley claimed was destitute of all independence and was so shackled as to render it useless. He confessed: "I do not see how the immediate and urgent demands upon its time, labor and intellect can be met in any satisfactory way; or how the necessary legislation which will be absolutely required before the 1st of August next can be completed unless the Board of Council be in many respects reformed, and a few more individuals directly interested in the welfare of the colony, in whom the community has confidence be introduced into it."[5]

As the day of emancipation approached, Burnley became more anxious about the contents of the abolition act and the new relations that were to ensue between the employer (former slave owners) and the apprentices (formerly enslaved). Although he had submitted his comments on the bill to Lord Stanley he had heard nothing in return. Such was his anxiety that between January 1 and August 31, 1834, Burnley wrote over twenty letters, some as long as thirty pages, to the colonial officials, seeking to understand what had become of his comments and adding even more recommendations to the regulations that were being framed to govern the relations between the former masters and the apprentices. Between 1834 and 1835—suffering from hypergraphia, an obsessive need to record his concerns on paper—a profusion of feelings gushed from Burnley's heart that he transmitted to all the parties involved.

On January 11, 1834, Burnley resumed his communications with Lord Stanley. He reminded him of the "numerous remarks in detail [he had made] upon a manuscript draft of regulations for the government of apprentices with which he had previously the kindness to furnish me." Although he had heard nothing from him in this regard, he was prepared to add a few more remarks to those he had made previously. He recognized that things could change rapidly before the abolition bill came into effect. "The scene is now reversed," he said; "Freedom is proclaimed, and the power of the master annihilated."[6] Since such sympathies were likely to continue in the direction of the apprentices, it was more than likely that the feelings of the special magistrates would also be swayed in favor of the apprentices. Therefore, he thought it was necessary to enlighten the colonial officials about the realities of the local situation.[7] Although it may have been construed that he was "advocating exclusively the interest of the class to which I belong," he could not help but offer his "impartial" view on the subject. He was expansive in his comments:

> The consequence of transferring unimpaired that sympathy and protection, which was not unnaturally bestowed upon the slaves, to the Negro apprentice, will be an abandonment of the leading principle by which alone can the measure be made to work successfully. A slight consideration of the subject will show that the power of the law will now be principally required to keep the apprentice to the honest fulfillment of his engagement. The employers would have no power to evade this share of the contract; substantial lodging he must furnish at the outset—clothing he must provide six months in advance, and food once a week. His consideration being thus paid in advance, he is afterwards to depend upon the honesty of the Negro laborer for the faithful discharge of the debt he has contracted. We cannot expect to find the latter a higher degree of moral feeling than Britons possess and the history of the Australian apprentices sufficiently prove that a sense of benefits received, on a knowledge of debt incurred, afford no security for the performance of engagements, unless accompanied by the fear of judicial and executive power.[8]

Given that the terms of the agreement called upon the apprentice to render forty-five hours of work a week to his employer, Burnley wanted to know who would reimburse the employer when the apprentice was imprisoned. He also protested against the form of punishment that was proposed for the apprentices. Although the order called for the confinement of apprentices "to hard labor and the stocks for the women, with addition of whipping for the men," that was not sufficient for Burnley. As an insider he knew the most effective way to punish apprentices, particularly the women, his bête noire, whom he believed to be the eminence grise behind all the conspiracies; or that is what he thought.[9] Thus he advised: "The occasional substitution of confinement at night in a room furnishing all that may be necessary for comfortable repose, would in numerous instances be more efficacious, particularly with the women, in deterring from the commission of offences, than any other description of punishment; and have at the same time a favorable influence upon their habits and their manners."[10]

On January 13, 1834, Burnley was at it again. He wrote to John Shaw-Lefevre regarding the recommendations that he had made about the abolition act. He felt the governor may have been a bit reluctant to carry out some of the new measures because the governor was not sure what Secretary Stanley's feelings were on the matter. On the other hand, Burnley felt he should have known what was taking place and, more to the point, the governor would have expected him to know. Cutting through the superficialities, he went to the heart of his concerns: "The object of my communication is not to add by multifarious questions to the entanglement of the subject but honestly to ascertain whether any of the measures I have recommended are deemed by Mr. Stanley inadmissible that we may lose none of our remaining time in contending for improbabilities, but earnestly devote one's whole attention to the perfection of those regulations which we may ultimately expect to be approved of here." The officials at the Colonial Office did not seem especially concerned about Burnley's anxieties. One of them scribbled the following note on Burnley's letter: "This letter may be put by. It relates to the proper method of framing the Law for the government of apprenticed laborers—which law has long since been framed and is now in full operation."[11]

Burnley was also bothered by the idea of a free labor class that would evolve as a result of emancipation. On January 24, he wrote a sixteen-page letter to Secretary Stanley in which the words "deepest anxiety," "fear," "dismay," "impending ruin," "injurious results," "valueless," and other such emotive terms inundated the first three pages of his text. It was almost as though, in their "microscopic, quantum way,"[12] these emanations of consciousness revealed an unknowing and unknowable future—perhaps what Camus would call "the absurd"—where everything was about to be thrown into inevitable chaos. Burnley was not sure how things were going to turn out or how the evolving situation would affect the wealth he had gathered over the thirty years he had spent working on the island, but he was concerned. This was his existential crisis.

Apart from, or perhaps together with, this intense anxiety, Burnley was riddled with four major concerns: (a) the fear of a limited African work force; (b) a large, fertile land, which as he said, "possessed the richest soil on the most favored part of the globe," and that he feared the apprentices would use to undercut his dominance and control; (c) an increase in the cost of production that was likely to render his machinery "inactive and valueless"; and (d) the ability of the workers to command whatever price they wanted for their labor thus raising the labor cost. It would be a disastrous situation for him and other planters; or, as he would say, it would bring them to ruin.

In his letter to the secretary of state, Burnley called upon the colonial government to ensure that the proprietors always had a ready supply of labor, which could be achieved by imposing a fixed tax on the sales of all parcels of land, whatever their quantity. This tax, he said, should "be sufficiently high to prevent the fractual [sic] division, whilst it presents no obstacle to transactions on a large scale." The taxes so raised, "together with all future receipts on account of the sales of Crown lands," should be "exclusively devoted to the encouragement of immigration to the colony." To ensure that all this took place, he advised that power be vested in the local legislature "to mortgage the revenues arising from these taxes in payment of the interest of any sums borrowed for the purpose of affording partially or wholly the means of transport to all laborers desirous of settling in this colony."[13]

Burnley's fear of being ruined also revealed a deep-seated racism. He called for the introduction of white immigrants, not to work in the factory, but to superintend the manufactory occupations for which they were "considerable qualified." He notes: "In every industrious department where skillful manipulation is more required than hard labor, their superiority over the African race would be manifest." He agreed with the experts who argued there are "some generic [in today's language he would have said "genetic"] difference in the African race, rendering them more prone to idleness and vagrancy than Europeans; which not a few have boldly asserted."[14] Burnley was not unique in his opinion. Europeans like William Cobbett believed the Africans were "dull, easily excitable and disposed to laziness."[15] A century later, after Europe had exploited Africans all over the world, Jean-Paul Sartre affirmed: "The only way the European could make himself man was by fabricating slaves and monsters."[16]

These were Burnley's views at the beginning of 1834, the year in which the emancipation of the enslaved was supposed to come into being. They found favor with the British government that feared if it freed the Africans "they would abandon the plantations, resulting in the bankruptcy of planters."[17] So that even before the enslaved Africans were emancipated formally on August 1, 1834, others sought to shape their destiny. The officials at the Colonial Office and the local legislators who endorsed Burnley's proposals made it difficult, well-nigh impossible, for Africans to buy lands so as to set up themselves and their families in this new situation. "Sell land in larger rather than smaller parcels" became their guiding philosophy. Such a plan, as was revealed later, was intended to make the Africans "tenants and renters" rather than owners of the land.

The second aspect of this plan involved encouraging immigration to Trinidad, thereby negating any gains the enslaved may have achieved through formal freedom; using the colony's revenues to ensure a new form of enslavement of African people; and extracting more surpluses from Africans through the legal stealing of forty-five hours of free, compulsory labor that was mandated by the abolition bill. In fact, between 1834 and 1835 close to two thousand new workers came to Trinidad from various parts of the world at a time when there were approximately twenty thousand apprentices in a population of about thirty-nine thousand.

That which seemed to be a well-deserved, hard-fought freedom turned out to be yet another guise to keep Africans tethered to their former masters and the land. Burnley, it turned out, was the chief architect of this plan that frustrated the aspiration of ambitious Africans. It was something that he spent his life fine-tuning and putting into effect even though in later life he would become an advocate of free labor. His plan, we would see, changed the entire social, cultural, and religious fabric of the island forever.

CHAPTER 15

Preparing for Emancipation

The just claims to the privilege of controlling their own taxation and expenditure and of making such reasonable laws and regulations as local circumstances of the colony may require may be regularly urged upon every previous government even when little hope of success existed. And now that they approach the goal of their wishes their exertion will not be relaxed; for they can entertain no apprehension that the liberal principles which animate His Majesty's present will permit them to withhold this boon one moment longer than the immediate safety of the colony under the important changes decided upon, may appear to require.

—William Burnley to John Shaw-Lefevre, 1834

HAVING ACCEPTED THE inevitability of the emancipation of the enslaved, Burnley turned his attention to influencing the arrangements that would govern the administration of the new order. On January 28, 1834, he wrote to John Shaw-Lefevre as follows: "Considering the changes that must take place in the colony in August next, in the civil and criminal codes—the new constitution and establishments which must be framed—the financial wants which their cost will create and the necessity in fact of building up a new structure of society from the foundation—it is to be regretted that a popular alteration in the form of the colonial government had not been made to take timely precedence over the Act for the Abolition of Slavery so that the first change might have been organized and satisfactorily settled before the other commenced." Yet he remained hopeful. He averred: "However late the change might be, even if simultaneous, I am convinced that if it comes in a shape satisfactory to the colonies that it will infuse into local proceedings, best calculated, if any human agency can have that effect, to render the impeding experiment successful."[1]

As hopeful as Burnley appeared, he had some critical concerns such as whether the local legislature would have the power to tax, be able to control expenditure, or have "anything worth left legislating about." He assured the secretary of state that the colonists would "cheerfully conform to the course of proceedings he may think most conducive to a successful issue of the measures contemplated; either by doing the best we can with the present form of government established in the colony; or by vigorously exerting ourselves under the sanction of the government in establishing without delay a more popular and efficient system." According to Burnley, the planters had always advocated the just claims "of controlling their own taxation and expenditure and of making such reasonable laws and regulations as the local circumstances of the colony may require." Only now, things had become more urgent, a claim with which the Colonial Office agreed. An official from the Colonial Office appended the following note to the bottom of Burnley's letter: "This letter has just come to light. It relates to several important topics, on which it would be necessary that the decision of the Secretary of State be proscribed."[2]

On February 11, following through on his concerns, Burnley wrote to Shaw-Lefevre to inform him that the colonists would do everything in their power "to promote the industry and secure the good conduct of the persons to be manumitted." He reasoned that while the colonists were prepared to defer their concerns on the substantial issues of the constitution they believed that slight alterations to the standing rules of the Legislative Council would "facilitate the quick dispatch of business which the preparations for the impending change will render essentially necessary."[3] If such changes (like the initiation of laws, which only the governor could do, and the record-keeping of council proceedings) were made it would allow for the more efficient transaction of the nation's business. He also suggested that members' positions on the council be based on seniority—except for the chief judge who, although an ex-officio member, was second to the governor—and that council meetings be regularized so that the unofficial members could plan in advance to attend them.

Such recommendations, if adopted, would have made the system more efficient, given the council better status, and attracted a better caliber of men (women were not considered) to serve in the council. He reminded Stanley: "The chief object in appointing unofficial members from amongst the proprietors of the colony, must be to satisfy the community that their local interests are discussed and protected in an independent and efficient manner. It follows that if dignity and power are withheld from them that their influence in society will be trifling, and their utility for the purpose intended rendered more doubtful."[4] Burnley was not unmindful that the constant changes taking place at the Colonial Office made it difficult for the officials to keep up with what was going on in the colony.[5]

The colonial officials concurred with many of Burnley's recommendations. In response to his letter, Thomas Spring Rice, the undersecretary of state, wrote that the solicitor general should have a seat in council "instead of the protector of slaves; the members of the Council should have the right to initiate measures except in cases of grants of public money and with the proviso that the Governor's final approbation should be necessary to only ordinances forwarded upon such measures; that the members of council should have precedence according to their seniority except as regards to the Chief Justice who should take precedence officially over other members; and that a clerk to the Council should be appointed—some inconvenience being felt from the circumstances that the minutes of Council are now being kept by the colonial secretary who is not the servant of the Board but one of its members."[6]

After dealing with the structure of the local legislative council, Burnley turned his attention to what he called "the development of just and correct principles in the experimental measures about to be adopted for the extinction of slavery." His particular concern was section 20 of the abolition bill that prevented the employer from prolonging the apprenticeship period beyond the six years as stipulated by the law and which he contended contradicted the preamble of the bill intended "for the purpose of compensating the owners and for promoting the industry and securing the good conduct of the persons to be manumitted." While section 20 provided that the employer be compensated for the loss of services, the problem revolved around whether the provision was intended "only to cover the loss arising from absence occasioned solely by voluntary desertion, and not when occasioned by other willful acts of an apprentice." Burnley believed that certain words ("willfully absent himself") had the effect of sabotaging the larger and more important intent of the bill, which led him to conclude: "The destruction of slavery by a legislative act was easy; but the reconstruction by the same means of a free and prosperous social system on its ruins, appears enveloped in doubt and difficulty."[7]

Burnley believed that it would be dangerous to propose a condition in which all the formerly enslaved would become free after six years (in 1840) regardless of their criminal behavior during the six years of apprenticeship. He could not understand how "the perpetrators of fraud, violence and rapine, as well as the moral and industrious shall be meted out the same prospect of future happiness. . . . The admission of such a rule will immediately throw the most serious obstacles in the way of the first legislative steps which the colonists will be called upon to take for the security of the social order, and the due administration of justice, under the new form which colonial society is expected shortly to assume." Such a bill, he said, only governed the relations between the apprentices and the employers and essentially left untouched "the more extended and complicated relations of individuals with each other and with the state."[8]

Burnley remained convinced that the ambiguities of section 20 needed clarification. The same was not true for an error caused by "the deliberate infusion of unsound principle," which led him to his rather unsound and exaggerated conclusion: "I can imagine nothing more disastrous in its moral consequences than the enactment of a law by which mere absence from work (which considering the Negro character must be esteemed a venial offence) will be visited with future punishment from which fraud, rapine and violence are to be exempt; and by which the convicted swindler, ruffian, and robber are all to be deemed worthy of being at loose on society on the first days of emancipation, whilst the lazy idler alone is to be kept under prolonged restraint."[9] Burnley believed that this one constitutional blemish was enough to ruin the apprenticeship experiment. The reputation of Britain depended on it.[10]

As Burnley prepared to leave England to return to Trinidad, he met with Secretary Stanley on April 1, 1834, to discuss issues facing Trinidad. His fundamental distrust/fear of the ex-slaves led him to insist upon selection of a chief justice with knowledge of local conditions to ensure that there was adequate coordination of the justice system (that is, the colonial magistracy and the police) on a countrywide basis. He suggested that a registry be kept of the apprentices. His rationale ran as follows:

> In a colony like Trinidad where more than nineteen twentieths of the whole surface is in a state of nature, covered with dense forests, it will be impossible to confine a barbarous race within the bounds of civilization unless there is a strict registry both of persons and domicile. This alone can prevent maroon settlements in the interior by checking the first attempts at desertion—for when effected, no physical force could remedy the evil. The regulations for these police registries must be adapted to the character and habit of the population, and copies of the latter must be kept in some central spot. A metropolitan registry will also be required of the extension of apprenticeship authorized by the Abolition Act; as the district records will be liable to loss and destruction for a variety of accidents.[11]

Secretary Stanley disapproved of Burnley's proposition that a compulsory process be established in which convicted vagrants were to be forced to become apprentices as contained in Edward Jackson's code of apprentice laws. Jackson's draft rendered vagrants liable to apprenticeship upon a conviction before a single magistrate. Secretary Stanley was unwilling to accept this exception. Even some members of the Trinidad council felt that "the terms under which vagrants are defined . . . extended the provisions of the [Abolition] Act too widely."[12] Given the strong feelings against the proposition, Burnley hoped that Secretary Stanley would adopt the remainder of the plan. The magistrates, he said, "will then only require to remit sentences passed upon vagrants, in the event of their voluntarily contracting to serve for a limited period, any person disposed to take charge of them."[13]

On May 20, as part of a delegation, Burnley held his final meeting with Secretary Stanley before he returned to Trinidad. The delegation that consisted of Joseph Marryat, Russell Ellice,[14] Henry Davidson, and Burnley presented Secretary Stanley eight resolutions "embracing the substance of the representations the deputation wished to submit to his consideration."[15] Marryat actually presented the resolutions. They hoped: (1) that the regulations that were about to be framed for the apprentices "will be assimilated as near as local difference will permit, to the provisions contained in the Act for the Abolition of Slavery in the island of Jamaica which recently received His Majesty's gracious consent"; (2) that sufficient legislative facilities be given to the Council of Government in Trinidad to enable them to carry into effect laws as the future exigency of the case may require; (3) that they be allowed "to introduce into the regulations for the government of the apprentices, the applications of fines, as far as they may be practicable, for the compensation of injuries and punishment of offences"; (4) that the British government grant them a loan to build police stations to control the apprentices; (5) that they receive government assistance to introduce "a free population from any quarter from which it may be redundant"; (6) that the liberated Africans be treated in the same manner as the apprentices; (7) that the government frame laws and regulations to repress vagrancy; (8) that the government's plan for banks in the West Indian colonies "embrace no plan for the introduction of a paper currency into the island of Trinidad, where for the purposes of a circulating medium it is not required, and which in its consequences would prove highly injurious"; and (9) that every measure be taken "to reduce the expenditure of the colonial government in Trinidad."[16]

Stanley expressed no objections to the substance of some of the resolutions. He was willing to provide proper facilities to the government "to enable them to complete the legislative measures which the early changes in the colonial system would render necessary." He felt there were sufficient buildings in the colony that could be rented to provide police stations for the apprentices even though the delegation was of an opposite view.[17] Although he agreed with certain aspects of the resolution that called for immigration, he was cautious lest "it was desirable to avoid exciting an opinion in Europe that we are capturing and liberating slaves [that is, the liberated Africans] for the purpose of working them in our colonies under regulations which might be supposed to wear the semblance of slavery."

Stanley did not agree that the vagrants be kept at hard labor for an unlimited period until they were disposed to enter into an engagement to work for reasonable wages, as prescribed in the 11th clause of the Earl of Ripon's plan of emancipation. However, he expressed "his readiness to accede to a modified arrangement by which a vagrant condemned to a definite term to imprisonment and hard labor might obtain remission of part or the whole of his sentence by engaging to work in the service of an employer disposed to take charge of him under proper regulation." Stanley also expressed his general inclination "to provide immigration to the colony by any proper regulated ordinance conducive to that important object."[18]

By the time Burnley returned to Trinidad in June 1834, arrangements were being made for the formal emancipation of the enslaved. In preparation for the great occasion Governor Hill sent copies of his proclamation in English, French, and Spanish to commandants of the various districts (or quarters as they called them), directing them to explain to the soon-to-be freed apprentices "the nature of the new state in which they will be placed on the 1st of August next as contrasted with what has been their state of slavery." He also advised the commandants to give copies of the proclamation to owners and managers so that "due care be taken to direct the minds of the slaves from any erroneous impressions or misapprehension of the operation of the Abolition Slavery Act they may have imbibed."[19] On July 20, Governor Hill sent a letter to Secretary Spring Rice informing him of the measures that he had taken to alert the enslaved about their proper mode of behavior on that glorious day of liberation. He even invited the runaway slaves, numerous in number, to return to duty assuring them that if they did they would be exempted from punishment. Thus, preparations were made for August 1, 1834, the most glorious day in the lives of the enslaved; a day Burnley and his fellow planters feared.

CHAPTER 16

Burnley's Views on Apprenticeship

≈

The term apprenticeship is held by the Negroes in utter contempt, particularly by the middle aged and old men who ask, "What have they to learn?" or "whether the white men are now going to teach them to dig cane holes after a new fashion."

—Young Anderson to Mr. Beldam, 1835

The apprenticeship is not popular among the planters nor would they prefer a system of wages. Their wish is to perpetuate a system of slavery under the name of apprenticeship or under any other by which the system may be designated.

—Young Anderson to Mr. Beldam, 1835

THE EX-SLAVES WELCOMED their day of liberation. After being treated as brutes for so many years, they displayed a new consciousness and a new understanding of their place in the world. By their actions they had annealed into one social body, joining in that free consciousness of their peers the world over. Such behavior, one may argue, was analogous to what was taking place among the English working class during the same period. Steven Marcus has argued: "In these scenes of early industrial life—as it came to its first great crisis in the 1830's and 40's—something new had happened. In part that newness consisted in the actual conditions that were being created and disclosed; in part it had to do with human consciousness struggling to make, and often resist, the radical alterations and accommodations within itself that these conditions required."[1]

The planters and the apprentices saw apprenticeship in two different ways. Governor Hill and the slavery party saw it as an opportunity to perpetuate the old system of coercion under a new guise and to run the system with an iron hand. Studholme Hodgson noted that it soon became evident that "the colonists had no intention whatever of employing the interval between the apprenticeship and the entire freedom of their former slaves, in allaying and reconciling animosities, or in creating a foundation for feelings of mutual kindness between the whites and the blacks."[2] The apprentices saw the new system as a cruel joke. "What can we learn from them?" they asked; "Is the white man going to teach me how to dig cane holes after a new fashion?" To them, apprenticeship was nothing more than "a cruel mockery of their degraded state to call them free, and still work them as slaves under the name of apprentice."[3] They were convinced the planters were determined to thwart the provisions of the emancipation bill.

Burnley, who was out of the island for most of the year, returned prior to the day of emancipation. Since he was away so long, the governor had to find a way to reinstate him as a member of the Council of Government. On Saturday, August 9, as the agitation around emancipation began to settle down, Governor Hill sent a note to Sir John Shaw-Lefevre, undersecretary of state for a short period, to inform him that Burnley had returned to the country and was trying to regularize his official status. Shaw-Lefevre, in his turn, wrote a note to Governor Hill asking him to "introduce" Burnley to him. Hill responded: "He merits your commendation. He is intelligent and conciliatory in his manners and has a marked disposition to co-operate with me which has given me much satisfaction."[4] Governor Hill relieved Mr. Roxboro, a junior member of the council, of his seat to accommodate Burnley. He assured Roxboro that he would reappoint him to the council when the first vacancy for a nonofficial position arose.

While Burnley was abroad he had also cultivated a close friendship with Nassau W. Senior, the Drummond Chair of Political Economy at Oxford University and a member of the British Poor Law Inquiry Commission of 1832. Burnley looked after Mrs. Laurence Nihell's interest in the El Dorado sugar estate at the request of Senior, who was probably a trustee for the family under a marriage settlement. The Trinidad Register of 1813 showed that Laurence Nihell owned the El Dorado sugar estate. It consisted of 191 slaves. Mrs. Nihell inherited the estate at the death of her husband.[5] The El Dorado estate was located to the west of Burnley's Orange Grove estate in Tacarigua.

On August 9 and September 3, Burnley wrote two letters to Senior describing his views on apprenticeship.[6] In his letter of August 9, Burnley assured Senior that he had not "neglected his affairs entrusted to my charge" and that "El Dorado has made a good crop and the proceeds will not be short of the results I led you to expect." He also enclosed a copy of the *Port of Spain Gazette* of August 5 to give Senior an idea of what was taking place in Trinidad. He explained:

> The Negroes will not comprehend the system of apprenticeship, which when fairly explained presented generally no great advantage to them. These principally benefitted on the few that had hard and tyrannical masters, but throughout the island their treatment was humane and their work moderate. As such they do not hesitate to abuse the king for making any law at present on the subject. "If no free for six years, better let we tand as before till that time come." They show themselves excellent lawyers—all who have come before me plead as a defense for deserting their estates, that the managers called them together some time and read them a paper saying "All we free on the 1st of August," but when questioned as to the restrictions and reservations explained at the same time, they will give no answer.[7]

Burnley reported to Senior that apprentices on the El Dorado estate were behaving "no worse than their neighbors, and in the course of the month regular labor will be restored."[8] He suggested that Senior get in touch with Hume, Burnley's brother-in-law, if he wished to get any further information about what was taking place on the island. That was not difficult. Hume was a friend of Senior and a frequent guest at his house.[9] Burnley doubted whether he could keep the El Dorado estate in Mrs. Nihill's possession "through the next crop, as they will do their utmost to have a sequestrator appointed, when she can no longer be benefitted by incurring costs of suits." Apparently, the estate was not making enough money to keep it going. On September 3, he informed Senior that "the grand appointment of apprenticeship," in the colony was "*politically . . .* perfectly successful."[10] He had nothing but contempt for black people. He condoned Governor Hill's harsh treatment of the apprentices, suggesting that they deserved nothing better. He continued:

> The bribe of 20 million has effectively neutralized the opposition of the upper classes and the Negroes are too ignorant to understand the real position in which they are placed. They made a strike to obtain what they considered to be freedom, but being promptly met by force, they have relapsed into their former obedience and terror of their masters; and incapable of nice distinctions are satisfied now that slavery exists for them until 1840, whatever may be the term given to their existing condition. It is the impetus of past slavery [a phrase he used previously] therefore which now carries apprenticeship onward in this colony at a smooth and steady pace. But as intelligence spreads, will the impetus slacken, and the system in my opinion work less efficiently every day?[11]

In Burnley's estimation, slavery had a capacity for good. As it sickened and died, he wondered if the replacement system would have the same impact upon the apprentices' capacity for hard work.

Two years later, in spite of his acting on behalf of an owner of slaves in Trinidad, Senior praised Gustave de Beaumont's *Marie, ou l'Esclavage aux États-Unis*, a novel that criticized slavery and racism in the United States. Senior was a good friend of Alexis de Tocqueville, with whom he had corresponded for several years. Beaumont had accompanied Tocqueville to the United States in 1831 and wrote this companion piece to supplement Tocqueville's *Democracy in America*. Senior commented: "I have read *Marie* with great delight and instruction. It is very powerfully written, though perhaps with too much *onction* [sentimentality] for our colder [English] tastes."[12] Burnley may have been acquainted with *Marie*, having met Beaumont when Tocqueville visited the United States in 1831.

Burnley believed that apprenticeship was just another form of slavery and predicted its failure. Its demise, he said, would be "slow and gradual" although its promoters would proclaim its success to the world. He, for one, feared the island would relapse into a "New St. Domingo." He also feared a repetition of a lack of laborers on the island of which he had always complained. Antigua did not undergo an apprenticeship period, and that held out some hope for Burnley on the labor front. He wrote: "The further experiment in Antigua will very soon show us what may be expected from African free labor under the most favorable circumstances of density of population." He wondered what would transpire in the interim (1834–1840) and what would happen when apprenticeship ended. He says that if the Antiguan results were favorable, "then it would be a concern in this colony, where without a considerable influx of population we shall find but few hands to cultivate our estates after 1840. And whether we can even cultivate them up to that period will altogether depend on the fiscal measures pushed in Great Britain with respect to foreign sugars."[13] The absence of an apprenticeship period in Antigua did not make any appreciable difference in terms of the labor situation in Antigua.[14]

On September 3, 1834, Governor Hill reported to Thomas Spring Rice, secretary of state for war and the colonies, that the apprentices had returned to work "with contentment. . . . My expectation is that in a short time all the labor will be performed by task [work] and the apprentices will have many extra hours to dispose for good wages."[15] Burnley was more positive at the end of the year. He wrote to Spring Rice: "I am sure that you will receive with gratification my report of the universal good of the apprentices during the festivals of the holidays. In fact, all classes of society have enjoyed themselves with cheerfulness and good order."[16]

However, all was not rosy for the apprentices. The planters who had become the special magistrates in this new dispensation were determined to vent their vengeance upon the ex-slaves. One hundred and forty planters were made special magistrates. Therefore, they were able to administer special punishments to the apprentices. Since the managers of these estates did not wish to lose any man hours from their slaves, they simply sent them to another slave master (now a stipendiary justice) to administer punishments. Between August 1 and December 31, 1834, 560 apprentices were the recipients of corporal punishment, each receiving 6 to 39 stripes. The most severe punishment occurred in August, the month of emancipation, when 301 apprentices were beaten.[17] The apprentices at Burnley's Orange Grove also felt the brunt of his cruelty. Governor Hill made Mr. Lee, manager and part owner of Orange Grove estate, a stipendiary magistrate, permitting him to administer punishments. By July of 1835, over four hundred punishments were inflicted upon the apprentices at Orange Grove estate.

By 1835 the apprentices were totally fed up with the cruelty that was being inflicted upon them. Apart from some small wages and additional allowances they received when they worked in their spare time, they could not tell the difference between slavery and freedom.[18] In July 1835 Young noted that at no period within the last twenty years of working with the enslaved, "have the Negroes been so discontented as they are at present. In fact, more coercion is required and exercised to make them work as they did before. They certainly consider apprenticeship a hardship."[19]

Burnley did not stick around to follow the evolution of this new social system. By the beginning of 1835 he had departed to Europe. He had to discuss matters of compensation and determine how best to carry forward his immigration plans. He also had to visit his family in Europe. His younger son, only about twelve years old at the time, needed his father's guidance and love, at least some of the time.

CHAPTER 17

Apprenticeship
Making It Work for Him

The case which I so urgently represented to Your Lordship on the 20th instant has exerted the greatest discontent throughout the colony; . . . who will perceive with alarm the impossibility of any man of honor and independence continuing [to serve] as a member of a Board where his intention and his motives may be underhandedly calumniated, his conduct and character traduced, and his disinterested exertion in His Majesty's services rendered nugatory and useless without his possessing the constitutional means—not merely of redress—but of ever arriving at a knowledge of the source from which the calumny had flowed.

—William H. Burnley to Lord Glenelg, 1835

O NCE IT BECAME evident that the emancipation of enslaved Africans was inevitable Burnley decided to think about how best to make the new system work for him. He explained calmly and dispassionately to the House of Commons Select Committee on the Disposal of Lands that once he saw there was determination in Britain to emancipate the slaves, "I very naturally and anxiously turned my attention to the means by which we should be enabled to cultivate our estates when that period ended." In pursuance of that goal, Burnley visited Martinique (French); St. Thomas and St. Croix (Danish); St. Vincent, Barbados, Jamaica, and Antigua (British); Curacao (Dutch); Cuba (Spanish). He also visited Venezuela and the United States in 1834 "for the particular purpose of making inquiries relative to the free and slave labor in those states" (*DL*).[1] When asked by William Gladstone, a member of the committee with whom he had corresponded, why he did not visit Haiti, he replied that although he was anxious to do so, "from Curacao I could find no opportunity of proceeding to Hayti. I went in consequence to Jamaica direct; and, in fact, I had not the sufficient time, without renouncing my visit to Havannah, for it was then the month of June, and I found it necessary to be in England by the month of October."[2] It is clear that Burnley wanted to cover all of the bases before he encountered the realities of apprenticeship.

Burnley departed for Europe at the beginning of 1835, staying off at St. John's, Antigua, for a short while. While he was there he saw a letter in the *Antigua Free Press* that made him jump to the defense of his island and justify the flow of black Antiguan laborers who were leaving their country to go to Trinidad to share in Trinidad's prosperity. Burnley claimed that "a character of high respectability and of the most perfect honor and veracity," in order to discourage Antiguans from immigrating to Trinidad, was spreading rumors that Trinidad was treating its black citizens horribly. This anonymous writer said that in Trinidad there was "no provision for the moral or religious instructions of the negroes," inferring that it was better that black Antiguans stay in Antigua rather than travel to Trinidad (*PG*, January 23, 1835).[3]

On January 10, Burnley's response to this defaming article appeared in the Antigua's *Weekly Register*. He noted that the ecclesiastical establishment in Trinidad consisted of "a Bishop, permanently residing in the colony, a Rector, a Vicar-General, and nine churches who with their assistants receive annually from the Colonial Treasury above 3,000 pounds sterling and who administer their sacred duties." He assured the anonymous correspondent (and black Antiguans by extension) that "no more affectionate pastors, devoting their time and energies to the moral and religious improvement of their flock, can be found in any Christian community" (*PG*, January 23, 1835).

Burnley took particular exception to the anonymous correspondent's assertion that "he never met with a plantation slave who knew the letters of the alphabet." Burnley assured him that the island possessed "a national school for males and another for females in which the poorer classes are instructed gratuitously, beside numerous private schools." In fact, he promised his anonymous correspondent that if he finds himself in Trinidad he could "show him Negro laborers on our own estates [his and Mr. Jackson] who can not only read, but write. Burnley also assured him that Trinidad Negroes were supplied adequately with food and clothing and did not have to work extra hours to supply their wants. He hoped his "slight review" would give the correspondent an appreciation for the real character of the island and thereby encourage others to

Trinidad "where labor is always in demand and wages high" and where they would meet with "affectionate pastors to provide for the moral and religious instructions of their children" (*PG*, January 23, 1835).

As he traveled to London, Burnley was preoccupied with the lack of laborers in the colony where slave prices were high, labor scarce and costly, and the availability of fertile lands plentiful, a point that Burnley made in the *Weekly Register*. On June 27, after taking a hard look at the conditions in the colony and evaluating its future prospects, Burnley informed Hume that although the abolition bill would not take effect in 1840, "the change in the interim from slavery to apprenticeship being more nominal than real. The Negro still works for his master by compulsion and without wages; and so long as the system exists, the cultivation, more or less, of exportable products will be kept up." In Trinidad, where private individuals held large tracts of uncultivated lands, "there must be a deficiency of laborers in 1840—unless an additional population be introduced; and from the fertility of the soil giving very large returns for even superficial cultivation, it is supposed that proprietors of the land can afford the expense of procuring it."[4] The prospects, then, weren't that bad.

Between 1834 and 1835, the population of Trinidad increased by about two thousand persons, mostly through the immigration of people from Fayal and Madeira, the neighboring West Indian islands, and liberated Africans from Havana.[5] One thousand liberated Africans came to the island from Cuba. The emigrants who arrived from Fayal in July 1834 were the first indentured laborers to come to the island. They seemed to have fared better than the apprentices. They received six Mexican dollars per month out of which they had to repay the speculators who bought them for sixty dollars during their indentureship or what Burnley called their "term of apprenticeship." Additionally, they were given three and half pounds of salt fish and seven quarts of Indian corn as rations weekly and "a comfortable cottage and garden ground of half an acre to each individual to cultivate on their own account in their leisure time. . . . They profess to be well pleased with their situation, and are only anxious that more of their country folk should join them. Up to this period therefore the experiment may be said to be perfectly successful."[6]

Burnley envisaged the Fayal experiment as the model upon which to pattern immigration into Trinidad. The whole plan, he said, was to procure a race that was best suited to the climate. Initially, this was the driving force behind bringing Africans to the plantations of the Caribbean. It would seem that Burnley was thinking of reintroducing a similar scheme into Trinidad under a different guise. In order to achieve his goal, he requested from Hume "at which of the two groups of islands, whether at the Canaries or the Cape de Verds [*sic*] would there be the best probability of success in inducing emigrants to move" to the island, what he thought the responses of the various government might be, and what would be "the most economical mode of conveying the immigrants to their destination—whether by an English or an American vessel?" The scheme turned out to be unsuccessful although Burnley reported that the emigrants liked living in Trinidad.

While he was in London, Burnley discussed his plan with the officials at the Colonial Office and members of the House of Commons, many of whom were favorable to it. On March 3, he wrote to Mr. Hay to thank him for letters of introduction to His Majesty's commissary judge and to the British consulate in Havana, Cuba.[7] Thereafter he returned to Trinidad. However, by May 21, he was off to Europe again, but not before he and Edward Jackson started a big fight with Governor Hill as to how the liberated Africans from Cuba were to be distributed amongst the planters.[8] This dispute led to a lot of harsh words and finger-pointing between Governor Hill and Burnley. It was a fight in which the Colonial Office had to intervene.

In February 1834 the first batch of 207 liberated Africans came to the island. There were three other shipments, the last group landing in September 1835. The planters welcomed these Africans with "aggressive enthusiasm" because of the "economic uncertainty engendered by the ending of slavery."[9] Necessarily, there was much jockeying for this precious cargo. The task fell to the governor to determine the persons to whom these Africans should be apprenticed.[10] The first group was distributed evenly in divisions of ten to twenty planters. Seven of them, too young to go to the plantations, were placed in the homes of "respectable families." Many of the larger and more prosperous planters disagreed with how the governor distributed the Africans.

By the end of 1835, the prospect of recruiting liberated Africans seemed to be a promising way of providing labor for the island. Governor Hill "made no secret of his desire to demonstrate Trinidad's willingness and suitability to receive a large group of such immigrants," and a group of local employers expressed their desire to employ "no less than 5,000 refugees."[11] On April 26, 1835, in the light of this enthusiasm, the council passed an amendment proposing rules for the distribution of the Africans that disregarded the governor's responsibility in favor of what Stephen Rothery, the attorney general, called the planters' "selfishness." It devolved upon Rothery to advise the governor why he should disregard the advice of the members of his council and follow the Colonial Office's instructions that called upon him to be "the guardian and protector of these helpless beings."[12]

Rothery felt that the council's rules were based on "a distrust of the Executive whom it supposed incapable, if not restrained, of using the power that it would otherwise possess, with partiality and as a means to conferring benefits upon private or political friends, made of abandoning the interest of the Africans." He believed that the proposed rules totally lost sight of the welfare of the Africans who were treated as so much property "which the colony by chance or favor has become possessed of; and then a mode is fixed upon for dividing up the booty among the applications for a share."[13] This criticism was harsh but true. The leading proprietors viewed the distribution of the Africans as an opportunity to acquire as many free laborers as possible.

Rothery was on even more solid, perhaps novel, ground when he interpreted apprenticeship as an instrument to establish "a respectable middle class of society in the island, would be assisted and forwarded by a more general distribution, and by allotting the services of some of the new apprentices [the Africans] to tradesmen—shopkeepers, captains and owners of droghers and passenger boats—and the proprietors of small cultivations of cocoa, coffee, provisions or cotton, and to those whose crops are the produce of free labor." The society, he argued, could not achieve this goal if the Africans were sent to the large plantations where a majority of the owners, being absentee landowners (they lived in England for the most part), would result in the Africans being placed under managers who had little interest in their welfare. Rothery believed that if the governor located large numbers of Africans in one place as the rules suggested "they will form a society of themselves and will retain the savage habits of their nation, whereas by a more general distribution amongst small proprietors of land resident on their own property and superintending the work of their own laborers, habits of industry would with a greater faculty be formed in the man heretofore totally unaccustomed to any system of regularity whatsoever."[14] These sentiments may have been a reflection of Rothery's biases, but he certainly thought it was only through close supervision that the Africans could be prepared to live independently after 1840 when all the apprentices would be freed.

By May 13, the council had withdrawn the rules and given the governor (perhaps more accurately the governor had asserted) the right to distribute the Africans as he saw fit. By then, however, Burnley and Jackson had lodged two protests, one made jointly by Burnley and Jackson and the other from Burnley, against the new authority. The protests were given to the governor who promptly submitted them to the secretary of state for his advice. In his cover letter to the secretary of state, Hill offered the following evaluation:

Mr. Burnley, I observe in the conclusion of his protest seeks for the restrictions on the governor, and urges the necessity of them from the danger of the members of Council being particularly favored. As nothing has occurred to justify that apprehension I do not consider his suggestions worthy of further notice than to express the satisfaction I shall feel in receiving Your Lordship's instructions for my guidance.

Mr. Burnley has lived with me most harmoniously. But I could not avoid perceiving that he was much disappointed in Council at not receiving the support from unofficial members he expected.[15]

Hill also drew the secretary of state's attention to a letter from Rothery that he enclosed in the same package he dispatched.

On July 15, Lord Glenelg wrote a response to Governor Hill in which he praised the clarity of Rothery's advice and his "luminous and powerful remonstrance against them [meaning the members of the Council]." He also demanded that "the employer of each African be selected by yourself [that is, the governor] with a due regard to the well-being of the African; that you do transmit to this office a report on every such occasion, stating the names and residences, and the occupation of the employer, and the motives by which you may have been guided in the selection. You will assent to no rules which fetter your discretion as to the choice of the employers to whose charge the Africans are to be consigned."[16] The secretary concluded his letter by asking the governor to convey his thanks to Mr. Rothery for "the very valuable assistance that he has afforded the Government on this occasion."[17]

The governor's emboldened response enraged Burnley. On November 28, writing from his Bryanstone residence in London, Burnley requested that Sir George Grey, undersecretary of state for war and the colonies, provide him with a copy of the order-in-council regarding the distribution of the liberated Africans that was sent to Lord Glenelg on July 1. Addressing Grey in the third person, Burnley reminded him that as a member of the Council of Government he took much interest in the provisions of the bill framed for that purpose; and as the regulations for these distributions, considered by the board as necessary for their future welfare having been disallowed, he was "naturally desirous of knowing the points on which the members of the Board were mistaken in forming their opinions."[18]

Burnley's first impulse was to argue that the members of the committee were not directed "to frame rules of protection of the Africans but simply for their location and distribution." This was a fine distinction that had little to do with their setting up of the rules to their benefit rather than the welfare of the Africans.

Second, Burnley contended that Rothery impugned the reputation of every member of council who had no avenue of redress. Such a stinging letter, Burnley opined, made it nearly impossible to entice any "man of honor and independence continuing [to serve] as a member of a Board where his intention and motives may be underhandedly calumniated, his conduct and character traduced, and his disinterested exertion in His Majesty's services rendered nugatory and useless without his possessing the constitutional means—not merely of redress—but of ever arriving at a knowledge of the source from which the calumny had flowed."[19]

This was clearly a difficult moment for Burnley. Once more he was being resisted in his demands to control the affairs of the island. In spite of his protestations, he did not quite realize that things had changed and that other interests were now involved in setting a new agenda for the colony. As he left for Paris that December to ring in the New Year with his family, he reminded Lord Glenelg that his only desire was "to support and to render the Colonial Government popular with the community, by making it at the same time satisfactory."[20] As he relaxed in Paris with his family, he assured Lord Glenelg that he remained available to explain any aspect of his letters that needed clarification.

After enjoying Christmas and New Year's Eve with his family, Burnley visited Alexis de Tocqueville. He met him five years earlier when Tocqueville visited the United States to investigate the prison system and also took the opportunity to evaluate the progress of democracy in the United States, which he celebrated in *Democracy in America* (1835). Aware of the publication of *Democracy in America*, Burnley used his friendship with Nassau W. Senior (Tocqueville had sent copies of the book to Senior to garner reviews in the British press) to secure a meeting with the great French thinker. On November 20, 1835, Senior penned the following to Tocqueville: "The bearer of this note is Mr. Burnley, an old friend of mine, and the brother-in-law of Mr. Hume. He is anxious to make, or rather renew, his acquaintance with you. I say renew, because he once went over one of the American prisons in your company."[21] When Burnley met Tocqueville on January 20, 1836, Tocqueville was mourning the death of his mother, Louise, which occurred on January 9 of that month. He was not in the best frame of mind to receive Burnley. On January 27, he wrote Senior:

> I received that gentleman [Burnley] as well as I could, but much less hospitably than I wished. I had, unfortunately, only too good an excuse for this. I have just had the misfortune of losing my mother; and you will feel that in the first moment of the grief cause by this sad event, I was not in a fit state to do the honours of Paris to a stranger. Happily Mr. Burnley proposes to spend the whole winter here, and I intend to do all I can to make myself agreeable to him. I am all the more sanguine as to my powers, as I have now an excellent interpreter.[22]

Tocqueville had just married Marie Mottley, an English woman, on October 26, 1835, which allowed him to communicate better in English although Burnley spoke and read French fluently. One does not know if Burnley ever met Tocqueville again. Yet, the question remains: why would Burnley, a major slave owner and opponent of democracy, be anxious to meet Tocqueville, an aristocrat who was preaching the virtues of democracy and theorizing the need for "the general equality of conditions among people"?[23] Burnley, to be sure, was schooled amongst aristocrats and certainly associated with them in his adult life. At the very least, it showed another side of Burnley: an intellectual curiosity in social and political topics that will be illustrated in the next chapter. Indeed, it may not be too much to claim that such curiosity reflected the Jeffersonian tendency in the man.

CHAPTER 18

The Virtues of Land Possession

It is clear to any person acquainted with their present condition that a larger portion of the sugar estates in the old island will, at no distant period, cease to produce that article. It seems necessary, therefore, to encourage in time a more extended cultivation in the new colonies to meet this expected diminution in our import (export) of sugar; which must otherwise, from the enhancement of price . . . inevitably give an extraordinary impulse to the extension of sugar cultivation in the foreign colonies [non-British colonies]; and consequently to a more extended and determined prosecution of the traffic of slaves.

—W. H. Burnley to Lord Glenelg, November 1835

WHILE BURNLEY WAS in England he came into contact with the economic philosophy of Edward Gibbon Wakefield that would have a tremendous effect on how he understood the use of wasteland in carrying forward the business of colonization.[1] In 1833, Burnley read Wakefield's *England and America: A Comparison of the Social and Political State of Both Nations* and was "immediately struck with the new principle developed in that work, which completely and entirely tallied with all the experience I previously had acquired amongst unsettled and uncultivated lands, and I completely read it with the greatest attention" (*DL*, 148). Burnley also read "A Letter from Sidney" in which Wakefield explored how "capital and labor in the colonies could make the best of the land to their mutual satisfaction."[2]

Burnley was struck by three major ideas Wakefield espoused in his work. First, there should be a "sufficient price" at which wastelands should be sold—high enough for labor to be available to capital and yet not so low as to allow settlers to be able to purchase land before they had worked for their employers for a considerable period of time.[3] Second, the wastelands should be sold and taxed. The revenues resulting therefrom should be used to fund the passage of emigrants from the motherland to the colonies. It was a way to ease the overcrowding and poverty in England. Third, a judicious mix of men and women (preferably young) should be sent to the colonies to prevent open prostitution of the inhabitants settling in these new lands.

Given the large tracts of fertile land in Trinidad and the anticipated desertion of Africans from the estates in the post-apprenticeship period led Burnley to conclude that crown lands should be sold and taxed. The monies derived there from should go to an Emigration Fund that would be used to transport laborers to the island free of charge. Crown lands, he said, should be preserved against intrusion and occupation by "unauthorized settlers" and should be disposed of at such a price that will "oblige the great body of the lower classes to work for wages."[4] When asked by H. G. Ward, the chairman of the Select Committee on the Disposal of Lands, what price he thought should be placed on the crown lands, Burnley responded:

> The chief object in putting a price upon the land is to prevent any laborer from ever hoping or expecting to become a proprietor, who is not by nature or by education qualified to undertake successfully the cultivation of land on his own account. This I consider to be the foundation of the whole scheme, and if it cannot be defended and supported by showing that it is for the good of the laborer in the first instance, I do not think that it will be found correct throughout; but as far as I have given attention to the subject, I think that the natural consequence of obtaining the first object, will be to produce all the other results which have been pointed out as desirable. (*DL*, 152–53)

Burnley did not believe that the ex-slaves would ever save enough money to purchase lands: it was not in their nature to do so. He told the select committee that "the great majority of them will expend their wages, whatever they amount may be, from day to day, or from week to week." Asked by Poulett Scrople, a member of the select committee, if he believed the apprenticeship system could induce Africans to change their ways, Burnley retorted: "I look upon the African race to be improvident, luxurious in their tastes, very imitative, and disposed to go to any expense in their power to copy from those who are settled around them; so that I do not think that more than one out of ten could ever be induced to save his wages for a whole twelve months" (*DL*, 152–53). V. S. Naipaul could not have said it better.

In Burnley's way of seeing, black people were consigned to be perpetual wageworkers in the foreseeable future. He did not see his suggestion as being disadvantageous to the blacks. On the contrary, he saw it as a measure that would benefit everyone. It would not repress the energies of the laborers nor discourage any industrious effort. In his letter to Lord Glenelg, he argued: "The patient and frugal laborer, exercising forethought and forbearance, will soon become the purchaser and owner of land; giving by this act alone, the best guarantee of his capability to manage it to advantage. But the great mass of the lower classes, deficient in these prudential qualities will be compelled to labor for wages, by which their general maintenance and comfort would be most effectually secured."[5]

Burnley was also influenced by the study that Nassau Senior and Edwin Chadwick had done on the English Poor Laws and which Tocqueville used in his study of poverty in France. He was particularly attracted by the section, "Occupation of Land by Laborers," that inquired into "the mode in which the occupation of land by laborers had been effected" and the "probable effects of any legislative measures for the purpose of enabling laborers to become [permanent] occupiers of land."[6] From this section Burnley extracted the following observation that he included in his letter to Lord Glenelg: "If the laborer ceases to rely on his wages; if he becomes, in fact, a petty farmer, before he has accumulated a capital sufficient to meet, not merely the current expenses, but the causalities of that hazardous trade; if he had to encounter the accidents of the seasons, instead of feeling them at second hand after the force has been broken on the higher classes, his ultimate ruin seems to be almost certain."[7]

Burnley was convinced that blacks were disinclined to work on the plantation because all of their wants were provided for by nature or their natural surroundings. It was the old canard that the English had used against the blacks in the West Indies. Since their wants were fewer than those of Europeans, the planters could not count on them to work continuously and intensely on the plantations. As distinct from the white laboring population in the United States and Canada, Burnley believed that the ambition of the black laborer was limited "to a small garden, and a small and miserable house, something he could build in three or four days out of the forest in his neighborhood, which he could remove and replace when he required it, and which, as far as regards to taste and habit, probably affords to him a pleasanter residence than a house built in the European style" (*DL*, 156). Immigration, he believed, would also solve the labor problem that faced the colony.

Although Burnley was one of the first persons to argue that the British should use Indians (from India) to work on the island, he seemed to be unaware that

Britain was using Indians in Mauritius as laborers. Asked by the chairman of the Select Committee on the Disposal of Lands if he was aware that Mauritius had imported laborers from Bengal, Burnley responded: "I have never heard of the importation of any of the natives of Bengal into the West India colonies; but about 25 or 30 years ago Chinese were imported into Trinidad; and from the little experience which we derived from that experiment, if the Bengalese are at all equal to them, it would be a most advantageous measure. But I think the extreme expense of bringing them from that distance would prove an insuperable obstacle" (*DL*, 163–64).

At this point, Burnley could only contemplate Africans in the role of laborers and saw them as the savior of the West India colonies. When the chairman of the select committee observed, "You seem only to contemplate the establishment of a race of negro laborers in the West India islands," and asked whether Europeans should be brought in to work the land, Burnley responded: "I see no advantage in English laborers going to a West India colony, when we have the whole of Australia open to us; and my opinion is that the cultivation of the exportable produce of the West Indies can only be carried on advantageously by people of the African or other southern races" (*DL*, 163).

He believed that Trinidad was of greater value than either Puerto Rico or Cuba. Its soil, he said, was as fertile as those of Puerto Rico and Cuba, and its proximity to the continent of South America gave it greater commercial advantages. To add to these advantages, Trinidad, he writes, "is always exempt from the scourges of droughts and hurricanes, to which both these islands, from their geographical positions, are occasionally subject." He claimed that with additional laborers, Trinidad could provide all the sugar Great Britain needed. From the productive return of the soil "the planters could afford to pay higher wages [to laborers] than any other British colonists."[8]

However, there was one obstacle to this source of labor. The majority of the liberated Africans were males. To compensate for this shortcoming, the colony needed to attract more black women as spouses for the males who were already on the island and the others they were expecting in the future. Burnley believed that a ready supply of female slaves was available from Virginia, Delaware, and Maryland in the United States. All that was needed was a well-arranged plan, "under the sanction and guarantee of the colonial Government, which can provide for the hospitable reception, passage, expense, comfortable location, and immediate employment of this class of persons."[9] To attract the female slaves, the government was encouraged to offer a bounty of twenty to twenty-five dollars for every female who immigrated to the island. On June 7, 1836, the Council of Government approved a resolution to this effect and asked the acting attorney general to prepare the necessary ordinance to achieve this goal.

The United States was not the only source of female immigration. Given the constant political turmoil in South America, "a considerable immigration of females might be expected under a well-digested plan for their reception." But one had to be cautious. There was a fear that in bringing all these women to the island, it would either encourage the tendency of polygamy, "so general in the African race, or induce them to emigrate after the expenses of their introduction had been incurred, in search of partners elsewhere."[10] Even as he recommended the introduction of more black women to the island, he was obsessed with their sexual proclivities and the tendency of black men to have many partners (or so he thought), he could not recognize that he had similar tendencies.

· The success of these plans rested on the future management of the crown lands. Under no circumstances should these immigrants become independent of the planters to whom they should always be available as laborers. Without their availability as laborers, "no capitalist would expend money on machinery without a well-grounded expectation of procuring laborers to help it profitably in motion. Nor will he erect cottages, without a fair prospect of their being occupied by a peasantry disposed to labor for wages. . . . And if this material question is not promptly and satisfactorily settled, the monies to be received from the Compensation Board will be invested in other and possibly foreign securities."[11]

On February 5, 1836, Lord Glenelg sent a copy of Burnley's letter to Governor Hill. After reiterating Burnley's central points (his insistence on the reservation of the "waste" lands, the introduction of captured male Africans, and the introduction of black women from the United States), Lord Glenelg informed the governor that he was not necessarily endorsing Burnley's position "but rather to place yourself and the Council of Government in possession of his sentiments upon these subjects and to recommend them to your attentive consideration."[12] In spite of his charming introduction, Lord Glenelg made it clear that the reservation of wasteland, the principal view espoused by Burnley, had been adopted by His Majesty's government. He also advised the governor that if a practical way, under proper conditions, could be found to introduce "Negro women" from the United States into Trinidad, His Majesty's government would have no objection approving it providing they do not "increase the existing disproportion of the sexes in Trinidad." They also had to be "of marriageable age and unmarried." On the whole, the colonial officials seemed pleased with Burnley ideas of colonization which were in sync with theirs. At the suggestion of James Speeding, who had recently joined the Colonial Office,

Sir George Grey appended the following note to Burnley's letter. It said: "I have read it [Burnley's letter] and think it like all his papers, very clever and very clear."[13] That was high praise indeed. His views would not always merit such a ready reception from the Colonial Office.

Burnley was not entirely appeased. On November 10, 1835, Grey moved that the poll tax that was paid previously on the enslaved Africans—that is, twenty shillings for each slave—should be reduced by one half for the year 1835. Burnley, however, was not supportive of this measure which he opposed on the grounds that it was "unconstitutional . . . harsh and unnecessary." On December 26, 1835, in a letter to Lord Glenelg, he avowed that his objection to the tax did not arise from his irritation about the emancipation of the slaves but from his belief that the "the public treasury neither calls for, nor required the imposition of additional burdens upon the inhabitants."[14]

Burnley also had another objection to the imposition of this additional taxation upon the inhabitants. He believed that the changed constitution of April 23, 1831, that instituted the Council of Government placed relatively little meaningful power into the hands of the legislators. Although it appeared to concede more power to the unofficial members, it was "shackled" with so many restrictions that it was almost ineffective. The governor, he claimed, as president "possesses an original as well as a casting vote, thus establishing a permanent majority on the official side of the Board. Further, every member is declared utterly incompetent to propose for discussion at any time the propriety or altering or reducing the taxes in the colony or the number, the salaries, or allowances of the public officers paid by the colonial funds alone."[15] This objection to the apprentice tax was based also on constitutional grounds, the inability of the unofficial members of council to have any meaningful say in how their taxes were being spent and how their country was being governed.

Although Hill agreed with much of Burnley's proposal on the land question, he could not accept the rationale for his rejection of the apprentice tax. He argued that employers who were accustomed to paying the tax were relieved that it was only half of what they paid previously. However, he attributed Burnley's objection to "the natural anxiety of our class to relieve themselves from [their] burdens by passing it upon another class." He even suggested that although Burnley positioned himself as representing the views of the majority, it was not always so. "When I have not concurred with Mr. Burnley, even the unofficial members have more frequently preferred my views. Witness the important discussion on the distribution of Captured Africans, nay I have seen Mr. Burnley make and lose his motion for want of a seconder."[16]

Hill averred further that although he felt as strongly as Burnley in terms of introducing more democratic institutions (such as trial by jury and taxation by representation) into the society, he could not but feel that Burnley was concerned primarily with one segment of the society, the planter class, at the expense of the lower classes. As he explained: "Mr. Burnley is an agreeable cheerful gentleman. I like and have cultivated his society. He is a superexcellent planter *but he is a Planter*" (italics in the original). His sympathies did not embrace the whole society. In the light of this, the Colonial Office had to scrutinize Burnley's sentiment very carefully. Thus he warns:

> When Burnley speaks of the Public Voice or of the principles or the sentiments of the community here he would be understood no doubt as likening Trinidadians to Englishmen, as yet a few, a very few individuals *announce* the opinion of the Public, whilst the Public really care very little what opinion is attributed to them. That whilst Mr. Burnley intimates to be the community, would sign any memorial or vote at a Public meeting for any proposition under the influence of a half a dozen of leading proprietors . . . I would not for the present advise His Majesty's Ministers to transfer their prerogatives and powers. The interests of the colony will for some time longer be best fostered and secured by the superintendence, instructions, and the Orders of the English administration.[17]

Hill wanted to advise the Colonial Office that a new order had arisen in the colony and Burnley was not necessarily its chief spokesman. Whereas prior to emancipation sugar had occupied the minds of every able-bodied Trinidadian, the new emphasis was on the general improvement of "all classes of the inhabitants as forming a country," which if properly tended to, "will increase and brighten and ultimately exhibit this island as one of the best regulated and most improved foreign possessions of Great Britain."[18] That was the challenge that the British government faced. The new order could not be achieved without listening to the views of the newly freed class of people. How could one do this in a crown colony?

CHAPTER 19

An Artful Enemy

⁓

This letter I have written (much against the advice of my medical atten-
dant) from my chamber to which I have been confined by violent and
repeated attacks of fever. My illness alone prevented me from sending
my explanation by the last packet—and even now I feel it deprives me
of the equanimity of temper and judgment so essential to a person when
defending his character from the attack of an Artful Enemy.

—Stephen Rothery to Lord Glenelg, 1836

I cannot but believe in the truth of the solution which Mr. Rothery has
given of Mr. Burnley's anger on the occasion, and if he be accurate, Mr.
Burnley must be a person who tho' qualified by property, talents, and
education for a legislator, is very deficient in the yet more essential qualification of honesty of purpose.

—James Stephen, on Rothery's letter

O N DECEMBER 29, 1835, before he left for Paris, Burnley addressed a letter to Lord Glenelg concerning how Governor Hill had distributed the
liberated Africans to the various estates and the integrity of the advice Stephen
Rothery, the attorney general, had given the governor in this regard. He felt it
was his duty to call Lord Glenelg's attention to yet another breach "of that honorable procedure requisite to make public men in any country to act together
with confidence. I feel satisfied I have only to lay the case before Your Lordship
to induce you to mark it with your severest reprobation."[1]

Burnley was interested in the correspondences that had been exchanged
between Lord Glenelg and Governor Hill regarding the issue as well as a
letter Rothery had sent to Lord Glenelg via Governor Hill in which Rothery

contended that Burnley and the planters did not have "the smallest concern for the welfare of the Africans" and the majority of the council members, being large proprietors of praedial apprentices, framed the rules and regulations in such a way that "debarred every class but their own from participating in this essential benefit."[2] Burnley interpreted this letter to be Rothery's character assassination of all of the unofficial members of the council.

Alarmed by such charges, Lord Glenelg sent Burnley's letters to Governor Hill on February 15, 1836, requesting that the latter report to him, with the least possible delay, his "opinion upon the topics to which Mr. Burnley refers, together with your views of the facts which that gentleman has represented to me."[3] Lord Glenelg also requested that Rothery respond to Burnley's complaints as quickly as possible. On the same day that Lord Glenelg sent his dispatch to Governor Hill, the Colonial Office assured Burnley that it "will lose no time in requiring from Mr. Rothery such explanations as it may be in his power to give, respecting the various matters laid in his charge. As soon as Mr. Rothery's report shall have been received, the subject will undergo the careful consideration of His Majesty's government."[4]

On April 22, 1836, Rothery responded to Burnley's charges. In his cover letter to the Colonial Office, Hill concurred with and courageously supported Rothery's actions. He noted that Rothery acted consistently and fairly throughout all the proceedings that he had witnessed. Rothery's chief object, according to Hill, "was to throw the distribution and responsibility of locating the Africans into the hands of the Executive and to prevent the operation of rules proposed which would have most injudiciously placed them almost exclusively on the estates of the largest proprietors. I concurred with and co-operated with him in opposing and defeating this project which was quite apparent and would have expected from Mr. Burnley that such reference to the conduct of members in Council cannot produce useful results."[5]

Rothery did not flinch from Burnley's charges. He gave as much as he received. In fact, Rothery's response was so stinging that Lord Glenelg retracted a paragraph from the response that he sent on to Burnley.[6] Rothery reminded Lord Glenelg that he had been pleased to express his approbation of his work on the rules and regulations "in terms most flattering" and which he termed "luminous and powerful. . . . After this strong expression of Your Lordship's opinion it would be superfluous in this my answer to defend the sentiments contained in my letter to further observe upon the Rules which Your Lordship has so justly reprobated."[7]

This being done, he proceeded to demonstrate the groundlessness of Burnley's objection, arguing that some of Burnley's charges were "contrary to the Truth." He insisted that Lord Glenelg had the responsibility to select the most eligible persons to whom the Africans should be sent. If they had accepted the committee's recommendations (of which Burnley was a part) the larger planters would have been given a decisive advantage over the smaller planters (thereby getting more than their fair share of the Africans). Under the amended rules proposed by Rothery, three of Burnley's estates (Orange Grove, Providence, and Cedar Hill) lost twenty-four Africans, which, as Rothery suggested, may have been why "Mr. Burnley's anger against me and a feeling not entirely unconnected with revenge may possibly have led to the groundless accusation preferred against me."[8]

Rothery noted that "when the rules first came from the hands of the Committee—they exhibited such a studious care to exempt all but the wealthy from a participation in the benefits to be deprived from these Africans, that I apprehended that the honor of the Legislative Council and its character for impartiality would suffer if ever the rules became law and were made public." He explained that the rule requiring every applicant to provide a security in the sum of 120 sterling for each African "was calculated further to deprive the tradesman, the shopkeeper and the respectable middle classes of this island of any chance of obtaining an African apprentice. I therefore moved that it should be expunged."[9] This, in other words, was an attempt by Burnley to perpetuate and reinforce the system. Although Rothery was plagued with illness, his desire to clear his name demanded that he respond to Burnley, whom he called "an Artful Enemy," without much delay.

Perhaps Rothery's most devastating critique was an exposure of Burnley's negative views about the Africans. He pointed out that Burnley's committee did not show the smallest concern for the welfare of the Africans. In their view the words "comfort" and "misery," when associated with the African race, were "out of place and unintelligible."[10] Rothery was convinced that Burnley did not view Africans as human beings but only saw them as so many items of labor to be used for his and the other planters' benefits. It was a rejection of the implicit notion that African's lacked humanity that Rothery was striving to assert when he objected to the rules and regulations that Burnley and his friends proposed.

Rothery defended himself well, earning the approbation of Lord Glenelg, who wrote that Rothery had "completely and satisfactorily exonerated himself from all blame in the transaction to which you have directed His Lordship's attention."[11] Stung by Lord Glenelg's endorsement of Rothery's position, Burnley made a complete about-face. His major concern, he said, was not the conduct of the attorney general but whether the members of council could discharge their duty because it was "reversed by His Majesty's Minister, upon the view and consideration of an ex-parte statement from one of their colleagues, by which their motives, and conduct and the nature of their proceedings, may be maligned and misrepresented, without their possessing any official means of defense, or even arriving at a knowledge of the existence of such a document."[12]

Burnley could not have known that James Stephen, the British undersecretary of state, had also sympathized with Rothery's position. Apart from his opposition to slavery, it was a case of one attorney admiring the legal and literary skills of another lawyer. He averred that one could not read Rothery's defense against Burnley's charges "without being convinced that Mr. Rothery has been injuriously calumniated; that he is a man of very considerable talents, and that if as he says his temper has occasionally failed him under the pressure of illness, he has on the whole maintained it very successfully."[13] In Stephen's view, the entire episode reflected badly on Burnley whom he depicted as a person who "tho' qualified by property, talents, and education for a legislator, is very deficient in the yet more essential qualification of honesty of purpose."[14] Nothing could have been more devastating to Burnley's ego and credibility.

No doubt Burnley knew that he had lost favor and needed to regain his reputation with the Colonial Office. In a private note to his colleagues, Stephen had written that "Mr. Burnley will understand Mr. Rothery's acquittal as invaluing[15] [sic] his own condemnation and it seems to me that there is good reason why he should so understand it."[16] Burnley also realized that if he wished to recruit Africans from the continent or the United States that being seen as a racist was not in his best interest. To regain his credibility, Burnley requested that Glenelg send him copies of the minutes of the Council of Government, lodged in the Colonial Office "to substantiate, by the same evidence, the correctness of the statement which I had the honor to submit to His Lordship on the 29th of December last."[17]

It took Burnley three months before he responded to Rothery's report. It consisted of thirty pages and was sent to the Colonial Office on August 2, 1836. Chafing that although Lord Glenelg had found it necessary to suppress two sentences of Rothery's reply, there still remained "a tone, and a language, so offensive as applied to myself coupled with statements so opposed to the real facts of the case that I am compelled again to trouble Your Lordship on the subject." Burnley was most troubled by Rothery's charge that his behavior was activated "by the strongest motives of personal enmity; and he has gone so far, as to characterize my proceedings as unfair, because I did not institute charges against him in the island of Trinidad prior to my departure instead of deferring them until December last, for the sole purpose (as he alleges) of availing myself of the time and distance, which now divide us to calumniate him with great security." Burnley complained that Rothery misquoted him, built up a case against him on misrepresentations, and created the impression he had no feelings for the Africans' humanity. "I feel almost ashamed," he said, "at being compelled to defend myself before Your Lordship against such puerile and irrelevant attacks."[18]

Burnley even accused Rothery of duplicity. He wondered whether his accusations resulted from a "mental inability on the part of the Attorney General to understand the question [posed] or from a desire so to confuse the whole subject as to render it difficult for Your Lordship to comprehend it." He denied most vehemently that the proprietors on the board were motivated "by a selfish policy, and a desire to debar every other class but their own from a participation in a public benefit." Yet, the accusation that hurt him the most was his being accused of "being deficient in humanity towards the unhappy Africans; constituting in the present times, a charge of so odious a nature, as to require a mind of the highest order to decide correctly wherever it may be imputed; and unavoidable to fasten, in public opinion, some discredit and injury upon the party against which it is directed, in spite of the clearest acquittal."[19]

Such an accusation went against how Burnley saw himself and how he wanted to be seen by others, particularly those in the Colonial Office. Yet, his behavior and his words supported Rothery's charges against him. His complaint that he had no avenue to respond to Rothery's accusations that were sent secretly to the secretary of state had some merit. George Scotland, the chief justice of the island, whom Lord Glenelg had asked to review all the circumstances surrounding the case, believed that Rothery had misrepresented some of Burnley's position; doubted that Burnley acted out of a feeling of revenge; and stated that Rothery's conduct was not "wholly free from liability to censure."[20]

Yet the damage was done. Burnley had played such a dictatorial role in the affairs of the colony that the members of the executive felt they had endured enough of his tyrannical power. He could not agree with the praise that Lord Glenelg had given to "His Majesty's principal Law officers in the colony" and regretted that those gentlemen who had devoted their time to public service "in the hope of meriting the approbation of His Majesty's Government and of their fellow colonists . . . and with the most anxious desire to promote the benefit of the colony and the cause of humanity, have been indignantly rejected upon unfounded and private allegations; without their being allowed a hearing in explanation or defense; and that impressions derogatory from their honor and

integrity have been created in Your Lordship's mind, by the un-candid representations of one of their colleagues, who has managed whilst traducing them,
to obtain one of the highest rewards to which a public officer in the colony can
aspire—Your Lordship's approbation."[21]

These were high-flown sentiments. George Orwell, in his comments on politics and the English language, helps us to understand Burnley. He observes:
"The inflated style is itself a kind of euphemism. . . . Where there is a gap
between one's real and one's declared aims, one turns as it were instinctively to
long words and exhausted idioms, like cuttlefish squirting out ink."[22] Rothery, it
seems, had unearthed and exposed Burnley's insincerity and his racism. Burnley's response was an attempt to mask his Eurocentrism with elevated words
and sentiments. One could not but think that they were the ruminations of a
defeated man who was caught out at his own game.

CHAPTER 20

Changing Fortunes

There would be but little justice or wisdom in exaggerating the darkness of the past, in order to give the greater éclat to the dawn which appears to be rising over these colonies; or, in forgetting, that, whether the chain of servitude galled the body of the slave to the degree which some will believe, or not, there can be no dispute as to the abasing moral influence which its presence exercised, more or less over every class of society in the countries where its existence was endured.

—C. J. Latrobe, *Negro Education, British Guiana and Trinidad*, 1838

AFTER THE BIRTH of their younger son, Joseph Hume Burnley, in 1821, Burnley's wife Charlotte left Trinidad and lived in London and Paris until her death. Burnley visited Paris frequently to be with her and his younger son, but she resolutely refused to live in Trinidad in spite of her husband's blandishments. She may have been aware of the allure that Augusta Farquhar, his mistress, had on him or she just did not like Trinidad. Yet, Burnley's separation from his family caused him much uneasiness and perhaps loneliness. He had much reason to worry about his wife living in Paris. Between 1801 and 1856, Paris grew in size from 457,000 people in 1801 to 1,539,000 in 1856. For the most part, these cities were "dens of high mortality" and, as the population grew, "at the lower end of society, vegetated a population of casual laborers, tipping into vagrancy, crime and prostitution."[1] In 1836 Burnley made a more determined effort to repair his family ties. He wrote a series of letters to his wife pleading with her to return to Trinidad so that they could reestablish a stable marital life.

By this time, William Frederick, his elder son, had settled in Glasgow, where he was a merchant and a partner in Eccles, Burnley and Company that conducted his father's and the Eccles's business in Scotland. He also became a partner in William and James Eccles and Company as well as in George Eccles and Company. On January 21, 1835, he was elected a director of the Glasgow West India Association that was founded in 1807 to support the work of the planters. It became "the strongest pro-slavery group outside of London. It vigorously opposed the passing of the Abolition Act in 1833."[2] For example, on May 9, 1832, the association recommended that Burnley be a witness to provide expert testimony to a parliamentary inquiry that was being conducted by the House of Lords on the condition and treatment of "the Negro Population" in the West Indies that sat between May and August 1832.[3] After emancipation, it mounted a fierce campaign to assist West Indian plantation owners, both in the Caribbean and absentees in Scotland, to receive greater financial compensation from the British government.

In 1838, in keeping with the practice of cementing business interests through marriage, William Frederick married Rosina Eccles, the daughter of James Eccles, at Renfren, Scotland, thereby uniting the Eccles and Burnley families.[4] However, the Eccles and Burnley companies were not managed properly. They eventually became a drain on Burnley's wealth. On October 4, 1842, the *Edinburgh Gazette* announced that two of the companies with which William Frederick was associated were in financial trouble and that Eccles, Burnley and Company would assume their debts. Charlotte Burnley urged her husband repeatedly to sell his Trinidad estates, but he rejected her advice "on the plea that such action would cripple the business of their son's Glasgow business" (*OG*, 17). Despite Burnley's loyal support, the economic climate had changed and Eccles, Burnley and Company went bankrupt in 1847. This time Burnley did not come to the rescue of his son. He realized too late that his son was not an astute businessman.

At fifteen, Joseph Hume, Burnley's younger son, whom he affectionately called Humy, needed his father's guidance and love. Prizing the value of education and wanting to make up for his parental neglect, he sought to enroll him into one of the better schools in Europe. In October 1836 Burnley visited Amsterdam and Germany in search of an adequate school for his son, keeping his wife informed of the progress that he had made. His son must have given an indication of the career he wanted to follow. Burnley settled on sending him to Karl Ferdinand Becker's school at Offenbach, calling it "a more appropriate [school] for the future diplomat" (*OG*, 6). As a seasoned traveler, Burnley felt that the scenery of the Rhine was inferior to that of Caracas and Lake Aragua, which he had visited years earlier. By December he was back in London visiting the theater and enjoying the nightlife there. Still, with an eye on the ladies, he found "the only objects there worthy of notice were the legs of Madame Vestries, the dancer, which, he is happy to say, were as perfect in symmetry as ever" (*OG*, 7). Joseph went on to serve in the diplomatic services. On June 12, 1850, he married Emily Adelaide Heath at St. Pancras Parish Chapel, Camden, six months before his father died. It is not known if his father attended the wedding.

In Trinidad, during this period, a new social order was emerging. The suppressed African element began to assert itself and make demands upon the society. The Colonial Office, seeing the turmoil that was taking place in the other British West Indian islands, recognized the need for the planter class to loosen its grip on the society. In August 1836 when Governor Hill informed Lord Glenelg he planned to replace Robert Neilson (an unofficial member of the Council of Government and a wealthy merchant) with John Losh, Lord Glenelg suggested the governor consider appointing "some gentleman of African descent, by whom the duties at the Council Board could satisfactorily be discharged."[5] Lord Glenelg assured him: "I should be well disposed to approve of your nominating him [a person of African descent] to this or any future vacancy as I view it of great importance that some members of this class should have a place in the Colonial Legislature, which is now the case in almost all of the West Indies."[6] On July 25, 1838, when Thomas Bligh Darracott, an unofficial member of the Council of Government and son-in-law of Neilson, objected to placing Trinidad under the administration of the governor general of the Windward Island (a short-lived experiment), he was fired immediately by Murray Macgregor, the acting governor of Trinidad, and St. Luce Philip, "a respectable gentleman of color,"[7] was appointed to replace Darracott thereby becoming the first black member of the Legislative Council of Trinidad and Tobago.[8]

The Colonial Office also wanted to know how the apprentices were being treated and adapting to their new conditions. The responsibility of responding to Lord Glenelg fell upon Thornton Warner, stipendiary magistrate of Tacarigua, who informed him that the feelings between the employers and the apprentices were "generally good," that the apprentices worked "willingly" and preferred to do "task work"[9] rather than work standard hours during the day. When apprenticeship ended, task work or piece work was introduced into 253 estates. Although they were supposed to labor without wages for their former masters, the apprentices found ways to enter into the wage economy. Warner reports that during this early period of apprenticeship, few opportunities were provided for the formal and religious education of the apprentices. There was one Catholic church in the district of Tacarigua, which was well attended. Arrangements were being made for a Protestant clergyman to conduct divine services in the village. Warner also reported that "the erection of a church and school in the district is in contemplation."[10] Eventually the contemplated church was named St. Mary's Anglican. Although the first Anglican service was held at the police station, "the first entry in the 'Registrar of Baptisms in the quarter of Tacarigua and Arima, including the settlements of Caura and Turure and La Seiva 1825,' [was made] on April 2, 1825, administered by John H. Pinder."[11] On August 30, 1837, John Hamilton's name appeared in the "Officiant's Column" of the church, which suggests that he may have been the first clergyman of the parish. He arrived on the island in 1837.

The contemplated school to which Warner referred was St. Mary's Anglican, which was constructed in 1837 with the assistance of the apprentices. In 1834 the British government allocated an annual sum of £25,000 to promote "Negro education" in the British West Indies of which Trinidad received £500 in 1835.[12] In 1836 Trinidad did not get any of those Parliamentary funds. The British Parliament also allocated £20,000 to build school houses for the instruction of the emancipated population in the British West Indies. In the summer of 1837, C. J. Latrobe, "a great traveler and one perfectly well qualified for the duty, [was] sent . . . in the capacity as inspector to examine what had been done in the West India colonies with reference to [Negro] education."[13] After spending seventeen months in the West Indies, Latrobe authored three reports on Negro education in islands.[14] In his third report, *Negro Education, British Guiana and Trinidad* (1838), Latrobe noted that in British Guiana and Trinidad the laboring classes had "shown a disposition to assist by subscriptions, or otherwise, in the efforts of making for their especial advantage, and in several instances have done so to a very considerable amount."[15]

Latrobe observed that Negro education in Trinidad was still in its infancy. Yet the desire among the laboring class to educate their children and themselves was enormous. Latrobe reports that by 1837 "a school-house was built on land given and conveyed by Captain [Samuel] Span; wood on stone pillars, shingled (master's apartments included)."[16] The villagers and the bishop of the diocese contributed 636l and 150l sterling respectively toward the construction of the school that seated 250 persons and which on Sundays was used as "a place of Divine worship."[17] Additional funds came from the Society for the Propagation of the Gospel in Foreign Parts (SPG), the local proprietors, and the proprietors of the district. In 1838 the Council of Government appropriated another £250 for the school. As fate had it, Alfonso Nurse, George Padmore's father, taught at this school before he went on to devote his life to agriculture. It was also the school that my family and I attended. My grandparents' house was built on the side of the school.[18]

Even as efforts were being made to "formally" educate the apprentices, many of them were becoming disgruntled about their labor conditions while the liberated Africans began to chafe under the conditions in which they lived. This resentment toward the whites burst forth on the morning of June 17, 1837, when the war chants of the African soldiers of the First West India Regiment encamped at the St. Joseph Barracks interrupted the blissful slumber of the residents of that village. Initially the residents did not recognize the chants, but after listening more intently, the African chants became clearer as a sonorous voice intoned: "Come to plunder; come to slay" to which his followers responded: "Master, we are ready to obey!"[19]

This call and response pattern was repeated incessantly. A European visitor in the village reported: "This wild song consisted of a short air and chorus. Although the tone was wild, it was not inharmonious. The words were rather uphonious [*sic*]." Little did he realize that he was listening to an African war chant that called upon the children of Africa to bring fire and brimstone to their kidnappers who had stolen them from their motherland and brought them to Trinidad against their wishes. Then he saw the flames that lit up the morning skies. He was hearing the voice of Daaga, an African chief who was captured aboard a slaving ship on the coast of West Africa and impounded into the service of the West India Regiment. The white men called him Donald Stewart, a name he despised. He was the adopted son of Madershee, a childless king of Togo, a country between present-day Ghana and Benin in West Africa. The Yorubas and Ibos called him *longa-longa* because of his height. They believed that *longa-longa* would keep his word and eventually set them free.

When Dagga and his men revolted that morning, they believed that the ex-slaves would join them in their rebellion. Many of the ex-slaves were wandering over the country with little to do while others squatted on crown lands. Although apprenticeship was meant to alleviate their conditions, many of them were being exploited by the system. Daaga believed he could defeat the whites and thereby ameliorate the conditions of the blacks on the island. Later, when the opportunity arose, they would return to their homes in Africa. According to Burnley, about a third of all the ex-slaves on the island were African-born

(*DL*, 156). Many of them believed they would return to their country, even after death, which is why many slave owners decapitated them so that they would not know how to get back to their homes.

Daaga was captured on July 18 and court-martialed the following day. He was found guilty and ordered to be shot to death. On August 16, he and the other prisoners were taken to the site of the mutiny to be executed. Daaga was dressed in a white gown trimmed in black. He showed no remorse. At eight o'clock in the morning Adjunct Meehan, the chaplain of the forces read a Christian prayer after which he shook hands with Daaga and the other condemned men. As they lowered the nightcap over his eyes, Daaga pushed up his nightcap in defiance. He wanted to face his death in a soldierly way. The provost marshal gave the command, "Ready! Present . . ." to the firing squad. Before he could finish his sentence, Daaga's deep metallic voice rose up in defiance as he uttered his final challenge to the white world:

> THE CURSE OF HOLLOLOO ON WHITE MEN. DO THEY THINK
> THAT DAAGA FEARS TO FIX HIS EYEBALLS ON DEATH?[20]

As the firing squad leveled their muskets at Daaga, he turned around in a squatting position and received their fire from behind. In an instant he was dead. Even in death his ferocious demeanor excited awe in the men around him. The blacks present were stunned into silence at his courage. The whites did not know whether he was saint or sinner. He accepted his death with stoic acceptance. He believed that his God, Holloloo, had sent him to the white man's country to be killed so that his death would embolden his people making them fearless and courageous.

We cannot be certain of the effect Daaga's defiance had on the system and on the blacks in the society. The disturbance only lasted for five days. However, as Daaga and his men traveled from St. Joseph to Arima they must have caused the blacks to see their situation in a different manner. Colonel Busche, in trying to explain the cause of the rebellion, felt that too many captured Africans were placed in the same company, which made it easy for them to conspire against their superiors. He also felt that it was not "prudent to have so large a force as nearly as three hundred ignorant, newly-arrived Africans with so small a force as 32 men of the First West India Regiment to secure their subjection." It must have been quite an unnerving experience for the rulers of the society.

CHAPTER 21

Burnley's Immigration Initiatives

And now that the golden beams of the morning have lighted up the arch of heaven, and happiness is depicted on every countenance, we are pleased to hear the sound of church-going bells; these inform us that this is a day which calls to mind a pleasing fact, whilst the groups of people which are to be seen repairing to the several churches for the purpose of devout thanksgiving all contribute to creating strong devotional praise to that great being who is loving every man, and whose tender mercies are over all of his works.

—*Berbice Advertiser*, August 5, 1839

ONE OF THE first indications of Burnley's attitude toward the apprentices revealed itself in the contradictory position he took toward their education. Although many initiatives were being taken by the religious bodies and the philanthropic organizations such as the Mico Charity and the Society for the Propagation of the Gospel in Foreign Parts (SPG) to educate the newly enfranchised apprentices, Burnley opposed Negro education adamantly. In 1839 when Mr. and Mrs. Sicard opened a school in Maraval to educate youths and adults, Burnley opposed giving any such assistance to them. He argued: "Gratuitous education should only be afforded to those who were really unable to pay for it, and who, but for the gratuitous education, would remain in ignorance. . . . It was very bad policy, too, to teach the laboring classes to rely on the exertion of others rather than on their own exertions" (*TR*, February 26, 1839).

Burnley had displayed a similar recalcitrance toward the distribution of the liberated Africans. He wanted to achieve every possible advantage he could get from the system. In 1834 it appeared that he supported public-funded education when it seemed expedient. Yet after extracting the labor of Africans for over thirty years, Burnley wanted to impose a new spirit of self-help upon them since laziness, as he argued, prevented them from educating themselves and their children. Burnley found a willing supporter in John Turnbell, the colonial secretary, who argued: "Many laborers, perhaps, were only working four days in the week now, and idling the other two, when, if they had to pay for their children's education they would work the whole six" (*TR*, February 26, 1839). One month later Colonel J. A. Mein, the acting governor, made a similar complaint to the Marquis of Normanby. He noted: "At present, the laboring population is generally idle and careless of obtaining employment. Principally, this arises from a want of competition. They know they can always get any engagement however idle and worthless they are whenever they choose to return to their employment."[1]

The laboring class who had just come out of slavery and apprenticeship needed all the assistance and encouragement they could get to prepare them for their new condition of freedom. Burnley's denial of educational assistance to the ex-slaves and his exhortation that they rely on their own efforts could be contrasted with the vigor with which he demanded public funds to support an immigration policy that encouraged the arrival of laborers to the island and his unstinting desire to cut back on the high wages the Trinidadian laborers commanded.

As far as Burnley and his colleagues were concerned, Trinidad's problem was largely their inability to get the ex-slaves to work six days a week. They were willing to work on their former masters' plantations for three or four days and spend the next two or three days (allowing one day for the Sabbath) on their provision grounds, hence Burnley's complaints: "I have heard it calculated that every able-bodied laborer in this island can grow and manufacture 4 hogshead of sugar. In some of the more fertile districts, they may certainly do more. The managers of some of my estates have told me that if I can guarantee them the services of thirty able-bodied people who would work willingly, and work six days in the week, they would guarantee me a crop of 200 hogshead of sugar."[2]

Burnley felt he would get the best results to his appeal from the manumitted slaves in the southern United States, a position that he reiterated at a hearing of the Select Committee on the Disposal Lands in the British Colonies in 1836. Referring to the efforts of the American Colonization Society to settle free blacks in Liberia, Burnley observed:

They are very anxious at the present moment to get rid of their free coloured population and have attempted to do so by the establishment of the colony of Liberia. I think therefore that the inhabitants of the United States would be glad to see some foreign colony opened, where, at no expense, the free population could be removed, and find themselves comfortable. . . . If it were a known and established fact that our colonies in the West Indies presented a sure asylum where free negro laborers could be comfortably located, and furnished with profitable employment, I think that a very large number would voluntarily emigrate from the United States of America, and give additional encouragement to future manumissions. (*DL*, 164)

Burnley concluded that "the emancipated Negro" in the United States lived in a state of perpetual apprehension and degradation and therefore was anxious to change his situation. Immigration, as Burnley understood, was the only possible way to achieve this objective. At that time, four options loomed in the horizon: free blacks could immigrate to Haiti, the West Indies, Liberia, or Canada. Many rejected the possibility of relocating to Liberia. To many, Haiti was a symbol of Black Nationalism. The Philadelphia elite, for example, "had a stronger sense of cultural affinity with Haiti than with Africa."[3] Haiti, then, was one of the first countries to which Blacks were willing to relocate. In 1824, Jean Pierre Boyer had put on a full-court press to win over African Americans to relocate in Haiti. A pamphlet from the Haytien Emigration Society for Colored People that was formed to promote the goal of Haitian immigration reminded the free blacks of America: "We are your brethren in color and degradation, and it gives us a peculiar delight to assist a brother to leave a country, where it is but too certain the colored man can never enjoy his rights."[4]

Burnley, however, had his reasons why the Haitian experiment did not succeed. He believed that Henri Christophe's (and later Boyer's attempt) to encourage those free blacks to emigrate and stay in Haiti failed because of the differences in language and the "antipathy of habits" between the two peoples of the same race but products of different aspects of the slave system. He said to his colleagues in the Trinidad Legislature: "Many of you, perhaps, have read the Code Rurale of Hayti, and you cannot wonder that these immigrants, who had left the shores of South[ern] America in the search of freedom, were not disposed to work at Hayti at the point of the bayonet." Speaking as a seasoned capitalist and acolyte of Wakefield, he added: "Christophe was anxious to introduce labor, but labor without capital is valueless. Now the laws of the country, which preclude any white man from holding property in Hayti [this wasn't quite true] shut out European capital and enterprise from the soil, and the labor Christophe had thus acquired, he found of little value" (*TR*, April 2, 1839).

Burnley believed that Trinidad provided a more fruitful environment for these emancipated African Americans, having had to integrate similar immigrants who came to Trinidad after the American War of 1812 in New Orleans. Trinidad absorbed them more successfully because it located them "on large and fertile tracts of land, placing them at once in a state of comparative wealth—making that a condition of location which should have followed as a reward, and been held out in perspective as a spur to their exertions" (*TR*, April 2, 1839). Burnley also provided an interesting explanation as to why these emancipated African Americans were willing to relocate to Trinidad. Although it is a long statement, it needs to be quoted:

> There are a number of highly philanthropic religiously-disposed proprietors in Southern America anxious to emancipate their slaves, but entertaining the strong and conscientious belief that, in doing so, they shall not be able to secure the future comfort or welfare of these whom they seek to serve, unless they could at the same time ensure their departure from the States. Their mere passing over to the Northern States, where slavery does not exist, will not ensure the proper enjoyments of their freedom. The prejudices of color are very strong throughout the States; and I regret to say, that, from this state of feeling the free colored people, in very many cases, are considered a complete curse to the Northern States. It is a melancholy fact that on a calculation founded on the comparative numbers of the two classes of population, and the punishments awarded for crimes committed by either, the crimes committed by the free colored and black people in the Northern States are as ten to one compared with those of the white. Yet this arises not, most certainly, from any moral or physical inferiority on their part, but from the persecution they undergo, and their being shut out by the prejudice of the other inhabitants from every honest and useful avocation. (*TR*, April 2, 1839)

Although the government would have had to advance the money for this scheme, Burnley felt his plan would yield benefits within four years. The financial panic in the United States in 1837, the severe racial climate in the society (there were four major race riots in Philadelphia between 1834 and 1842), and the recent emancipation of the Africans in the West Indies gave free blacks and people of color in the United States new hope that they could better realize their freedom in the British West Indies in spite of the experience of their fellow Americans in Haiti. Julie Winch notes that by 1839, "blacks all over the North [of the United States] were showing an interest in the possibility of emigrating to the British West Indies. Particular attention was focused on Trinidad because the island's authorities were actively recruiting settlers."[5] Since Trinidad was an "experimental colony," and seemingly crying out for labor, it seemed only fair that it take its chances with these new immigrants.

Meanwhile the emancipated blacks in Trinidad (that is, the ex-slaves) began to organize themselves around their new freedom rather than the schedules of their former owners. All their lives they had been considered property. Now they were able to sell their labor to the highest bidder. Nor, for that matter, did they have to work six days a week, a fact that became a major issue for the planters. The ex-slaves simply divided their time to working in the fields, planting their provision grounds, and entering into new labor specialties. One year after apprenticeship ended a report in the *Trinidad Standard* stated that while the enslaved, under slavery and apprenticeship, devoted all of their time to the cultivation of sugarcane and other crops, after slavery the ex-slaves devoted themselves to "establishing their provision grounds."[6] Many of them devised "various modes of life to avoid that of agriculture: [such as] servants, hucksters, boatmen, fishermen, and jobbers of all descriptions; but absolute idlers are not as numerous so far as we can ascertain."[7] Women, for example, perhaps following their mothers and grandmothers of West Africa took to small trading. One report notes: "Hucksters with perhaps a few mangoes to sell or a load of guinea grass on their backs became a familiar sight in Port of Spain and along the roads."[8] Such reports belie the notion of the extreme idleness by which the ex-slaves were categorized and the allegation that they had abandoned the estates.

By the end of the first year of apprenticeship the newly-freed began to settle down to a new rhythm of life. The laborers began to spend more time on their provision grounds and to follow other pursuits while the planters began to use coercive force to get them back onto the plantations. Although new workers began to trickle onto the island, the planters were determined to superintend the national work force. To achieve their objectives, the planters created a rule that laborers who did not perform five days of work per week on their estates would be made to pay rent for their homes and grounds for every day they did not work. The *Trinidad Standard* concluded that this was a good system in that it "induced many who were idly disposed to work with tolerable regularity" (*TS*, September 6, 1839).

In spite of the planters' rhetoric, production had not dropped as dramatically as the planters had claimed (see table 2). In fact, things had gone so well in 1839 that the *Trinidad Standard* could argue that while the planters believed a turbulent future lay ahead for the colony after the end of apprenticeship, they were pleased to note that "the laborers were not likely to disturb the order of society in their mode of enjoyment of the recent boon which had been conferred on them in that there as much, and perhaps more, safety for life and respect for property, than previous to emancipation." Although the planters feared that all would be chaos after 1840, the year in which apprentices were carded to end officially, the newspaper could report that the planter could look upon post 1840 "with renewed hope and brighten prospects—let us trust that ere its close, it will behold her sure of her future fortunes, and emerging from her secondary position, taking that place to which here natural and geographic advantages eminently entitle her—as one of the first sugar colonies of the British Empire" (*TS*, January 3, 1840).

TABLE 2. ECONOMIC PRODUCTION IN TRINIDAD, 1838–1839

	AUGUST 1838	AUGUST 1839
Sugar	19,837 hogshead	17,470 hogshead
Molasses	2,337 barrels	3,144 barrels
Rum	130 puns	85 puns
Cocoa	2,294,936 lbs	2,382,108 lbs
Coffee	393,089 lbs	211,212 lbs

Compiled by the author.

CHAPTER 22

The Road to Prosperity

On looking at the resources of this island and its great capacity of production, it must be apparent to the observer that labor is all that is wanted to render it a highly valuable colony—a soil most fertile, a position well adapted for commercial transport, and its produce always commanding a ready sale. There appears only one evil to depress its agricultural and commercial importance, and that is the deficiency of its laboring population.

—Governor Mein to the Marquis of Normanby, 1839

THE PROSPECT OF the ex-slaves controlling the tempo of labor in the Caribbean was abhorrent to the planters. On January 4, 1836, John Gladstone, an absentee owner and father of William Gladstone, future prime minister of England, wrote to Gillanders, Arbuthnot and Company, a Calcutta shipping agency, about the dangerous monopoly that black workers would have on the West Indian economy when apprenticeship expired in 1840. He noted that it was important "to provide a portion of other laborers, whom we might use as a set-off, and, when the time for it comes, make us, as far as is possible, *independent of our Negro population*; and it has occurred to us that moderate number of Bengalese, such as you were sending to the Isle of France . . . [Mauritius] might be suitable for our purposes."[1] Such a concern led inevitably to the importation of East Indians to the Caribbean. It was this fear of an African monopoly in labor that led planters and the mortgagees of the estates to abandon their plantations after apprenticeship ended and to order their managers "to spend no more money and do no more work than

137

was barely necessary to take off the crops" (*PO*, "Mr Guppy's Reasons for being a Reformer," July 13, 1888).[2] Such a position had disastrous consequences for the island. Robert Guppy, an English barrister who arrived on the island in 1839 and worked with Burnley for a short while, made the following observation:

> The first day of August 1838 found the plantations in Trinidad in a state of ruin of which people who see the country now can form no sort of idea. The owner's dwelling house, the laborers' cottages, the mule pen, sugar works, and machinery were all in a complete state of dilapidation; the stock of mules and cattle diminished and inadequate; the cane fields full of bush and grass. There were some few exceptions to this state of things in Tacarigua, in South Naparima, and elsewhere, where the proprietors [such as Burnley] had capital of his own, and more courage and confidence in the future. Amongst other evils the roads throughout the colony had fallen into a state so bad that it could not be worse. (*PO*, October 18, 1887)

Then things changed. In 1839 the price of sugar rose and the planters became frantic to get more workers to reap those rewards. Although the ex-slaves had continued to work and respect the property of their former masters, the question became, "How to take care of this new opportunity that the rising price of sugar offered?" The island was entirely unprepared for the change. Guppy notes: "As the slaves and apprentices had received no wages, there were no shops. There were no villages, no places to establish shops. Nothing could be bought outside the large towns. The owners and managers of plantations got salt fish, pork, and other provisions to see to their people, for which they charged high prices which the people were forced to pay. The laborers demanded high wages, and in most cases were able to exact them" (*PO*, July 13, 1888).

Then the fight-back started. To get the laborers to return to the fields, the managers began to destroy their provision grounds "in order to force them by hunger to comply with their terms, and that without any notice" (*PO*, July 13, 1888). Without fail, the stipendiary magistrates supported the planters' actions, accepting that the planters had a right to treat the ex-slaves in this manner. These arbitrary actions forced the laborers to move away from the plantations and to seek out new ways to maintain a living. It also led the ex-slaves to break their ties with their old plantations; to form new villages and to squat on open land. Such legitimate action on the part of the ex-slaves allowed the planters to complain of an artificial labor shortage and to increase their cries: "We can't get labor! We can't get labor!"

On April 18, 1839, Colonel J. A. Mein who had replaced Governor George Hill, who had died in office on March 8, 1839, wrote to the Marquis of Normanby to inform him that the planters and merchants of the island were issuing the same threats that they had always offered before; that is, "unless steps be taken to increase the amount of and industry of the laboring population, the cultivation of this island will be most seriously impeded, and I fear a state of agricultural distress will be produced among the proprietors of the estates, which will, in its reaction, ultimately fall on the laborers themselves."[3] Needless to say, the merchants and planters were being unnecessarily alarmist since they, through their actions, had contributed to the alienation of the workers, creating a situation that would ultimately result in the detriment of all the inhabitants of the island.

On April 1, 1839, a few months after he opposed the granting of funds to educated black children, Burnley brought a motion to council to permit the introduction of laborers from Malta, Sierra Leone, the Isle of Man, and the free people of African descent from the southern states of America who were "accustomed to agriculture, and inured to labor in a tropical climate" (*TS*, April 2, 1839). An undersecretary in the Colonial Office, afraid that Burnley's proposal, particularly regarding Sierra Leone, resembled an attempt to revive the slave trade, appended the following note to Burnley's letter: "The coast of Africa is out of the question." The *Anti-Slavery Reporter* called this proposal "the bondage ordinance of Trinidad" (*AR*, November 14, 1842). Burnley made it clear that the people in the Caribbean (that is, Trinidad, British Guiana, and the Eastern Caribbean) were "all agriculturalists, all embarked in one species of cultivation—sugar, coffee, cocoa, or cotton—and when a defiance of labor occurs, we have no internal source to look for supply. In such a case, immigration is our only resource" (*TS*, April 2, 1842). He made a similar point to the Select Committee on the Disposal of Lands in the British Colonies.

A few days later the planters and merchants held a major public meeting in Port of Spain, chaired by John Lamont, a close friend and confidante of Burnley who was the principal speaker. A major outcome of this meeting was the formation of the Agricultural and Immigration Society, of which "the indefatigable Burnley" was named chairman (*OG*, 7). Guppy, a member of the society and "a man of education and totally independent of class feelings,"[4] as Governor Henry George MacLeod described him, noted that the principal objectives of the society were "first, a combination to keep down the wages of labor, [and] second to put pressure on Government to import laborers at the public expense" (*PO*, October 18, 1887). When Governor Mein informed the Marquis of Normanby about this meeting, he recommended that the British government do everything in its power "to facilitate such measures as will tend to produce that effect." He believed that, if the British government supported such a move, in four years there would be sufficient laborers for the colony, which would provide enough revenues to conduct the colony's business. He prophesied that "when a large number of Africans had found out the road to this island, where they could obtain high wages and constant labor the present bounty to immigration would after a time be no longer required and we should be ultimately supplied with those who had discovered the advantages afforded by this island." He estimated that the island could absorb ten thousand additional laborers, the effect of which would be to encourage laborers on the island to work more industriously and "to do a fair day's work which is not the case now, and would induce them to enter into contracts for a limited time which is done in all civilized countries." Such an undertaking would lead to a more stable society and produce "a very beneficial moral influence upon the laboring classes."[5] The blacks were afraid to enter into contracts with their former slave masters. Intuitively, they understood that contracts involved consensual relations among equals, which they did not have with their former slave masters.

Then, Burnley attempted a major coup against the governor and the Colonial Office. On April 22, 1839, he managed to get the Council of Government to pass a resolution making him the agent for the colony. In this position he supported "promoting the immigration of agricultural laborers into the colony, and the disposal of Crown Lands therein, with power and authority to confer and correspond with all persons or public bodies in England, in the United States of America or elsewhere for these purposes."[6] The council also appointed a "Committee of Correspondence" with the responsibility of conveying instructions to the agent that effectively bypassed the governor's responsibility in these matters. Such sweeping authority in Burnley's hand was bound to create conflicts with the Colonial Office and undercut the governor who conducted Britain's business on the island. Armed with this resolution, Burnley felt empowered to act on behalf of the Trinidad government on all matters that had to do with bringing laborers to the island.

As was to be expected, Governor Mein was not comfortable with this resolution. On April 25, 1839, he sent a copy of the resolution to the Marquis of Normanby, noting that he had tremendous misgivings about the resolution although he allowed it to be proposed and voted upon. He recognized that such an agent acting independently of the executive would undercut the governor's authority, particularly when the agent "receives his instructions from a Committee of Council with whom he corresponds, and from whom he receives his directions. Whether he lays the communications before Council or not, they still emanate from a body by which a majority may oppose the views of the Governor and even frustrate the intentions of Government at home [meaning England]."[7] While he harbored no animosity toward Burnley, whom he considered "a man of talent,"[8] he felt that such an appointment would interfere with the governor's duties, his being the sole medium of communication with the English government.

If Governor Mein had doubts about the appropriateness of Burnley's appointment, James Stephen, the undersecretary of state for the colonies, had no such reservations. Noting that the governor was "an essential and integral part of the Council," he reaffirmed that the governor was the only channel through which the Colonial Office can properly communicate between the council and the ministers of the Crown. If Burnley was given the power he sought, in effect, he would interpose himself "between the Governor and the Secretary as a channel of communications, and the inconvenience of communicating with Her Majesty's representatives in such a manner requires no proof or explanation."[9] However, the use of diplomacy was the way out of this embarrassing situation. Stephen intimated that no decision should be made about Burnley's title until Sir Henry MacLeod, the prospective governor (Mein acted for a year as governor), assumed his role on the island: "Until then, it will not be possible to recognize Mr. Burnley in the character which has been assigned to him."[10] This recommendation was confirmed in a letter that the secretary of state sent to Governor Mein in June of 1839.[11]

Just as Burnley was making his move at home, William Frederick and William Eccles were doing everything in their power through the Glasgow West India Association, of which they were directors, to help Burnley and his colleagues achieve their objectives in Trinidad. On February 25, 1839, Eccles, representing the "Planters and Merchants interested in or connected to the island of Trinidad," held a meeting in Glasgow in which they requested that African workers be allowed to move freely between the West Indian islands without hindrance, selling their labor to the highest bidder. In their plea they seemed to be reading from one of Burnley's scripts:

> The proprietors in Trinidad are in a very critical situation. Although their soil is extremely fertile and their island possesses every advantage calculated to render it a splendid province their laborers are so few that unless they work regularly— which unfortunately they have not hitherto done—the cultivation cannot be maintained, though every arrangement has been made to substitute machinery for the limitation of labor. They do not ask for any law to retain a laborer or tradesman in the island one moment longer than he is prepared to remain—but, while the personal freedom and protection of every individual, without exception or distinction, is effectually guaranteed with the colony, they claim the right of employing servants in any part of the world—and more especially in the West India colonies in the same manner as they may now do in Great Britain.[12]

The Colonial Office reasoned that reiterating their objection to the free movement of laborers within the West Indian islands was like "robbing Peter to pay for
Paul." The loss of laborers from any one of the colonies could result in the reduction of productivity on the islands that lost their laborers. Burnley seems to have
recognized this position. In April 1839, in making his motion for an ordinance to
procure immigrants from outside of the British West Indies, he remarked: "The
planters of the other colonies are of opinion, whether correctly or not, that they
require all their present stock of laborers—that they can find profitable employment for the whole—and they are therefore decidedly averse to parting with any
portion however trifling of their laboring population" (*TS*, April 5, 1839).

Meanwhile, on May 22, 1839, in his capacity as chairman of the Chamber of
Commerce of Glasgow, William Frederick sent a letter to Sir Richard Doherty,
the governor of Sierra Leone and apparently an old friend of his father, to
enquire whether Trinidad planters could recruit laborers from that country to
work in Trinidad. His uncle-in-law, Joseph Hume, who wrote to the Marquis
of Normanby on March 25, urging him to approve William Frederick's request,
assisted William Frederick. It fell to James Stephen, the undersecretary of state,
to inform the marquis that he had no option but to decline William Frederick's request, reminding him that "the establishment of an agent on the coast of
Africa for hiring laborers to work in the West Indies would be a measure justly
obnoxious to the charge of [continuing] the Slave Trade under a new form." He
continued: "Slaves would be brought from the interior to the coast, in order to
supply the demand and such persons could only be nominally free agents in
accepting or rejecting the terms proposed to them."[13] The marquis sent a similar
note of rejection to Eccles informing him that the persons who would be called
to make contracts as they went from one island to the next in the West Indies
could only enter into such arrangements "under extreme disadvantage arising
from the superior knowledge of the persons with whom they would negotiate
on the subject."[14]

As the need for labor became more intense, Burnley and the Trinidad
planters eventually procured laborers from Sierra Leone and the other West
Indian colonies, many of whom were smuggled onto the island. Yet it is clear
that the Trinidad planters and merchants had the assistance of an international
movement of people who were dealing with slave labor upon whom they could
call anytime they needed. Given the porous nature of Trinidad's borders, the
Trinidad planters found ways to evade the restrictions placed on them by the
Colonial Office and recruited workers to the island.

CHAPTER 23

Burnley's Changing Racial Rhetoric

When we attacked slavery, we boldly proclaimed to the world that all men had an indefensible right to the labor of his own hands, with liberty to dispose of it when and where they demand most advantageous; and that all men were possess of even natural rights, without distinction of color or complexion, and were equally competent to judge of that which would best promote their own happiness. If these principles, My Lord, solemnly invoked for the destruction of our old colonial system, are now discarded, when appealed to in aid of the difficult task of reconstructing a new one, what hope of success can remain in the breast of a colonist?

—William Burnley to Lord John Russell, 1839

"WE WANT AN increase of hands" became the cry of the Trinidad planters at the end of 1839 and the early 1840s (*AR*, April 15, 1840). This time around, the planters set their sights on the presumed availability of free colored laborers in the United States of America and Canada. In August 1839, Burnley set off for Nova Scotia, New Brunswick, and the eastern seaboard of the United States to ascertain "whether any portion of the free-Negro population inhabiting those countries could be induced to remove to Trinidad."[1] To achieve his objective Burnley had to change his rhetoric even though he did not change his fundamental views on Africans. In fact, his venture into North America and the rhetoric he used to entice African Americans to come to Trinidad did not represent so much a case of his having changed his thinking about black people as his having changed his tactics to regain control over the blacks in the colony. Julie Winch notes that at this point in his career, Burnley "was not exactly committed to equal rights, although he was adept at tailoring his message to his audience."[2]

Burnley made initial stops in Nova Scotia and New Brunswick. He was not successful in those provinces because the colored people there were described as "a thriving and useful portion of the population of Canada who were not desirous of emigrating"[3] to Trinidad. His efforts, however, were more successful in the United States where he spent three months (from August to October), traveling from Maine to Virginia, informing free blacks about the glorious opportunities that awaited them in Trinidad. He noted that everywhere he went, he got the impression that the free Negroes were ready to immigrate to the island provided the host country could ensure them "political and social stability without distinction of color." Burnley noted: "In the United States neither jealousy nor prejudices seem to oppose themselves to this step [that of immigrating to Trinidad]. I frankly spoke everywhere of the object of my mission, communicated openly with the Negro population; addressed them in public rooms and chapels without fear of molestation; and attached my name to the invitations printed and distributed everywhere among them."[4]

Burnley was quite a salesman for his island. Madhavi Kale describes him as "the colony's most ardent booster and a most tireless promoter of immigration to the British Caribbean colonies."[5] In *Description of the Island of Trinidad* that he printed for his recruitment effort, he reminded his audience that unlike all the West Indian islands, Trinidad was free from hurricanes and droughts and that given "its happy position, it cannot fail to become the great commercial emporium—the 'New York,' in fact, of that part of the world."[6] This is a sentiment that many Trinidadians still hold. However, given the arduous fight he had made against the abolition of slavery, one could not be but surprised when he declared:

> The great inducement, however, to an emigrant who wishes to raise himself in the scale of society, is the political and social advantages which the colored inhabitants of Trinidad enjoy over that of any other part of the world. Slavery has been utterly and entirely extinguished therein by the British government and no exclusive privileges now elevate a white man above his colored brethren. A Council of Government, consisting of twelve gentlemen, in which white and colored are mingled, are appointed by the Queen to legislate for the whole colony. Judges are also appointed and paid by the Queen, to administer justice cheaply, and, as it were, at every man's door throughout all the rural districts. One of these judges is at the present time a colored gentleman and more will be appointed whenever they can be found qualified by education for the office. A perfect equality, therefore, of respectability and dignity is enjoyed by the colored population, not only by law, but socially and practically throughout the colony.[7]

A year later, on an immigration mission in England, Burnley repeated similar sentiments. He informed the editor of the *Colonial Gazette* that Trinidad was one colony in the West Indies "in which all distinctions on account of colour had ceased, and the white and coloured races were as one in all civil and political matters." The *Anti-Slavery Reporter* countered: "A grosser misrepresentation of the colony—of the condition of the coloured classes, and the sentiments and policy of the whites towards them—could not have been made, than that which Mr. Burnley, with the full knowledge of the real circumstances of the case, imposed for truth upon Lord John Russell and the editor of the *Colonial Gazette*" (*AR*, 1840, 328). It pointed out that the colored classes in Trinidad enjoyed the worst conditions in the West (an exaggeration), fewer privileges, and a smaller measure of rights given the proportion of their property on the island.

While he was in America, Burnley assured the potential colored emigrants that they had nothing to fear if they decided to relocate in Trinidad. He reminded his audience that there were many examples of successful colored entrepreneurs on the island: "There are now not less than a dozen coloured proprietors, owning valuable sugar estates, besides many in possession of plantations of coffee and cocoa." All these brilliant opportunities awaited an industrious man "although he should now leave these United States without a single cent in his pocket" (*D*, 7). Burnley, however, could not tell them what the Trinidad correspondent of the *Barbados Liberal* reported: "Of the ninety-one white burgesses [in Port of Spain], . . . twenty-eight of the most conspicuous characters are not householders [one had to be a householder to vote], and one, but a few months since, in open court, declared he had nothing, and prayed to be allowed to pay a small sum due by him in monthly installments. The object was to swell the list of whites as much as possible; and, if men of property could not be found for the purpose, why not take men of straw?" (*AR*, 328). Such a position did not necessarily reflect an equal playing field among blacks and whites in the society.

During this period many supporters of segregation in the United States saw emigration to countries such as Liberia, Canada, and Haiti as a way to solve the race problem in their country. Therefore, Burnley was not incorrect when he observed that from Maine to Virginia the white population wished him success and echoed the following sentiment: "The two races could not exist advantageously together on terms of equality, and that policy as well as humanity would rejoice if a separation could be effected, and a happy home provided elsewhere for the free colored population."[8] Burnley's views were so enticing that a group of black leaders in Philadelphia asked him to send them five thousand copies of his pamphlet so they could study the details of his plans. He immediately complied with their request and sent them the required number of copies they requested (*D*, 1). The last page of the pamphlet contained directions as to how potential emigrants could apply to be a part of the scheme and the various agents that were appointed in New York (Robert S. Buchanan), Philadelphia (Frederick A. Hinton), and Norfolk, Virginia (Robert Soutter). The trades and employment that were listed as being in demand were agricultural workers, carpenters, coopers, wheelwrights, sawyers, masons, blacksmiths, drivers (accustomed to driving oxen and mules), and domestics of all kinds. He also reminded them: "Brickmakers and lime burners would find steady employment, as both these articles [*sic*] are imported in large quantities from Europe" (*D*, 8).

Antislavery advocates in the northeast of the United States opposed Burnley's effort or what they called the "Trinidad Scheme." In a letter to his supporters at home Burnley announced "that so strong an opposition to emigration had been raised in the northern states of America by the Anti-Slavery Party that he should not be able to procure emigrants from that quarter" (*AR*, February 24, 1841). William Whipper, a black leader in Philadelphia, saw the scheme as being "pregnant with evil forebodings to the antislavery cause"[9] even though he admitted there was considerable support for the idea. Soon, however, enthusiasm for the project began to wane on the grounds that the Trinidad scheme was nothing but colonization in reverse. It suffered a fatal blow when George Shannock reported that "illness, high mortality rates, low wages, poor food, and an unhealthy climate in Trinidad"[10] were not conducive to the well-being of those who had immigrated.

In spite of his extolling the advantages Trinidadian blacks enjoyed and the genuine equality he said existed on the island, he also hoped to attract "a superior class of persons possessed of superior education and pecuniary means"[11] to act as a middle class (his words) in order to achieve the successful transition from slavery to what he called "the experiment of emancipation."[12] Only the addition of such an intermediary class could thwart the ambition of slave owners in foreign states who wished to destroy the dreams embodied in the liberation of a free people in the West Indies.

Burnley was interested in acquiring the skills of these free people of color so that Trinidad planters could embark on the cultivation of tobacco and cotton, which was the subject of another of his missives to Lord Russell.[13] But he had another grandiose, perhaps Edenic, vision of the region. He envisaged a "free, numerous Negro population, under the protection of the British Government, prosperity, social happiness, and equal rights. The effect of such an imposing scene," he wrote, "would be soon to attract around it, as a nucleus, all the loose floating colored population at present scattered throughout the Antilles and the Gulf of Mexico, which is everywhere depressed and generally degraded." This was not all; he believed that the "gradual accession of such a population would give everywhere throughout our West Indian colonies, highly gifted as they are by nature, and so admirably located for the commerce of the Western continent, a stirring impulse to agricultural exertion, furnishing an extended market for our manufacturers and a constant source of profitable employment for our capital."[14]

Burnley did not see colonization (the removal of blacks to Africa) as a viable solution to the African American situation. He was so excited about the possibility of their creating a new civilization in the West Indies (it was "no idle delusion") that after his visit to the United States he wrote Lord Russell it was reasonable to believe "the negro race is more likely to acquire in the tropical west the same advantages which their white brethren have obtained by emigration to the same continent, than by making an attempt in any other quarter. The fact to which I before alluded to, of the determination of the Negroes of the United States not to proceed to Africa, coupled with the history and actual condition of the American settlements on the coast, fully confirm this opinion."[15]

The planters of the island were no doubt excited at seeing the first contingent 239 colored Americans arriving in the society, "the first fruits of the arduous work of the Honorable Mr. Burnley in originating and promoting immigration here from the free colored population in the United States." Although the journey from New York to Trinidad took nineteen days, the immigrants were in the best of health and extremely cheerful when they arrived. The *Trinidad Standard* saw their arrival as opening an important era for the island, hoped that this stream of immigrants from the United States would continue, and praised them for "abandoning a country where they are firmly exposed to oppression, contumely, and insult and adopting in its stead, a land whose inhabitants are most willing and anxious to afford them refuge, and enroll them among its free citizens" (*TS*, November 15, 1839).

This was an extraordinary declaration coming from a society that was less than one year out of slavery. Like Burnley, it saw these immigrants as leavening the society and providing human materials for the middle class it wished to encourage, hence its declaration: "From what we have heard and read of the colored population of America, we think they will be found imbued with much of the active speculative turn of their white brethren of the States, and are likely to infuse a fair proportion of these qualities in our African and Creole laborers, and render them more willing to undertake extra work for extra wages" (*TS*, November 15, 1839). The newspaper did not see this evaluation as being insulting to the Africans already on its soil. It thought it exemplary and one of the values the new immigrants were bringing to Trinidad. The newspaper ended its report by informing the population, rather excitedly, that the next vessel of immigrants would sail from Philadelphia five days later on November 20, 1839.

Although Burnley would make more trips to America to recruit more colored Americans, they would soon lose interest in the island. Burnley would look to other places to satisfy the need for what he considered the shortage of laborers. However, his trip to the United States was not entirely unsuccessful. He would have taken much pleasure from the fact that he managed to persuade Samuel Ringgold Ward, an ex-slave, that his salvation lay in emigrating to Trinidad. Prevented from joining the Literary Society in Poughkeepsie, New York, where he taught; discouraged from furthering his education in the land of his birth; and denied equality with his fellow white Christian citizens, Ward decided to leave the United States for good. He writes in his autobiography:

> Then, thought I, what is the use of my acting uprightly, seeking to win fame, and gaining it, if in this country a professed friend, a man who goes with to the house of God, hearing me preach, visit my house, after all treads upon me to please his neighbor? My determination was formed to leave the country. I accordingly wrote to Mr. Burnley of Trinidad Legislature, a relation of the late Joseph Hume, Esq., M.P., who had kindly encouraged my going to that island.[16]

Ward did not go to Trinidad. Shortly after writing to Burnley, he took up an appointment as an antislavery agent for the American Anti-Slavery Society. In 1841 the Congregational Church of New York ordained and inducted him into its South Butler church ministry, an all-white congregation. This created a paradoxical, though not unwelcome, situation for him: an African American preaching to an Anglo-American congregation in the age of slavery. After spending two and a half years in South Butler, Ward moved to Cortlandville Congregational Church in New York, where he was the pastor. While he was there, he edited two antislavery newspapers: *The True American* (1847–1848) and *The Impartial Citizen* (1849–1851).

As a Christian abolitionist, he preached that the liberation of African Americans "would not materialize by prayer alone. Oppression had to be abolished, he believed, by Christ-like labors which would be in the form of improving the social and moral conditions of the black people."[17] In this context his approach to the African liberation struggle was different from those that were captured in *The History of Mary Prince* and *Narrative of the Life of Frederick Douglass, An American Slave*. Kenny Reilly says that Ward's "writings show the emergence of black people in the British Empire attempting to construct a British identity and a belief that compared to other empires, the British was the best option."[18]

One is not sure if Burnley responded to Ward's letter. However, apart from winning over a convert to his cause—a black abolitionist at that—Burnley's name entered into United States literary history via Ward's autobiography.

Ward believed that he could be of service to himself, his people, and his religious master, by spreading God's words if he had settled in Trinidad. He did not go to Trinidad for reasons unbeknown to us. Trinidad's loss might have been Jamaica's gain. In 1855 he retired to Jamaica where he witnessed the Morant Bay Rebellion of 1865. He died there in 1866.

TABLE 3. RETURN OF EMIGRANTS TO TRINIDAD 1839–1842

COUNTRY OF EMIGRATION	1839	1840	1841	1842
Grenada	355	203	428	274
Tobago			2	
Dominica	39	21	43	66
Barbados	27		128	
Nevis	49	223	503	˙757
Tortola	58	112	57	86
Carriacou	13	19	7	34
Montserrat	44	77	304	264
Antigua	14	104	50	17
St. Lucia	20	7	2	109
St. Kitts	32	261	113	109
St. Vincent				
Saba		61	3	
Anguilla	28	2	3	
United States	314	909	63	
Sierra Leone			170	514
St. Helena				402
TOTALS	1,006	2,015	1,952	2,872
Number arrived in 1839	1,006			
Number arrived in 1840	2,015			
Number arrived in 1841	1,952			
Number arrived in 1842	2,872			
TOTAL NUMBER ARRIVED	7,845			
Amount paid in 1839	L2,691 7s. 4d			
Amount paid in 1840	L6,345 13s 2d			
Amount paid in 1841	L5,951 10s 4d			
Amount paid in 1842	L12,320 18s 51/2d			
TOTAL AMOUNT PAID	L27,309 9s 3 1/2d			

Compiled by the author.

CHAPTER 24

A Continuing Quest for Labor

In our great social experiment it will be impossible for us to proceed successfully without them [free colored people of the United States] in Trinidad. With every disposition on the part of the white inhabitants to discard preexisting prejudices, we can only be expected to associate with them of similar attainments with ourselves and beyond a limited number of individuals they are not to be found in Trinidad.

—William Burnley to Lord Russell, 1840

AFTER HIS VISIT to the United States, Burnley returned to London at the end of November where he immediately requested a meeting with Lord Russell (which was granted on December 1, 1839) to explain the results of his United States undertaking. After meeting with Lord Russell, Burnley proceeded to Paris where he found his wife "suffering under indisposition" and needing his attention. It was the first time he had seen his wife since he arrived in London in May of that year and one of the few references he made to her in his official correspondences. Once he had settled in Paris, he informed Robert Vernon Smith, the undersecretary of state of the war and the colonies, that he would be happy to reply to any further questions Lord Russell wished to ask him with regard to his practical acquaintance with issues that faced the West Indian colonies. He ended his letter by reminding Smith that he would be willing to return to London immediately if there were any pressing issues that Lord Russell wished to talk about.

Burnley spent most of the next two years enjoying the enchantment of Europe, discovering the excitement of traveling by steam, looking for ways to attract new workers to his island, and reconnecting with his American family that his father left in Virginia. Of immediate importance was a letter Lord Russell had written to Burnley on January 6, 1840, asking if the British government should extend the cultivation of cotton or tobacco in the West Indies and what laws, in his estimation, were opposed to the introduction of those articles in the markets of Great Britain. Having come from a cotton and tobacco background when he visited the United States, Burnley had paid specific attention to the possibility of cultivating these crops in the Caribbean. Responding at length to Lord Russell's inquiries, Burnley reminded Lord Russell that the planters of the United States have long been the chief suppliers of cotton and tobacco for the European markets and that through time and patience acquired "much skill in their cultivation and dexterity in the best mode of preparing them for consumption that a mere equality of duty will now enable us to enter into successful competition."[1]

Burnley noted that the first obstacle to the cultivation of these crops in the West Indies was the export duty of 3.5 percent that Trinidad growers paid in advance of the shipment of their goods to Great Britain, which he calculated "may be fully equal to 5 percent levied upon the same article when delivered for home-consumption and sometimes to considerably more, when it is liable to diminution in quantity and weight during the voyage." In the United States, he said, no duty was paid upon the export of any article of native growth, which led him to suggest "the removal of this colonial duty would place us far on a footing of equality and enable us to contend with any competition starting from the same point of departure."[2]

Since the West Indian planters had suffered many disadvantages in competition with the United States over the previous years, Burnley concluded that they could not compete with their United States counterparts unless they received a temporary bounty on those articles that were shipped to Great Britain. It was the only way West Indians could profitably cultivate these items for a British market. Until now, governments in the West Indies had made similar arguments to the mother country.

Burnley's paper left a favorable impression on some of the officials at the Colonial Office who read it, one of whom found it "a most valuable paper, but the subject of it belongs rather to the Board of Trade than to this office, and to that Board I think it ought to be communicated for their opinion."³ This was done the following day. The board of trade agreed that the export duty of 3.5 percent was harmful to goods grown and manufactured on the island in that it was likely to exclude them from the British market by making them compete on unfavorable terms with countries whose goods were exempt from such duties. They did not agree with Burnley's proposition that bounties should be used to encourage the cultivation of tobacco and cotton on the island, which "the nature of our commercial relations with the United States would cause such an interference with the freedom of trade in articles like tobacco and cotton to lead to the most injurious consequences."⁴ Britain was not prepared to disrupt its economic relations with the United States to accommodate the wishes of such a small market as existed in Trinidad.

In April 1840 another threat to the prosperity of West Indian planters emerged when the British Parliament proposed a bill to equalize duties on foreign and British sugars. The merchants and planters of Trinidad, led by Burnley, saw the equalization of duties or what they called "the withdrawal of the protection which West India products now enjoy in the markets of the United Kingdom" as harmful to their interests and a devastating blow to their investments in the Caribbean. They argued that the passage of such a bill would be analogous to entailing "the sin of slavery on one of the parties for the sake of the pecuniary advantage to the other in order to afford a relief to the consumer trifling in amount and of no long duration [and which] would seal the certain and no slow ruin of the colonists."⁵

Burnley wrote that he was thankful that the "great experiment of emancipation" had proceeded with "less injury and less positive injustice" than he and his colleagues had predicted and anticipated. Economically, however, the experiment of emancipation resulted in a large decrease in agricultural products and a heavy increase in the cost of production. They reasoned that if unfettered immigration were allowed, there would be no need to fear the island's prospects once "our peasantry acquire the skilled and provident habits which their new social condition at once requires and creates, the British West Indies will abundantly supply the wants not merely of the mother country but of all the Europeans markets."⁶

The planters were convinced that the conflict they faced revolved around the economics of sugar production by slave labor as opposed to sugar produced by free labor. To compete with the former, it was necessary to continue to grant the islands that produced sugar by free labor a continuing advantage on the British markets. In their view the ruinous consequences of the British action would fall not only on the planters and merchants. Given their education and their finances, they could immigrate and start their lives anew. A different fate would befall the emancipated laborers. Without capital and/or the availability of industries, their decline was almost certain. More important, "deprived of all the better influence of a higher class of society, they would retrograde in civilization until they descend again into a savage state."[7] As per usual, the image of Haiti and savagery was never far from the horizon.

By June of 1840, Burnley was making plans to return to the United States aboard the steamship *British Queen* to continue the work he had commenced the previous year. Before he left, he appealed to Lord Russell to relax the British policy that called for the importation of an equal proportion of the sexes among the emigrants who were being taken into the colonies. He also called on Lord Russell to intervene to bring down the high duties that were imposed on the salted provisions that were imported from the United States. While Lord Russell agreed to relax the provision with regard to the importation of an equal amount of men and women, the board of trade, to whom Lord Russell had referred Burnley's second request, refused to act in Trinidad's favor. Governor MacLeod also refused to support the reduction of duties on salted provisions from the United States.

Governor MacLeod also had another problem with Burnley. He could not come to grips with Burnley's designation of himself as the "Agent for the Council of Government in Trinidad." Governor Mein had alerted the Colonial Office about this issue, but the Colonial Office refused to deal with it at the time. On August 6, 1840, MacLeod informed Lord Russell that when he was in London earlier in the year, he got the impression that "Her Majesty's Government were not prepared to encourage Mr. Burnley in any such capacity and I find on record a dispatch from the Marquis of Normanby to Sir Evan Macgregor in which His Lordship declares it to be impossible for him to receive Mr. Burnley in the character to which had been assigned to him."[8]

MacLeod, it seems, had to act because Burnley was beginning to create a few problems for him and, in the process, was undermining his authority. Burnley had made certain promises to potential emigrants that were outside of his purview and of which the governor was unaware, such as "the expectation of public employment and other advantages that had been held out to the colored Americans generally as inducement to them to immigrate thither." MacLeod wrote to Lord Russell: "I do not think that the success of the cause in which Mr. Burnley is engaged will be much promoted by exciting fallacious hopes of this description, but when they are made by one presumed to be acting in a public capacity, I respectfully solicit Your Lordship's consideration of the inconvenience to which such proceedings must expose my Government."[9]

On October 2, Lord Russell assured the governor that he had no intention "to recognize any claim of that gentleman to act generally as the Agent or representative of the Government of Trinidad in this country [meaning Britain]." The title, Lord Russell suggested, only referred to what the Trinidad council had conferred upon Burnley to conduct any transaction he had to do on behalf of his colleagues. However, "a special employment of this nature could of course carry with it no other powers than those which had been expressly committed to the party employed or which were necessarily implied in the mere fact of this employment. If Mr. Burnley has assumed any more extensive authority or has entered into engagements which he was not expressly empowered to make, the responsibility must rest with himself alone."[10]

Lord Russell was treading on a fine line of little distinction. He had to appease his governor, who was in charge of conducting the business of the British government in Trinidad, and someone whom Lord Russell had come to know and perhaps grown fond of in the course of their encounters at the Colonial Office. The Colonial Office, located at 14 Downing Street, was close to the seat of power, 10 Downing Street. Burnley knew many of the powerful players in the realm, and Lord Russell genuinely respected Burnley's ability. He offered a compromise: Burnley might use the title "Agent," but he should be careful that he did not usurp the functions of the governor.

CHAPTER 25

Visiting Family in Virginia

≋

Like all British Governors he is infected with jealousy, and we are not likely
to be very thick together. In fact, I am considered to be too great for a
subject, but I am unfortunately also independent, so that I shall go in my
own way without requiring his assistance.

—William H. Burnley, 1841

BURNLEY WAS AN inveterate traveler. Given the time required for voyages
before the introduction of steamships, it is remarkable how many times he
crossed the Atlantic, the many countries he visited in Europe (all of which he
couldn't have gotten to by land), and the many forays he made into the West
Indies and Venezuela.[1] Burnley's own fleet consisted of four ships: *William*,
Calypso, *Arethusa*, and *Louisa*, which he used for business and for pleasure—
traveling around the island (the roads were in bad shape at that time), around
the West Indies, and to the United States. Therefore, Burnley was in his glee
when steamships began to ply the waters of the Atlantic. It was a development
that he welcomed, a voyage that he yearned to experience.

Burnley's first transatlantic trip aboard a steamship took place on the *British Queen*, named after Queen Victoria. Launched in 1838 shortly after Queen
Victoria ascended the throne, it was the largest passenger ship of its time and
the second ship to complete the transatlantic journey on steam. Charles Robert
Vernon Gibbs observed that steamers "offered more comfortable travel than
their contemporaries, being roomier and probably better equipped."[2] The
saloon of the *British Queen* was thirty feet wide, superior by far to the "'long

narrow apartments' [Charles] Dickens found in the Cunard *Britannia*."[3] It carried 104 passengers in its aft and 103 forward. On June 19, Burnley embarked upon the *British Queen* for New York "to follow up the measures which have made such a successfully commencement" (the recruitment of free persons of African descent in the United States).[4] Traveling on the *British Queen* to the United States proved to be an immensely pleasurable experience for Burnley. When he arrived in New York on July 17, he wrote to his wife as follows:

> I left London on 1st [July] in the Southampton car, and on arrival there found a steamer in waiting to carry the passengers on board the *British Queen,* lying at Ryde, where we arrived in time for dinner at half past four, and before dark were well on our voyage down the Channel notwithstanding a westerly wind in our teeth. No sailing vessel would have left the harbour. The shortness of the passage constitutes only half the value of steam-conveyance. You move on the day appointed. And well do I know the misery and expense of being detained at a hotel until the wind chooses to change! Our passage has been long, nearly 16 days, the wind contrary the whole way. But never will I go any other way. In fact, it is not a sea-voyage, in a vessel like this, even in wind and rain. We have a fine deck to walk upon under shelter. No hurry and commotion, however rough the weather. Our bottles and glasses [sit] comfortably upon the table and the vessel generally upon even keel. Turbot and salmon (preserved in ice) every day. Champagne drunk like water. I never touched it, but even if I had a taste that way, the gluttonous, vulgar manner in which I see it consumed around me would give me a distaste for it. (*OG*, 8)

After spending a month and a half in New York, Burnley traveled to Baltimore to recruit more laborers. In Baltimore he revealed another sleight of hand (some may call it business acumen) in terms of his business dealing. He complained to Lord Russell that one of the impediments that prevented the American laborers from settling in the country was "the extreme dearness of their food." No British interest would be injuriously affected by an alteration of duties upon salted provisions from the United States "whilst the great object of supplying our W. I. Colonies with a sufficient population, and raising tropical produce by free labor would be most materially promoted."[5] Such action would lower the cost of food on the island.

Burnley did not wait for a response from Lord Russell about this matter. To get around his having to pay duties on the salted provisions that he was taking back to Trinidad for his workers, he decided "to go to New York for a few days, where I have a parcel of salted beef and pork to purchase. [I will] send it on to New Brunswick, where, by being landed and put into the British warehouse at one door, and passed through another, and shipped again, it becomes British Colonial and is landed in Trinidad without any duty; otherwise, I would pay five dollars a barrel." Burnley, ever the shrewd businessman, knew how to get around restrictions even as he pleaded with the British authorities for assistance in the matter.

At the end of October, Burnley traveled to Norfolk, Virginia, to visit his family whom he had not seen (or perhaps known) since he left the United States to live in Britain. His family members who still resided there welcomed him. After his father left Virginia, the other Burnleys had done quite well in the commonwealth, becoming, as Burnley described them, "among the first people" in Virginia.[6] When his uncle Zachariah died in 1800, he was described as "a man of prominence and wealth and ranked among the most patriotic citizens of the state."[7] Zachariah and James Madison, president of the United States, had served as census enumerators in Orange County, Virginia, and enjoyed a close relationship. Emma Dicken observed: "The families of President James Madison, the Taylors and the Burnleys seemed to be intimate. There is mention of a social circle in Orange County, 1786–1799, and among the members are the Burnleys, Bells, Taylors and others."[8] Zachariah was also the godfather of Elizabeth, the sister of President Monroe.

Hardin Burnley, Zachariah's son, played an important role in Virginia and United States political and constitutional history. After attending the college of William and Mary, he studied and practiced law in Orange County where he was born. In 1787 he was elected to the first four successive one-year terms to the Virginia House of Delegates. That same year, he sent a letter to James Madison regarding the implementation of a new replevy that was about to be implemented in the Virginia House of Assembly.[9] On November 5 and 28, 1789, Burnley sent two letters to James Madison informing him of his concerns about the meaning of the Ninth Amendment of the United States Constitution. Madison "agreed with Burnley's reasoning and appended his language in a letter he sent to George Washington" on December 5, 1789.[10] The National Governors Association asserts: "[Burnley] worked with friends of James Madison on behalf of the amendments that were submitted to the states in 1789, ten of which became the Bill of Rights when the Virginia legislature ratified them in December 1791."[11]

In 1790 he was elected to the Virginia council of state to replace Thomas Madison who had resigned from the council.[12] He also served as the lieutenant governor of the state for several years. In 1799 he was elected president of the council and acted as the governor of the state for three days (December 7–11) pending James Madison's swearing-in ceremony. At the end of the year, Burnley left the council because of ill health. He retired to his one-thousand-acre plantation until his death on March 11, 1809. The *Enquirer* of Richmond, Virginia, spoke of the love and respect the commonwealth had for him. On Friday, March 17, 1809, it published the following obituary:

> He had a humor and wit of the most exquisite flavor—a mind clear, penetrating and strong—principles of action, that were the most incorruptible and honorable stamp—and a soul, that was eminently fitted for all the excellences of patriotism and friendship. No man was more zealously devoted to the principles of a republican—no man burnt with a more disinterested ardor in the service of his Country. . . . He exerted his fine talents for the benefit of the State. But the friend of virtue, the friend of his country and of man, is gone forever. He has left behind him an affectionate wife and six children to mourn his irreparable loss.

Other members of the family did quite well. David Meriwether, son of his aunt Judith, became a member of the Georgia State Legislature and speaker of the House from 1797 to 1800. He represented his district in the United States Congress from 1802 to 1809 and served as a presidential elector in 1821 and 1824. Meriwether County in Georgia was named after him. Richard Thomas Walker, grandson of his aunt Keziah, became a member of the 41st and 42nd U.S. Congress and a colonel in the Virginia Regiment of the Confederate Army. Other members of the family also became prominent in the state.

Life, however, is not without its ironies. When Hardin Burnley, son of Zachariah, died, he decreed that his very large estate should be divided equally between his six children: Hardin, Hardenia, Elizabeth, Mary, Edwin, and Judith. However, in April 1834 when Hardenia died, she left her land, slaves, and most of her other property to her mother, Mrs. Henry Pendleton, with the provision that at her mother's death, "the slaves were to be freed and sent to Liberia with clothing and comforts for the voyage and their introduction into that country. The other slaves were to be allowed their choice of going to Africa or remaining in slavery."[13] Such a bequest, it seems, was made at a time when her first cousin William Hardin was striving mightily to prevent the British from freeing their slaves and who, a mere six years later, would be struggling to buy laborers from Africa (Sierra Leone) to work on his plantations in Trinidad. However, he enjoyed the warmth of his family during those cold days of November and early December. Most of them were affectionate and loving and that pleased him immensely.

When Burnley returned to Baltimore on December 26, the city was experiencing such severe weather he simply had to sit tight and manage the cold as best he could. Yet, his focus remained the same: to recruit as many immigrants as possible to take to Trinidad to work on his plantations there. In January

1841 John Lamont joined him in Baltimore to assist him in recruiting laborers. Their yield was small. They managed to recruit only fifty Americans, which turned out to be a huge financial loss to Burnley, but all was not lost. He learned that his nephew, William Hume, was about to sail from Glasgow to Trinidad to assist him on his plantations. By the end of January the weather broke, and Burnley left for Trinidad where he arrived on February 8 after having been abroad for almost two years.

Three days after he returned to Trinidad, he convened a meeting of the Agricultural and Immigration Society to inquire into the degree with which the society (or the state of agricultural affairs in the country) had changed since the end of slavery and apprenticeship. The subcommittee was also tasked with recommending measures that should be taken to establish a free-enterprise or free-labor system where wages would become the major mode of labor transactions. He was convinced that "the most injurious consequences will ensue to the laboring classes, unless the present system of gratuitous allowances, in the shape of houses, provisions, and spirits, is put to an end."[14] The worst aspect of that system was the allowance of rum as part of the workers' wages, which had negative effects on the workers.

In order to conduct a successful hearing, Burnley needed the cooperation of the executive and the participation of the clergy, the magistrates, and other public servants. On March 8, two weeks before the hearings began, Burnley wrote to the governor asking that he use his influence to assist him to achieve his goals. On July 7, as the hearing drew to a close, John Losh, secretary of the Agricultural and Immigration Society, invited the governor to send anyone of his choice to give additional evidence to the committee to correct any errors he may have detected in the hearings. Resentful that the hearings had gone beyond the society's mandate, the governor politely declined the committee's invitation (*O*, 135).

Never one to back down from his position and conscious of his importance in the larger colonial world, Burnley informed Governor MacLeod that he and the members of the committee "felt it to be their duty to occupy the widest field which the subject required, whilst, they trust, they have abstained from overstepping its legitimate boundaries." He noted that it was primarily from a desire to maintain its impartiality that the committee invited the governor's representative "to qualify or amend the evidence previously obtained" (*O*, 136). Moreover, he had no desire to relieve himself "from the slightest portion of the responsibility which necessarily devolves upon me as chairman of the Committee" (*O*, 137). Governor MacLeod's position seemed to have been vindicated when an official of the Colonial Office appended the following note to MacLeod's letter: "This [meaning the report] should be referred to the Land and Emigration Committee, although there is very much in it which is rather out of their province, and to which it may be necessary hereafter to advert after this report shall have been recorded."[15]

Needless to say, the tensions between these two men were building up over MacLeod's governorship as they had done with other governors who had trespassed upon Burnley's domain. Burnley was off of the island when MacLeod became the governor in April 1840. Therefore, he could not have had much acquaintance with him. Yet, on March 11, 1841, a month after Burnley returned from his two-year hiatus abroad, he complimented MacLeod's business acuity and capacity for hard work, but added: "Like all British Governors he is infected with jealousy, and we are not likely to be very thick together. In fact, I am considered to be too great for a subject, but I am unfortunately also independent, so that I shall go in my own way without requiring his assistance" (OG, 10). In spite of MacLeod's resistance, Burnley used the hearing as a basis upon which to make his case for importing more laborers into the society and spreading his views about his conception of a colonial society.

CHAPTER 26

Burnley and the Question of Free Labor

There exists in that island an equality among all ranks, unparalleled elsewhere: the proprietor of large estates having no more political weight than the poorest laborer. None of the evils, therefore, which have arisen in that colony can be imputed either to the power or hostility of the planters. Further, there has existed no combination among them to depress wages; nor have any efforts been made to exact rents. . . . Finally, no religious differences have tended to increase the difficulties of the experiment.

—William Hardin Burnley, *Observations on the Present Condition of the Island of Trinidad*

B URNLEY'S DETERMINATION TO hold his hearing after he returned from the United States was neither an impulsive nor accidental gesture. It was all part of his and the planters' attempt to maintain their hegemony over the laboring classes, reduce their wages, and retain the profits they enjoyed prior to emancipation. Faced with a laboring class that was organizing itself in a new social and political environment, the planters had to develop strategies to stymie these activities. Opting to do task work, attending to their provision ground, and looking for plots to live on became symbolic of this new thrust. The planters, on the other hand, depicted every initiative of the ex-slaves in a negative manner and placed several obstacles in their path to prevent them from liberating themselves.

By 1840 Burnley was one of the most knowledgeable men in the Caribbean, particularly as it had to do with British colonial affairs. Not only was he a well-read and well-traveled man, but he was the darling of the proslavery forces in the English-speaking world. He traveled throughout the Caribbean, the Americas, and Europe, which gave him a good understanding of what was taking place in those countries. Henry James Ross, a fellow planter of Grenada, noted that Trinidad was fortunate to have "one so talented and meritoriously active as their valued 'Agent' and quasi-representative, much of whose time has been so usefully, of late, divided between Europe, America and Trinidad in the improvement of the latter."[1]

Burnley used his hearings to examine how "the great experiment of Negro emancipation succeeded." In so doing, he was using the Trinidadian backdrop to answer an important and pressing issue that faced the advocates as well as the detractors of the use of free labor in the West Indies. The resulting product of these hearings, *Observations on the Present Condition of the Island of Trinidad and the Actual State of the Experiment of Negro Emancipation*, fed into a larger debate that was taking place among the planters, the abolitionists, and the Colonial Office "about the results of what Lord Stanley had dubbed 'the mighty experiment' of slave emancipation."[2] The *Morning Herald* in London remarked: "In seeking to achieve their own future prosperity, the Trinidad planters are assisting their brethren in all our sugar colonies. They are doing more, they are working out the claims of the British people to cheap sugar, and they are asking to fill the empty coffers of the British treasury" (*M*, January 8, 1842). In other words, by holding his hearings and writing about them Burnley was making a major contribution to a problem about which the planters in these newly freed societies and colonial officials were keenly interested.

Many of the proslavery forces believed that the ex-slaves enjoyed a better economic status, worked fewer hours, and exerted themselves less than their English counterparts, so good were their conditions in the West Indies. Like many of his European colleagues, Burnley was entrapped by the notion that the energetic northerner possessed a progressive work ethic, whereas the lethargic and lazy southerner on the plantations of the West Indies avoided work whenever he could. Henry Ross saw things differently. The Negro, he argued, was not a lazy person. However, Burnley believed that by implementing a false sense of democracy in the West Indies, the Colonial Office erred in applying one standard at home (what he called a constitutional monarchy) and a beggared form of democracy in the colonies that prevented the "judicial and official rank to the upper classes of the community" from deploying "the social and political influence which not only naturally attaches to property under such an institution, but is essentially necessary to its support." This, he says, "is a dangerous experiment, at whatever distance from the heart of the empire it may be made" (*O*, 12).

Burnley's efforts were directed to the importation of laborers to expand the profit of the merchants and proprietors of the island. "Sound policy," he argued, "prescribes that as little time as possible should be lost in introducing the number of laborers required, by which means alone can a wholesome competition be created amongst them, wages reduced to a fair rate, and the idleness, vagrancy, and other bad habits now rapidly increasing, be speedily and effectually checked" (*O*, 13). He believed that everything should be done to protect the proprietor so that the laborers, for whom this new system was created, could enjoy the freedom envisaged by the originators of "the great experiment." In order to do so, Burnley's Agricultural and Immigration Sub-Committee suggested that the colony be allowed to import a sufficient number of laborers of both sexes and that the legislative code be framed in such a way that it embraced "*provisions for regulating the condition of the Negroes*, by which they may be trained and educated as moral and useful members of society in the station of life to which they belong" (*O*, 38; italics added). In other words, for Africans to be successful, whites must provide guidance, schooling them into accepting an inferior position in the society.

To consolidate their position, Burnley insisted on the sanctity of contracts of services, the *sine qua non* of the capitalist system. A rigorous respect for contracts, as they favored the whites, was the only way to keep order in the society. It was imperative to teach the laborer, "through the instrumentality of the law, a moral lesson of the first importance in civilized life—viz., to enter into all contracts cautiously, and then, whatever may be the consequences, to keep them honestly" (*O*, 22–23). If such a principle was not embedded into the minds of the laborer, he asked, "how will it be possible to protect the sanctity of the marriage contract, which we are so anxious to promote and encourage among them"? Hence their recommendation: "The whole influence of Government should be directed to the encouragement of contracts of service; and the most advantageous mode in which it can be exercised is by legalizing those made out of the colony" (*O*, 23). Needless to say, after being enslaved for so many years, the ex-slaves were suspicious about signing any "paper" that seemed to bind them to their former masters.

To counteract the challenges posed by the ex-slaves, the committee proposed a large increase of the labor population though vigorous immigration.

The planters, it was suggested, should look for laborers in latitudes within forty degrees of the equator "to whom the climate of the island would be as genial as their own. Asiatics would answer well, but the natives of Africa are greatly to be preferred, for many reasons: they are naturally docile, and open to new impressions; even their ignorance is in their favor, for they have no bad code of policy, morality or religion to unlearn" (*O*, 26). The committee decided to look to Africa for labor. Although such a proposal would entail enormous expenses, the committee confidently expected that the government of the colony would defray the cost of such a program. He had to convince the Colonial Office that the introduction of his plan would not result in the reimposition of the slave trade in another guise. Burnley, however, remained convinced that his plan would result eventually in the extinction of "the second slavery" that was practiced in Brazil and Cuba.

The hearings ended on July 20. By then Burnley had left the country. Unable to submit a detailed report of their hearings to Governor MacLeod, the Agricultural and Immigration Sub-Committee offered eight resolutions that embodied the substance of their findings which they believed would lay the foundation for the future prosperity of the colony. On August 20, Governor MacLeod transmitted a copy of the evidence to Lord Stanley, who immediately forwarded it to the Colonial Land and Emigration Board. On December 3, 1841, the commissioners of the board asserted that the "Minutes of Evidence" offered a "very full picture . . . of the industrial condition of the Colony, and of the means at present existing for raising produce from the soil" but were unable to determine "how correct and complete" it was in all its parts.[3] They pointed out that none of the ex-slaves were examined. Of the twenty-one witnesses called, only three were sympathetic to the plight of the Africans and could be counted on to be unbiased. When Sir Charles Douglas pointed out that omission, Burnley confessed he "was under the idea that they could not give us any useful information. I regret now that some labourers were not examined, in order to satisfy public opinion in this country [England]" (*SC*, 60). One did not have to look any further to see what Burnley thought of the laboring population; they had nothing useful to offer to an understanding of the situation.

The commissioners agreed with the Agricultural and Immigration Sub-Committee that the wages of labor in Trinidad were "extremely high, both with reference to the cost of living and to the rates in other places; and this fact may of course be assumed to indicate the scarcity of labor compared with the capital applicable to its employment." They noted correctly "the unquestionable competition amongst employers to secure laborers sufficiently proves that labor is deficient in respect to capital." However, they did not see this relative advantage of the laborers "as a growing evil, or that the demoralizing consequences of it to the laborers are so pernicious as they have been represented." It was merely a case of gross exaggeration by the planters. While the commissioners conceded that there was a certain amount of squatting, they believed that immigration, a policy it endorsed, "would more than balance the withdrawal of the squatters from the labor market—a withdrawal, moreover, which is never complete, as when pressed for money they return to work." They also felt immigration would make "available the fertile districts, which are now lying waste over a large proportion of the island,"[4] although the Agricultural and Immigration Sub-Committee did not specify how best to achieve this desired condition. The colony would have to call upon the Colonial Treasury to assist them in this regard.

Burnley was convinced his plan would lead to the extinction of the slave trade and the happiness of the African emigrants who would be brought to the West Indies where they would enjoy the benefits of a superior civilization. It would also prove the superiority of free labor over slave labor and bring enormous benefits to the West Indian planters. The people of Great Britain would also profit from his scheme in that they too would enjoy the benefit of cheaper sugar. Burnley decided to spend at least six months of the year at home to attend to his business affairs. He had allowed affairs of state to consume too much of his time, thereby neglecting Orange Grove in the process. He even suggested that his wife should come out to Trinidad to join him each winter. It would have been a welcome relief from the dreary cold of Paris, and it would have pleased him much.

As he sought to adapt to the colony after his stint abroad, his relationship with the governor continued to decline. On May 29, Burnley reported that he had attended a ball that the governor gave on May 26 in honor of the Queen's birthday. "I went out of civility," he said, "seeing that there has been some coolness between us, but stayed only one hour. It seemed a very poor concern, not sufficiently lighted up. From general manner and deportment his is not likely to add much to Society; though an honorable man with good common sense; and so far a good and safe governor." He accused the governor of being "extremely jealous" of his hearings that were taking place at the time "but cannot help himself." Yet eight days before the hearings ended, he would say of their relationship: "There is much civility between us, and I have an invitation to dinner at St. Ann's [the governor's residence] about once a fortnight, but he will not be sorry to see me quit the island. He is a better man than his immediate successor, but will never be a Sir Ralph Woodford" (*OG*, 11).

Burnley did not remain on the island long enough to see the report of his Agricultural and Immigration Sub-Committee turned in to the governor. He left that honor to his fellow committee members, Henry Murray and Robert Dennistoun, who took the resolutions to the governor. By August, Burnley had arrived in New York, having traveled to the United States via Philadelphia. As was to be expected, straightaway he went to see Mrs. Farquhar and Augusta. On October 17, he arrived in London, having traveled from New York to Bristol on the *Great Western*. This time it took him thirteen days to cross the Atlantic. In spite of his relationship with Augusta Farquhar, he was still determined to have his wife live with him at Orange Grove. Thus, he wrote to her encouragingly: "The steamers will begin to move next month, and will not exceed 16 to 18 days on the voyage. They are, besides, so large, so airy, and so sweet, and well provided with every comfort that the voyage will be a different thing to what you were accustomed" (*OG*, 12). He also informed her that William Hume, his nephew, would go out to Orange Grove to learn the sugar-planting business: "I shall place him under Lionel Lee's direction. He will live and mess with him at O.G. [Orange Grove] House, and not be mixed-up with the other overseers" (*OG*, 12).

From London, Burnley traveled to Paris hoping once more to persuade Charlotte to come to Trinidad to live out her last days with him. He must have seen hopeful signs for he and his wife began to look for furniture for their home in Trinidad. Burnley remained in Europe until August 1842 before returning to Trinidad. Although the *Isis* steamer was not as luxurious as the *Great Western*, it offered many of the essential comforts he had come to expect from the previous steamers on which he had traveled. As he reported, "The berths are roomy, comfortable, and on the upper deck; and I have a port-hole so high that it can be opened in any weather. A huge stock of food is laid-in. We have had fresh green peas every day; always two soups and fish and fowl of half-dozen kinds. Wine you pay for at 3/- a bottle for sherry, Madeira, and port of tolerable quality" (*OG*, 13).

By September 1842 Burnley was back on the island, ready to deal with problems there, especially the rash of squatting that was taking place. On September 6, together with Charles Warner, John Losh, and others, he was present in the council chambers prepared and eager to address the matters of the society.

FIGURE 1. *Residence at Orange Grove Estate, Tacarigua*. Reproduced from Michel-Jean Cazabon, Album of Trinidad, 1857. Photograph courtesy of Geoffrey MacLean.

FIGURE 2. A photographic print of a daguerreotype of William Hardin Burnley, in *From Colonial to Republic: One Hundred and Fifty Years of Business and Banking in Trinidad and Tobago, 1837–1987* (Port of Spain: Paria Publishing, 1987).

FIGURE 3. Charles William Warner, circa 1842, in *Aucher Warner, Sir Thomas Warner, Pioneer of the West Indies: A Chronicle of His Family* (London: West India Committee, 1933).

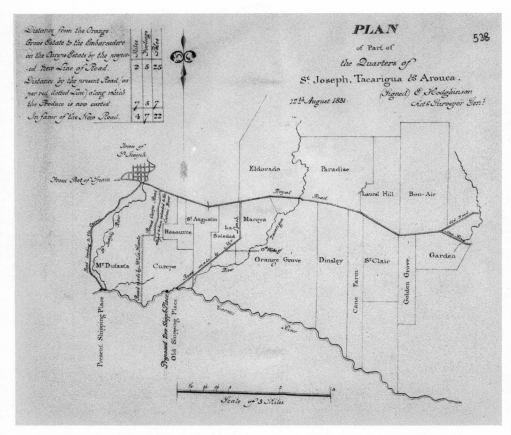

FIGURE 4. Plan of Part of the Quarters of St. Joseph, Tacarigua and Arouca, including the various estates of the area, 1831. This was the second most important sugar-growing area of Trinidad. Photograph courtesy of the author.

FIGURE 5. *Orange Grove Estate.* Watercolor by Michel-Jean Cazabon, 1849. Photograph courtesy of Geoffrey MacLean.

FIGURE 6. St. Mary's Anglican Church, Tacarigua, built on lands donated to the community by William Hardin Burnley, 2015. Photograph by Richard Howard. © Richard Howard.

FIGURE 7. Tombstone of William Eccles, in the St. Mary's Cemetery. Together with William Frederick Burnley (son of William Hardin Burnley), he was responsible for setting up the St. Mary's Children's Home. Photograph by Richard Howard. © Richard Howard.

FIGURE 8. An aerial photo of St. Mary's Children's Home (formerly known as the Coolie Orphan Asylum), taken by the Royal Air Force, circa 1942. The Children's Home was built in 1857 on ten acres of land that was donated by William Frederick Burnley (son of William Hardin Burnley) to the community. Initially, it was meant to serve Indo-Trinidadians who had lost their parents. Photograph courtesy of the author.

FIGURE 9. Prime Minister of Trinidad and Tobago Eric Williams, right, shakes hands with British Prime Minister Harold Wilson on the steps of No. 10 Downing Street, London, on October 20, 1964, after their meeting. Donald Wood, author of *Trinidad in Transition* (1986), described Burnley as "a founding father of British Trinidad." Citizens of Trinidad and Tobago describe Williams as "the founding father of the Nation." Associated Press.

FIGURE 10. *West View of Burnley's Mansion at Orange Grove, Tacarigua.* Watercolor by Michel-Jean Cazabon, 1849. Photograph courtesy of Geoffrey MacLean.

FIGURE 11. Photograph of Selwyn R. Cudjoe, author. © Richard Howard.

FIGURE 12. The residence of Selwyn R. Cudjoe on Bailey Street, Tacarigua, which runs horizontally to Richard Street, that borders the St. Mary's Children Home. © Richard Howard.

CHAPTER 27

The Evil of Squatting

The general conclusion of this report [Agricultural and Immigration Sub-Committee] seems to be that for the present nothing remains to be done but to take more effective precautions against squatting either by partial surveys or the amendment to the law—or by more effective execution of the law. . . . My own belief however is that squatting is one of those evils which admits of no effective remedy—the temptation being too general, too constant and too strong to be counteracted by mere penalties. We have no colony in which it [squatting] has ever been successfully resisted and many where it has been, by mere necessity, expressly sanctioned and regulated. It is like the attempt to interdict the fisheries to a whole population dwelling on the sea coast.

—James Stephen, 1841

WITH SO MUCH available land, it was next to impossible to prevent inhabitants from using land for housing and for planting. The commissioners of the Colonial Land and Emigration Board recognized that there was "a great temptation to the poor to possess themselves of land, and to dispense with labor for their support." Reflecting on this tendency of the laboring classes to squat on unoccupied lands, Governor MacLeod remarked that it was "a circumstance which tends to retain the people of this island in an uncivilized condition, and to check any species of industry."[1] With his usual prescience, James Stephen, a liberal, noted that "squatting is one of those evils which admits of no effective remedy—the temptation being too general, too constant and too strong to be counteracted by mere penalties. We have no colony in which it has ever been successfully resisted and many where it has been, by mere necessity, expressly sanctioned and regulated. It is like the attempt to interdict the fisheries of a whole population dwelling on the sea coast."[2] Needless to say, the law in force against this practice, as Burnley's Agricultural and Immigration Sub-Committee found and the Colonial Land and Emigration Office asserted, was ineffective. This was why Burnley held his hearings in the first place; he wanted to ensure that new laws against squatting were formulated to prevent this practice that was ruining the planters on his island.

Faced with this evil, Burnley and his fellow planters were intent on bringing immigrants onto the island to reduce the advantage the laboring classes had over them. To achieve this goal, a deputation from the Agricultural and Immigration Sub-Committee, composed "of all the most respectable inhabitants [of the colony],"[3] visited Governor MacLeod on November 29, 1841, with a proposal to purchase a ship of sufficient size to run between Trinidad and Sierra Leone to bring immigrants to the island. The governor had no objection supporting such a proposition although he had some reservations about it.

Stephen, sympathetic to the Negroes, had his own take on these matters. After reading all the reports regarding this issue, he raised several questions to the British Treasury about the cost of such immigration.[4] He wondered whether consideration should not be given to bringing immigrants from places other than the British dominions; whether publicity should not be given to the dangers that awaited European immigrants from France and Germany; and whether the law against squatting should be amended. He advised against encouraging British laborers to immigrate to Trinidad. He also wondered whether "we have been doing harm instead of good by the extent to which gratuitous education has been afforded to the children of the Negroes and whether therefore there be any real cause to regret the gradual reduction of the Education Grant."[5] After reading these recommendations, Stephen noted that the advocates of slavery,

grossly misunderstood and misrepresented the real character of the Negro race—that the Abolition of Slavery has yielded fruits better and earlier than even the authors of the measure dared to anticipate—that the countervailing disadvantages are incomparably less than it seemed reasonable to expect—that society is on the whole in a healthful and improving state—that the falling off in profits on capital though a great evil is yet largely compensated [for] by an increase in the material comforts and in the moral and intellectual state of the people—that the decline in profits is however great—that this is an evil not only in itself, but as it promotes the interest of the slave as against that of free labor—and that it is the duty of government to do what can be done for the abatement of this evil. Immigration may do something, but I believe that the efficacy of it to be exaggerated for many reasons, and especially for the following: every imported laborer increases the demand for labor in a greater proportion than he contributes to supply and demand. Where wages are so high he straightway becomes a consumer, and needs a house, furniture, food, dress, and many things which he once thought superfluities. He enhances the demand for builders, tailors, provision growers, and so on.

I think it a nice problem whether immigration will for a long time raise, rather than reduce the wages of labor. In these attempts to recruit a defective laboring population by artificial methods, I suspect that we engage in a real though undesigned struggle against one of the fundamental Laws of human society, and that is only by the natural increase of the species that Trinidad or any other place can ever attain to the balance between capital and manual labor which secures to capital the maximum of profit [which Burnley was about] which is compatible with the general prosperity of the hand laborers.[6]

These penciled notes reflected Stephen's evaluation of the findings of Burnley's Agricultural and Immigration Society Sub-Committee. It is clear that Stephen considered Burnley's (and his committee's) obsession with squatting exaggerated at best and his emphasis on immigration overblown. He certainly did not see it as the way out of the challenges that faced the West Indies. And it was entirely true that immigration would not necessarily result in a decrease of wages and a lowering of the cost of living. However, he still appreciated Burnley's findings and the importance of the documents on which they were framed. He noted that they constituted "a useful addition to our stock of West Indian statistics."[7]

No sooner had Stephen offered his evaluation than the reviews on Burnley's *Observations* started to come in.[8] Burnley wanted the information he acquired from his hearings to reach "the public of Great Britain . . . [and] every impartial inquirer . . . [who wanted] to ascertain the true state of this great and interesting experiment" (*O*, 4–5). He must have been quite pleased by the international as well as national recognition his work received when it was published in 1842. As fate would have it, Burnley's book coincided with the publications of Henry James Ross's *Thoughts on the Objectionable System of Labour for Wages in the West India Colonies* and *A Letter to the Right Hon. Lord Stanley, M. P. on the Sugar Question, with Some Account of the Anomalous Position of Barbados* by a late member of Parliament, each of which was published in 1842. They examined the effects of apprenticeship on the planters and workers and sought "to influence the outcome of the debate that had started at the termination of the apprenticeship [and which continued until the 1850s] about the results of what Lord Stanley had dubbed 'the mighty experiment of slave emancipation.'"[9]

Ross encountered Burnley's book quickly after he sent his pamphlet to the press. Burnley, in his turn, also read Ross's pamphlet (*SC*, 48). In a postscript to Burnley's book, he noted: "Such is the information contained therein that no one interested in the welfare of the West India colonies and in 'the great experiment,' now in operation in that part of the British Empire, should fail to read and carefully digest it" (*SC*, 111). Stephen had made a similar point. Yet it was the *Colonial Gazette* of London that offered the first, rather extensive, review of the book. It opened its review by quoting the first paragraph of Burnley's book. It noted that *Observations* reflected the great weight of the matter "put forth on behalf of one of the most active communities in the West Indies, Trinidad, as part of a series of energetic efforts to redeem those colonies from the ruinous effects of crude legislation." It argued that although one may be tempted to see Trinidad as an exceptional case, "we shall not be far wrong if we take the case of Trinidad, here most ably and forcibly developed by Mr. Burnley, as representing the case of the West Indies generally; and in the case of the West Indies are involved all of the interests which are concerned in the suppression of the slave-trade and the regulation of intertropical labor and commerce" (*C*, "The Destinies of Tropical America and the African Race," Janauary 5, 1842).

Burnley sent a copy of his work to the *Trinidad Standard* just to be sure it reached his home audience. Describing Burnley as a "valued and indefatigable friend" of the colony, the editor of the newspaper, John McSwiney, argued that *Observations* contained a concise view of the present conditions of Trinidad and the West Indies and offered "bold and convincing suggestions as to the advantages that must accrue to those colonies, as well as to the unfortunate Africans, by the establishment of a regular system of emigration from the latter country upon the principles of perfect freedom." The editor believed that if Burnley's advice was followed, it "would destroy that horrid and debasing trade which is a stain upon Christianity, and would raise this race of our fellow creatures to the rank of civilized beings, as well as promote in a prominent degree, the prosperity of the colonies whose natural advantages have hitherto been but very partially developed from the want of enlightenment and just regulations in their natural management" (*TS*, February 10, 1842).

The *Port of Spain Gazette* celebrated Burnley's achievement with unrelieved enthusiasm. It boasted that it was "like everything which has fallen from this gifted author: a clear and comprehensive performance, and not less remarkable for the soundness than for the boldness of his views on Colonial Affairs." The reviewer noted that the book contained what every man of commonsense on the island knew. He remarked: "We are not without a hope that this Report and the evidence on which it is founded, will have considerable influence in

England. It is altogether free from passion and anger and does not contain a single passage capable of being tortured into a triumph over, or provocation of, the Anti-Slavery Society." The editors could not be prouder of the achievement of a son of its soil—at least that is how they considered him—and were enthralled "with the labors of such a profound and powerful thinker on subjects as deeply interesting to us all." They concluded: "Trinidad may well be proud of possessing the ablest living advocate of Colonial claims to fair play and impartial government—a man whose energy and perseverance in the cause and demand our admiration as much or more than the ability and talent which he brings to the support of it, great as these are universally admitted to be" (*PG*, February 15, 1842).[10]

The *Morning Herald*, a proplanter newspaper, also offered effusive praises and welcomed this remarkable pamphlet "by one of the most intelligent and energetic planters on an island—Trinidad—equally remarkable for intelligence, energy, moderation, and freedom from party squabbles and disputes between masters and slaves" (*M*, January 8, 1842). A few days later the editors of the *Morning Herald* pulled back from their unequivocal endorsement of Burnley's book. Feeling that they may have spoken before they realized the full impact of Burnley's ideas, they countered that although they had allowed Burnley "to speak in his own language" in doing so, they ought not to be considered "as adopting his reasoning in all its details, or his conclusions to their whole extent. To his general views we see many formidable, but not insuperable objections" (*M*, January 13, 1842). They proposed to visit Burnley's views again once the public had an opportunity to study them.

The *Naval & Military Gazette* offered a more restrained analysis than either the *Colonial Gazette* or the *Morning Herald*. It noted that it had perused Burnley's book "with much satisfaction," the object of which was "to prove that sound policy prescribes that as little time as possible should be lost in introducing the number of laborers required, as emigrants, by which means alone can a wholesome competition be created—wages reduced to fair rate, and the idleness, vagrancy, and other bad habits, now rapidly increasing, be speedily and effectually checked." While they did not endorse Burnley's plan to bring laborers from Africa, they argued that "his work will amply repay the perusal, and we consider he deserves very great credit for the labor he has bestowed on this subject, and which he has treated with considerable talent and judgment" (*N*, January 22, 1842).

At the end of January, the *Morning Herald* had received a copy of Ross's book and the pamphlet by a late member of the House of Assembly and thus could congratulate Burnley on the excellent example he had set for the West Indian proprietary body. The newspaper thought that the two pamphlets were valuable. However, it preferred Ross's rather than Burnley's plan. It argued: "Immigration is an effective expedient, but only on such an immense scale as to make subsistence difficult. Drops of immigrants may, Mr. Ross inferentially suggests, only more quickly ruin the planter. We must adopt some plan, he urges, to induce the present population, as well as the immigrant, to devote continuous labor to the cultivation of our stables" (*M*, January 29, 1842). It promised to return to the matter in a subsequent issue.

The *Anti-Slavery Reporter* was not as receptive or as respectful of Burnley's views as were the other proslavery newspapers and even the local media. It saw it was an encouragement of the continuation of the European slave trade to the West Indies if Burnley's malevolent prescriptions were followed. It complained vociferously about the unfairness of his brochure and saw as contradictory Burnley's recommendation of importing Africans to work in the Caribbean while simultaneously promoting such immigration as a means of extinguishing the slave trade. It described his recommendations as nothing more than an attempt to increase his profits and his writing under the ambit of the Agricultural and Immigration Society as "a device for bringing forward with more of pomp and circumstance the views of Mr. Burnley." It asserted: "There is nothing new in the whole pamphlet; but that it is merely a repetition, with a show of documents, of the sentiments which the world has known Mr. Burnley to hold for some years past." Even the title of Burnley's pamphlet came in for criticism. The *Anti-Slavery Reporter* claimed that it unfairly represented the conditions in Trinidad as the general conditions in the West Indies and, as to be expected, was especially critical of how he represented the Negro condition (*AR*, January 26, 1842).

The *Anti-Slavery Reporter* was particularly repulsed by Burnley's claim that purchasing Africans in Africa and bringing them to the West Indies would result in their enjoying greater freedom on the island and would lead ultimately to the end of the slave trade. The newspaper had two responses to this proposition. First, "No one so purchased will have the name of freedom until he reaches Trinidad or the substance of it when he arrives there. The thing intended is a *forcible expatriation*, and a state of compulsory servitude; and this is called conferring liberty." Second, that "the systematic purchase of slaves on the coast of Africa, . . . [would] generate such enormous crimes and miseries on that unhappy continent, that we are utterly amazed how anyone professing regard for its improvement can entertain it for an instant" (*AR*, January 26, 1842). Nothing in Burnley's plan, according to the *Anti-Slavery Reporter*, would contribute to improving the conditions of the people on the island. It would only increase Burnley's profits and give the false impression that he was concerned with the well-being of Africana people.

After due consideration, the *Morning Herald* reviewed Burnley's book in another of its issues. It was even more alarmed by the aspect of Burnley's plan that called for the purchasing and manumitting of Africans who were held "in bondage" in the interior of the country. It was in agreement with the concerns of the *Anti-Slavery Reporter*. Arguing strongly against such an approach to acquiring African laborers, the newspaper noted: "It would stimulate the curse of Africa, the curse of its desolation and misery—the internal slave trade. . . . The slave-trading wars and incursions of the chiefs of the coast of Africa would be increased and thousands of human beings would be yearly slaughtered, that a few might be captured and sold into freedom." Hitting at the heart of Burnley's plan, it pointed out that "the prosperity of the West Indies and the success of the 'great experiment' cannot be worked out by so dreadful a process" (*M*, February 1, 1842). The editors remained convinced that when Africans realized the benefits to be derived from being free laborers in the West Indies, they would be glad to emigrate there.

On March 8, the *Glasgow Courier* reviewed Burnley's book, incorrectly identifying him as a member of the firm Messrs. Robert Eccles and Company. Making no bones about its proslavery stance, it endorsed Burnley's position that Trinidad was capable of producing enough sugar to supply Great Britain, but "the impediments interposed by the remissness of the home government, and the prejudice which have been so diligently created against the planters, and in favour of the blacks, made this impossible and that the only remedy for these evils, which affect all our West Indian dependencies with nearly equal force, is, the institution of contracts between the labourer and his employer, and the importation, under suitable regulation, of free negroes from the coast of Africa." Like Burnley, it believed that abolition of the enslaved was "hurriedly conceived and bunglingly executed" without preparing the formerly enslaved for their new condition. Thus, it took men of Burnley's character and experience to come forward to consider "whether, upon the new system, it be possible [any] longer to cultivate these magnificent islands to advantage?" (*G*, March 8, 1842).

Burnley's book was very successful in that it engendered an important debate about the role of free labor in its attempt to dislodge slave labor. It elicited views from a broad spectrum of the slavery and nonslavery community: those from the proslavery camp such as the *Colonial Gazette* and the *Morning Herald*; those from the antislavery camp such as the *Anti-Slavery Reporter*; and those from the racist camp such as the *Glasgow Courier*. No one, of course, could mistake the pride the local newspapers (*Port of Spain Gazette* and the *Trinidad Standard*) took in the accomplishment of their man and to some, their savior, William Burnley. He had reached a broad sector of the British public, but one could not help but remember the brooding commentary of the *Glasgow Courier* and its strange caution:

> Although we are much impressed with the deliberate and calm tone of Mr. Burnley's book, which we would earnestly recommend to the attention of those who are interested in the question, we would caution him, however, against being too sanguine in his expectations as to the results of an appeal to British reason. That faculty has been under an eclipse for the last ten years, and we should doubt if it will ever shine forth with the splendor which once characterized it. (*G*, March 8, 1842)

Quickly after the reviews (together with those of Ross and the late member of the assembly) appeared in the newspapers, Lord Stanley appointed a "Select Committee on West India Colonies" on March 22, 1842, to inquire into "the existing Relations between Employers and Labourers, the Rate of Wages, the Supply of Labour, the System and Expense of Cultivation, and the General State of their Rural and Agricultural Economy" (*SC*, iii). In this sense one can argue that Burnley had achieved his objective of bringing a seminal question to the attention of the English public, "How has the great experiment of Negro Emancipation succeeded?," even though many of his readers were not entirely satisfied with his answer to the question.

CHAPTER 28

Policing the Negroes

They [the Negroes] have a great deal of pride and ambition, and do very handsome and very liberal things every day, but it is steady good conduct in a small way which is most required in the foundations of society. . . . The Negro laborer is very acute and very intelligent, and understands his own interest perfectly.

—William Burnley, *Report from Select Committee on West India Colonies*

THE SELECT COMMITTEE on West India Colonies held its first meeting on April 11, concluded its hearing on July 14, and submitted its report to the British Parliament on July 25, 1842. The committee[1] interviewed proprietors and managers from St. Vincent, Trinidad, Barbados, Guyana, Grenada, Antigua, St. Kitts, and Jamaica in addition to people who "differ materially from the West Indian Proprietors as to the causes which have led to that distress [in the West Indies], and believe that the great advantages which have resulted from Emancipation" (*SC*, iii). The committee agreed unanimously that "the great act of emancipating the Slaves in the West Indian Colonies has been productive, as regards the character and condition of the Negro Population, of the most favorable and gratifying results" (*SC*, iv). Burnley, however, was convinced that neither greater church attendance nor increased marriages among Africans implied that their morality and quality of civilization had improved. "Marriage ceremonies in themselves alone," he said, "are no sufficient test of an improved state of morality amongst the Negro population" (*SC*, 60). He was also critical of the degeneracy that he saw taking place among the apprentices.

The select committee met with Burnley on April 28, May 2, 5, and 9 in his capacity as the chairman of the Agricultural and Immigration Society and used his *Observations* as a basis upon which to examine him. These hearings allowed Burnley to elaborate upon the findings of his Agricultural and Immigration Sub-Committee and gave him an opportunity to voice his opposition to the post-emancipation labor regime. In fact, the first question the committee raised dealt with the issue of squatting by the former slaves, which Burnley deemed "one of the great grievances which we have to complain of" (SC, 46). Burnley believed that within the four years after apprenticeship one third or eight thousand field laborers had retired from the fields, although immigrants from the other West Indian islands had filled the labor gap (SC, 75). The planters anticipated that immigrants from Sierra Leone would alleviate the labor problem. This hope never materialized.

In the light of this labor shortage, the planters attempted to get the laborers to devote more time to working on the estates. The laborers, however, were more inclined to work when and where they pleased and opted to do task work instead of working set hours on the plantations. They worked three or four days a week on the estates and spent the remainder of their time on their provision grounds. After emancipation, they formed villages just outside the boundary lines of the existing estates so as "to establish themselves where they can get a house and ground of their own, without any rent, and at the same time, make themselves independent of the solicitations of the proprietors and managers to work for them, they would only have to return over the line to occupy houses on the estates they had previously vacated" (SC, 47).

This independent spirit characterized most of the laborers. Burnley acknowledged that the best and most industrious workers preferred field work "because when they work in the fields they depend wholly upon themselves, and if they are active, industrious persons, they can make two tasks per day easily, and gain a large sum of money." The women worked hardest during the weeks prior to Christmas and Easter since these were occasions where "a great deal of splendour in dress and feasting [were] displayed. I have known them before those holidays, for two or three weeks, work two tasks a day for several days consecutively" (SC, 53).

The apprentices also looked out for one another. Friends and relatives took care of the aged and infirm, which resulted in pauperism being "quite unknown" in the country. Burnley testified that he "never heard of a person being in distress in the agricultural districts" (SC, 54). These newly freed people also provided a few houses for the refuge of destitute persons and "several benefit societies supported by the labourers themselves, in various parts of the rural districts" (*SC*, 90). These nascent modes of self-help represented the start of what was to become the friendly society movement that emerged in Trinidad, which lasted well into the twentieth century. My parents and grandparents were members of the friendly societies in Tacarigua and Arouca.

The select committee devoted much time to discussing how to attract labor from abroad so as to reduce wages and to create competition among the laborers. Burnley made it clear to Mr. Hawes that increased immigration would create greater competition amongst the laborers "but if by regulations, as some may suppose, you can induce or compel the present population to work better than they do—to work, in fact, three times more in a week than they do at present, the result of that would be equivalent to trebling the actual population" (*SC*, 81). Failing such exertions by the existing laborers, the country had to introduce one thousand Africans a year under "contracts of service for 12 months" to solve the labor problem on the island (*SC*, 104–5).

Burnley believed that the apprentices (that is, the Africans in the land) were making much too much money, which, according to him, led to retrogression in their condition. He noted that this was "why, instead of advancing in moral improvement, they are rather retrograding at the present period; for I hold that it is impossible for any moral improvement to take place in a community where the want of a good character and good reputation interpose no serious obstacle to a man's gaining a lucrative employment" (*SC*, 86). Once apprenticeship ended, Burnley's saw his principal activity as securing more immigrants, which he considered to be "radically necessary for the improvement of the moral condition of the labourers, considering that, until there is competition among them, wages will remain higher than is favorable to the moral improvement of labourers in any part of the world" (*SC*, 85).

Given this concern for their moral improvement, Burnley contemplated setting up a restrictive/oppressive state (or a big-barrack type system) to monitor and restrict the movements of Africans (or new immigrants) and to ensure that they keep on working in the fields. He suggested that the commandant (or someone possessing such authority) be given the power to determine who would live in the various districts (or quarters) and who possessed the right to restrict their movement in and out of the various quarters. These issues resulted in a testy exchange between Burnley and Lord Stanley.

Lord Stanley continued to probe Burnley's desire to create this restrictive/oppressive state. He asked him if leasing land to Africans would not tie them sufficiently to the soil and thereby ensure a steady pool of labor that Burnley saw as the prerequisite for the continued growth of the island. Burnley did not accept Lord Stanley's position. Instead, he differentiated between the financial sophistication of the superior Africans as opposed to the lack of thrift and unreliability of the lower class Africans who constituted the majority of the black population. The lower classes, he argued, were not "in that advanced state of civilization to take leases on property. They are ready to work out as day labourers but I really know very few that would be disposed to take leases." He believed that the superior Negroes knew how to make money and how to keep it. They were "generally a different class of persons from the ordinary labourers in the colony" (SC, 71).

Although the laborers made some money (after all, their wages were high), it is doubtful whether they saved as much as they could. Burnley noted: "They spend it in the most extravagant way, which I consider is the great cause of their present demoralization" (SC, 69). Those who saved their money purchased houses and land and engaged in the setting up of small shops. While they did not produce enough to meet their needs, they imported a lot of "plantains, poultry, pigs, and other provisions brought from the Spanish continent" (SC, 70). Burnley attributed this condition to the apprentices' abandonment of their provision grounds since many of them began to diversify their occupations.

Burnley opposed any plan "to educate their [the ex-slaves'] children gratuitously when they have the means of paying for them liberally" (SC, 50), even though he admitted that the ex-slaves "paid very liberally" for religious education for their children. When asked if they should be forced to pay a tax to send their children to school, Burnley responded: "I do not think they are so advanced in civilization that they would prevent in general their children from loitering and idling about; many of them, however, are extremely anxious that their children should be educated" (SC, 51). Nonetheless, the government and the planters paid the salaries of the twenty-three teachers on the island with a population of forty-five thousand (SC, 52).

One of the chief objectives of Burnley's Agricultural and Immigration Sub-Committee hearings was to bring this "sinful" and "evil" practice of rum drinking to an end. He suggested that the laboring population brought this curse upon themselves but made no mention of the part the planters played in encouraging the use of this intoxicant among the slaves. Seeing the apparent contradiction in Burnley's statement, Hawes asked him what steps he had taken during his time as a member of the legislative council to prepare the laboring classes for their new condition. Burnley responded defensively: "Up to the period of my departure [for England] no preparations were made. On the contrary, the labourers were distinctly informed by a proclamation, that the abolition of apprenticeship would not take place until the year 1840." Pressed as to whether he felt he had any obligation to assist in preparing the enslaved for their new condition, Burnley responded defiantly: "None at all. I considered myself that the abolition of apprenticeship should not have taken place" (*SC*, 85).

Rum drinking was not as simple nor as straightforward as Burnley made it out to be. Rum drinking and a general culture of alcohol were integral to the modus operandi of the society, a form of social behavior that was "loaded with symbolic meaning." Among Africans, rum itself and rum drinking possessed both spiritual and secular uses. Enslaved Africans embraced rum as "a sacred fluid that enhanced connections to the spiritual world and strengthened ties to African culture." They used it for religious reasons and oath-taking at important ceremonies. In fact, any time African began to drink rum together, one of the participants always poured "a drink for the dead."[2] That, at least, was part of the popular superstition. In the secular sphere, rum drinking was symptomatic of the social tensions and pressures that many of the apprentices, so recently enfranchised, felt within the system.

Rum drinking was not confined to the enslaved population. A. L. Joseph, an Irishman who lived in Trinidad during the same period as Burnley (he managed the Chatham Estate in 1825), gave a different picture of the use of alcohol among the blacks as opposed to the whites. As far as he was concerned, rum was "scarcely as injurious as gin, whiskey, or brandy, unless it be taken in greater quantities. Rum is the bane of nine-tenths of the lower order of English, Irish, and Scots who come to these islands; other Europeans are in general less addicted to intemperance, yet are, on the whole, not so sober a set of people as Africans and Creoles."[3]

Therefore when Burnley raised the peril of rum drinking and drunkenness among the apprentices he was really hitting at a practice that had its origins in seventeenth-century Barbados and Martinique and which has come to characterize the behavior of many contemporary Trinidadians and Tobagonians. He might have been somewhat disingenuous in his concerns in that he said nothing against this practice during slavery even though he knew it was harmful to the enslaved. To his admirers, however, he was "one of the most intelligent and energetic planters of an island—Trinidad—equally remarkable for intelligence, energy, moderation, and freedom from party squabbles and disputes between masters and servants" (*PG*, January 8, 1842). I am not too sure that Africans shared in this evaluation or saw him in the same light as many of his admirers.

CHAPTER 29

Waging War against Africans

≈

Give a man a seven years lease of a highly cultivated garden, and at the end of that period the chances are that you will find it a desert—give a man a portion of a desert as a freehold, and in less space than seven years the chances are that you will find it a highly cultivated garden.

—William Hardin Burnley, "*Letter to the Colonial Secretary*," 1842

AFTER TESTIFYING BEFORE the select committee in May 1842, Burnley visited his friends in London and then hurried across the channel to see his wife Charlotte. This must have been a difficult visit since Burnley had been away from his wife for such a long time. While he was in Paris, he and Charlotte discussed the possibility of her returning to Trinidad to live. At sixty-two he felt the need to be closer to his wife and his family and to regularize his domestic relations. After spending two restful months in Paris, he left for Trinidad at the end of August aboard the steamer *Isis*. As he approached Porto Santo, that beautiful Portuguese island to the northeast of Madeira, he wrote his wife to tell her how much he missed her and wanted them to resume their family life together in Trinidad.

In his letters to Charlotte he asks that she bring some of her French servants with her to Trinidad, especially her coachman and his wife. Burnley always seemed to have a problem getting good local help. He also requested that she acquire other home comforts for Orange Grove. He asks that she bring a kitchen range (stove), softer mattresses, wax candles, more furniture, and selected items they needed when they hosted their dinner parties. He also suggested that Charlotte acquire a secondhand piano, telling her where to buy it and how much to pay for it. He sent her a ground plan of the house, with measurements of rooms, "to enable her to visualise the furniture required" (*OG*, 13). Paradoxically, even as he was planning a new life for Charlotte and himself, Mrs. Farquhar and Augusta suddenly arrived at Orange Grove, the former in a delicate state of health. Burnley was either mixed up or didn't quite know what he wanted.

As he rested at home the increasing tendency of the African laborers to occupy the land continued to bother him. As they became more independent they began to occupy more lands. Consequently, Burnley became more hostile against them and raved against what, in his opinion, was a grievous crime. He felt that if the government did not deal with "this problem" immediately, it would ruin the colony completely. Moreover, the loss of productive labor (labor on the estates, as he saw it) and the cost of importing immigrants to replace them would impose an enormous financial burden on the island. In a letter to the colonial secretary, he noted: "Every squatter who retires from cultivation of our exportable produce to a mode of life which may be vastly agreeable to himself but contributes nothing to the advancement or resources of the Colony, so retires at a loss to the Colony of $30, the sum required to supply the deficiency from Africa" (*PG*, November 8, 1842).

The immigration of workers into the colony continued to be an urgent issue. On October 2, 1842, during one of its legislative sessions, Charles Chipchase, Collector of Customs, moved that the acting governor authorize the immigration agent "to hire a suitable and proper place for the reception and accommodation of all immigrants arriving from the neighboring West India islands and colonies; . . . to provide (if necessary) proper food and sustenance for immigrants located at such place, for space of three clear days at least, after their landing; and that they may be at liberty to remain in such place during one week and no longer" (*PG*, November 3, 1842). They needed to acquire a new place to receive and accommodate the new arrivals because the most prosperous planters had the first pick of the new immigrants when they landed at the private wharf of a gentleman in town. A majority of the members of the Legislative Council voted that the immigrants should be brought into a public space where all the planters could have an equal chance to recruit them and where the immigrants themselves could be given more time to decide where and with whom they wanted to work. This proposal did not sit well with Burnley and John Losh, two of the most prominent planters in the colony and senior members of the Legislative Council.

The collector argued that the resolution was designed so that African immigrants coming to the island "should not be cast upon the community as it were to the best bidder, who might offer for their services." When these immigrants were kept in a special place, they were "'snapped up' and carried away to dark holes and dungeons" (*PG*, November 3, 1842) by selected planters. In defending the motion, Henry Fuller, "the Father of the Trinidad Bar" (*PG*, "Sketches of the Trinidad Bar," March 17, 1843) and member of the Legislative Council, argued that the provision for such a place, as envisaged by the collector, was necessary. His analogy was simple; in so doing, the immigrants could make the best bargains for themselves and not be overcome by the blandishments of the first planters they encountered since they knew nothing of the land or had no friends in the colony.

Burnley believed that such a judgment should be left to the discretion of the governor who "had shewn the greatest inclination to do the best in his power in the question." He was concerned that the negative statements that were being made about the ill-treatment of the immigrants once they arrived on the island were likely to give outsiders the impression that immigrants were subjected to enormous deprivations. He noted "that after thousands of laborers had been landed here, such was still the demand for labor that parties were running after them with money in their hands, begging and praying for their services." If a house was to be provided "for the mere purpose of competition, for the benefit of the immigrants, the Government were bound to look into the character of the people competing for them; and after it came to this—the immigrant on going down to an estate, would after a week sit down and quietly and coolly calculate all the advantages he might obtain by changing his employer" (*PG*, October 3, 1842).

In a way, Burnley was still fighting the "emancipation" battle, still struggling to keep the workers under his control, and still calling upon the government to limit the choices of those living on the island and of those coming to work there. He was still trying to find the right balance between free and slave labor in a society in which there was an abundance of land. This was the same battle—determining the "sufficient price" of these laborers—that Edward Gibbon Wakefield was assessing in colonies such as Australia and Canada and which he might have discussed with Wakefield when they met earlier at one of the parliamentary hearings. Burnley reasoned that given these available tracts of land, there could be no chance of the planters obtaining labor. He argued: "If this system was permitted to continue, the people coming here would settle as squatters under their chiefs, to whom, it was known, they had a great attachment, and be of no benefit to the Colony, and all the expense incurred in aiding immigration would be thrown away" (*PG*, October 3, 1842).

Charles W. Warner, solicitor general, friend and sometimes antagonist of Burnley particularly during the governorship of Lord Harris, disagreed with Burnley.[1] He did not see how a provision that provided for "proper and salubrious habitations" on different estates could lead to an increase of squatting. He observed that there was so much competition for them among the planters, that there could be no want of food among them. He did not think that the government was encouraging more squatting by providing the immigrants a house and food for three days. He felt that the new immigrants, by associating with those who had come to the island earlier, would make better decisions and increase the possibility of their settling on the island. He reasoned: "It was not only necessary that these people coming from Africa should be provided for, but on the broad principle of justice, that the law should not only be administered but administered well, for the equal benefit of all" (*PG*, October 3, 1842).

Ultimately, the motion to secure a suitable place to receive and accommodate the Africans was carried by 6 to 3 vote. Burnley, however, was not satisfied with the results. On November 8, in a letter to Arthur White, colonial secretary, he elaborated upon his objections to squatting. He argued that any time a laborer deserted the plantation to work on his own provision ground the result was a net loss for the island. More important, such a tendency redounded to the destruction of the moral fabric of the worker. Such a bad habit was transferred unto the third and fourth generations of Africans, and the planters would always be at their mercy. Since laborer's only aim was "to enjoy the present moment. Recklessness of the future becomes a necessity, in *his* case an *absolute, virtue*" (*PG*, November 8, 1842). Such behavior, Burnley argued, would only sap the moral energies of the laborer and lead to further acts of larceny, violence, and bloodshed, which eventually terminate in guilt, shame, and misery.

The editor of the *Port of Spain Gazette* called for the prevention of this pernicious practice of squatting to counteract these violent outcomes. He argued that these establishments by the Africans and the local population should not be allowed to take root. They should be eradicated at once when they spring up. And just to make sure that this evil was eradicated from the land, he advised that the governor issue and circulate a proclamation throughout the rural districts, in English, French, and Spanish, reprobating "the practice of squatting in plain and decided terms, and declare the intention of government to suppress it by every possible means" (*PG*, November 8, 1842).

In February of 1843, speaking at the Council of Government, Burnley argued that nothing short of the elimination of squatting must be achieved in order "to carry out the work of Emancipation." He argued further that squatting should be seen as a crime in the same way that vagrancy in England was seen as a public offense. In carrying out this great work of emancipation, magistrates must show no sympathy for squatters. He declaimed: "What would be thought there [in England], when a vagrant was brought before a magistrate, and it was said, 'This man has been a vagrant for 20 years and surely you would not trouble him now.' It might be said that it was a hard case individually; but it was putting down this as a public evil and a public crime. He hopes they would not allow the little sympathetic feelings of their nature to interfere with a public duty which they had to perform" (*PG*, February 7, 1843).

Burnley believed the government should prohibit squatting and declare war against squatters. The society should show no mercy toward them. The coddling of these outcasts was acting against the public good and holding back the progress of the island. The workers themselves had no right to tend their private gardens or provision grounds. Theirs was the responsibility of making their labor available to the estates thereby ensuring the prosperity of the island and, in the process, realizing the promise of emancipation—that is, making the planters prosperous and keeping the formerly enslaved people tethered to the land. In Burnley's view, that was the destiny of the ex-slaves, being at the constant service of the planters. They could never become yeomen farmers as was the case of the laborers in the United Kingdom; such possibilities were never on the horizon.

CHAPTER 30

Domestic Matters

After passing St. Josephs, on a rising ground, to the left, the roads
became rather deep from the heavy rains we had had; we passed several
estates, and some neat looking houses. The houses of El Dorado struck
me as a very English-looking place, and extremely beautiful. The view
of the ford of Tacarigua river, is decidedly English scenery; and such as
known the river Teme, at the village of Bransford, in Worcestershire, will
find a strong resemblance.

—Mrs. Carmichael, *Domestic Manners and Social Condition*, 1833

TACARIGUA, THE VILLAGE in which Burnley's mansion was located, could
boast of its rustic charms. Alison Carmichael, a member of "the upper end
of the social spectrum of Scots in the Caribbean,"[1] arrived in St. Vincent in 1820.
Five years later she went to Trinidad. She was greeted by Sir Ralph Woodford,
the governor, and stayed at the home of the chief justice, Ashton Warner, who
accompanied her to her new residence at Laurel Hill. Warner had provided her
with his "carriage—a smart English equipage with footmen behind—she could
hardly believe that she was still in the West Indies."[2] In her book, *Domestic
Manners and Social Condition of the White, Coloured, and Negro Population of
the West Indies*, she described Laurel Hill (or Five Rivers), a village adjacent to
Tacarigua in which she settled, as being the nearest thing to an English village
in the Caribbean. She was also enthusiastic about the splendor of Burnley's
house. She observed:

One of our near neighbours was the Honorable William Burnby [sic], at Orange-Grove; and I was much charmed by the aspect of this place. Not that I considered its natural beauties at all comparable to Laurel-Hill, but it remains a marvel to me to this day, how the remarkable neatness of that place was effected by Negro labourers. The house stands in a park of some extent, studded with fine natural wood, and dotted with abundance of better-looking sheep than one usually sees in the West Indies. . . . Orange-Grove was, however, a very charming place to look at, and a very delightful place to visit.[3]

St. Mary's, the second Anglican church built on the island, added to the beauty of the village. Burnley, a committed Anglican—he was a commissioner of the Anglican Church in Trinidad from as early as 1827[4]—donated the land on which St. Mary's was built to the diocese. It opened just in time for Charlotte Burnley's anticipated return. On May 6, 1843, the Lord Bishop of the Anglican Diocese "consecrated the Church and Burial Ground of St. Mary the Virgin in the district of Tacarigua, and confirmed 26 persons." John Metivier, a former pastor of the church, in one of his musings wrote: "It is a splendid and graceful work of architecture, in what must have been the loveliest setting of any church in the country. In its original setting with the river on the south, the village green on the east, the road on the south, with sugar cane laden ox-driven carts inching along the Estate road and the high road passing by; while in the distance the cattle lazed around the pond—the closest bit to old England—it would have provided pastoral scenes fit for the brush of Constable or Mallet."[5]

To accommodate Charlotte's every possible desire, Burnley decided to renovate and expand his mansion at Orange Grove. In spite of his parsimoniousness, he wanted to make his mansion as perfect as he could for his wife's return. Although he was upset at not hearing from her through no fault of her own—the steamer bringing the mail to the country had been wrecked at Corunna—he persevered. John Lamont, Burnley's best friend, explained: "New plans were accordingly got out for the enlargement of the old house, and the erection of another house adjacent, thus greatly increasing the accommodation" (OG, 14). The necessary advertisements were placed in the Port of Spain Gazette for masons and bricklayers so that everything could be in readiness for when his wife would arrive.

In July, Burnley was still trying to convince his wife that the village had changed much since she was there last and of the exciting company that awaited her upon arrival. On July 15, he wrote to her as follows: "There is a pretty little church, at the entrance to Orange Grove, close to the River, where service is performed every Sunday by the Rev. Mr. Hamilton, who married Miss Jesse. They live close to it; and Mrs. Span, with very pretty daughters at Paradise; these with the Paseas, and Mrs. Henry Johnston at Laurel Hill, and Mrs. Dr. Carmi-chael, constitute our lady society in the Quarter" (*OG*, 14–15). In 1840, Isabella Carmichael, Alison's husband's elder daughter from his first marriage, married Charles Warner, the solicitor general of the island. Burnley considered Warner one of the three most accomplished intellectuals in the colony. William George Knox and Edward Jackson were the other two. The only problem with Burnley's praise of Alison Carmichael's company to his wife was that Carmichael had left the island in 1833. There seems to be no record of her having returned to the island after that date.

Even as he courted his wife and sought her return home, Burnley was not as transparent about his fortune as his wife thought he should be. While he was urging her to return to Orange Grove, Lamont visited Charlotte in England and gave her a good estimate of Burnley's wealth. It may not have been deliberate but the result of this information seems to have dissuaded Charlotte from rushing back to Burnley's arms. At any rate, Burnley had to write Charlotte as quickly as he could to counter whatever impression Lamont had left on her mind (*OG*, 15). After his death, Charlotte questioned the accuracy of his fortune.

All of a sudden, Burnley reported delays in his renovation plan. On August 13, he wrote to his wife that she had better not leave her "sweet tranquil cottage at Blackheath" in East London where she was staying until she heard from him. He equivocated about the progress of the building operations at Orange Grove. He said: "A spell of heavy rain has injured the tapia walls of the east wing, now up for 22 years." (Tapia, a clay-like material made from mud and leaves, was used to construct the walls of buildings in those days.) But his ardor had cooled. He wasn't sounding as enthusiastic about welcoming Charlotte back home as he had before. One month later, on September 18, he told her that there would be further building delays; that tradesmen were likely to be all over the house for months to come, and therefore "I am really in hopes that you will find it more agreeable to remain in Europe" (*OG*, 15). And then, inadvertently, he let the cat out of the bag. He sought to assuage her: "You need not fear for Willie and me. We shall have Augusta Farquhar to keep house for us. She will occupy the bedroom next to the drawing room." At this point, as his biographer points out, "the long series of letters to Mrs. Burnley ends" (*OG*, 16).

Charlotte may have smelled a rotten rat in the bag. Without any written explanation she refused to return to the island. There were too many references in his letters to Mrs. Farquhar and her daughter Augusta. For several years Burnley had been begging his wife to come out to Trinidad to live with him, even if only for the winters, which were very cold in Europe. Then, just when it seemed that she had decided to come out to the island, Burnley asked her to stay a year longer because the workmen were likely to prove worrisome and disruptive. Then she learns that Augusta, who had left for New York in April of that year to mourn her mother's death, had returned to the island and was staying at Orange Grove, with Burnley. Not only was she staying at Orange Grove, but she was declared to be an excellent housekeeper occupying "the best bedroom, next to the drawing room—for which Charlotte has been choosing furniture for the last two years" (*OG*, 16). Something was not right with that scenario. Charlotte must have opined that their relationship was over and that Augusta had taken her place in her husband's affection. On the other hand, she might have lost interest in the relationship or, at any rate, began to question Burnley's sincerity.

Augusta, a younger woman than Charlotte, had made herself much more available to Burnley when he needed a woman's comfort and her sympathy. Nor, for that matter, was she unaware of how much he was worth and that may have played into her calculations. Taking his cue from those around him, Burnley decided that Augusta could have substituted for his wife until she returned to the island. As a matter of fact, he must have been romantically involved with Augusta from the late 1830s. While Charlotte lived in London and Paris, Augusta had the opportunity to get closer to Burnley. Their relationship intensified after Burnley returned to Trinidad at the end of 1842 when Burnley began to reduce his travel abroad. Even while he was courting Charlotte intensely during the early part of 1843, Augusta was laying her claims for the man. Before Charlotte knew it, Burnley had succumbed totally to Augusta's charms. This is one reason why the letters between Burnley and Charlotte ceased so abruptly after September 1843.

Finally, around 1845, the renovations on the mansion were completed. The finished product was breathtaking in its beauty. In 1849 Burnley commissioned Michel-Jean Cazabon, one of Trinidad's leading landscape painters of the nineteenth century, to paint twelve of the most beautiful scenes on the island. He chose Burnley's newly renovated mansion as one of his subjects. In his *West View of Orange Grove, Water Color, 1849* (the title Cazabon gave to the painting), he captured this magnificent building with its tall porticoes, dormer windows, and imposing structure. As if to replicate Carmichael's earlier description of the place, Cazabon placed in the foreground some cattle grazing on the savannah and a water pond with lilies at the lower left of the painting. He located the mansion at the center of the painting, with two stately palm trees in front of the mansion that highlighted its magisterial presence. He even included a coolie pistash tree at the side of the building to give a flavor of the local landscape. Today, the coolie pistash tree still stands as a reminder of a time when that luxurious building graced the Tacarigua savannah.

In 1856, L. A. A. de Verteuil commented on the grandeur of Burnley's mansion. He observed: "Several country residences can bear comparison with English and French villas, viz., that of the late Mr. Burnley, Tacarigua; or late Mr. L. Agostini, St. Ann; [Fritz] Zurcher, Dr. de Boisiere and Cipriani, in the neighborhood of Port of Spain."[6] His book was designed "to make Trinidad better known to the British public in general and to its own inhabitants.[7] In 1946, when Norman Lamont, grandnephew of John Lamont, delivered his lecture on Burnley to the Historical Society of Trinidad and Tobago, he reminisced about Orange Grove recalling "the magnificent pasture, like a fine English park, with its spreading saman trees, its well-kept fences and its ornamental water" (*OG*, 14) that was still available for viewing. It was the fading grandeur of that magnificent structure that I saw as a boy when I was growing up in Tacarigua, Trinidad.

Even as he sorted out his domestic affairs, Burnley made an effort to integrate himself into the social life of the island. At the beginning of July, he announced that his nephew dined with Sir Henry MacLeod and that he, too, had participated in an evening party and quadrille dance at the governor's home. Burnley, however, was not very enthusiastic about the event. He said, "The Governor and his Lady seem sensible, quiet people, and I think we shall respect and esteem them, but they will not be very conducive to society, as their manners are reserved and distant—at least his; and she seems disposed to be led by him" (*OG*, 14). Around the end of July, Duncan Stewart, Burnley's partner in the Savanetta estates, visited Charlotte and informed her that Burnley was doing fine and that "it is delightful to see how active, and cheerful he is, and his interest in everything" (*OG*, 15). One does not quite know what he told Charlotte about Burnley's "fine princely fortune."

Burnley even attempted to pass on to his wife the gossip of the island and indulged in talk about female society so as to interest his wife about the womanly ways of the society. On August 13, 1843, he told Charlotte about the growing unpopularity of the governor and his wife (*OG*, 15). Burnley had good reason to malign them. They were exact opposites in policy and temperament. While MacLeod was a liberal in his political views, Burnley was a conservative; while MacLeod was sympathetic to the aspirations of the newly freed blacks and the coloreds, Burnley was determined to keep them in their place. On October 26, 1846, Alexander Fitzjames, a colored man of property and an attorney (called to the English bar in 1847), remarked: "No man I believe landed on the shores of Trinidad with more liberal views. No governor ever secured so suddenly the good feelings of the oppressed population than did Sir Henry MacLeod. My heart beat with joy at his inauguration when he stated that he would use his endeavors to put down the prejudices of cash and complexion."[8]

Fitzjames had special reason to welcome MacLeod. The colored population, or the free mulattoes, had suffered tremendously under the oppressive rule of previous governors, beginning with Sir Ralph Woodford, who went out of their way to deny the coloreds the advantages they had won under Spanish rule. Fitzjames argued that MacLeod's public announcement that he would do everything in his power to eliminate the prejudice of money and race must have offended Burnley. Such a threat was strengthened by the reputation for fairness that MacLeod had gained in St. Kitts where he had previously served as governor. When MacLeod's councilors realized how liberal he was and his determination to treat the nonwhite population fairly, "They resorted to their old intrigue and ensnared him. And if it be enquired into I have no doubt but that he soon regretted his fellowship with his councilors and moreso his separation from the Chief Justice."[9]

Five months after Burnley's comments about the governor's unpopularity, MacLeod resigned from his post because of "violent and repeated illness."[10] Although there were other complicated political reasons for MacLeod's resignation, there can be no doubt that Burnley's negativity contributed to his departure from the island but not before he was able to accomplish some good for the society. On the eve of his departure, Burnley had many complimentary things to say about MacLeod's tenure as governor. One is not too sure it erased totally the many harmful things that Burnley had said about the man and his tenure.

CHAPTER 31

Land Occupation

It requires no great experience amongst the lowest orders of society to discover that many will become useful members of society if allowed to cultivate their own lands, who if forced to labor for wages, would only turn to the idle and dissolute life of smugglers or poachers in England, and to that of squatters in Trinidad.

—Lord Harris, 1847

AFTER APPRENTICESHIP, THE question of squatting (or what I prefer to call land occupation) remained one of the most pressing issues for the planters. While the planters saw squatting as a plague upon their house, the ex-slaves saw this mode of land acquisition as a vital avenue through which they could achieve their freedom. In fact, the ex-slaves saw their ultimate liberation as consisting of their ability to possess a plot of land to house themselves and their families and a space to grow and cultivate their crops. Hence, their first act after apprenticeship was to occupy the land (what else could they do?) to make a new life for themselves. C. L. R. James has argued that the ultimate aim of all revolutions and revolts is the acquisition of land. He noted that after the Civil War, African Americans "tried to take land. They had fought with an instinctive confidence that it was going to be theirs, so much so that much of the idleness and discontent in certain areas after the Civil War [and their emancipation] could be traced to the fact that they had not got what they expected. In certain areas they actually seized the land and refused to return it."[1]

The ex-slaves in Trinidad and the West Indies displayed similar traits as their American counterparts. They wanted land. Had they been able to settle peacefully on the land, their social evolution may have taken a different trajectory. They may have become a body of peasant proprietors working side by side with the owners of central sugar factories seeing themselves as *partners* rather than *antagonists* of their former masters. In 1847, when Lord Harris had to decide what to do with ex-slaves who had occupied crown lands, he described seeing "a thriving village with a respectable and loyal population and which I shall loath to disturb and most distressed to see harshly dealt with, which is composed almost entirely of settlers upon Crown Lands. To force them to buy now would very likely ruin many, and any attempt to oblige them to return to the state of hired laborers would certainly render them discontented and probably fail."[2]

During the period, land-occupancy patterns among the ex-slaves were a pressing matter for Burnley consuming much of his time. On February 7, 1843, the governor laid before the Legislative Council a report from John Carter, whom the governor had sent to Naparima on a special mission to report on the extent of squatting in that area. Stemming from his findings the governor directed the stipendiary magistrates to proceed against those who had occupied crown lands for less than twelve months and asked Edward Jackson, the attorney general, to be more considerate of anyone who had held lands for more than twelve months.

On June 12, 1843, the governor met with members of the Legislative Council to discuss the final settlement of the squatting question. The editor of the *Port of Spain Gazette* was delighted by the governor's declaration that "to treat parties who had cultivated land under permission of the Commandants—who had been 8 to 11 years in possession of their locations—as mere Squatters, would be cruel and unjust." The newspaper was even more pleased that Burnley, "the originator of the movement with regard to Squatting, express[ed] his entire concurrence in that opinion (we say this, because the honorable gentleman once seemed to entertain somewhat sterner opinions on the subject) and we should have been sorry to find the originator of a measure which had our approbation, and which was in itself most wholesome and beneficial, spoiling a good cause by anything which savored of hardship and oppression." The *Port of Spain Gazette*, however, could not help but draw its readers' attention to the ill-effects of such "an indiscriminate and extensive donation of land as regards the general polity and good government of the Colony." Granting land on such easy terms, it said, would lead laborers to withdraw from the cultivation of sugar, which "can never be of any use to the mass of society." They felt that "the greatest evil in the settlement of this Colony was the dispersion of the inhabitants over such a vast extent of country—and though this evil cannot now be remedied, there is surely no occasion to go on increasing it" (*PG*, June 20, 1843).

The governor's decision to allow some of the squatters to remain on crown land left in limbo the fate of the ex-slaves who had occupied private lands. On July 20, a committee appointed by the governor to come up with a "final policy" on land occupation met with the attorney general to see whether it had any jurisdiction over squatting on private lands.[3] When the Colonial Land and Emigration Board, set up by the Colonial Office in 1840 to superintend emigration and the disposal of wastelands, met in early 1844, they divided the squatters into those who were on the land before January 1, 1834, and those who occupied the land afterward. While lenient terms were to be accorded to the former class who would be permitted to acquire a title on making certain reasonable payments for same, "the others are to be more strictly dealt with, and in their case it is to be the exception instead of the rule, to permit them to acquire a right to the lands on which they have settled" (*PG*, February 16, 1843). There was little sympathy for those squatting on private land.

Although Burnley was harsh against squatters, he seemed to have some affection for the village in which his mansion was located. On September 5, 1843, he voted with other members of the Legislative Council to provide the sum of five hundred dollars to purchase a quarry of land for the Tacarigua parsonage. In October 1845, he persuaded the Legislative Council to allocate £2,500 to repair St. Mary's Anglican Church in Tacarigua (*PG*, August 5, 1845). Yet when it came to allocating funds to support the education of ex-slaves, Burnley felt that "as a general principle that the parents were well able to pay for the education of their children, and it was only right that they should pay for it." Arthur White, the colonial secretary, felt that many of the teachers "were incompetent and should be examined by a competent Committee of Education" (*PG*, September 5, 1843).

Besides being dead set against their squatting, Burnley was willing to prosecute the ex-slaves for walking on his estates. At one of the Legislative Council meetings, he wanted to know what were the laws respecting the right of persons going about his estates without permission. He argued that the proprietors in the country were "much aggrieved by persons trespassing on their lands. . . . They were in great danger from fire, from these people passing through the cane pieces with lighted segars [*sic*]." He asked: "If he had a field ploughed up, and a man chose to walk diagonally instead of straight across it, or was firing at birds through the cane piece, or shooting whatever he chose; if the proprietor could not get redress, they should bring a law to prevent these trespasses, and that the laboring population should be made to know what their relative duties were" (*PG*, November 3, 1843).

Burnley felt there were so many laws buried in the Spanish code that he did not know where to find the appropriate law governing such behavior. George

Scotland, the chief justice, suggested that one need not turn to the old Spanish laws to find an answer to that question. Anyone who felt that his property was trespassed upon could bring an action in the court of the first instance or the complaint court "where actions were generally tried before the Chief Justice, or, at least, before one of the Judges of the land. Burnley wasn't satisfied with this answer. He pointed out that in 1838 a trespass ordinance was passed but was disallowed because of a protest by the then chief justice" (*PG*, November 3, 1843).[4]

Charles Warner came to the aid of the chief justice by explaining to Burnley that the common law in Trinidad was the same as it was in England or Spain, no man had a right to trespass on another man's property. He advised Burnley that if an owner found a man trespassing on his land, he "could tell him to leave softly; then he could urge him a little more strongly if he did not leave; then he could take him gently at first; and if that would not do, take him not quite so gently; and if he still resisted, get assistance and bundle him off neck and crop, as it was called" (*PG*, November 3, 1843). However, he cautioned the planters that any trespass ordinance they passed that prevented the ordinary laborer from walking on an estate would not be regarded kindly in England.

Burnley was pleased that the planters could bring matters of trespassing to the stipendiary magistrates. He reminded the solicitor general that planters in Trinidad enjoyed a different relationship with their workers than landowners in England. However, he was not inclined to accept the solicitor general's suggestion as to how to remove trespassers from his lands. He informed the solicitor general that the use of "neck and crop" to remove trespassers off his estates was "rather a dangerous experiment, particularly where there were 300 or 400 persons living on an estate, and the proprietor or manager had only his overseer to assist him" (*PG*, November 3, 1843).

Just when Sierra Leone was turning out to be barren soil in terms of recruiting workers for the island, the example of East Indians going off to Mauritius and British Guiana proved to be welcome news for the planters of Trinidad.[5] In July 1844 the *Port of Spain Gazette* revealed that a plan had been drawn up by the West India Body in England and George William Hope, undersecretary of state for the colonies, for the bringing of Indians from India to relieve the labor shortage on the island. However, on July 25, Warner let the cat out of the bag when, at a meeting called by the Presbyterians at the Greyfriars Church to discuss the Ecclesiastical Bill, he announced that "We are shortly expecting a large increase in our population by the importation of Coolies. I believe these people are capable of instruction, and it would be a great check to their returning, if they adopted a purer religion than their own."[6] Such was the glee of the planters' voice—the *Port of Spain Gazette* was considered to be "the voice of the planters"—at these announcements, it could not help but pour scorn upon the hold that these "unfortunate blacks" had upon the market:

> The boon, so long and loudly called for by the planters of British Guiana and for which not a few of our Trinidad Agriculturalists have been secretly sighing, is at last conceded to us. The Hill Coolies of the East are to be summoned to the aid of the "field Negroes" of the West, diminished in number by the advancement of many to a higher step in the social scale and the retirement of very many more to the *otium cum dignitate* [leisure with dignity] of a Guinea grass patch, a plantain walk, or a cassava garden. (*PG*, "Immigration from the East Indies," July 2, 1844)

As if in anticipation of this move, at a special meeting on June 29, Burnley's Agricultural and Immigration Society adopted a resolution to be debated at its general meeting on July 12 that demanded an immediate reduction in the money expenditures of all the sugar estates in the country. They believed that such a reduction in wages was imperative for the future success of the industry (*PG*, "Proposed Reduction of Wages," July 2, 1844). Whatever may be said of the planters, they were not merely crying wolf. Besides the duties that the British government placed on sugar, the slave-grown sugar of Cuba, Brazil, and the United States combined to have devastating effects on the Trinidad owners' free-grown sugar. David Hughes observed: "In possibly the first 'fair trade' movement, Anglo-Caribbean growers pleaded with Parliament for the application of an import tariff or boycott against slave-made sugar—but to no avail."[7]

On September 24, the *Port of Spain Gazette* announced the great news. Two thousand and five hundred Hill Coolies were destined to come to Trinidad. The newspaper implored the planters to make adequate preparations for the new arrivals. It suggested that the planters use the houses that the ex-slaves had vacated. They had preferred to erect their own houses "at their own cost on their land, and although they continued to work on the property, gave up their cottages to their employers as an object of no value" (*PG*, "The Coolies," September 24, 1844). The newspaper also urged the planters to be considerate about the feelings of the ex-slaves and remarked: "Up to the present hour much credit is due to the native population for the way in which they have behaved as regards the immigrants introduced from various sources. True there was no just ground for jealousy; for Trinidad is large enough, and can afford employment for everyone" (*PG*, September 24, 1844).

As far as the ex-slaves were concerned, the pending arrival of the Indians merely represented the coming of another set of workers onto the island. Their major concern revolved around how best to accommodate themselves to their new condition of freedom by becoming owners of land and useful members of their society.

CHAPTER 32

The New Order of Things

≷

> You will probably be aware that we are very particularly situated with our negro apprentices in the West Indies, and that it is a matter of doubt and uncertainty, how far they may be induced to continue their services on the plantations after their apprenticeship expires in 1840. . . . It is of great importance to us to endeavour to provide a portion of other laborers, whom we might use as a set-off, and, when the time for it comes, make us, as far as possible, *independent of our negro population.*
>
> —John Gladstone to Messrs. Gillanders, Arbuthnot & Co., 1846

ON MAY 30, 1845, after ninety-six days at sea, the *Fatel Rozack* arrived in Port of Spain, Trinidad, from Calcutta, bringing 225 East Indians to the island. Six Indians died en route to the colony. This voyage was simply the continuation of a policy that began on January 4, 1836, when John Gladstone, an absentee owner, wrote to Messrs. Gillanders, Arbuthnot and Co., informing them that his company, in light of the upcoming end of apprenticeship, carded for 1840, would have to institute different arrangements to make itself, "as far as possible, *independent of our negro population.*"[1] As a result of this policy, 419 Indians landed in Guyana in 1838 where they were assigned to plantations owned by Messrs. Gladstone, John and Henry Moss, Andrew Colville, and James Blair. A majority of the Indians (229) went to Gladstone's plantation.[2] It was only a matter of time before the Indians were sent to the other British colonies to replace the Negro workers there. Although a few of the Indians went to other counties, the bulk of them came to Guyana and Trinidad.[3]

The morning after the Indians arrived in Trinidad, Governor MacLeod visited the *Fatel Rozack* to inquire into their conditions. He discovered that "several of them [the Indians] who had been in Mauritius and who spoke terrible French afforded me the opportunity of conversing with them freely. From what I could learn they all seemed perfectly contented and in good spirits."[4] Of the 1,938 Indians who came to the island between May 30, 1845, and May 2, 1846, ninety settled on Burnley's plantations (Cedar Hill, Union Hall, Phoenix Park, and Esperanza). Twenty-two others settled at Otaheite Estate that was jointly owned by Burnley's son William Frederick, George Eccles, Robert Eccles, William Eccles, and John Ronald (*TRG*, June 3, 1846).

On April 17, at a sitting of the Legislative Council, Burnley moved that an address adopted by the Board of Council be presented to Governor MacLeod at the end of his governorship on the island. The address—read by Thomas Johnson, clerk of the council—praised the governor for introducing trial by jury, encouraging the recruitment of new immigrants (particularly Indians), supporting the agricultural interests on the island, and the establishment of the Colonial Hospital and the Leper Asylum. It also acknowledged that the governor had secured "the respect and confidence of the community by an honest, manly and candid discharge of the trust confided to you devoid of all affectation or display" (*PG*, April 17, 1846). Interestingly, Burnley's signature (followed by Charles Warner and William George Knox, barrister and chief justice of Trinidad, 1849–1869) was the first of over three hundred distinguished inhabitants who offered their "sincere respect for your person, and our deep sense of the many benefits which we have derived from your government" (*PG*, "Valedictory Address to Sir Henry MacLeod," April 21, 1846).

The next evening, Saturday, April 18, thirty-eight of the most distinguished inhabitants sat down at the Union Club, one of the most luxurious clubs on the island, to a "tastefully arranged and well devised banquet" to bid Governor MacLeod his final farewell. Burnley was extremely sentimental on this occasion. In a toast "replete with good taste and feeling," Burnley admitted that although he was pleased to be at the banquet he would readily have foregone "all this pleasure and all this gratification could they only retain His Excellency for some time longer" (*PG*, "Dinner to His Excellency, Sir Henry MacLeod," April 21, 1846). Although Burnley was "personally acquainted, sometimes intimately," with every British governor who had ruled the island since its capture in 1797 and had the highest regard for Governors Picton and Woodford, he claimed: "It could never be said of them, what might be most truly and conscientiously asserted of Sir Henry MacLeod that he closed his official career without leaving behind him, amongst the honest and well disposed and intelligent portion of this community, a single enemy" (*PG*, April 21, 1846). This was praise indeed.

Burnley took the opportunity to explain his differences with MacLeod's administration. He claimed what MacLeod had done in the colony was "well and ably done." This, he said, was the "universal feeling" of the inhabitants. Resisting suggestions that he bore malice toward MacLeod, he insisted that "any difference of opinion which might have existed amongst them with respect to the nature of Sir Henry's Government went only, as to the *extent of its merits*" (italics in the original). He believed that MacLeod's most outstanding achievement was the "lucid order, method and arrangement of the public accounts" which he felt "might advantageously compare with any of the best regulated of Her Majesty's dependencies. . . . In his humble opinion this was merit of the highest order" (*PG*, April 21, 1846).

On April 20, "our respected and beloved governor" left for England, so said the *Port of Spain Gazette* (*PG*, "Departure of Sir Henry MacLeod," April 21, 1846). Some of the most respectable inhabitants of the island accompanied him to the wharf and bade him farewell. Prior to his departure, a deputation consisting of Messrs. Richard Darling, Louis Boissiere, T. B. Darracott, Joseph Andre, and Henry James Mills presented him with the "Valedictory Address" that Burnley and his other colleagues signed in appreciation of MacLeod's service to the colony. Having served as governor from 1840, they appreciated how well he guided the state of ship in those turbulent years after apprenticeship. Even a poem, "The Good Sir Henry," was composed in memory of his service to the colony.[5]

The arrival of the Indians represented a partial triumph for the planters and held out the possibility that a resolution of their financial problems may be close at hand. It also gave them more power to appeal to British capitalists to invest in the island's economy. An editorial in the *Port of Spain Gazette* proposed three ways in which to exploit this new condition: the introduction of a railway to the colony to provide for the better transportation system to take the sugarcane and other produce to the factories, the creation of factories to centralize the manufacture of sugar, and the introduction of tramroads that would be "the arteries through which a new and profitable impulse and extension of cultivation would be introduced and thus add to the traffic and consequent profits of the Trinidad Railway Company" (*PG*, "The Trinidad Railway," November 28, 1845).

The introduction of a railway to the island captured the fancy of the planters and other business people on the island. Burnley brought up the subject during the hearings of his subcommittee of the Agricultural and Immigration

Society. On June 30, 1841, he asked Frederick Brown, one of the witnesses, about "the practicality of forming railroads in this [Trinidad] colony," to which the latter responded in the affirmative. Asked if he thought it would be a profitable venture, Brown replied that such was "the fertility of the soil, that with a sufficient population the establishment of sugar estates would be close and concentrated on each side of the line of the road, and the quantity of produce passing over it would amply repay the cost of formation and annual repairs" (*O*, 92). Horatio Nelson Huggins, a planter who had moved to Trinidad in 1820, was also excited about the possibilities of introducing rail service to the island, particularly in terms of the tremendous savings that would accrue to the planters. He was "the proprietor of the Bronte estate, and half proprietor of Nassau estate and Union Hall plantation in South Naparima."[6] His nephew of the same name wrote *Hiroona: An Historical Romance in Poetic Form*, which Paula Burnett called "the Caribbeans' first epic poem."[7]

In October 1841 the Trinidad Railway Company was formed "to supply the valuable island of Trinidad with the advantages of railway communications. No part of the British dominions appears to present greater natural facilities to the construction, or to afford a better prospect of return for the capital required to invest" (*PG*, "Trinidad Railway Company," October 14, 1841). Once Lord Harris became the governor of the island, one of his major objectives was to make the construction of the railway a reality. On May 21, 1846, less than one month after he took office, he informed William Gladstone, secretary of state, that after studying the correspondences between Gladstone and Governor MacLeod, he (Harris) had concluded that "energetic support should be given to this company at the present time. I do not think that any better method of doing so could be proposed than that of giving them a certain quantity of Crown Lands, under certain conditions."[8]

In 1845, Jamaica established the first railway line in the Caribbean while Barbados was raising funds to do the same (*PG*, "Railroads in the West Indies," July 22, 1845).[9] In speaking about the feasibility of a similar project for Trinidad, the editor of the *Port of Spain Gazette* observed that the "only difficulty in the matter that presents itself is the want of capital—and that difficulty got over, there would be no question as to the success of a TRINIDAD RAILWAY COMPANY." The editor insisted that the capital for this enterprise must come from England "for every shilling of available capital in the colony has already its full employment" (*PG*, July 22, 1845). The article called upon the influential residents—a virtual Who's Who in the colony—to urge their associates in the United Kingdom to invest in this project (*PG*, "Railroads in the West Indies, July 22, 1845).

On October 17, 1845, E. Taverner of New Broad Street, London, and Henry Stone and S. N. Rooks, solicitors, ran an advertisement in the *Port of Spain Gazette* reminding the public that a company had been formed to carry out "a complete system of RAILWAYS in Trinidad and negotiations on the subject with the most influential Residents and Proprietors of Estates and the Principal Mercantile Houses in this Kingdom interested in the Trade with that Island, are now pending." It also informed them that the company would soon ask the Legislative Council to adopt an ordinance to allow the company to conduct business on the island.

William Macredie, who was sent to Trinidad by Phoenix Fire Insurance Company of London in the 1830s to establish an insurance agency, became the secretary of the local committee of the Trinidad Railway Company. On December 5, 1845, he intimated the company's intention to ask the Legislative Council to bring forward an ordinance in February 1846 to allow the company to make and maintain railways or tramroads with proper warehouses, wharves, landing places, tunnels, bridges, viaducts and suitable and commodious erections, road communication and conveniences. He also laid out the proposed routes of the railway and tramways. On March 6, 1846, Macredie informed Governor MacLeod that the company was about to complete its survey of the lines upon which the projected railway would be laid down but felt he had a duty "to ascertain the full extent of encouragement which the government of Trinidad may afford to the company to induce the shareholders to proceed in their construction of the railway and other important works therewith connected."[10]

On December 26, 1846, Sir John Rae Reid wrote to Earl Grey, the new secretary of state for the colonies (who assumed the position on July 6, 1846), to remind him of the encouragement the British government had given to the company during its infant days and to inform him that the cost of the project had escalated to £1,000,000. He repeated some of the same points that Horatio N. Huggins had made at Burnley's hearing in 1841, which suggests that he and his colleagues had studied the hearings of Burnley's subcommittee carefully. Although the Committee of Management felt assured that the project would generate "a considerable and increasing return, they regret to find, however, that they cannot impart the same confidence to the shareholders of the company."[11] The committee was not prepared to proceed with the project unless the government was willing to guarantee a yearly dividend of 5 percent to the company. In the event that the company profits exceeded 5 percent, the surplus would be paid to the government (*PG*, "Legislative Summary," June 1, 1847).

Reid and his committee were confident that the Trinidad government would support their project given their believability in its potential profitability; the power of their lobbying efforts in London (after all, Reid was a director of the Bank of England for ten years and a director of the London and Bristol Railroad Company); and the eagerness of the Trinidad government to establish a railway to open up the country and to alleviate its financial crisis. At that time, a government's guarantee of a yearly dividend (5 percent was the normal rate) was practiced in some countries that were engaged in the railroad industry. Trinidad's need for capital infusion would trump all other considerations. More to the point, Earl Grey and Lord Harris supported the project enthusiastically and unequivocally.

The company did not count on the stubbornness of Burnley, "the only resident capitalist in this colony . . . worthy of the name" (*PG*, "Capital and its Application," June 26, 1846), who was riding out the financial crisis fairly unscathed and who was deathly afraid that the establishment of a railway would have a devastating effect upon his business. While absentee proprietors suffered greatly from the crisis, resident proprietors "having proper command of capital . . . yielded . . . a fair interest for the capital invested" (*PG*, June 26, 1846) and Burnley was "one of the largest resident slave owners in the Caribbean."[12]

Although Burnley might have been enthusiastic about the railway project in 1841, by 1847 his ardor had cooled. More concerned with consolidating his wealth and protecting the advantages he had gained during the previous years, Burnley felt tremendous unease at the prospect of a new economic venture in "his" territory. He also felt that the construction of the railway would draw laborers away from his estate. As a resident proprietor, Burnley believed he had more to lose than the railway investors who saw Trinidad as just another avenue of generating an assured profit on their capital, which led him to describe the introduction of railroads as antithetical to the "existing propriety interest of the colony" (*PG*, "Railway Debated," June 18, 1847). Although he felt tremendous uneasiness at having this infrastructural project placed in his backyard and saw it as a potential threat to his capital and his wealth, the importance of this facility led to intense discussion about its usefulness for the island's development.

CHAPTER 33

The Great Railway Debate

The Trinidad Government has a strong motive to render every assistance in its power, for it cannot fail to be perceived that the construction of the lines of railway exhibited on the plans, will greatly tend to advance the prosperity of that colony, and there is no doubt that the inhabitants generally will duly appreciate their importance.

—"Trinidad Railway," *Railway Record*, November 21, 1845

ALTHOUGH BURNLEY WAS the preeminent voice in the colony during the first fifty years of its history, by 1847 his voice had begun to fade and Charles Warner, twenty-five years his junior, began his ascendancy in the island's social and political hierarchy. While Burnley was a product of an earlier age, Warner instinctually had a better understanding of the colony's requirements as it sought to launch itself into a new era. In an age of "railway mania," he understood the important role railways would play in a country's development. In England railway mania led to the laying down of thousands of miles of railway tracts that sped up the delivery of goods and mails and released an essentially agrarian population "from bondage to the land into relative prosperity."[1] Karl Marx, drawing on India's example, recognized that the railway system would become "the forerunner of modern industry."[2] Warner saw the introduction of the railway into Trinidad as a means of launching the country into modernity (that is, into a new colonial-capitalist path) and a way to further his Anglicization project of the island.

Warner's political trajectory was similar to Burnley's. His long tenure as attorney general made him the power behind the throne. While governors came and went—many of whom were his classmates at Eton—he remained a constant in the government's structure. Without his knowing it, he was being groomed by the colonial establishment to take Burnley's place in the official hierarchy.[3] During the first two weeks of June 1847, Warner had the responsibility of piloting resolutions on the Trinidad Railway Company through the Legislative Council. On June 1, he laid before the board a dispatch from Earl Grey covering the correspondence between the Colonial Office and Sir John Rae Reid, chairman of the Board of Directors. He informed the council that the company proposed to lay down ninety miles of railroad at a cost of £1,000,000.

The company promised to limit its first outlay to £300,000 and to carry out "the most advantageous part of the work." They also required that the government grant them one thousand acres of crown lands for every mile of rail they laid down and that the land thus granted to the company should be put up "by them to private auction and disposed of at not less than the minimum price of other Crown Lands, and one fifth of the net proceeds paid over to the treasury." They also demanded that timber on such crown lands should be considered "the exclusive property of the company;" that the mineral in the land, if any, should also belong to the company; and that the company "have permission to enter on any Crown Lands, and to cut and carry away timber for the purposes of the railway" (*PG*, "Railway Debate, No. 1," June 8, 1847).

Although it was not alluded to in Earl Grey's correspondence, Lord Harris wanted to know whether the company intended to import European workmen to carry out its project or to employ Trinidadian workers "in which case it would have a serious effect on the labor market" (*PG*, "Legislative Matters," June 1, 1847). He raised this concern in his correspondence with Gladstone on May 21, 1846, when he sought to encourage support for the construction of the railway.[4] He was also concerned about the amount of lands that would be granted to the company but thought it best to consider this and other such matters when the full debate on the issue began on the subsequent Monday.

The council began its discussion on Monday, June 7, on the resolution guaranteeing a 5 percent dividend on the £300,000 the company invested. Burnley reminded the council that he was the first to point out the great advantages of having railroads in the colony and that William Curtis, the company's engineer, in preparing his report on the feasibility of establishing such a railroad, drew on the findings of his subcommittee hearings of 1841 to arrive at his conclusions.

Therefore, Burnley was "justly entitled to consider himself as the father of the scheme for establishing railways in Trinidad and he wanted to assure his learned friend [the attorney general] that he was not going wantonly only and wickedly to throw his bantling overboard." Although he strongly supported the establishment of a railroad, he wanted to be sure it existed "for the advantage of the community not for the exclusive profit for any monied company in London." In the light of this, he considered the proposition to guarantee the company an annual dividend of 5 percent from the Colonial Treasury "to be monstrous and extravagant and calculated beyond every other measure to render it impossible for the company to succeed" (PG, June 8, 1847).

As a former slave owner and capitalist, Burnley believed in the sanctity of private property. To him, a government guarantee was one way to ensure that a company would fail. Such guarantees, he said, were not in keeping with the traditional approaches of capitalist development as found in the image of Adam Smith's "invisible hand" and Jean-Baptiste Say's "law" that production creates its own demand.[5] He averred: "To give a bounty in the shape of a guaranteed dividend to the railroad company, would be a bonus in favor of negligence, waste and mismanagement. He doubted under such circumstances whether the foundation of the railroad would be well and substantially performed" (PG, June 8, 1847). Given his wealth, he preferred to see minimal state activity and a greater emphasis on the ingenuity of the entrepreneur in a developing economy.

Although such subsidies were given in India and Europe, Burnley believed that they had no place in Trinidad. In India, for example, Sir Henry Hardinge, governor general of the country and an Etonian like Warner, played a significant role in the development of the railway. The railway there was granted subsidies to assist in its development. Burnley held that such a subsidy was given at "the emphatic recommendation" of the governor general because of "its immense military advantages and the saving it would create in the war and ordinance departments. Such a work could never be cited as a precedent bearing on the present subject—it was principally for military and not for commercial purposes, and was entirely excluded from the category of free trade principles" (PG, June 8, 1847).

Warner rejected Burnley's objections, which he said might apply to a railroad "in an old settled country but when they came to a new country it was entirely different." In a new country, the entire burden of developing a new industry such as the railway depended on government's assistance. Although he accepted Burnley's paternity of the railroad, "nothing," he said, "could justify Burnley "treating his child with the unmitigated severity with which he had treated it." In his view, the £20,000 per month the Home Government paid to the Royal Mail Steam Packet Company to deliver mail to the West Indies was similar to the dividends for which the railroad company was asking. As to the economic viability of the project, Warner felt assured about its prospect: "When I see the names of Sir J. R. Reid, Barclay, Hankey, Marryat, Wilson, and others, gentlemen so largely connected with the island, it proves to me that this is no bubble company got up by men who have no capital or anything else to lose" (*PG*, June 8, 1847).

This was the most important of all the propositions offered, the guaranteeing of a yearly dividend of 5 percent to the shareholders of the company. If, at the end of the year, the railway made no profit on the £300,000 it proposed to spend, then the government would be liable to the company annually for the sum of £15,000 or about one-fifth of the colony's annual revenues. The *Port of Spain Gazette* noted: "This is the extreme risk of the case, as it appears at a first glance but by a little management, the risk can be considerably managed, and on closer examination, the real loss to the colony would not be by any means so great a loss as it first appears" (*PG*, "The Railway Propositions," June 15, 1847). One can only assume that the members of council took this financial calculation into consideration when they voted for this proposition by 9 votes to 1. Only Burnley voted against it.

Burnley also opposed the second proposition that called for granting the railway company one thousand acres of crown lands in alternate blocks for every mile of rail it constructed, subject to the company paying over one-fifth of the proceeds of those lands, when sold, to the Colonial Treasury. Burnley considered this giving away of the colony's lands to be "more extravagant and extraordinary" than the 5 percent dividend agreed upon in the first resolution. He also believed that the railway company would draw workers away from the surrounding estates and that would prove to be "a ruinous nuisance to his neighbors." Indeed, two of Burnley's estates—Orange Grove in Tacarigua and Golden Grove in Arouca—were situated along the first line of railroad that was proposed to be constructed between Port of Spain and Arouca, so Burnley stood to lose if the company went ahead with its proposal.

John Losh, a fellow board member and local proprietor, sided with Burnley, fearing that without some stipulation "as the prices and quantities in which those lands were to be re-sold by the company, the stock of labor of the colony would be drawn away from the present proprietors, and the ruin of these latter would be the inevitable consequence" (*PG*, June 15, 1847). Pierre Antoine Ganteaume, the only Creole member of the board, also shared Burnley's fears.

He argued that he was not disposed "to sacrifice his position in society as a pro-prietor, and the future prospect of his children who were dependent on him for a very hazardous benefit. He considered that the measures would be the ruin of the present proprietors if they did not provide largely for the introduction of laborers into the country" (*PG*, June 8, 1847). Ganteaume was prescient. Within one year after this debate he declared bankruptcy.

The acting chief justice, William George Knox, made a case for the larger public good that would result from the introduction of a railway even though initially some people were likely to be impacted negatively by its presence. Ulti-mately, the whole population stood to gain from the establishment of such an industry. He observed: "If Mr. Burnley's idea was to be carried out, there would never have been railroads in England. There were thousands of Innkeepers and Postkeepers ruined in England from the introduction of Railways; and this was foreseen, but this was not considered an insuperable objection to railroads, as it was considered railways would be a great benefit to the large mass of the public." He felt that granting the land to the railway company was of enormous benefit to the country. The railroads "were a great public benefit and should outweigh any objections made by the honorable member [Mr. Burnley]" (*PG*, June 8, 1847).

Burnley envisaged that giving the company so much land and the right to sell that land as it chose could result in a reduction in the price of crown lands. Since Burnley owned much of the country's private land, he feared that he stood to lose the most in any such transaction. To him, the question was "whether all the old proprietors were to be denuded of their property that would benefit their posterity." To prevent that possibility, Burnley offered an amendment to the resolution that would have made it illegal to grant any crown lands to any public company other than on the same terms to which they were granted to private individuals. He thundered:

> Let the railway be supported by its own regular traffic which an influential mem-ber of the board, who had looked at the statistics and calculations of the company, had declared to be amply sufficient. [It should] not look for further profit by a sys-tem of land-jobbing which was foreign to their original object, and could only be made advantageous to them by interfering with the regulations which had been framed for the general welfare and protection of the colony. (*PG*, June 8, 1847)

In speaking thus, Burnley cast himself as the major defender of the private landholding interest in the colony. He posited that the proprietors' interest coincided with his private interest. However, he could not get another unoffi-cial member of the board to second his amendment. The official members who got their orders from London refused to support him. Burnley had come to a humiliating moment in his public life; one of his former admirers described his fears as "an aggravated form to the imagination of Mr. Burnley" (*PG*, June 15, 1847). His amendment could not be put to a vote because none of the other members seconded it. The members then voted for the original resolution—that of granting one thousand acres for every mile of railway—which was carried by a 7 to 4 vote. Knox, one of Burnley's best friends, asserted: "I never doubted Burnley's affection for railways, but he has a strange way of showing it" (*PG*, June 8, 1847).

At the end of the day, all the council members were exhausted. The debate which began at noon ended at ten minutes past eight in the evening. Frustrated by his many defeats, Burnley asked for an adjournment in the hope that his colleagues would be better enlightened "by the opinion out of doors. If they were wrong, they would hear it" (*PG*, June 8, 1847). This had been one of the most agonizing days of Burnley's life. The council was to reconvene on June 16. Burnley hoped for a more productive day when the debate continued.

CHAPTER 34

Toward Modernity

Do not allow yourselves to be misled by any circumstances, which had been alluded to with respect to railroads in England. No doubt, those who at first rejected railroads had bitter reasons to regret their folly, but their case is not analogous [to our own]. In our consideration of the subject, the labor question stands prominent. In England the question was limited to having railroads or no railroads. Here it was totally different. It is: shall we have a railroad or labor? Is the advantage of the former so great that the labor is to be sacrificed to it? I insist it is the height of folly to do so.

—William Hardin Burnley, "Railway Debate," June 16, 1847

THE VERBAL BASHING that Burnley had received during the first part of the railway debate did not lessen his intensity when the debate continued on Wednesday, June 16. John Losh, supporting Burnley, reiterated the devastating effect that the construction of the railway would have on the society and the possibility that many of the present proprietors would suffer greatly when their laborers were enticed away from their estates to work on the new railway properties. This objection allowed Lord Harris, an English landowner in Kent, to reflect on what had transpired in his county when a railway line was built there some years previously. He said that when it was first announced, many people of his area cried out they would be ruined. After the line was built, their lands "doubled in value, and such would be the case here. The Council should be careful in what they did, for if they refused these propositions of the company, they never would get such an opportunity again" (*PG*, "Railway Debate, No. 2," June 16, 1847).

The governor also noted that many people in the Trinidad countryside lived a miserable life. Out of a population of 60,000 to 70,000 people only 10,000 to 15,000 labored on the estates. This led him to ask, "What were the unemployed doing?" The attorney general, Charles Warner, chastised Losh for repeating Burnley's suggestion that the railway company did not pay any regard to the existing interests in the country and said that since crop time was over, "his honorable friend Mr. Burnley wanted something to amuse him, and was carrying on in this discussion. He hoped they would go on with the propositions with the same good humor they had at their previous meeting" (*PG*, June 16, 1847). It almost seemed as though Warner was making fun of Burnley's contribution.

Burnley took umbrage at Warner's assertion that he was opposing the introduction of capital into the country. He even suggested that Warner may have been working for "the monied corporation" who were likely to sell out and leave the country once they had made sufficient profits. Burnley was correct. Warner acted as an agent for British merchants, which "was more profitable to him than his Attorney Generalship" (*PO*, July 13, 1888). Burnley, however, believed that the country's main problem revolved around the question of labor, which led him to ask rhetorically: "What was the use of capital without labor to keep it in motion? It might as well be at the bottom of the Gulf [of Paria]" (*PG*, June 16, 1847). In this regard, his analysis was similar to that of Herman Merivale, Britain's permanent undersecretary of state for the colonies and professor of political economy at Oxford University, who pointed out that "land and capital were both useless unless labor could be commanded."[1]

The attorney general was not in the least persuaded by Burnley's argument. In fact, he poured scorn upon it. He termed it "a most amusing speech," the musings of a man at the twilight of his powers. "It was all: 'Youthful poets dream at twilight eve.'"[2] Twilight describes a period or condition of decline following growth, glory, or success. This might have been how Warner had come to view Burnley. He insisted that Burnley felt threatened by the possibility of having new capital come into the island that would open up the country and allow laborers to move more easily within it. Such a possibility went against Burnley's policy of keeping the laborers tethered to their estates and "the old school of Planter Policy," championed by Burnley, which was designed "to make everything consumed by the laborer as dear as possible so that he might be kept, as it is termed, 'from hand to mouth' and be compelled by actual necessity to work daily, and for each day's subsistence" (*PG*, "The Rum Ordinance," September 7, 1847). The policy of the new-school planters was "to make all the necessaries of life as cheap as possible, so as to attract immigrants and induce them to remain among us" (*PG*, September 7, 1847).

Warner saw nothing disruptive about labor moving from one part of the country to another. In fact, he welcomed it. He argued that if labor was paid adequately, they would never move from their employers. "Although he had been reproached with saying what he did not say, he would ask if it was not a benefit to draw labor from one part of the colony to the other, if the public benefitted thereby. They had a right to do it." The introduction of capital into the island should not be rejected because it was not in the interest of a few individuals. It should be welcomed because it benefitted "the general interest of the island. He asked for a railroad only because he thought it would do good" (*PG*, June 16, 1847). Therefore, the members of the council had to decide if they were prepared to take the railway on the modified principles submitted to them or reject it altogether.

The coming of the railroad threatened to reduce Burnley's empire. As he said, "No man liked to see himself ruined." Musing on his future, he could picture himself in his mansion, on a hot balmy tropical evening, as the Tacarigua River flowed gently by: "When I think of a time which might come, when my agricultural friends and I might sit at our verandahs and look on the railroads with no sugar to send by them, for the want of labor to cultivate our fields, I think it better to oppose the railroads at the existence and expense of the proprietary interests of the colony" (*PG*, June 16, 1847). These were the last words Burnley offered on the resolutions that the members of the Legislative Council passed. None of his amendments were carried nor did any of his objections prevail. Truly his "twilight eve" had arrived.

Burnley did not take his defeat lightly. He opposed the concessions that were granted to the railway company and defended the breach made in his position at the earlier meeting, "with a courage and determination worthy of a better cause; that is, what we should consider a better cause. The honorable gentleman is clearly of opinion that his is the best cause of all—a struggle for self-preservation—a battle *pro aris et focis*" (*PG*, "The Railway Company's Propositions," June 18, 1847) or, as the translation of the Latin phrase suggests, a struggle to uphold all he held to be dear and venerable. He insisted that the question was "not whether we should have railroads or no railroads, but whether we should have railroads and an inadequate supply of labor on the Estates, or no railroads and an adequate supply of labor on the Estates" (*PG*, June 18, 1847).

As sympathetic as the editor of the *Port of Spain Gazette* was to Burnley's sentiments, he could not accept his argument. He felt that the introduction of a railway to the island would be better for the inhabitants. It would increase the mobility of laborers allowing them to get from one point of the island to another very quickly. Laborers residing at St. Joseph, Tacarigua, and Arouca "who have friends to visit in Port of Spain . . . would be in town in twenty or sixty minutes (according to distance) by the morning train, arrive without fatigue, make their visits and purchases, and return by the afternoon train in time for their hour of repose, and in readiness for their accustomed occupation on the morrow" (*PG*, June 18, 1847).

There were many advantages in having the railway. It would facilitate the movement of people during the rainy season when the roads were almost impassable. It would also prove invaluable to the sick who wanted to see a physician as quickly as possible. In short, the opening up of a railroad was a movement toward modernity or, as Lord Harris said, "would bring them within the precincts of civilization."[3] At the very least, it would go a long way toward lifting the society out of its narrow provincialism. As the editor of the *Port of Spain Gazette* bemoaned:

> It is painful to us to witness the *nonchalance* and *incurie* of many of the native inhabitants of the town, of the laboring class, or even a grade a little higher, who have never been further eastward of Port of Spain in their lives than the St. Juan's River, or westward than the village of Cocorite. The Railroads will "whisk" these people about, and enable them to form a little better idea of the extent of the Colony, and the folly of remaining crowded and cramped together in the metropolis, whilst both in the mechanical and agricultural line they could do so much better in the rural districts.[4]

On Saturday, June 19, the members of the Legislative Council were called into session to review the resolutions and to revise verbal inaccuracies. However, there would be no discussion "regarding any question of principle adopted by the board" (*PG*, June 18, 1847). Although Burnley could not attend the meeting, he informed the board that he intended to protest against the resolutions that were passed. By July 21, Burnley wrote up his objections, which Lord Harris transmitted to the Colonial Office. He reiterated most of the points he had made during the debate. On July 23, several proprietors and other interested parties sent an elaborate memorial to Earl Grey protesting the propositions favoring the construction of a railroad on the island (*PG*, "Railways," July 23, 1847). Losh and Pierre Antoine Ganteaume presented a joint protest while Horatio Huggins, John Lamont, and St. Luce Philip protested on behalf of the proprietors of the Naparimas and Savanna Grande.

As fate would have it, the collapse of Reid, Irving, and Company, of which Sir

John Rae Reid was the senior partner, did more to end the railway venture than the protests of Burnley, Huggins, and Ganteaume. The *London Times* noted that the failure of Reid, Irving, and Company, "irrespective of its amount, derives importance from the circumstances of the head of the firm being one of the senior directors of the Bank of England" (*L*, "Money-Market and City Intelligence," September 18, 1847). With Reid gone, the funding of the project was gone. For the poor people of the island who had poured their money into this venture, the end was sad enough. One can hear the pain in Alexander Anderson's voice as he tried to come to terms with the failure of the company that promised so much:

> A company was formed under the auspices of a number of influential names, some of whom had large interests at stake in this island, and were considered men of capital. As soon as the project was made public, the scheme was swallowed up with avidity which can only be accounted for by the infatuation of the times. Subscribers flocked from every quarter; the shares were immediately at a premium, and many a shareholder laid up his money in hopes of reaping a golden harvest only to be disappointed.
>
> By the mere fact of this insolvent baronet, the scheme is blown to a thousand atoms and an "enterprise" of great pith and moment thus made to turn awry and loose the name of action. (*PG*, November 12, 1847)

On October 1, Amory, Sewell and Moores, a prestigious solicitor's firm in London, wrote to William Curtis, the engineer who had done the preliminary work for the railway company, to state that if "suitable interest was being taken in the project by parties in the island, there would be no difficulty in finding other parties in England disposed to complete the share list"[5] of a new railway company. A few days later a public meeting was held in Port of Spain, attended by Lord Harris, "and the bulk of the most respectable people in the island, when it was determined to give to the project all the support the means of the colonists admit. A Committee was formed, prospectus and advertisement issued and active steps taken to promote shareholders."[6] Henry Scott, a merchant and member of the Legislative Council, was named chairman of the local committee. The profitability of this new company would be realized through the exploitation of the valuable timber the island possessed and the land the company would acquire rather than the transportation of sugar and passengers.

Curtis, the new leader of the team, was quick on the job. He spent six months in Trinidad (from October 2, 1847, to March 30, 1848) organizing a new company to carry out the lines of railway that he had projected and surveyed in 1846. On November 5, 1847, the *Port of Spain Gazette* called attention to the preliminary prospectus of the Trinidad Colonial Railway Company that was formed to carry out the project of the defunct Trinidad Railway Company. It observed that "Hardly have the directors of the latter association announced the abandonment of their undertaking, then Phoenix-like, we find a company rising out of the ashes of its predecessor" (*PG*, "The Trinidad Colonial Railway Company," November 5, 1847).

No reason was given for the demise or abandonment of the Trinidad Railway Company except that the company "was got up in the hey-day and glitter of Railway mania—when every man, ay, or every woman, who had a guinea, was anxious to invest it in Railways shares; when schemes, the most wild and romantic, were hailed with unbounded confidence, and the only cry was for more of them." As if to soothe the dashed hopes of the past experiment, the newspaper summarized the disappointment of a nation when it described the Trinidad Railway Company, as "the child of prosperity, born in sunshine and summer. The other, if it struggles into existence, will do so amid the wintry gloom of adversity, and in spite of obstacles the most detrimental to its proper growth and development" (*PG*, November 5, 1847).

Lamont announced that Burnley's greatest success took place in November 1847 "when he triumphantly defeated the proposal for a Trinidad Government Railway" (*OG*, 17). One is not too sure how to access this statement. It is true that Burnley protested the construction of the railway even after it had passed the Legislative Council, but the very passage of the resolution in spite of Burnley's objections suggested that his power and persuasiveness had begun to wane. The evidence suggests that the establishment of the railway was terminated because of the collapse of Sir Rae Reid's firm rather than Burnley's protests. The passing of slavery called for a different approach to economic planning and social problems and more forward-looking leadership that Burnley was unable to offer. In a way the railway debate, conducted between these two intellectual giants, signaled the passing of the leadership of the English segment of the community from Burnley to Warner, ushering "the age of Charles Warner."[7]

This tendency to oppose or place a negative spin on every progressive idea, evident in the railway controversy, replicated itself in the colony's attempts to introduce Indians onto the island. Although he was among the first to acknowledge the desirability of bringing Indians to the island to relieve the shortage-of-labor problem he was surprisingly tepid about having them settle in the colony and eventually became opposed to it. It was just too costly for his frugal and economic tastes to bring these immigrants to the island especially when the colony could secure African laborers at a much cheaper rate, a point he made at a special meeting of the Legislative Council when he observed: "No Colonial Minister could have supposed for a moment that the sugar growers of Trinidad paying $75 for the lease of the services of an Indian for 5 years, with an obligation to send him home at the expiration of that period at the colonial expense, could for an instant compete with the slave owner who commanded the compulsory services of his laborer for the whole term of his natural life, for about $300" (*PG*, "Council of Government," October 20, 1846).

On October 17, 1846, Lord Harris announced the government's intention to stop the intercolonial bounty that was being paid for West Indian immigrants and the bringing of more Indian immigrants to the colony. While several planters disagreed with the cessation of Indian immigration, Burnley was adamant that the imperial government should have ended Indian immigration "the moment the last Sugar Duty Bill was passed [in 1846]" (*PG*, "Council of Government," October 20, 1846). The editor of the *Port of Spain Gazette* reminded Burnley that the West India Body in England had failed, by their silence, to represent the interests of its constituents properly. He noted that if such "an influential gentleman as Mr. Burnley with interests so extensive at stake" wished to put an end to such an objectionable source of expenditure, he ought to make his objections known to the Colonial Government (*PG*, "Legislative Proceedings," October 20, 1846).

In December 1846 the high cost of Indian immigration came up for discussion again. Government officials, such as J. A. Allen, treasurer of the Legislative Council, asserted that Indians "would never amalgamate with the people of the colony and then they were under an engagement to send them back to India at the expiration of the five years" (*PG*, December 25, 1846). These officials hoped that African laborers would fill the labor gap that existed in the country. They also felt that Africans would have been more compatible with the existing laborers on the colony since they possessed similar habits with most of the inhabitants, and it was cheaper to bring them to the island.

Burnley was therefore ecstatic when, in January 1847, Lord Harris announced that the secretary of state proposed to use one of Her Majesty's steamers to transfer immigrants from Africa to British Guiana and Trinidad. He declared: "These people would be conveyed here in a government vessel and should she meet with a slaver she would take her and bring any people she might have along with her" (*PG*, "Council of Government," March 2, 1847). At this time the British navy intercepted ships that were trading illegally in Africa and brought the human cargo found on those ships to the Caribbean. They were called "liberated Africans." Just to be sure that the Trinidad government would not be participate in reinstituting the infamous slave trade, the governor sought to temper Burnley's enthusiasm by reminding him that "these people should understand upon what terms they should come here, and should know this before they went on board a ship. The best thing they could do would be to appoint a committee to determine upon what terms they should come here." In a burst of frenzied rhetoric, Burnley retorted: "Let the committee, when appointed, be like a jury, not allowed to separate until they came to a decision" (*PG*, March 2, 1847). Burnley was selected as a member of that committee to look into the possibility of introducing these new laborers onto the island.

Burnley, who never saw anything inherently wrong with slavery, welcomed the desire of the British government to purchase laborers from Africa. It was left to the Anti-Slavery Society to demonstrate the pitfalls of such a plan. The society noted sarcastically that the principal function of the British agents in Sierra Leone, where the agents would be placed, would be to announce when the British vessels arrived "and to diffuse such information respecting the kind of labor required in the West Indies and the average rate of money wages and other advantages to be obtained by laborers, as may enable the people to exercise an intelligent choice in accepting or rejecting the offer made to them."[8] Fortunately, the Africans rejected this enticement to be re-enslaved. The *Port of Spain Gazette* explained: "The poverty which formerly prevailed there [in Sierra Leone] has now disappeared; so likewise has the motive to emigrate. Whilst the rise of wages at Sierra Leone, and the reduction which must shortly ensue here, will so equalize the two, that the great inducement to the laborers to come hither can no longer be held out to him, and the captured slaves ['the liberated Africans'] are our only resource in this quarter" (*PG*, May 26, 1848). By June 1848, only 392 Africans had immigrated to the island (*PG*, June 6, 1848).

Later in the year Burnley came in for more denunciations, particularly when the government tried to revive the old railway under a new name, the Trinidad Colonial Railway Company. This time around Lord Harris took the initiative to push this revival. At a public meeting at the Theatre Royal in Port of Spain on November 12, 1847, Lord Harris reminded his audience that he was always in favor of building a railroad on the island and had even written William Gladstone to that effect. He outlined the advantages that would be derived from having a railroad in the country and called on the local population to make their financial contribution to the project even though he predicted that "the biggest portion of the capital will be provided by England and one can believe that we will receive the same conditions as those which the local government offered to the company that withdrew." Meanwhile, the objective of the railroad had changed. The new directors believed that the trade in time "would form a source of very great profit to the company, which can only be obtained by the introduction of a railroad company upon the plan laid down by the prospectus (*PG*, November 16, 1847).

Earlier, Burnley had opposed the establishment of the railroad as proposed in London. Now, at the meeting, he explained his change in thinking. "If the calculation of the considerable profit demonstrated by the plan submitted to the assembly was well founded, he would support it with all his might." He was pleased that this new plan was in the hands of Trinidadians and that, indeed, "It would be a family affair." In spite of this welcome development, the major criterion for his support would be whether the railway could pay for itself. He argued that "no man in his senses when he looked at the present position and future prospects of the colony could be made to believe that the railroad could be supported by transportation or the ordinary colonial production." He did not feel that it made economic sense to be asking for concessions on the sugar duties while the island was destroying its capacity to raise enormous money from its timber. He thundered: "Why give it away to the railroad company?" (*PG*, November 16, 1847).

Mr. Anderson, a member of the provisional committee of the new company, was the first person to respond to Burnley's objections. He believed that the company would make a considerable profit by establishing a timber trade in the colony. He recalled the enthusiasm shown by many of the local people who had rushed to support the initial venture. Anderson came down hardest on Burnley, "the soi-disant 'Father of the Railway in Trinidad' who like the progenitor of Jupiter and other of the heathen deities, has a most unfortunate propensity for devouring his own offspring—who came forward in speech of witty sarcasm and well-concerned irony to throw ridicule on the whole undertaking" (*PG*, November 19, 1847).

Anderson was angry that Burnley had used his influence to prevent the building of the railroad initially and feared he was likely to do so again. This time around Anderson was insistent that "the existence of a big capitalist such as Mr. Burnley would not stop the progress of the railway. There was enough energy to carry out the measure without Mr. Burnley. We do not need those who blow both hot and cold." This last remark drew Burnley's ire, and he defended himself vigorously. It was Burnley's most forthright and clearest assessment of why he had done so well in the society:

> The learned gentleman has called me a capitalist. I disclaim the title. Sugar estates productive of a loss were sorry capital. The learned gentleman can know nothing of my other pecuniary resources. I am always prepared to pay every just demand

that is made upon me and limit my expenditure to my means. I never borrow from others. In this respect I am rich and if the learned gentleman pleases—a capitalist. In this sense every member of the community who exercises the same forbearance might be a capitalist also. (*PG*, November 19, 1847)

Lord Harris was offended by Burnley's bombast and what he interpreted to be his disrespect for "the motherland." He castigated Burnley for the discouraging tone in which he spoke of the proposal, thanked him sarcastically for the amusement he provided members of the assembly, and denounced his ability, "on lightweight grounds, to oppose, one of the most effective measures for the [advancement] of the colony." He ended by explaining why he interrupted Burnley so frequently during his presentation:

I do not hesitate to declare that whether against one person or against ten thousand, neither in my position as representative of Her Majesty, or as a private individual, I will never allow that this, so dear a motherland, to be mentioned ironically without interrupting the speaker. I am proud to belong to a nation that has never hesitated to sacrifice their blood and treasures for the cause of freedom and humanity. (*PG*, November 19, 1847)

In the earlier debate on the desirability of establishing a railway in the country, Charles Warner had poured scorn and sarcasm on Burnley's positions. He, rather than Burnley, would become "the great advocate of East Indian immigration."[9] Lord Harris, in his turn, was more pointed in his denunciation of Burnley's behavior. His peroration may have been a bit overblown, but he had achieved his objective. He was tired of Burnley's proprietary rights over the island and his tendency always to look out for his interest rather than those of the country. Although Burnley was the biggest capitalist in the country, Great Britain still ruled the island. One suspects that Lord Harris took pleasure in bringing this fact to Burnley's attention.

CHAPTER 35

The Agony of Despair

There was but one simple proceeding to which they must come at last, or renounce all hope of making free labor supersede slavery in the Tropics, namely: To purchase Africans on the coast, as has been done for centuries past, and then emancipate them in our colonies. I have not shrunk from recommending this publicly in London some years ago and, to the present hour, I have not heard one single valid argument against it.

—William Hardin Burnley, "Council of Government," 1848

B Y THE END of 1847, the economic fortunes of the island began to worsen, no doubt because of the effect that the Sugar Duties Act was having on the sugar industry. In August of that year, the Colonial Legislature passed a bill that called for "the immediate reduction of duties on all foreign sugar—both free and slave grown—to 21s. The differential tax on the foreign product was to be systematically reduced by 1s. 6d. a year until by 1851 the duties on all sugar entering the United Kingdom would be equalized."[1] Needless to say, this bill had devastating effect on Trinidad's economy because the Trinidad planters had to compete with slave grown sugar in Cuba, Puerto Rico, and Brazil that was being produced at a cheaper rate.

At a meeting of the Legislative Council on November 21, 1847, John Losh alerted the board that "the great depression of the agricultural interest of the colony at the present moment, which was known and admitted by all" (*PG*, "Council of Government," November 22, 1847) was having a devastating effect on the island. In December 1847, "several vessels lay at anchor in Port of Spain unable to sail or discharge cargo as a result of the inability of the colony's merchants to pay custom duties."[2] Since the British Parliament was likely to meet on the matter in February of 1848, Losh advised the council that it had precious little time to ascertain "the causes which during the succession of years had led to the aggravated distress which prevail so generally at present." He warned that if the depression continued for the next year "there would be no hope that the cultivation of sugar in this island would continue much longer" and moved that a committee be appointed "to inquire and report upon the existing depression of the agricultural interests of the colony, the causes which have led thereto, and to suggest such measures by way of remedy as may occur to the committee in the course of their inquiry" (*PG*, November 22, 1847).

In responding to Losh's contribution, the attorney general declared that the British Parliament would ignore any British minister who came before it with a proposition to promote West Indian planters. He was not sure whether the crisis in which the planters found themselves was attributable to the low price of sugar. He suggested that the proposed committee that would be set up to inquire into the crisis should compare the production cost of sugar in Puerto Rico and Cuba, two slave countries, with that of Trinidad (*PG*, November 22, 1847).

As was his wont and as his interests dictated, Burnley offered a different position. By then, he was working closely with his brother-in-law Joseph Hume "to secure the restoration of protective duties."[3] He argued that the Colonial Office was indifferent to the crisis on the island while many planters were being ruined by it. He argued that while there was a monetary crisis in 1831, "at that time the planter had not to contend with free labor. Although the price of sugar was low, now the whole of the profits in making sugar went into the pockets of the laborer, not into the planter" (*PG*, November 22, 1847). In other words, the laborer was now the culprit. Irredeemably against Indian immigration, which he called "an unprofitable speculation" (*PG*, October 5, 1847), Burnley believed that the solution to Trinidad's labor shortage lay in bringing African laborers to the island. His reasoning was somewhat disingenuous but consistent:

It should not be called slavery to go to Africa and buy them there, and make them free here. They were not going to Africa to procure people and put them aboard vessels and jam them up like herrings in a barrel; but let them be brought here like free men, and remove all restrictions on emigration from Africa. There would be no new purchases in the market: they would not raise more sugar than what they could make a profit. People were not going to die at ten percent, because they were made free. They would live longer, and in 8 to 10 years they would put an end to it [the slave trade] altogether. He still believed free labor could compete with slave labor, if it had a fair chance; but this he did not think it had at the present. (*PG*, "Council of Government," November 22, 1846)

Nature also seemed to be against the inhabitants. On October 11, 1847, a severe storm ravaged the island for sixteen hours nonstop. It began at 11:00 p.m. on the eleventh and lasted until 4 p.m. the following day. The governor reported that "the wind which blew south was very violent and being accompanied by torrents of rain has caused considerable damage in some parts of the island." The cocoa plantations in the valleys of the Northern Range suffered the worst damage, with over thirty thousand cocoa trees destroyed. The laborers were also hit very hard; their provision grounds were laid to waste as were those on the Spanish Main from "whence the chief supply of provision [for the island] is derived."[4] That October night—dark, fuliginous, and foreboding—seemed to anticipate what nature and the blind forces of economics had in store for the inhabitants of the island in the coming year.

In 1848 the society felt the full impact of the economic depression. At the Legislative Council meeting of April 3, the governor reported that the secretary of state had approved the running of a trading vessel along the African coast "to convey captured Africans and others from Africa, Jamaica, Demerara and Trinidad" (*PG*, April 4, 1848). The governor also informed council members that he had received a dispatch from the secretary of state informing him that he disapproved of the regulations that he (Lord Harris) had drawn up regarding Indian immigration. The governor explained Indian immigration was simply too expensive and the planters were not accepting the workers. Between 1846 and 1847, the government had spent half of its revenue on Indian immigration.[5] Of the 4,300 Indians who had arrived on the island, the planters had applied for only 1,200 of them which led the governor to complain: "This last cargo of Indians which arrived had been two days here and no one would take them. The Immigration Agent at last got people to take them without paying anything for them" (*PG*, April 4, 1848). Many Indians left their estates within a week after entering into their contracts thereby exacerbating the situation. There were no laws to deal with desertion or to regulate their movement on the island.[6] This gave Burnley the opening he was looking for:

> We must make some law for the government and the laborer. . . . The regulations for the government of the Indians worked well but were rescinded by orders from home [that is, the British government]. In Couva and Savonetta, where I have large interests, there are numbers of these people employed and there is no law when they leave their service without cause to put them in irons or otherwise. The planters have just as many wheels in the machine as I require but the people who leave their employment put everything out of joint. *This is one reason why I would not employ a single Indian.* I would be happy to employ 200 to 300 Indians in my estates if they could be made to do the same work as laborers in any other part of the world. I will have no hesitation in carrying on all the estates in the colony even

at the low rate of produce at present at the home market, provided I could depend on the continuous labor which an employer in every other country in the world received. However, under the present system things are going from bad to worse, sinking money from year to year in the vain hope that a better time will come. (*PG*, "Council of Government," April 4, 1848; italics added)

Burnley, acting in collusion with the protectionist element in the House of Commons, believed that squatting compounded the problem. He felt that the government dealt too leniently with formerly enslaved workers. The attorney general proposed that every person in the country, "from the highest to the lowest," should be registered in order to prevent laborers "from roving from one end of the island to another." Yet the fear remained that a substantial number of the laborers "would be thrown out of employment, and the people thus thrown out of work would go to the neighboring estates that were still under cultivation, but they would not be able to employ them." Burnley theorized that the problem, which faced the country, resulted from the absence of a law against vagrancy. If such a law was introduced and strongly enforced, he would not hesitate "to continue and carry on any estate in the country" (*PG*, April 4, 1848).

By then, the problem was so bad that laborers on some estates had not been paid for over two to three months and public servant did not receive salaries for the final quarter of 1847. When the governor brought up the question, Mr. Fuller, an unofficial member, reminded the house that in Barbados when the estates went bankrupt, the laborers had the first claim on the estates. This led Burnley to reply: "That would be re-establishing the old claim of tactic mortgage." One is not too sure if Burnley was comforted by the chief justice's response that the introduction of such law in Trinidad would shake confidence of any mortgage on estates, open the door to fraud, and lead to a great deal of mischief. He remarked: "If they attempted a law of this kind, they must strictly outline it to estates ceded under the Insolvent Committee" (*PG*, April 4, 1848). The extent of the economic downturn really hit home when Lord Harris informed Earl Grey on May 22 that "his coffers are quite empty. Our hopes of their being replenished are but small." He also feared that discontent that already gripped the laborers would be spread amongst government officials. He felt that "the regular payment of salaries would guard against" such a possibility.[7]

While Burnley was declaiming against the evils that had befallen the country, the depression had hit his family as well. On June 16, 1848, came the news that Messrs. Eccles, Burnley and Company of Glasgow, Scotland, of which Burnley's son William Frederick was a senior partner, had suffered insolvency. The company was indebted to Colonial Bank for the sum of £38,000, an enormous sum of money. William Eccles was in Trinidad when this tragedy occurred. On his return to Scotland he wrote C. A. Calvert, the secretary of the London branch of the bank, as follows: "I expressed to William Rennie [manager of the Trinidad branch of the bank] how anxious I should be to place your claims on the best footing and how deeply I regretted having been instrumental in involving the bank so deeply; although unknowingly done."[8] Since the tentacles of his son's company had reached into the Trinidad economy, the failure of that house had tremendous consequences to the lives of laborers and merchants of the island. It held mortgages for "nearly one third of the crop of the sugar made here. By this stoppage, labor had been suspended on thirty-four estates, the cultivation of which must have furnished food and other necessaries for at least 5,000 souls, who, by this time, are suddenly out of the means of existence" (PG, June 16, 1848). Of the 193 estates in the colony, seventeen were making a profit, while another seventeen were running even. The rest of the estates were running at a loss. According to Lord Harris, of all the estates operating in 1848, only six seemed likely to make a profit in 1848.[9]

The insolvency of Messrs. Eccles, Burnley and Company also resulted in the failure of Losh, Spiers and Company through whom Eccles, Burnley and Company conducted its business in Trinidad. On March 1, 1848, Calvert reprimanded William Rennie, manager of the Trinidad branch of the bank, for accepting "a letter of guarantee given you by Mr. Eccles which we consider very informal in as much as it is simply his personal guarantee, and not, as we presume both he and you intended it to be, that of his firm. . . . [It also] contains a very objectionable claim, viz, that funds are to be applied solely for agricultural purposes. How can you be certain that Losh Spiers & Co., will apply the funds you supply them with under this guarantee to none but 'agricultural purposes.'"[10] The Colonial Bank had limited the monthly overdraft of Messrs Eccles, Burnley and Company to £1,500. It was also aware of the economic difficulty which the island and necessarily the company were undergoing.

John Losh was the senior partner of that firm, which made him Burnely's business partner. Such a failure reflected on both Burnley and Losh's financial abilities. On August 1, sizing up his difficulty, Losh wrote a rather sorrowful letter to Harris informing him that he considered it his duty, "on public grounds to tender my resignation on the seat which it pleased Her Majesty to assign me."[11] Although Lord Harris agonized over Losh's plight and the propriety of accepting his resignation, in the end he had no choice but to accede to Losh's request.

When Eccles, Burnley and Company went under, William Frederick Burnley resigned the chairmanship of West India Association of Glasgow, an association that always supported the efforts of William Burnley, the father, in pursuing his causes both on the island and in London. In a long letter to the secretary of state, William Hamilton and C. D. Donald (chairman and secretary respectively of the association) praised William Frederick, whom they described as "so ably residing over their interests and whose character stands so high both as a merchant and as a man." They also bemoaned that their company had been sacrificed in the name of "all the struggles which they have made in the great experiment for the profitable production of sugars by free-labor, [which] will be rendered abortive" (*PG*, June 13, 1848).

Burnley, the father, regretted Losh's resignation. He revealed his views on October 2, 1848, when the council was debating a petition that was submitted by the planters to be relieved from a 3.5 percent export tax that was to be imposed on them in January 1849. He believed that, like him, every member of the house regretted Losh's absence from the council. He contended that Losh's services could never be replaced, downplayed the circumstances that led to Losh's resignation, and disagreed with the "necessity" that induced Losh to take that step. He believed that it was only Losh's "sensitive feelings" that induced him to do so. Given the severity of the depression, not even a conscientious man could escape from its claws (*PG*, "Council of Government," October 3, 1848).

When Losh alerted the board of the economic crisis that was unfolding in the colony, little did he know that he would become a victim of that catastrophe and that he would find himself in that "agony of despair" as Hamilton and Donald described what was taking place on the island. Burnley, in paying tribute to Losh's contribution to the island, had noted: "Their honorable friend had certainly failed, but from no fault of his own. He had been the victim of a succession of unwise political acts, against which no talent and no industry could stand. The blow which had felled him had laid the whole colony prostrate" (*PG*, October 3, 1848). Burnley, no doubt, was referring to the devastation that the Sugar Duties Act of 1846 was having on the island, particularly on men like Losh and Pierre Antoine Ganteaume.

CHAPTER 36

Burnley's Callousness

No man in Trinidad is more indebted to the laboring population than is Mr. Burnley, and yet in none have they ever had a more crafty and determined antagonist. Whoever yet heard the man who has become immensely rich and influential in the island through their sweat and toil, speak of them with gratitude and respect? Even when found to act far more faithfully and honorably than their employers, in affording continuous labor for months, though unrequited, their noble and praise-worthy conduct, which deserved his highest commendation as a planter and a legislator, is only noticed for the purpose of damaging their interest!

—X, Letter to the Editor, 1848

ON JUNE 1, 1848, the Burnley Committee (a committee the Legislative Council appointed in February 1847 to look into the great distress amongst proprietors) reported its recommendations to the Legislative Council. Burnley's committee believed that the imposition of stringent measures against the working population was the only way to solve the crippling economic crisis that gripped the society at the time. They felt that more workers should be brought into the colony, the cost of which should be paid for by the imperial government; that a few simple regulations should be enacted to suppress vagrancy; and that a more determined effort should be made to prevent squatting, which should be treated as "an offence against the public instead of a trespass upon private property" (*PG*, "Council of Government," June 16, 1848).[1]

Burnley offered his own evaluation of the economic distress that had befallen the country. He declared that the "natural course" in dealing with the crisis would be to reduce the wages of the laborers "until our staples could be produced at a remunerative cost." Such a measure would not affect laborers unduly because they lived in a climate "where clothes were required more for decency than for comfort and a house with a thatched roof and basket frame constituted sufficient protection against the weather." The high wages they received insulated them from the suffering to which the other members of the society, particularly the elite class, were exposed. These new capitalists, as he called them, possessed sufficient resources to withstand the economic distress that had crippled the society. "Witness," he said, "the stories in circulation that laborers who have not been paid for six months or more are not at work upon the estates—these are the real capitalists who can live on their means and give credit. So independent are they that many would not submit to a reduction of wages to that extent, but would prefer to turn their attention to the raising of provisions on their own lands, from which natural and useful course they have been hitherto seduced by the extravagant wages paid to them."

Anyone listening to Burnley—particularly after his son's company had gone under and wrecked the lives of five thousand workers and their families— would have thought he had lost his grip on reality. His paranoia seemed boundless. Without flinching, he declared: "I do not mean to be understood as asserting that widespread privations and distress do not exist in the colony, but it is not to be found amongst the laborers. It is confined to the proprietors, the shopkeepers and others immediately dependent upon them." Nothing, he said, could prevent the latter group from falling into eventual bankruptcy. They were "trembling upon the verge of a precipice, from which any additional calamity would inevitably precipitate them into the gulph of ruin below." Importing workers to the colony was the only recourse to solve the problem.

Once the decision to import workers was taken, another question arose: from what source would these workers come? Although Burnley had concluded that there was little hope of getting laborers voluntarily from Sierra Leone, he could not let go of the idea of purchasing them from Africa to work on the island. Although the fearful reimposition of the slave trade loomed in his proposition, this time around he made his case with more conviction. "I have not shrunk from recommending this publicly in London some years ago; and to the present hour I have not heard one single valid argument against it." To him, the virtue of his proposition consisted in the immense benefits of civilization that would accrue to "the unhappy African." As he said, "The true doctrine was to do good whenever and wherever they could, without regard to consequences which might safely be left to the Almighty Disposer of all events

to regulate." Although people in the twenty-first century may think that this
was a pernicious doctrine, Burnley believed that he was following the will of
"the Almighty Disposer."

It followed necessarily that if one were going to bring more of these uncivilized people into the colony, there had to be "wholesale and efficient regulations" to govern their movement and their behavior. Since all races were not
governed by the same motives—a false and mischievous idea that had capti-
vated the minds of philanthropists and economists in Great Britain—Burnley
contended that separate laws had to be established for these new immigrants
since they differed from Englishmen. They were at "a different stages of civilization." He therefore concluded that it savored of insanity "to suppose that
African savages could be beneficially, either for themselves or the community,
governed by the same code as English laborers, or even as the Creole laborers,
who had been educated for a generation or two in the colony."

To justify his scheme, Burnley argued that these savages should not be
considered as citizens or be entitled to the full privileges of British laws "until
the next generation, when some education in school and church might enable
them to understand and exercise them." They should not be able to leave the
districts in which they were first placed except by the permission of the government and then, only for good and sufficient reason, "to be ascertained through
the medium of a Protector to be appointed to watch over them in each district."
They also had to be kept in a stage of "pupilage" for their own benefit and those
of future generations. In keeping with his Christian persuasion, he pleaded
for the institution of this system "in the name of humanity, of justice and of
religion."

Burnley thought that such vigilance was necessary to combat vagrancy, "the
besetting sin of the African race [and] . . . the incalculable evils which flow from
it." Therefore, the implementation of a pass system, more akin to the system
of apartheid, was necessary to control the savagery of such natives. In a sense,
Burnley's musing predated the racist preoccupations of Cecil Rhodes of South
Africa and Zimbabwe.[2] To soften its harshness, Burnley used his chauvinism
to make his case. He said: "Something decisive must be done immediately to
bring this experiment of free labor to a successful conclusion, or it would ultimately prove to be an utter failure, and the reputation of Great Britain would
ultimately be branded with eternal disgrace." Believing the proprietors could
not be too lenient with these savages, Burnley drew on the wisdom of Charles-
Maurice de Talleyrand, Bishop of Autun, who admonished Napoleon that "in
all government matters, the most heinous of sins is a blunder."[3] Cecil Jenkins,

former dean of European Studies at Sussex University, described Talleyrand as "an ex-aristocrat, ex-bishop, ex-exile, who has become a byword for diplomatic deviousness and inscrutability."[4] Interesting enough, Burnley relied upon Talleyrand's words to support his argument on the introduction of one of the most repressive laws in the society.

The governor concurred with many of Burnley's remarks. His concern was whether it was cheaper or more profitable to carry on immigration or to permit those estates that could not be cultivated with the supply of immigrants to be abandoned. Like Burnley, he believed the government should control the movement of Africans who immigrated to the island both for their benefit and that of the community. He reiterated his ongoing concern of finding a principle that would bind "the various races, creeds and dispositions" into one community. Lord Harris believed: "A race had been freed, but a society has not been formed. Liberty has been given to a heterogeneous mass of individuals who can only comprehend license." He also added that to assist in civilizing the lower classes, "every encouragement should be given to the easy circumstances of a superior class, the Europeans, amongst the population."[5]

Although Lord Harris believed that the colony should institute a strong vagrancy law for "the idle," he did not think it was a good policy to have them registered. Such a process, he felt, would interfere with their freedom of movement thereby restraining the free supply of labor. He did not agree with Burnley's notion about the pupilage of these citizens for life. Instead, he was willing to concede that the immigrants should be distributed to those planters who were willing to pay attention "not only to their physical welfare but also to their religious and intellectual instructions so that every opportunity should be given them of becoming good members of society."

The secretary of state, Earl Grey, agreed with much the officials were saying in terms of the forcible apprehension of these workers and making them work for the state. He felt that anyone who was not working should be picked up and sent to a workhouse established by the state. These workhouses would be maintained by levying a tax upon the laborers or their houses which would provide for hospitals, poorhouses, and additional policemen to enforce the vagrant law.

Earl Grey also suggested that the law "might enact that every laborer occupying a house not taxed should be considered a vagrant; and, that vagrants might be employed either on roads or in gangs to work on estates, under the superintendence of the workhouses. This would give the laborer a stimulus to exertion." In other words, if the workers would not work voluntarily for the estates, the state would conscript them to do so either by introducing vagrancy laws or taxing them to the max. Under any circumstances, these new capitalists would be expected to support the state and help it out of its depression.

If these measures were not far-reaching enough, the attorney general proposed that squatting be seen in the same light as vagrancy. Squatting, he said, would also be made an offense against the public. He believed that every person on the island should be registered. "If a man was found in any district in which he was not registered, and could not give an account of himself, I would say to him, you have been found here without any ostensible means of support (for it is said that man by the sweat of his brow shall earn his living)." These were the draconian measures being proposed against the black people of the colony.

At the end of that very strenuous debate, only Henry Fuller, one of the unofficial members of the council, spoke out against those racist laws and defended the right of the workers to control their labor. He felt that a system of registration "would be the most cruel, the most unjust and the most unfair system that could possibly be effected." He even challenged Burnley's promulgation of such a law by asking him: "Suppose he met a man going to Tacarigua, with an old checked shirt and straw hat on, and you ask him his name? 'John Thomas,' he says. Then you ask: 'Are you a vagrant?' The man says 'No' and pulls out four dollars, and says, 'What have you got to say to that?'"

Burnley retorted: "This might be all very well but what has that to do with the question before the Board?" to which Fuller riposted: "You have amused the Board for two or three hours with a disquisition on the African slaves. What I am saying has quite as much to do with it [the issue] as what you said had to do with it. I would not debate the issue much longer." He felt that if the governor had released the dispatches that Earl Grey had sent to the governor "it would do more good than all the preaching for the last ten years." Perhaps it would have given the citizenry a better sense of how the officials were thinking about them.

Burnley did not respond to Fuller's intervention. Even though the board eventually voted for the recommendations put forward by Burnley's committee, supported in the main by the governor and the attorney general, there still remained a man of conscience who was brave enough to tell the council that what it was doing against the laboring class was wrong. These people should not be asked to bear the brunt of the crisis for which they were not responsible. If the economy had gone bad, it was because of the competition of cheaper sugar from the slave-producing states; the less-than-frugal manner in which the proprietors, especially the absentee proprietors, lived; and the enormous salaries paid to the government officials.

True to his convictions, on June 20, Fuller submitted the following resolution to be debated at the next meeting of council scheduled for June 24. In the light of the "unprecedented state of distress that now prevails in Trinidad," he proposed that "from and after the 1st of January 1849 one fourth part of all public salaries, pay, emoluments and pensions that are above two hundred pounds sterling" be disallowed. Second, since about four-fifths of the public revenue was collected by the Department of Customs and then turned over to the Colonial Treasury that both departments should be consolidated after January 1, 1849, and that "a committee of this Board be appointed to devise the means of effecting such an objective."[6] Third, that certain efficiencies be made in government to see the colony through its crisis. Fuller must have been pleased when the council, at its June 24 meeting, agreed with his proposals and reduced the salaries of public officers considerably (*TR*, June 24, 1848).

The public was not amused by the irresponsible manner in which the legislators addressed the question, nor were they pleased by Burnley's backward and racist views. Two local readers, writing in the *Trinidadian*,[7] a newly established local newspaper, poured scorn on Burnley's views: one, through outright criticism and the other through satire. One of the writers, using the pseudonym "X," described Burnley's speech as "vile in the extreme" and noted that "so much of it [was] characterized by the spirit of by-gone days, that it is difficult to conceive of the author of such diabolical views as were then expressed with even common respect." He reminded his readers how much Burnley's wealth depended on the labors of the black people of the island, yet "in none have they ever had a more crafty and determined antagonist." Burnley, he believed, should be grateful to people who had worked willingly without pay for six months rather than denouncing and rebuking them. He regretted that no one uttered a word "against the heartless wickedness of the swindlers who could so grossly impose upon helpless laborers, while profiting by unpaid toil" (*TR*, June 21, 1848).

"Humanitas," another reader of the *Trinidadian*, offered a stinging critique of Burnley's false philanthropy. Humanitas, it seems, could come to grips with Burnley's callousness only through the use of satire. He pointed out that "the comprehensive mind and humane disposition of the Honorable William Hardin Burnley" alone could have conceived a plan whereby one could bring Africans from Africa and then liberate them to work on the plantations of the island. He added sarcastically, that in proposing his scheme, Burnley had endeared himself to Africans and the cause of suffering humanity, by discovering a mode by which "the barbarous practice of the slave trade could be abolished and the regenerating light of Christianity and civilization made to pierce the cunerian darkness which wraps heathenish Africa." Because of such extraordinary insights and touching humanitarianism, Trinidad could lay claim to having won "providential favor of possessing within her bosom that man, whose wisdom doth confound all the wise things of this earth. This, she will preserve as a bright heirloom of unwonted glory, shedding its radiance on future admiring generations" (*TR*, June 21, 1848).

Burnley had never been assailed so openly in his adopted land. The people who had nursed and fed him and made him prosperous were becoming fed up with his ingratitude and his callousness. They could not understand how a stranger whom they had taken into their bosom could act and think so unfeelingly toward them. Within the legislature, at least one man, Henry Fuller, was looking out for the working people. Fuller proposed that the segment of the colony that received the most from its bounty should also share in the burdens that resulted from their extravagance. To the laboring population, Burnley was becoming more a part of the colony's problems than a part of its solution. His dominance of the island was fading. For the next two and a half years of his life, he would feel the full weight of the people's scorn and resentment.

CHAPTER 37

The Voice of the People

≶

We are strangers to nationality. Our platform is as broad as humanity. We repudiate, with unutterable loathing and disgust, that narrow spirit which would confine our duties to one quarter of the globe, to the exclusion of another, that can see nothing good or great in any land but our own.

—Frederick Douglass, "Pioneers in a Holy Cause," 1847

The British Nation acted generously, but blindly, when she gave Twenty Million as compensation to the slaveholders. The lowest principles of justice demanded that more than half of that sum should be given to the slaves—the victims of cruel wrong and oppression.

—George Numa Des Sources, *Trinidadian*, 1848

As was stated previously, the Trinidad economy was in a precarious state at the middle of 1848. It did not help that Messrs Eccles, Burnley and Company of Glasgow and their agents Messrs Losh, Spiers and Company in Trinidad declared bankruptcy nor, for that matter, that the early rains "arrested in the fields, at least, one-third of the abundant crop." For many Trinidadians this unfortunate situation resulted in heartbreaking scenes of poverty, homelessness, and despair on the island. Even the Indians who were brought to the colony at the public expense suffered grievously from this downturn in the economy. The *Trinidadian* reported that "Indians from the country are crowding our streets, and, it is said, are begging the Government to send them back to their native India, as they cannot live on the wages allowed them for their labor here" (*TR*, June 17, 1848). Something had to be done to reduce this suffering.

The advent of the *Trinidadian*, "a radical and apparently widely read" grassroots newspaper,[1] introduced the laboring classes to a wider range of views on the challenges that faced a newly freed people. It allowed them to perceive themselves in a different way, to verbalize their criticism of Burnley and the local colonial authorities, and to imagine themselves as a people or a nation.[2] Michael Toussaint called it "a pro-black and coloured newspaper."[3] It allowed brown and black people to confront Burnley's racist views and to challenge his contention about the purported shortage of labor that became his cause célèbre. However, the evidence suggests that Burnley used this so-called problem of a labor shortage to feather, or certainly to protect, his own economic nest.

In making itself relevant, the *Trinidadian* began to reprint a review of Burnley's *Observations* that had appeared in *The Colonial Magazine* in 1843. In a touching, even somber, introduction to the article, the newspaper declared: "As it is possible that our readers are partial, like us, to reminiscences, even though painful, we willingly echo 'A Voice from Trinidad,' which found utterance in *The Colonial Magazine* for 1843" (*TR*, June 7, 1848). One would remember that Burnley's hearing of 1841 was designed to attract more laborers to the island. No doubt, the republication of this "painful" reminiscence of Burnley's longrunning concern for new labor was linked to his desire to rid the country of its 3.5 percent export tax after it had spent enormous sums of money to bring East Indian immigrants to the island.

The immigration issue came up again in October when the government introduced its immigration ordinance that called on the government to pay the return passage of Indians who had come to the island in 1845. The *Trinidadian* wanted to know how many Indians, according to law, possessed the right to return and where was the country to get the funds to pay for these passages? In spite of the hardship the working people were undergoing, Burnley called upon the government to remove the export duty even though, "the present revenue, including the 3 1/2 per cent on Exports fall lamentably short of the expenditure" (*TR*, "Further Remarks on the Proceedings at the Last Meeting of the Legislative Council," October 7, 1848).

Burnley proposed "no other taxes to meet the serious defalcation which carrying out the motion would of necessity cause" (*TR*, October 7, 1848). Des Sources described Burnley's performance as "a clever, laughable and illogical farce" in which he "attempted to confound and contemn the eternal principles of even-handed justice, and effectually succeeded in despising or neglecting the crying claims of humanity." "Happily for Trinidad and the world," he continued, Burnley "has as much capacity and cunning as the fox, and as much principle, compassion and feeling as the vulture, the alligator, and the shark." Such a call, he felt could only come from "a fool or a knave" (*TR*, October 4, 1848). Burnley had met his match.

Des Sources kept his most stinging remarks for Burnley's unwonted greed and ingratitude. He insisted that Burnley was indignant because the British government paid only half of the price for his slaves for which he "boldly claims the other half. This is superlative effrontery." Comparing Burnley to a common thief, the editor asks: "What would Mr. Burnley think and say of the detected thief who dare to prefer a claim half the value of the time and toil and cunning, which is the thief's capital, expended in robbing Mr. Burnley's cane field, sugar house, dwelling house or cattle pen, or any other premises or property pertaining to the honorable gentleman." To justify his behavior, Burnley, like many of his slave-owning colleagues, "pleads a case for full compensation, on the ground that the British government sanctioned slavery" (*TR*, October 7, 1848).

Publicly challenging the probity of Burnley's argument, he countered that when an injury is done to any party or parties "compensation is due to all who have suffered, and in the proportion to the amount of injury they have sustained." He asks: "What loss had the slaves sustained by their proprietors and the British Government?" He answers: "Why, they had suffered the loss of liberty, and their labor during the years of bondage. The proprietors of slaves were deprived, at emancipation, of an unrighteous and cruel source of gain, and might, in some cases, lose a portion of the purchase price of their human (but inhumanly obtained treated) stock. The claims of the slaves were never thought of, and yet they were superior and prior to that of their proprietors" (*TR*, October 7, 1848). This was a superb refutation of Burnley's position. It was the first time that a local person, albeit a black person, had publicly challenged Burnley's imperial right to the property in black and brown bodies.

This issue came up again on November 13, when the Legislative Council passed a series of resolutions, which had the effect of overwhelming the local labor force and reintroducing slavery into the country via the backdoor. Taking exception to Burnley's "long desultory speech, the drift of which (slavery) was unmistakable," the newspaper fumed that Burnley's vast benevolence induces him "to desire such an influx of immigrants, alias slaves, as would swamp the laborers at present in the colony. As we understand him, he cares not though that our present laboring population starve, providing he gets labor for less than two bits a task—a rate not adequate to supply the necessary wants of a man or woman, although unblessed with a simple dependent. The heartless barbarianism of his unblushing avowed desire could hardly be surpassed" (*TR*, November 15, 1848).

In December the *Grenada Chronicle* argued that the only hope of resolving the crisis that had hit the West Indies lay in the hands of "the wise and righteous Providence of Jehovah, and, secondarily, in the Christian people of Great Britain" (*TR*, "A New System of Slavery for the Queen's Subjects in Trinidad," December 9, 1848). It continued: "We are therefore pained and deeply concerned to observe that a portion of our brother colonists of Trinidad are clamoring for unlawful gain, and appear not to care how much suffering may be inflicted on the unfortunate Africans, so, that their wicked purpose may be accomplished." However, the newspaper kept its worst rebuke for Burnley whose remarks, they said, were "peculiarly offensive. He evidently longs to see the black population reduced again to the state of vassalage, and in his erroneous effects to save the Colony from further embarrassment, enquires, what are the planters to do, whilst the newly imported Africans are learning to wash their nasty, filthy carcases [*sic*], and to eat with a spoon instead of putting their dirty fingers into the dish" (*TR*, December 9, 1848).

In addition to following the events in Grenada, Des Sources and his colleagues observed the conditions of enslaved Africans in the United States, particularly the activities of Frederick Douglass, an escaped slave, that were inspiring to them. Douglass was also inspired by the emancipation of the blacks in the West Indies, which he saw as being closely connected to the fate of his brothers and sisters in the United States. On August 1, 1847, at Canandaigua, New York, in the presence of over four thousand people, of whom one third were black, Douglass delivered his first of four speeches commemorating the abolition of West Indian slavery.[4] Embracing the enslaved West Indians as "our brothers and sisters,"[5] Douglass declared West Indian emancipation an event "which may be justly regarded the greatest and grandest of the nineteenth century . . . a splendid achievement, a glorious triumph of justice, love, and mercy, over avarice, pride, and cruelty."[6] Even as he celebrated the emancipation of eight hundred thousand freed Africans, he saw their liberation as a prelude to the future when, as he said, "we shall be summoned to rejoice over the downfall of Slavery in our own land."[7] He also likened West Indian emancipation to "a city set upon a hill"[8] and treated its emancipation day, August 1, "as more sacred than the Fourth of July."[9]

On September 3, 1848, on the tenth anniversary of his escape from slavery, Douglass wrote a letter, "I am your fellow man, but not your slave," to Thomas

Auld, his former master, which he published in the *North Star*, an abolitionist newspaper he had founded on December 3, 1847. In doing this, Douglass was merely following up on another daring gesture he had undertaken previously, that of sending a copy of his *Narrative* to Auld, daring him to challenge the authenticity of his account.[10] On January 10, 1849, almost as though it was responding to Douglass's quest to draw the public's attention to the horrors of slavery, the *Trinidadian* published an excerpt from Douglass's letter that reminded Trinidadians about the harrowing aspects of slavery in their country (*TR*, "Frederick Douglass and His Family," January 10, 1849). Des Sources wanted to tell his Trinidadian antagonists, the proprietors, that black people were their equals rather than their slaves, and they were bounded together in a common destiny, whether they liked it or not. Treating the ex-slaves fairly was an indisputable condition for the freedom of all.

One and a half years later (July 1850), in an even more direct admonition against Burnley and the planters, the *Trinidadian* serialized Douglass's *Narrative of the Life of Frederick Douglass* (1845), accompanied by the following remarks: "We commence in this number the insertion of the autobiography of Frederick Douglass, formerly a slave, and presently the proprietor and editor of the *North Star*, We invite the Honorable Mr. Burnley, and others, to begin its perusal at once. They may therein find some remedy for their infatuated dislike of 'African Materials'" (*TR*, July 10, 1850).[11] In deploying Douglass's autobiography against Burnley and the planters, Des Sources wanted it known that, like their brothers in the United States, blacks were dissatisfied with their conditions on the island. He also wanted to tell Burnley and the world that "slave-owners, rather than being gentle, Christian folk, were coarse men and women who dared not follow truly Christian teachings or their own humane and civilizing instincts."[12] When the *Trinidadian* reprinted the extract from "I am your fellow man, but not your slave" and serialized *Narrative of the Life of Frederick Douglass*, it wanted to remind Burnley that the scars of slavery still lingered in their hearts and the hurtful messages Burnley was sending through his rhetoric pained them tremendously.

The enduring link between enslaved African Americans and Trinidadians remained. Maxwell Philip, the author of *Emmanuel Appadocca*, the first novel of Trinidad and perhaps the West Indies, had the sufferings of his enslaved brothers and sisters in the United States in mind when, in 1854, he wrote his novel. He noted in his preface that he was inspired to write his novel because his feelings were roused up by the cruel manner "in which the slave holders of America deal with their slave-children." Unable to imagine how slavery could hide "the hideousness of begetting children for the purpose of turning them into the fields to labor at the lash's sting, he ventured to sketch out the line of conduct, which a high-spirited and sensitive person would probably follow, if he found himself picking cotton under the spurring encouragement of 'Jim-boes' or 'Quimboes' on his own father's plantation."[13] There can be no doubt that a growing spirit of solidarity had emerged among these children of the dark in the immediate aftermath of (and during) their slave experiences in these Americas and that Frederick Douglass had become a standard bearer of those relations.

CHAPTER 38

Burnley's Declining Significance

The object of immigration when first commenced was to supply a deficiency of labor resulting from the change of habits in the Negro population occasioned by the possession of freedom. This labor was required to work the sugar estates, which had been produced by an entirely artificial system, supported by the compulsory labor of slaves and afterwards carried on in the hope that the losses which were incurred in the first year after the change would be recovered at some future period; this hope being formulated on faith in the promise of production held out by the British Parliament.

—Lord Harris to Earl Grey, 1849

B Y THE BEGINNING of 1849, it was clear that Burnley's power and influence, or what a later activist called "the Burnley School," had begun to wane (*PG*, "The Great Reform: Monster Mass Meeting in the Savana," January 18, 1887). Although he was still a powerful presence on the island, his clout and influence were being superseded by Lord Harris's exuberance and Charles Warner's continuing rise to power. The vociferous opposition from Des Sources and the blacks also contributed to Burnley's declining significance. Lord Harris was fortunate to have at his disposal a princely fortune of £10,000 or £12,000 per year whereas Warner, apart from the power of the attorney general's office, was an agent for British merchants on the island. Together Lord Harris and Warner worked to transform the island into their own likeness.

Given the bankruptcy of Pierre Antoine Ganteaume and John Losh, Lord Harris was beginning to question the wisdom of having so many sugar proprietors and heads of other speculative industries as members of his cabinet. He reasoned: "Not only is their time occupied on matters foreign to their public duties but as such undertakings generally entail risk and considerable anxiety of mind, they often become morally and mentally unfitted for performing the business of their office in a proper manner." Since financial losses frequently occur from such speculation, the embarrassment that results not only brings shame to the officers involved but causes "Government losses in public estimation."[1] This was surely a signal to Burnley and his fellow planters that they would not have the same power and dominance they enjoyed during the first fifty years of the country's development.

During this period three distinct dimensions within the planter class became evident: those who borrowed excessively to maintain their lifestyles and eventually were overtaken by the financial crisis that hit the island, capitalists such as Burnley who had their own capital and therefore did not borrow much, and the French planters who retained the services of most of the old slaves. The French planters treated their former slaves with "good temper and honesty. They were economically firm without tyranny. They attended in person to the work on their plantations; and it was well known that they made sugar at a lower cost than the others" (*PO*, July 18, 1887). Burnley argued that half of the island's ruin was due "to the facility with which owners of estates have hitherto been able to borrow money" (*PG*, "The Half-Million Loan," February 16, 1849), while the *Port of Spain Gazette* concluded that the other half of the island's ruin was attributable to the facility afforded to capitalists to swamp the planter "with exorbitant interests, commissions, and other charges; and if it be so evident that there was always on one side of our money bargains *a fool*, it may be fairly inferred that there was on the other side a knave to take advantage of his folly."[2]

While the first group favored East Indian indentureship, the latter groups resented having to pay for the exorbitance of the former group out of the public purse. They could see no reason "why they should be taxed to find labor for the gamblers, who were borrowing money at twenty to twenty five percent (interest and commission) to carry on their disastrous speculation."[3] By 1849 the colony had spent £148,000 for the importation of East Indian immigrants when the colony realized about £50,000 from import and export duties while the island's expenditure was about £90,000 per year. To discourage the reckless speculation of the first group, the state ceased to pay for this costly program. Instead, the proprietors were made to pay the full expense of bringing East Indian immigrants to the island who had to be "permanently located for a term of years on some estates."[4]

At this point, the East Indians were not better, nor more desirable, workers than the Africans. Yet they suffered from several disadvantages. Lord Harris noted that the East Indian "neither knows the language or the habits of the country. He is totally ignorant of the nature of the work he is to perform."[5] In the debate on the permanent loan from the British Parliament, William Rennie asserted "that East Indians, if properly selected, were as useful laborers in every respect as Africans. The great majority of those sent here from Calcutta and Madras were most injudiciously chosen, without reference to age, or their fitness for agricultural purposes; and although in particular instances, that immigration proved perfectly successful, generally it were not so" (*PG*, "Council of Government," February 13, 1849). He assured the Legislative Council that he spoke from his own experience.

Meanwhile, the black workers (sometimes called Creole workers) resisted the undercutting of their labor advantage by withdrawing from the estates and occupying the land. In places such as the quarter of Tacarigua, this practice had "utterly destroyed the cultivation of the estates." The attorney general believed that the only way out of this situation was to continue to pay the laborers high wages and to continue with his immigration process. Without such a combination, he could foresee no way out of the country's dilemma. He warned: "If the country relapsed into barbarism, it would entail misery on thousands and a loss of millions to the mother country" (*PG*, February 13, 1849).

The East Indians on the other hand were having a difficult time adjusting to the country. Burnley did not accept the argument that immigration per se was responsible for the death and diseases of the East Indians. He argued that this catastrophe started after Lord Grey nullified Lord Harris's regulations that were proposed to control the East Indians. According to Burnley, it was only after the abrogation of Lord Harris's regulations, "when these miserable persons were left at liberty to exercise their own idle and vagrant proclivities, that disease and death made such havoc amongst them. Let him not therefore impute to immigration those unhappy results which solely belonged to the neglect of all wholesome and proper regulations on the subject and which he trusted would be effectually guarded against in future" (*PG*, February 13, 1849).

As 1849 wore on the economic fortune of the island continued to deteriorate. At the council meeting of April 2, Burnley presented a petition to the government from one hundred and thirty planters who complained about their "perilous position" and asking the Home Government to increase the amount of immigrants that were being sent to the island. In their petition, the memorialists informed the government that they were daily "experiencing more and more difficulty, inconvenience, and uncertainty in taking off the present crop, in consequence of the increasing scarcity of labor for the purpose" (*PG*, "Council of Government," April 3, 1849). In their sorrow, they cried out to the Home Government: "Pray, remember the poor injured sugar planter" (*PG*, April 3, 1849). The Creole laborers, they said, had abandoned the plantations while the captured Africans squatted on the land. Their only hope lay in the work of the East Indian immigrants. It is the group to which they turned in their hour of economic need.

As was to be expected, the planters complained about the increased cost of production and their fears about competition from the slaveholding countries "which is yearly becoming more formidable, by the withdrawal of all protection [in the Home Market]." They called on the government to increase the number of East Indians and Africans, who were being brought to the island. J. A. Allen, the treasurer of the council, cautioned that there was a shortage of labor because the workers were not paid their wages. He argued that where workers "were regularly and properly paid—there was no want of labor on those estates. . . . He had not the slightest doubt that a planter who paid his people regularly could get all the labor he required" (*PG*, April 3, 1849). Lord Harris supported Allen's position. He agreed that more workers were reluctant to work on the plantations than those in previous years. He informed Earl Grey that the blacks were disinclined to work on the plantations mainly because of "the reduction of wages which had been attempted by the planters in consequence of the reduced prices of sugar."[6]

The attorney general agreed with the planters that immigration was absolutely necessary to ease the situation and offered that "without continued immigration there could be no hope for the large proprietary of the colony" (*PG*, April 3, 1849). But Lord Harris held a slightly different view. Although he supported the desired ends of the planters, he was not sure the answer to their problem lay in bringing more immigrants into the colony. He observed: "Even if the supply required would be procured, which appears from the information I have obtained more than doubtful, the expenses of the immigration must be considered and the success or failure or the experiment must depend very much upon that."[7]

During the original debate in April, Burnley referred to a letter written by "an Englishman" published in the *Port of Spain Gazette*, in which the latter argued that "Earl Grey had no power to adopt any national policy without the permission of the people of England" (*PG*, "Council of Government," February 13, 1849). Burnley agreed with the sentiments expressed in this letter, which led him to address the planters' petition to the "proper authorities in Great Britain" rather than Lord Grey. The governor did not miss Burnley's deliberate slight. After the resolution was passed, the governor observed: "The Board would observe that he [Mr. Burnley] had cautiously inserted the words 'proper authorities.' This gave to His Excellency the full and amble discretion to forward the memorial [petition] either to Earl Grey, or the sovereign people, as he might deem most advantageous to their interests" (*PG*, February 13, 1849).

Other Englishmen on the island shared the governor's view about Burnley's disparaging remarks about the mother colony. William Curtis, who was associated with the failed attempt to construct a railway in the colony and which Burnley had vigorously opposed, lost no time in registering his disapproval of Burnley's remarks by sending a letter to Earl Grey. He informed the latter that Burnley cherished "the most bitter antipathy against the British name and connexion and takes every opportunity of publicly and privately disparaging both." The fact that there was not even a whisper of censure by any member of the board made Burnley's statement more "reprehensible and calculated so deeply to injure imperial interests and the loyal feelings of the colonists."[8] Curtis was exaggerating the impact of Burnley's statement. However, he felt he could get away with such slander against Burnley because he sensed Burnley's declining significance in the colony and loss of favor at the Colonial Office.

Having attended to his official business, Burnley turned his attention to his domestic affairs. On April 7 he noted in his private notebook that "he left Trinidad in the *R.M.S. Tay*, accompanying 'Mrs. B' as far as St. Thomas, whence she sailed on the 15th in *R.M.S. Medway* for England" (*OG*, 16–17). Such an account was in keeping with the parliamentary record (*PG*, "Legislative Proceedings," April 13, 1849). He returned to the island on May 17. A year and a half later he berated the official members of the Legislative Council for not waiting until he returned so that he could participate in the debate on an important road ordinance bill. He complained: "These honorable members [that is, the unofficials] therefore pressed for a postponement. They could not wait for two or three days for the discussion, and yet they waited until the 31st December [1849] to pass the resolution, those very gentlemen who could not wait for two or three days when pressed by the unofficial side" (*TR*, "Legislative Council," December 14, 1850).

In spite of her disdain for the island, Charlotte had condescended to spend some time there with her husband. One does not know how long she stayed in the island. Norman Lamont concedes that Charlotte's long refusal to join Burn-ley in Trinidad gave him every reason "to side-slip in the direction of Augusta Farquhar" even though he insists that Burnley's letter to Charlotte proved that he was a devoted husband. This was only part of the truth. Although Charlotte returned, she might have been so shocked by what she saw that she was not inclined to stay on the island any longer than was necessary. By then Augusta was safely ensconced within Burnley's heart and hearth.

Charlotte's long separation from her husband had encouraged Burnley to seek solace in Augusta's arms. He might have been a devoted husband in terms of taking care of Charlotte's economic wants, but one is not too sure he was tak-ing care of the things that mattered most to her. His hot temper and stubborn-ness suggest a man who was more concerned about his needs and desires rather than those of his wife. And then he was about work and business. Charlotte became dispensable because Augusta was there to take care of his sexual and social needs. This, of course, was not unusual. Anthony de Verteuil, observed that during that period, "even some of the most respectable inhabitants of the town [Port of Spain] and well-known planters in the country could be found with a mistress."[9]

The short time Charlotte spent in Trinidad was not sufficient time to remove the deep fissures that separated the two. This was the last time Burnley saw Charlotte.

CHAPTER 39

Living Like a Lord

Emancipation in Hayti was no failure, but had proved an immense boon to the emancipated people. Some persons pointed to our West Indian colonies as a proof that emancipation had failed, and that slavery was better than freedom. Let such persons come to Trinidad, and ask the inhabitants whether they think so. He was willing to let the answer of the meeting decide the question.

—John Candler, Meeting of Friends of Freedom, Trinidad, 1850

O N JANUARY 5, 1850, at the behest of the Anti-Slavery Society of Britain, John Candler (an English Quaker and friend of Thomas Clarkson) and George William Alexander (an English philanthropist) visited Trinidad to study the effects of emancipation upon the recently freed Africans in the West Indies. Frederick Douglass, in the second installation of his autobiography, *My Bondage and My Freedom*, noted that Alexander, a friend of the Negroes, spent more than "an American fortune in promoting the anti-slavery cause in different sections of the world,"[1] which was why when Candler and Alexander arrived in Jamaica in June 1850, the *Falmouth Post* declared: "We have no reason to believe that Messrs. Candler and Alexander, would allow themselves to be imposed upon by the few 'malcontents,' who are ever ready to pour 'a leprous distilment' into the ears of those, who seek a knowledge of 'the truth, the whole truth, and nothing but the truth'" (*TR*, "Messrs. Chandler and Alexander, of the Society of Friends," July 24, 1850). They consoled themselves that "Messrs. Candler and Alexander are gentlemen of talent and keen observation—they will 'look with their own eyes' and judge for themselves as they contemplate our dismantled estates, and dilapidated buildings in our town" (*TR*, July 24, 1850).

Burnley and the Trinidadian elite felt a similar anxiety when Candler and Alexander visited the island at the beginning of the year. They met with Lord Harris (governor), William George Knox (chief justice), Charles Warner (attorney general), Thomas F. Johnston (colonial secretary of Trinidad), and other government officials. Aware of their influence in England and the United States, government officials and planters received them cordially and treated them with unusual respect. Lord Harris offered Candler and his party the use of his carriage "which we acknowledged thankfully, but declined."[2] They visited some of the more prosperous estates such as Aranguez (owned by John Severe Laforest, a black man), Le Valsayn (owned by Paola Maria Giuseppi), Corinth and Phillipine (owned by Dr. Philip), Union Hall (owned by Burnley), and Burnley's palatial mansion in Orange Grove. They may have expected to see the "dismantled estates and dilapidated buildings" they saw in Jamaica. However, they were shocked when they saw the grandiose way in which Burnley lived. He seemed to be living as "a Lord" in his castle. Candler described the atmosphere at Orange Grove during that first month of January 1850:

> This morning [January 16] early, a carriage and horses came to our door [in Port of Spain], sent by Wm. Burnley, member of the Executive Council, to convey us to his mansion in St. Mary's [Tacarigua] to breakfast. It is a mansion and he lives in it like a Lord. After breakfast we called on Wm. Hume, his nephew, who is son of Joseph Hume, MP, for Montrose, then rode through the Estate, which makes nearly 400 *tons* of sugar, inspected the sub soil draining of many of the fields, went through the Sugar works, and returned with our host to his dwelling house. . . . Dined at 5 o'clock. Wm. Hume and [Henry] Richards, the parish clergyman joined us and we spent a long evening in earnest conversation and friendly controversy. KA & MC [the wives of Candler and Alexander] spent the day at the mansion with an American lady and her niece, relatives of Wm. Burnley's.[3]

The next day Burnley provided a carriage to take Candler and his party back to Port of Spain.

On January 18, Candler and Alexander addressed a public meeting in Port of Spain that was held under the auspices of the Trinidad branch of the Anti-Slavery Society to which not "one planter or a merchant" attended (*TR*, "To the Editor of the Trinidadian," February 1850). In his address, Candler noted that ever since the abolition of the slave trade (he said he "remember[ed] the passing of the Abolition Act of 1807") his heart always beats in sympathy with "the Sons of Africa" (*TR*, "Anti-Slavery Meeting," January 23, 1850). He also explained that in order to get a more comprehensive picture of the Trinidad situation, they (he and Alexander) had accepted invitations from the planters to visit their estates and were assisted in their research "by all classes of the community. They had to thank the governor of all the colonies they had as yet visited for their urbanity and kindness, as well as their officers under them" (*TR*, January 23, 1850).

On January 20, Candler's party left the island, encouraged with what they had seen there. Although one cannot be entirely certain of the identity of the American woman of whom Candler spoke, it is possible that when, on December 29, 1849, Burnley left the Legislative Council expressing his fear about being "absent for two days from his family in the country" and anxious "not to keep out after dark on a Saturday night" (*TR*, "Council of Government," January 8, 1850), he was not referring to being away from his nephew for such a long time. It may be indecorous, but one can speculate that Augusta Farquhar was the woman to whom Candler alluded and who, it would seem, was then living openly with Burnley as his common-law wife.

At the council meeting of February 1, 1850, the governor directed the members' attention two dispatches that Earl Grey, the secretary of state for the colonies, had sent to him. The first dispatch dealt with the presence of Indian and Chinese immigrants on the island and whether the former, "after a term of years, should be entitled to a return passage with their wives and families to India, as [occurs] in the Mauritius" (*PG*, "Council of Government," February 8, 1850). The second dispatch dealt with the setting up of an internal postal system to distribute local mail better.

These matters were raised again at the March 1, 1850, council meeting in a way that demonstrated how much the October 1 rebellion had shaken up the confidence of the white elite in the society. William Rennie, a member of a committee and manager of Colonial Bank that was selected to prepare an immigration ordinance similar to the one in force in Mauritius, offered a motion that sought to increase the number of policemen and stipendiary magistrates in the colony. He assured the council that if such a measure was adopted "the expenditure on expensive criminal prosecution will be diminished without doubt, and the idle habits of the laboring population [will be] checked by the more certain and expeditious administration of the laws in the distant country districts" (*PG*, "Council of Government," March 5, 1850).

Rennie reminded the council that it was difficult "to introduce improved laws bearing on the relative duties of master and servants, with respect to their being efficiently carried out and the impossibility of getting them administered" when the laborers were so resistant to the dictatorial behavior of their former masters. This was particularly true in places such as Oropouche that, as he stated, "had recently gained so unenviable a [*sic*] notoriety for arson, assaults and murders," which suggested that a majority of the inhabitants "were ignorant of the existence of any law in the colony" (*PG*, March 5, 1850). He elaborated on his position: "There had lately been petitions and remonstrances laid before this Board from the proprietors of that quarter, urging the appointment of a resident Stipendiary Magistrate, and to such an extent had a lawless spirit got aboard there that when the Warden last week put a notification at the police station of the Ward rates becoming due this month, his notice was immediately pulled down, and his authority to collect rates was put at defiance" (*PG*, March 5, 1850).

Burnley did not let this opportunity pass. "It was," he said, "too important a measure to be voted in silence." He reminded his colleagues that he had always brought this matter to their attention, "pointing out that an economy in such a case [in the absence of the enforcement of the law] was detrimental to their pecuniary interests." He admonished: "Laborers upon estates [who] believe at present that they may almost do anything with immunity, and not without reason, from the difficulty and trouble of bringing cases quickly before a magistrate, so that nine-tenths of the offences committed were never investigated. If more Stipendiaries were appointed, this evil might be remedied." He reasoned: "They would then hear no more of such scandalous scenes as had occurred in Oropouche, where, according to the statement of the Colonial Secretary, the laborers had recently declared in a public meeting that they would not obey the laws. Resident proprietors would then feel themselves safe, and would be able to attend properly to their affairs. . . . No more important measure for the benefit of the colony than the present could have been brought before the Board" (*PG*, March 5, 1850). The resolution was carried unanimously.

At this time, the question of race was becoming a more heated topic both nationally and internationally. On February 20, 1850, the *Trinidadian* published excerpts from Thomas Carlyle's racist article, "Occasional Discourse on the Nigger Question," in which he described emancipated people in the British colonies as belonging to an idle, inferior race whom God had created to be servants to those "who are born *wiser* than you, that are born lords of you—servants to the whites, if they *are* (as what mortal can doubt they are?) born wiser than you. . . . And if 'slave' mean essentially 'servant hired for life'—for life, or by a contract of long continuance and not easily dissoluble—I ask, whether, in all human things, the 'contact of long continuance' is not precisely the contact to be desired, were the right terms once found for it" (*TR*, February 20, 1850).

Carlyle argued for the continuance of slavery since, in his opinion, emancipation had proven to be a farce. Many people of racist sentiments accepted his position, thus his article quickly became an important part of a transatlantic dialogue on slavery, emancipation, and the efficacy of race and class in the Caribbean and the United States.[4] A local reader called this essay, "a true work of the devil" (*TR*, "Mr. Carlyle and the Negro Question," April 3, 1850). Burnley's discourse was part of a racist dialogue that was taking place at a time when the formerly enslaved were trying to find themselves in their new society even as their former masters tried to keep them at the bottom of the social and political ladder.

At the February meeting of the board, the governor informed its members that he intended to set up an internal postal service that would be placed under an officer appointed by the colony "with the exception of the officer who would continue to receive and post the letters by the packets" (*PG*, "Council of Government," March 5, 1850). Burnley did not believe that the society would gain any advantages by setting up such a system. Dr. Philip, a resident of the south of the island, disagreed. He argued that "there was a strong feeling down the Coast in favor of it. They looked upon it as a great boon. He could not say what the feeling in Tacarigua [Burnley's home] was" (*PG*, March 5, 1850). Burnley rejoined: "All I wanted was to have some little doubts removed. I have heard nothing to assure me that the Post Office would work effectually" (*PG*, March 5, 1850).

This question came up again at the March meeting of the council. In spite of Burnley's objections, the governor announced he would establish a post office on the island, his views having "always received immediate attention and strenuous support from Earl Grey. Through his instrumentality I hope the difficulties have been got over. It is now in my power to recommend that the Council should authorize the expenditure necessary for its establishment" (*PG*, "Council of Government," April 2, 1850). It was a subtle way of telling Burnley that he would not allow him to frustrate his plan to transform the island into a modern state. When the proposed branches were announced, no branch post office was scheduled to be set up in Tacarigua, Burnley's home village, even though one was allocated to the nearby village of Arouca, which had a smaller population than Tacarigua.[5]

Lord Harris estimated that in any given year over one hundred thousand letters and an equal number of newspapers would pass through the several post offices that would be set up on the island. A half-penny postage stamp was also introduced into the system for the first time. Although the editor of the *Port of Spain Gazette* did not agree with the governor's figures with regard to the cost of the service, he believed it was a facility, "which will no doubt receive the best consideration honorable members can bestow on it, seeing the very great advantage of such a measure to the inhabitants of the rural districts" (*PG*, "Legislative Proceedings," April 2, 1850).

While the council listened respectfully to Burnley's views, the governor was not about to let Burnley derail his proposal. Burnley fought against this proposal up to his dying day. It was among the last dissenting petitions he sent to the secretary of state the week before he died. By this time, Burnley was seen more as an irritant than a force for good. Although he lived a lordly life in his palatial mansion, more and more he was being seen as a relic of the past.

CHAPTER 40

The Laborers' Rebellion

It had been mentioned to me previously that much discontent had been manifested by the people on this subject [that is, the shaving of the heads of debtors in the gaol]. I have heard also that the threats of violence and incendiarism have been pretty commonly bandied about amongst the lowest orders. These threats are only less wicked and foolish than the acts which they signify.

—Lord Harris, "Council of Government," 1849

AFTER CHARLOTTE LEFT the island, Burnley turned his attention to the business of government and the running of his estates. While he participated in most of the parliamentary debates, he did not initiate any major legislative measures although he clashed with the attorney general frequently as he sought to maintain his influence in the society. Increasingly, Burnley and Warner saw the society through different lenses. For example, during the debate on the territorial ordinance, Burnley refuted the attorney general's assertion that the unofficial members "considered themselves bound to oppose measures of government." He offered that the unofficial members were "bound to oppose the attorney general's encroachments, to which, on the present occasion, there seemed to be no end" (*PG*, "Council of Government," July 20, 1849). Nothing, of course, stopped Warner's powerful grip on government until 1870 when he was forced to resign.

On August 28, the quarrel between Burnley and Warner intensified. Joining with other unofficial members, Burnley objected strongly to a proposal brought by Warner that sought to increase the emoluments of government officials on the ground that one of the major objectives of the Legislative Council was to bring down expenditures rather than to raise them. "Necessity," he argued, "rather than their will compelled that they do so." Although the economic condition of the society had begun to improve, he warned that the island was still in a state of "great distress," primarily because of "the inability to sell sugar in the British market in spite of an actual protecting duty of 5s in their favor, at as low a rate as the planters of Cuba and Brazil. Their position, therefore, was a rapidly declining one, lower and lower until 1854, when the last vestige of protection [under the Sugar Duties Act] would be effaced" (*PG*, "Council of Government," August 28, 1849).

During this period the renewal of Indian immigration to the island became a more urgent topic. In September Burnley and his committee (comprised of Burnley, Warner, Henry Fuller, I. A. Allen, and Rennie) reported back to the Legislative Council on the need to increase the number of Indian immigrants to the colony. They declared that the source of all the economic problems that befell the colony lay in the inability of colonial officials to import more laborers after the enslaved were freed. In his dispatch to Earl Grey on September 6, Lord Harris wrote "a supply of Indian laborers would be of great advantage for all the sugar estates in the island and would probably prevent some from being abandoned, which without assistance could not be carried on." However, he cautioned that if immigration was to be renewed, "the expense ought to be considerably diminished to make it of any real use to the colony" (*PG*, August 28, 1849).

As sympathetic as Lord Harris was to the East Indians, he and his officials could not see the resentment that was boiling over within the breast of African workers and other members of the nonwhite society. The incident that led to the social explosion was harmless enough. On Monday, October 1, under a hot noonday sun, over five thousand laborers (out of a population of sixty thousand people) surrounded the Government House where the Legislature Council was meeting, demanding that they see the governor and Mr. Warner to sort out a horrendous wrong that was being committed against them. This was unusual.

The occasion itself was not unusual. The working people wanted to protest a law that was passed by the government that specified that all people who were imprisoned for debt under fifty dollars would have their heads shaven, wear the felon's dress (coarse, osnaburg canvas suits with black caps), and do the menial work of the prison. The *Trinidadian* reported that the legislation passed hurriedly, and contained a clause to the effect that people who were sent to prison for small debts "should be treated as criminals, should have their heads shaven, should be subject to jail fare, compelled to wear jail clothing, and perform the most menial and disgusting labor required within the walls of a prison while those imprisoned for large debts should not only be exempt from all such degrading impositions but be allowed to live at ease and in the enjoyment of such comforts and luxuries as their families thought fit to provide" (*TR*, "Riot, Loss of Life, and Incendiarism," October 3, 1849).

This was disturbing news. The West Indian colonies had a troubling history of abusing women. Although the abolition act demanded that apprentices "be freed from the atrocious system of irresponsible corporal punishment" the cruelty against women was unbelievable. The Anti-Slavery Society reported that during apprenticeship "the hardships of females, aged persons, and children, in most colonies, but especially in the Crown Colonies [such as Trinidad], have been greatly increased. . . . In Jamaica, wives, daughters, mothers and sisters, have been flogged, and may still be flogged for apprenticeship offence in reality, though under colour of prison discipline; and, that both in that and in other Colonies, they are still subjected to needless degradation."[1]

Studholme Hodgson noted the "cruel mockings and scourgings" to which these women were subjected. He reported that they had been "inhumanly lacerated and bruised; they have been loaded with galling chains and collars; they have been wantonly shorn of their hair."[2] This shaving of women's hair, he added, was "a most dreadful punishment in these climates: it leaves the skull unprotected, exposed to the rays of a tropical sun."[3] It is no wonder then, that these women became so alarmed when they learned that the government were planning to shave their hair while they were in prison. Angered by the implications of this regulation, the poorer classes (or "the lower orders" as they were called), together with their sympathizers, assembled at Eastern Market, Port of Spain, to discuss what action they should take to protest against such a reprehensible law.

First, they unanimously selected Edmund Saulger Hobson, a highly respected colored solicitor, to chair their proceedings. After some discussion, the people adopted a resolution that repudiated the enactment of the gaol regulation, as the law was called, which they described as being "tyrannical, unjust and impolitic for the following reason: because it visits a mere breach of contract, often times the result of uncontrollable misfortune, with all the pains and penalties of a crime of the deepest dye." Second, they appointed a delegation of six people—A. Radix, G. N. Des Sources, F. J. Scott, George Fitzwilliam, Louis Edouard, and Philip Rostant—to meet the governor with a view to resolving the problem.

Many of these men were distinguished members of the community. Des Sources was the publisher and editor of the *Trinidadian*, Fitzwilliam was the vice president of the Port of Spain town council while Rostant was a leading merchant of that city.

After the meeting, the people left Eastern Market and drifted toward Brunswick Square, opposite Government House, where the legislature usually met on the first Monday of the month. Although Hobson had asked the people to disburse peacefully and return to their homes and their business (he felt it was injudicious for them to stay since it may cause confusion), they preferred to remain and see how things turned out. About 10:30 that morning the people began to assemble around Government House. Jose A. Giuseppi, the Stipendiary Justice of Peace for the Eastern District, who was in Port of Spain that morning, described the scene: "The people began to collect at half-past eleven in tens, sixes, and so on, about Brunswick Square in front of Government House. . . . They remained there until 12 o'clock, when the meeting of the Council took place. I was with the Colonial Secretary when the messenger announced there was a deputation to the governor."[4]

The crowd filled Brunswick Square and the space between Government House and the Court House where the offices of the Supreme Court, the Nisi Prius and Complaints Court, the Registrar of Courts, the Registrar General, and the Solicitor General were located. They awaited the governor's response to the resolution they had passed in the morning. After meeting with the governor, Rostant and the other members of the delegation returned to Brunswick Square to inform their followers about the result of their deliberation. However, the square was so crowded that most of the people were unable to hear what they said. They were in a defiant mood. It was an appropriate place for them to congregate. Years earlier, two Amerindian tribes had fought a pitched battle there. They called it *Place des Ames*.

Like the earlier demonstration for freedom in 1834, the crowd consisted mostly of women. Some were carrying their babies in their arms. They refused to disburse. The gaol regulations intimately affected them. Unable to learn what had taken place between their delegation and the governor and what was transpiring during the debate in the council chambers, the people entered Government House and occupied the attorney general's office. The officers of the court demanded that the members of the invading party leave the office of the attorney general immediately. Joseph Celestin Surera, the leader of the uprising, refused to do so. He believed that the time had come to challenge the government for all the wrongs it had committed against the people. In an even more determined voice, he told his followers: "We must finish this today. This Government has trampled on the necks of the people far too long. It's time to resist. I am your leader. As long as I stay, you must stay. We must remain here until we get the Governor's answer."[5]

After Surera left Warner's office, he and his followers headed for the council where the debate on the gaol regulations was taking place. On his way there, he paused on the stairs and uttered a rally cry to his followers: "This country has been under the yoke of certain people for too long a time. It must be regenerated. You must remain here until you get a reply from the governor. I am your head. So long as I remain here you must remain also. If things remain as they are, this will become a country of cut-throats."[6] After that declaration, Surera and his followers went up to the council room. They occupied the galleries as they listened to the proceedings of the Legislative Council.

The attorney general proceeded to review the legislation. He assured his colleagues that this was not a piece of class legislation intended to protect the big capitalists. The rules, he said, were framed to protect the small traders and shopkeepers. His objective, he said, "was to show that the class of small traders suffered as the law now stood" (*PG*, "Council of Government," October 2, 1849). He produced statistics to show that eighty-three males and twenty-three females who were fined at the petty courts paid $1,200, a loss that fell upon the industrious small shopkeepers, all of which "was lost by them, who, of all others, were most deserving of protection" (*PG*, October 2, 1849). It was on those grounds that he thought the regulations should be considered. However, he was willing to modify the legislation if it created such a stir among the population.

Even the governor was willing to modify the regulation in the light of the serious objections of the laboring class, which he thought might have occurred because of "a purposed misuse of terms." He felt that people should have investigated the facts around the gaol regulations before they gave vent to their feelings. If they did, "they would have found, for instance, that as to the much talked of shaving of the head, there is none at all at the gaol. What has been done is solely this—that the rule has been acted on for years and years in the gaol of Port of Spain, viz: that for the promotion of cleanliness the hair of prisoners should be kept short cut. And I may here add, that the rules are all authorized by English precedent" (*PG*, October 2, 1849). In essence, if it was done in England, it should be good for Trinidad.

Burnley, on the other hand, felt no sympathy for the debtors or the rioters for that matter. He saw nothing wrong with shaving their heads, which, to him, was a necessary symbol of degradation. He was against making any changes to the regulations because he felt that to do so would convey to the rioters that the legislators had succumbed to "the noise and intimidation out of doors." He thundered: "Let them take up the vagabonds of this disgraceful riot—let them be brought to justice and be punished as they deserved."[7] He, for one, would not be intimidated by the lawless behavior that was taking place around the building. How could he be sure that some of the persons who had created the horrendous scene outdoor were not inside the building listening to him? He asked: "How can any member of this Board know, while he was performing his duty, he might not be a victim of that excitement that was taking place outside? I would do nothing until things have settled down" (*PG*, October 2, 1849). The government, he advised, should proceed in its usual manner.

At about 1:30 in the afternoon, the council chamber began to get stuffier. Although the stucco walled structure of Government House was designed to provide a cool interior, the number of people in the council room made it unbearably hot. The people who stood behind the governor's chair made the room even stuffier by preventing the free flow of air throughout the building. Sensing the governor's difficulty, Thomas Johnson, the colonial secretary, asked the people to remove themselves from behind the governor's chair. Several of them obeyed the order, but one man, Lewis Peter Gordes, remained. The attorney general then urged Gordes to move. He refused to do so. The governor then instructed Sub-Inspector Thomas to remove Gordes from behind his chair with a warning that if he did not do so he would be prevented from ever entering the council again. Not being near enough to Gordes, Thomas called upon Charles Edward Barnes to remove him from the chambers. A scuffle broke out when Barnes tried to arrest Gordes. The crowd inside the room intervened and liberated Gordes. At that precise moment, another man "waved his hand to the mob below and an attack with stones immediately commenced on the windows public building."[8] The building was inundated with stones. Nearly all of the panes of the glass on the southern side of the building were broken as a result. Some of the stones even passed over the governor's head.

Burnley must have been the most shocked person in the country. He could not understand the audacity of these formerly enslaved persons. He could not understand how these nonentities could ignore an order from him, the attorney general, and the governor and carry on their insubordination with such impunity. It frustrated him to no end, but the stones kept coming. One hour later, when things had subsided, the council proceedings resumed. The people on the outside kept shouting and the stones came in periodically but the council proceeded with its business. The governor even enlisted the help of the members of the deputation to go down to the crowd and tell them that the regulations were altered. The colonial secretary gave them a signed letter to that effect, but it was to no avail. The governor wrote later that "Nothing seemed to have any effect. They were evidently waiting for some other purpose."

As fate would have it, there were only ninety-one policemen on the island, thirty-eight of whom were located in Port of Spain. A majority of the policemen in Trinidad consisted of French and German immigrants since native Trinidadians refused to join the police force. It was only after Lord Harris divided up the island into wards and wardens were given power to recruit able-bodied men to act as special constables in their districts that native Trinidadians joined the force. When the rebellion broke out, the policemen on the island resembled an alien force. They had little in common with the native people. Some of them were also of questionable character. They could not prevail against such a large crowd who saw them as foreigners. This difference intensified the clash between the police and the people.[9] The governor had no choice to call in the soldiers and members of the West India regiment to quell the rebellion that was on his hands. When the tragedy had ended, three persons lay dead because of this terrible misunderstanding.

On December 21, 1849, at the trial of the patriots, Barnes testified about what happened when he tried to arrest Gordes. He noted: "The attorney general told me to move that man out. I attempted to do so by putting my hands gentle on his breast and pushing him. The Hon. Mr. Burnley told me to arrest him. I was prevented from doing so by the crowd which immediately came forward and cried 'No! No!' They came from both sides. They separated the young man and myself. The crowd remained a short time and then went down, the stairs being completely blocked by several people. I believe that they turned to the right. I was in the Council Room when the windows were broken. The stones came from the south side, fell on the floor and council tables, almost all the windows on the south side were broken."[10] Even within the chaos of the moment, Burnley displayed no sympathy for the police officers who were trying to maintain the peace. He complained that they had not done their duty efficiently. It was the most "disgraceful and disreputable scene it was his misfortune that day to witness" (*PG*, "Council of Government," October 2, 1849). It should not be allowed to take place again. In spite of his objections, several alterations were made to the regulations, which were ordered to be reprinted.

CHAPTER 41

Burnley Confronted

≈

Something must be done to infuse a salutary terror into the minds of the
ringleaders—something to assure them that the Colonial Government
possessed not only the power but the will and determination to crush
them. Something also must be done to support and encourage Her Majesty's loyal and well-affected subjects who are now trembling.

—William Hardin Burnley, 1849

O N OCTOBER 2, the morning after the rebellion, Burnley left Port of
Spain to return to his estate in Tacarigua where, he said, his presence
"was essentially required" (*PG*, "Council of Government," November 6, 1849).
Fires, it turned out, were set in seven places on his Tacarigua estate while several attempts were made to burn down his palatial residence at Orange Grove.
Remarkably, his servants and others in his employ extinguished the fires saving
his mansion from the fate that befell buildings on Macoya, El Dorado, and
Dinsley estates, which were located in close proximity to his property. Later
he noted: "Nothing but the merciful interposition of Providence, by suddenly
favoring them with a spell of showery weather, saved the whole district from
destruction" (*PG*, November 6, 1849).

Burnley did not evade all of the dangers with which he was confronted. In
fact, he may have been correct when, in his address to the council on the fateful day of the rebellion, he cautioned that persons within the council who had
heard his speech might have wanted to take revenge for what he had said there
and/or things he had done in the past. Margaret Mann, an English woman (and

wife of Gother Mann a young officer of the Royal Engineers who was stationed on the island), wrote her mother a letter the day after the rebellion. She reported that some of the rebelling laborers "met Mr. Burnley himself going out there [to Tacarigua] this morning and pulled him out of his carriage, beat him fearfully and left him in the middle of the road."[1] The next day she corrected herself. She wrote: "The report about Mr. Burnley's being beaten is contradicted. He was stopped and insulted but not touched. . . . However, I hope the rioters are satisfied with the mischief they have done at Tacarigua and the preparations made to repel them in Port of Spain."[2] At least, she had called the events of October 1 by its proper name; it was a rebellion rather than a riot.

By October 4, things began to settle down. Heavy downpours of rain (it was the middle of the rainy season) in the northeastern part of the island made everyone stay indoors. The presence of British soldiers and seamen guaranteed there would be few challenges to the government. The unrest, however, spread to Oropouche in the south of the island. W. H. Smith, a proprietor there, reported that on the evening of October 4 about forty people "mounted the steps of his gallery and with sledge hammers and felling axes, broke open the door, and entered his house. . . . They proceeded to break all my furniture and after doing this went down the stairs, cut away the galleries and steps, so as to cut away all egress, and began to fell posts which supported the house."[3] Smith and his family escaped from the house. After unleashing their violence on the house, the attackers then brought in their flambeaux and burnt down the house.

Burnley, however, offered his version of what had transpired. He noted that apart from their being in possession of the land for two days, they were following the example of what was taking place in the surrounding French-speaking islands. He charged they established a revolutionary club, made menacing speeches, and followed that up "by setting fire to the house of a gentleman who had rendered himself obnoxious to some of them, by acting as Agent for the owners of private lands, and he, with difficulty, escaped with his life." In the light of these circumstances, the government had no choice but to institute relevant laws that would ensure the safety of the community and protect property as is done "in every civilized country" (*PG*, November 6, 1849).

Not satisfied with previous debates on the issue, Burnley raised the subject once more when the council met on November 6 to finalize the gaol regulation ordinance. As he looked upon the countenance of his colleagues, he was surprised that there was "such a calm, placid, everyday composure, as would seem to imply that nothing had happened, and there was nothing to do." That did not bode well for Burnley or the country. With his voice rising with oratorical fervor, he reminded his colleagues that the occurrences of October 1 were too grave to be easily forgotten: "They constitute a sad and melancholy fact, clearly indicating the moral state and condition of their laboring population, and showing the miserable results of their training and education under British legislation" (*PG*, November 6, 1849).

Burnley advised that strong measures be taken against those who rebelled to avoid similar actions in the future. Something had to be done to support Her Majesty's well-attended and loyal subjects who were "trembling" in their shoes as a result of the rebellion. Something also had to be done to protect property. If not, the small amount of capital that still remained in the colony would be quickly withdrawn. Simply fixing the gaol regulations was not enough. The malaise among the population went deeper than that. The violation of the gaol regulations, he said, was never in their thoughts when they rebelled. It emanated from the reduction of wages that had taken place two years earlier, which resulted in "all their vindictive rage [being] leveled at the owners of property, at the magistrates, and at the head of the Government" (*PG*, November 6, 1849). As he saw it, the laboring classes were in full revolutionary mode, willing to overthrow their former masters and take control of the country.

Such was his paranoia, Burnley believed the brother of Faustin Soulouque, emperor of Haiti from 1847–1859,[4] had traveled from Haiti to be among the foreigners who had joined in rebellion against the Trinidad government. He put it this way: "On the day and night of the 1st October sinister forces were seen unknown to the Police and inhabitants, and menacing cries were heard savoring of the worst periods of Jacobinical France.[5] Individuals were continually passing to and fro, between Martinique, Guadeloupe and this colony. And amongst the rioters now under arrest, was one who boasted of being a relative, a brother, he believed, of Soulouque, the present Emperor of Hayti" (*PG*, November 6, 1849). Burnley interpreted the laborers' rebellion as being analogous to the Jacobins storming the Bastille in 1789. In his mind their actions demonstrated a readiness to overthrow the elite of the island, if necessary, to gain full freedom. Burnley, it seems, was carried away by his anxieties and the threatened diminution of his political power on the island.

Burnley cited three principal causes of the rebellion: the lowering of wages, the proposed taxation of inhabitants in the rural districts, and the ejection of the squatters who carried with them "the sympathies of the mass laboring population." The squatters possessed feelings and habits similar to those of the laborers who had rebelled and displayed "the same determination to work as little as possible and to pay no taxes. The sole distinction between them being that [while] one had been compelled, by the circumstances of his position to pay for the land he occupies, which the other had not" (*PG*, November 6, 1849). As it turned out, the squatters in Oropouche had nothing to do with the revolt.

What then was required to save the situation? Burnley believed it was important to institute a law of trespass, which placed the onus upon a stranger found loitering on an estate or far from his place of employment to prove that s/he was there for a necessary or innocent purpose; to put in place the promulgation of a vagrant law where a person could be found guilty if s/he were unable to support himself and/or engages in "desultory and idle conduct for any length of time"; and to make arson a capital offense of the highest magnitude; and to set up a general registry of all the inhabitants of the colony. Burnley referred to the use of arson as "the sudden effect of a Lucifer match in a densely cultivated cane district sweeping life as well as property before it in its overwhelming course" (*PG*, November 6, 1849).

Although such drastic measures differed from those that were enacted in the mother country (England), such an approach was necessary on the island because the behavior of English people differed so much from that of Caribbean people. Burnley noted that while the English people were prone to tumult and insurrection, Trinidadians revolted for different reasons. "It was an established historical fact," he claimed, "that misery and starvation alone moved the people of Europe to rise up against their Government. . . . When mills are in full activity in Manchester, and wages abundant, Government never apprehends danger." In Trinidad and the Caribbean such maxims are reversed. "The late riots were enacted by a pampered, overfed, over paid and over petted population, who work only a fractional portion of their time, and laugh and sing and dance away the rest, and who seem, in the last sad scene they had witnessed, to have destroyed property, and endangered life, from mere wanton petulance" (*PG*, November 6, 1849). One couldn't hope for a better caricature of the working people of the island.

Warner outlined a much more sophisticated approach to the issue. He realized Trinidad was in a transitional phase of social development, and the broad strokes Burnley painted did not capture its changing dynamics. He reminded Burnley that sociologically Trinidad was a peculiar society. "Not many years ago," he said, "it was divided into two classes, that of the proprietors and slaves. There was scarcely any middle class—none of those gradations of condition and fortune, which, by minute transition connected the highest and the lowest together. In this state of society, a change had been affected under such conditions as had materially interfered with the success of the experiment [of emancipation] and which would serve as a lesson to every other nation whenever entering on a similar experiment" (*PG*, November 6, 1849).

Warner felt it was important to renounce any position that might appear hostile to the laboring class. He was unable to support Burnley's suggested sanctions against arson. (He was not certain that a "mere increase in the severity of the punishment would have a greater facility and certainty in detection of the crime.") He could not make trespass on real property a criminal act, and he was uncertain whether it was appropriate to introduce a registry of inhabitants given the turmoil that was taking place at the time. He was convinced that the interests of the laboring classes and the proprietors were identical and believed the colony could overcome its problems if the proprietors showed the necessary "forbearance and a spirit of firm but tempered resolution" while the laborers displayed "good feelings and intelligence" of which they were capable. He was satisfied that "the laborers would not be long in discovering that those who endeavored to separate the interests of the employer and the laborer were not merely the open enemies of the employer, but the still more dangerous, because [they were] the covert enemies of the laborers themselves" (*PG*, November 6, 1849).

Unfortunately, the matter did not end there. On December 11, William Rennie brought a petition to council, seeking compensation for the damage that occurred to the properties of Messrs. Robert Bogle and Co. and Messrs. Losh, Spiers and Co., located in the Tacarigua area. Rennie claimed that there could be nothing more injurious to the credibility of the colony, particularly when an injury was committed against a nonresident of the colony. He also believed that it would go a long way to check incendiarism on the island if these petitioners were compensated. Given the poverty of the state, Mr. Fuller did not believe that the petitioners should be compensated.

Burnley, however, argued his case for compensation on what he called "much higher ground." Trinidad, he said, was a unique, experimental colony, in which the British government reserved the right to do as it pleased. He claimed that Great Britain "gave high moral lectures at the Congress of Vienna and Veronica" because it had abolished the slave trade in the West Indies and induced the other European powers to sympathize with the British in the "woes of Africa," and by holy alliance, to provide a remedy for the Africans. "Subsequently," he argued, "this natural impulse took a wider range, and it was determined to break the chains of slavery throughout the world; which could only be effected by showing that slave labor was more expensive than free labor; or, to use the emphatic language of the great leader of the movement, that 'Slavery was not only a crime but a blunder,' inferring that sugar growers were not only sinners but fools, to imagine that they could cultivate their estates more economically by slaves than by free labor" (*PG*, "Suffers by the Riot of 1st October, 1849," December 11, 1849).

This was quite a turnaround for Burnley who had made his fortune as a result of slave labor and had argued passionately in favor of slavery. Given the competition from Cuba and Brazil and the Sugar Duties Act of 1846, he began to see things differently. Yet it was remarkable that a man who believed in the power of slave labor should be arguing for the virtues of free labor. But the world had changed around him. He felt that the governor should be able to use his initiative to compensate the companies that had suffered losses during the rebellion. The inability to do so would result in the "instant failure of that great object, the success of which the British nation had so much at heart, and to prevent which, the extraordinary power vested in His Excellency had been purposely and expressly conferred" (*PG*, December 11, 1849).

Given the poverty of the colony, the attorney general inquired humorously if the council agreed to pay the petitioners would Mr. Burnley assume the responsibility of paying the bill. In his own inimitable manner, and believing strongly that the Home Government had not assumed its responsibility, Burnley responded: "When so many millions had been spent in the prosecution of a national object, its final success would surely never be risked by a refusal to pay a few hundreds. There should be no hesitation in cashing bills drawn for such a purpose. I feel satisfied that very little consideration on the part of my honorable friend, the manager of the Colonial Bank, would induce me to do the same. This conviction is grounded in my confidence in the honor and wisdom of the British nation and government" (*PG*, December 11, 1849).

In the end, the bill failed, and the petitioners were not compensated for their loss. In order to placate his friends—John Losh was a companion of Burnley's and a member of Burnley's firm at one time—Burnley willingly supported the petition. But more was at stake. Burnley really believed that the British government had forsaken the planters in the British West Indies by not placing a higher tariff on sugar produced with slave labor thereby making it more difficult for the cultivation of free sugar to survive in a world of competition. As he noted in his address to the council on November 6, 1849: "To this reduction [of wages] the laborers had never reconciled themselves. To this hour they believe it to have been the sole work of their masters and cannot be made to comprehend that it was the inevitable consequences of the British Sugar Act of 1846, of which both master and laborer have been the victims. Under these circumstances their condition as sugar planters seemed hopeless; for the reduction of

wages now complained of must inevitably be carried much further, whatever
may be the wishes of the Colonial Government or of proprietors to the contrary" (*PG*, "Council of Government," November 6, 1849).

Burnley was not far off the mark. The colonial government had failed the
proprietors and workers alike and the colony suffered as a result. The British
Sugar Act of 1846, which had such devastating consequences on Eccles, Burnley and Company, also had devastating consequences on the society itself.
Gerry Besson writes: "As a result of this Act the London market was flooded
with foreign-grown sugar, prices fell from £18 to £10 per ton. Some one hundred and forty West Indian sugar estates were abandoned and changed hands at
a fraction of their original cost. Estates that had been bought with its slaves in
1829 for £63,500 were resold eighteen years later for £3,000."[6]

Although Burnley was very much a villain, on this occasion Burnley spoke
out on behalf of the ex-slaves. Burnley, it seems, was the only person who was
equipped to keep the British feet to the fire on the issue. The newly freed subjects wanted to be treated as human beings, have their wishes respected, and
be compensated fairly for their labor. Warner and, to some degree, Lord Harris
understood the changing demands of the laborers more than Burnley who was
stuck in a past in which society was demarcated rigidly into masters and servants. Sixteen years after slavery the social relations in the colony had become
much more fluid and more accepting of the newly freed people. Burnley was
finding it difficult to adapt to this new way of seeing.

CHAPTER 42

Revolutionary Ideas

It was a mockery to say that the inhabitants are not yet fit to receive institutions of a freer kind; it was absurd and childish to assert that men who filled offices of high trust, and exercise the liberal professions were unfit to take part in the management of the affairs of their country. Everyone had more or less in him the elements of self-government.

—Alexander Fitzjames, Remarks at Public Meeting
for a New Constitution, 1850

THE LABORING CLASS, believing in the correctness of their moral position, was determined to free themselves from a system that treated them like children or mindless beings. They took their lead from Candler's observation that Haiti, under Jean-Pierre Boyer (president from 1818 to 1843), had kept the peace at home and with its neighbors and that the Haitian people "proved themselves more fit for self-government than many of their white neighbors" (*TR*, January 23, 1850).[1] Therefore they rejoiced when General Lafayette, an active participant in both the French and American revolutions, in his letter to President Boyer in 1830 observed that "the friends of humanity in all countries, were seeking the success of 'your republic' and hoped that black colonists from the United States would find in Haiti 'liberty, work and happiness.'"[2]

Burnley had criticized Toussaint and the Haitians consistently and what he called their savage disposition. He had to reduce Haitian people to a state of savagery to promote Anglo-Saxon purity. Burnley, it seems, needed an enemy to refract his own glory and he found it close at hand: the Haitians. Umberto

Eco observed in another context: "It seems we cannot manage without an enemy! The figures of the enemy cannot be abolished from the process of civilization."[3] Even Lord Harris, like many of his contemporaries, saw Africans as "half-savage, childlike creatures."[4] "Some races," Harris wrote, "by their own moral and intellectual powers and energies work out their own progress in civilization." "Other races," the majority of civilization, "are more disposed to remain stationary, and seldom make any advancement except by the adoption or imitation of those more advanced than themselves."[5] This process of *othering* allowed Europeans to always project themselves as being better than the natives. Since black people, as Lord Harris saw them, were still "very low in the scale of civilization" and "little removed from that of savage life,"[6] they still needed white people to direct them in terms of political governance.

Des Sources, the editor of the *Trinidadian*, was aware of Burnley's tendency to de-humanize Africans. He was also aware of the leading role Haiti played in introducing republicanism in the Atlantic world. Instinctively, he realized that John Candler's views had undercut Burnley's constant attempts to berate the demands of Trinidadians for self-government by associating their actions with the so-called "savagery" of the Haitians. He noted that any time a disturbance took place in the West Indies "a cry of alarm is raised, and Hayti pointed at as a bloody example of the danger of Negro emancipation." He noted further that any time a call for the introduction of the elective franchise was made, "Hayti is cited as an instance of the impossibility of self-government being a judicious exercise by the African race. Not one step is made towards certain parties, not one word spoken, not one wish expressed for a better state of things, but St. Domingo is on their lips as an irrefutable argument in opposition to our demands. St. Domingo is, in fact, the bear bug of the enemies of political progression in the Colonies" (*TR*, January 23, 1850).

Des Sources conceded that there existed "uninterrupted confusion, rapine and carnage" in Haiti. This was true for any people who sought to throw off the yoke of despotism that had remained on their backs for centuries. Many of Haiti's detractors refused to acknowledge the liberatory and ennobling effects of the Haitian Revolution on the Atlantic world. Des Sources even invited his detractors to take a look at Europe's long years of fratricidal struggle for freedom and asked: "Was not France, the most polished nation of civilized Europe, deluged in the blood of their best citizens? Is her internal condition much better than at the last century? Is not the whole European continent convulsed by the conflict between the people and despotism? Has not vandalism, from time immemorial spread furiously over that delightful abode of the arts and sciences?" (*TR*, January 23, 1850). In fact, Des Sources anticipated Fyodor Dostoevsky in reminding Europeans how much blood was shed in making their civilization. In *Crime and Punishment,* when Dunya confronts her brother Raskolnikov about the awfulness of his crime (he had killed a pawnbroker in cold blood), he replies almost frantically: "Everyone sheds blood . . . which flows and has flowed on earth, like a waterfall, which has been poured out like champagne, and for which they crown people on the Roman Capitoline and designate them benefactors of mankind."[7] If only Europe could accept its complicity in its crimes against his people.

Des Sources believed that slavery, as Harriet Beecher Stowe asserts in *Uncle Tom's Cabin*, "is brute force."[8] He was only asking his detractors to allow black people in the Caribbean to construct their democracy in a way that was appropriate to their needs. He was aware that the black inhabitants of that region had "smarted under the grip of tyranny, and of a monstrous system, and were driven to an appeal to physical force, which demoralizes and brutifies man" (*TR*, January 23, 1850). In fact, the notion that slavery "brutifies" a person was certainly analogous to Douglass's absolute certitude of slavery's tendency to transform an individual into a brute even as the latter sought to humanize or make himself human.[9] It is a term that would come up time and time again to describe the psychological condition of the enslaved.

Des Sources, a product of the Caribbean, understood the urgency of his people's demands. Caught up in the spirit of republicanism that gripped the region at the time, he used his editorials to counter the reactionary language and racist convictions of Harris and to persuade his readers about the justice of their cause.[10] This was true of Bolivar, General Lafayette, and Daniel Webster in their respective countries. Burnley, an acquaintance of Tocqueville, never understood what Des Sources was trying to do in Trinidad. In fact, Burnley had used every opportunity to vilify Des Sources and to discredit the *Trinidadian*. Through Des Sources, the Caribbean had found a powerful advocate for the cause of its freedom.

There can be no doubt that West Indian patriots were inspired by what had transpired in France during the Revolution of 1848 that proclaimed the liberty of the sovereign people "to make their own constitutions through an elected constitutional assembly, equality through universal manhood suffrage, and the avoidance of violence by fraternal union."[11] On April 9, 1850, Burnley raised his voice in the Legislative Council to oppose the new political trend that was taking place in the colony. He noted that he would be the last man to oppose any changes in the political order but argued that these changes ought to take place "in a proper manner and at the proper season" (*TR*, April 13, 1850). He informed his fellow councilors that he looked upon the anticipated changes with "a great deal of alarm" and reminded them that "there were two great revolutions in the affairs of the island: the revolution of 1834 when slavery was abolished, and the revolution of 1846 when protection was taken away." He contended that even those who supported those revolutions did so without "a sufficient knowledge of the state of things in the colonies, and without having received sufficient knowledge from the people in the island" (*TR*, April 13, 1850).

But the struggle of the laboring class for its freedom kept on apace. On April 20, St. Luce Philip, an unofficial member of the legislature, chaired a large public meeting of the progressive forces in Port of Spain that petitioned the British government to grant the colony the right to form a Legislative Council "elected by the people, in lieu of the present form of government" (*TR*, "Public Meeting at Juteaux's Room," April 20, 1850). Henry Fitt, an unofficial member, pointed out that the inhabitants did not control their own affairs and that the Legislative Council consisted "exclusively of gentlemen nominated by the Crown, and a majority of its members subservient to Government influence by virtue of their official appointments. The Government may, whenever so pleased, command a majority of votes, and thus render powerless any opposition on the part of the non-official section" (*TR*, April 20, 1850).

In seconding Fitt's resolution, Alexander Fitzjames, a distinguished Trinidadian lawyer who became a "queen's advocate" and acting governor of Sierra Leone (1858–1859), pointed out that while the existing constitution may have been appropriate for the slave period, it had long outlived its usefulness.[12] It was put in place for "the slaveholders to advise His Excellency in the enactment of laws to suit the exigencies of the day. Now that that state of things had ceased, that institution had become useless. But they had stolen power day by day until they had found the courage to oppose themselves to government measures" (*TR*, April 20, 1850). Being members of Legislative Council was not good enough. A new constitution should reflect the new realities of their country. They may have disagreed among themselves about which model (be it the constitution of the Cape of Good Hope or New South Wales) was suited to their needs, but they were convinced they could not be liberated by a constitution that was constructed to serve the needs of the slave era.

At this meeting, forty-six of the most distinguished members of the society signed the petition for self-government that was sent to the British government. Many of them were intimately involved with the October 1 rebellion. They included Henry Fitt, John Losh, and F. J. Scott, unofficial members of the legislature; L. A. A. de Verteuil, a member of the town council and author of *Trinidad: Its Geography, Natural Resources, Administration, Present Condition, and Prospect* (1858); August Thoulous, a member of the Port of Spain town council; and Alexander Fitzjames, lawyer and defense counsel for those who had rebelled on October 1; Philip Rostant and Des Sources, members of the delegation who met with Lord Harris on the morning of the October 1 rebellion. Edmond Hobson, the chairman of the committee, formulated the petition of the delegation that met with the governor before the rebellion of October 1, while George Savary, a member of the Port of Spain town council, was appointed to a corresponding committee to prepare the petitions that were to be submitted to the British Parliament and the two Houses of Parliament. It is not too far-fetched to argue that this event was the culmination of a revolutionary process that started when the enslaved Africans rebelled against their oppressors on October 1, 1849.

As was to be expected, the proprietors were offended by the audacity of these underlings. They sent a petition to Her Majesty the Queen opposing the resolution of St. Luce and his group and the introduction of a two-chamber legislature. They preferred a constitution in which a larger proportion of the council members should be proprietors. Without their being in the majority, they felt there would be insufficient members "to form an adequate check on the lower chamber of an exclusively popular election" (*TR*, April 24, 1850). They were convinced "that any change in our form of government will be productive of injury," if it did not keep steadily in view "the protection and preservation of property, and the promotion and extension of those agricultural interests which are the social basis of our existence as a society." Everyone knows, they said, that "any government OUGHT TO HAVE IN VIEW the protection and preservation of property, and the extension of ALL INTERESTS" (*TR*, April 27, 1850).

The progressive forces wasted no time in responding to these charges. They even sent their counter proposal as it were to the Queen and her representatives. They wanted a legislative council structured in a manner in which all views of all segments of the society would be heard without their voices being subordinated to that of the Crown. The *Trinidadian* editorialized: "We are certain, and it is well known that it is not limiting the legislative power in the hands of the A FEW, that this object will be attained." Des Sources was convinced that any single legislative form of government that the Crown controlled would be unmindful of the "UNREPRESENTATIVE MASS." He was so distrustful of the planter class that he asserted the aim of the opposition was "to secure and to perpetuate within their own circle, the whole control over the public affairs of the colony and thus establish for themselves the government of the few" (*TR*, April 27, 1850).

The opponents of popular government sought to create the impression that inhabitants who were seeking self-government were incapable of governing themselves. In order to counter these misgivings the proponents of self-government wrote an open letter to "the Queen's Most Excellent Majesty" affirming their fitness to govern themselves: "Your petitioners, however, most respectfully submit that Your Majesty has been misinformed, and that your loyal subjects of Trinidad are perfectly competent to fulfill the duties of popular representation." This letter which they advertised repeatedly in the *Trinidadian* on April 27, May 1, 8, and 18 reaffirmed "that the present form of Government in the island is totally unsuited to the altered circumstances of the colony" and called upon Her Majesty to introduce a legislature of two chambers, which they felt "will be conducive of great advantage to the colony and that such a constitution would ensure satisfaction and confidence to the community" (*TR*, April 24, 1850). They were convinced that they could achieve a greater degree of self-representation by reorganizing the Legislative Council.

CHAPTER 43

A New Consciousness

The heart of the speech [Frederick Douglass's "Self-Made Men"]
described how men and women could better their condition through hard
work and education. [Abraham] Lincoln too believed in these templates
as the primary means to self-improvement. But the ultimate goal of such
transformation was to improve society rather than to get rich. In remaking
the self, you reformed society.

—John Stauffer, *Giants: The Parallel Lives of
Frederick Douglass and Abraham Lincoln*

IT IS NOT coincidental that the demand for self-government arose at the
same time that society saw a rise in the number of educated black men and
women. Many of them who had supported the rebellion and the subsequent
call for self-government had studied in England and France, possessed a great
deal of intellectual sophistication, and were steeped in Enlightenment ideas.[1] At
a time when the nation was undergoing a radical social upheaval, a new group
of men and women who were willing to take their destiny into their own hands
started to emerge. In an age of self-made men, these men and women truly
believed that "in remaking the self, you reformed society." John Stauffer notes
that both Frederick Douglass and Abraham Lincoln, citizens of another slavery state, understood that "self-making was antithetical to racism . . . because
the idea of 'whiteness' (white skin) as a sign of superiority and justification for
oppressing blacks *depended* on believing that the self was fixed and unchanging. Douglass and Lincoln moved beyond the traditional idea of 'character' as

fixed and based primarily on heredity and social status, and instead saw the self in a state of continual flux."² A similar idea gripped this emerging stratum of the Trinidad society.

When Lord Harris informed Earl Grey about the conviction of the men who had rebelled on October 1, and the length of the sentences they received, he was genuinely pleased he had stemmed a sense of "lawlessness" that had emerged in the society. He even felt magnanimous for acting so generously toward these misguided people. What he did not know was that the impetus for rebellious forces at work in the society stemmed from a deep-seated nationalism and racial pride that was coming to birth in the people's heart. While these newly freed people appreciated the assistance they gained from the British people in achieving their emancipation, they were also aware that Lord Harris, Warner, and Burnley were attempting to repress many aspects of their freedom. For example, in February 1849 a law was passed that would have limited the movement of black and brown people in the colony, the violation of which would have led to their being imprisoned. The secretary of state for the colonies vetoed it.

These brave men and women displayed other aspects of nationalism and racial pride. On August 1, 1849, the Friends of Freedom sponsored a dinner in Port of Spain to celebrate the anniversary of their emancipation. Two hundred and fifty of the most distinguished black and colored citizens attended the dinner. The only government officials who attended the function were the registrar of the Supreme Court, the clerk of the Petty Civic Court of Port of Spain, and the police inspector. The men and women at this dinner were suffused with happiness. They were joyous at having been emancipated and proud of the achievements of their race in spite of the obstacles that had been placed in their way. Michel Maxwell Philip, author of *Emmanuel Appadocca* and later solicitor general of the colony, mentioned the achievements of the great men of the past who gave their lives that enslaved Africans might be free, saying "We honor them, because we believe ourselves to be honored." He then spoke of the horrors of the middle passage and the brutality Africans endured in their new land. He opined: "From the moment that his native sun dawns upon him, to the hour when he is restored to his mother-earth, or cast a loathsome carcase [*sic*] to the beasts of prey, his [the African's] whole life is one scene of unmitigated misery. Bereft of every consolation for the present, devoid of every glimmer of hope, tortured, torn, and taxed, he lives and dies a man of woe. . . . Such are the horrors of African slavery; such are the shocking evils that have been cured by the emancipation act" (*TR*, "Anniversary of Freedom: First of August Dinner," August 8, 1849).

Although black men were subjected to much woe and misery, John O'Brien, another speaker at the dinner, preferred to affirm the equality of all men and women by drawing on the Bible verse that proclaimed "[God] hath made of one blood all nations of men to dwell together on all the face of the earth."[3] Taking mankind's unity as his theme, O'Brien affirmed that "we should take it as our bounded duty to consider ourselves as belonging to the whole human family and to sympathize with each other as brethren." He saw their task as having to combat the errors "of those descendants of the African race who disclaim all sympathy with the slave, upon the simple ground that they, or their immediate ancestors, were not slaves (Loud Cheers). If these want an example, I would point them to that great man, Alexandre Dumas (Cheers). Does he deny that he is a descendant of a son or daughter of still degraded Africa? No! He prides himself upon it, and lest he should be mistaken, he nobly and exultingly points to his curly hair, and says, 'Here are my credentials!' (Loud Cheers)" (*TR*, "Anniversary of Freedom: First of August Dinner," August 8, 1849).

O'Brien was referring to the great black French writer who established himself in French literary history during the 1840s with the publication of novels such as *The Count of Monte Cristo* and *The Three Musketeers*. Anyone reading the French newspapers at the time (and many of these French-trained intellectuals in Trinidad were) would have been aware of Dumas's name and his father's history. During this time, close to 75 percent of Trinidad's population spoke French or patios.[4] Francine du Plessix Gray claims: "Never in the annals of French literature was there a fecundity comparably to that of Dumas between 1845 and 1855. Throughout that decade a score of his novels, each of them running to thousands of pages, were serialized in Parisian newspapers."[5]

What O'Brien left out of his story or took for granted (it must have been common knowledge of the educated people of the time) was that Alex Dumas, father of Alexandre, was one of the most famous generals during the French Revolution. What he did not have to tell his audience was that Alex, the son of Marquis de la Pailleterie and his black slave Cesselle, born in San Dominque, became "the most imposing as well as possibly the most respected" of Napoleon's officers when Napoleon invaded Egypt.[6] O'Brien's white counterparts in Trinidad could not have known the importance one's hair played in the psychology of black people. The author of the first biography of Alex Dumas written in 1797 observed: "The General is six foot one or two inches tall, and one of the handsomest men you will ever meet, his interesting physiognomy is accompanied by a gentle and gracious manner. His frizzled hair recalled the curls of the Greeks and Romans."[7] Alexandre's hair, like his father's, was an important part of his identity. It is something culturally conscious black men and women in Trinidad knew instinctively. It was a fact that Lord Harris, to his dismay, learned on October 1, 1849.

The black people of the colony hated the racist attitudes and practices that people such as Burnley, Harris, and Warner displayed toward them. By 1849 the time had come to take a stand. Like the famous seat that Rosa Parks took on the bus in Montgomery, Alabama, in 1955, the rebellion that took place in Port of Spain on October 1, 1849, represented nothing more than a bursting out of suppressed rage that had resided in black people's hearts for a long time. This sterling act of solidarity, together with the public meeting of April 1850 for self-government, announced new stages along the path toward the establishment of their personhood. It was the beginning of a fight to death. These deeply metaphysical and psychological acts coincided with Albert Camus's observation that when one rebels or revolts, he "identifies himself with other men and so surpasses himself, and from that point of view of human solidarity is metaphysical."[8]

In this sense, then, the *Narrative of the Life of Frederick Douglass*, published by the American Anti-Slavery Society in May 1845, turned out to be an invaluable document in the hands of those Trinidadians who were fighting for their liberation. Within three years the book sold over eleven thousand copies in the United States, and by 1850 it had sold thirty thousand copies, making it an international bestseller.[9] Des Sources, no doubt, must have been impressed with Douglass's life, particularly his battle with and overcoming of Edward Covey his overseer. Douglass described this event as a changing point in his life and "a full compensation for whatever else might follow, even death itself." He described this event as "a glorious resurrection, from the tomb of slavery, to the heaven of freedom. My long-crushed spirit rose, cowardice departed, bold defiance took its place; and I was now resolved that, however long I might remain a slave in form, the day had passed forever when I could be a slave in fact."[10]

Parenthetically, George Wilhelm Friedrich Hegel articulated a similar idea in *Philosophy of Right*. He insisted that "freedom cannot be granted to slaves from above. The self-liberation of the slave is required through a 'trial by death': And it is solely by risking life that freedom is obtained. . . . That individual, who has not staked his life, may, no doubt be recognized as a Person [the agenda of the abolitionist] but he has not attained the truth of his recognition as an independent self-consciousness."[11] Hegel had picked up this idea from the Haitian Revolution as he followed its progress in the pages of the *Minerva Journal*.

James Cone, "a central figure in the development of black liberation theology in [the United States] in the 1960 and 1970s"[12] used a similar argument to describe the impact that the theory and practice of Black Power had on the black people of the United States during the 1960s and 1970s.[13]

On October 1, when the nameless men and women rebelled in Port of Spain, they wished to reiterate a truism to which Camus alluded when he said: "In our daily trials rebelling plays the same role as 'cognito' in the realm of thought: it is the first piece of evidence. But this evidence lures the individual from his solitude. It founds its first value on the whole human race. I rebel—therefore *we* exist."[14] Subliminally or perhaps even metaphysically, the laboring population wanted to convey to Burnley and other members of the planter class that their reign of power and terror over them had ended. For these ex-slaves, it was a fight to death. One party had to be diminished or defeated for the other to exist, at least that was the message those black people were trying to convey to their former masters.

In this context Douglass's example was important to Des Sources and others of the laboring class. In July 1850 the editors of the *Trinidadian* began to serialize Douglass's *Narrative* in their newspaper. In the preface to the serialization, the editor invited "the Honorable Mr. Burnley and others to begin its perusal at once" and added: "They may therein find some remedy for their infatuated dislike of 'African materials.'" Des Sources's reference to "African materials" was not accidental. On January 19, 1850, Des Sources wrote a strong response to Burnley's address to the Legislative Council in which Burnley said that the operation of the municipal system in which "the English pride themselves . . . will never be successful within the tropics 'for this reason alone that the machinery must be principally composed of African materials'" (*TR*, January 19, 1850). In other words, self-government could not be practiced on the island because the blacks were incapable of running such a system.

Des Sources did not take such an attack against his people lying down. He was repulsed "at such language [being] used by someone born in a country where African slavery is held as a sacred and religious duty, where thousands have fattened on the blood of millions of the sons of Africa, and wallow in the mire of ill-gotten wealth." He was referring to Burnley's American birthplace. He questioned the absurd sentiments of someone whose fortune was due entirely "to African materials, but who has ever taxed his mind to vilify . . . those, who by their unrequited labor, *laid the foundation* and raised the superstructure of his fortune." He prophesied: "We are certain that he will sink into the grave with the black seal of ingratitude stamped on his hoary brow with the galling consciousness that the great leveler is at hand" (*TR*, January 19, 1850). It was almost as though this denouncement had sealed Burnley's fate and cast him into the realm of oblivion or the depth of abasement and public scorn.

Parenthetically Des Sources directed his scorn at the depreciatory manner in which Burnley depicted Africans and his assumption "that the African race was only destined to pamper their gaping avarice, and that the privilege of free birth and moral conduct are irreconcilable with their condition." He argued that this notion proceeds "either from that brutish and disgusting ignorance in which such men as of the mental caliber of a BURNLEY grovel for life, or from that deep-rooted hatred and malice which the reprobate portion of humanity so warmly nourish for all who resemble them not." He refused to believe that the "Supreme Architect of the Universe" had sealed all knowledge with any particular portion of the human family and concluded by reminding Burnley of the great gifts Africa has given to the world:

> As the great luminary of the day, by his command, rises for the benefit of all, so he has provided every one with an internal luminary [an inner light] to guide him through life, and this luminary, if not prostituted to base passions and filthy love of money, never fails to disclose to its possessor all the qualities that ennoble mankind, and raises it far above the brute creation. Nay, if by miraculous interference the form which suffuses the mental organs of those of the Burnleyan school were ever removed, they would discover that Europe is much indebted to Africa for the knowledge which she now boasts of, they would at all events, admit that it is much better to be composed of African materials, than to be renegade to one's country, and a disciple of slavery. (*TR*, January 19, 1850)

Many of the views expressed in this refutation of Burnley's diatribe were influenced by French Enlightenment ideas, particularly those of Jean-Jacques Rousseau, whose vision for individual moral transformation "highlighted man's capacity for self-mastery, transparency and virtue by means of an inward journey towards greater perfectibility." Des Sources's two major ideas, "the Supreme Architect of the Universe" and the notion of the "internal luminary" as a guide to human behavior, were taken from Rousseau who, in *Emile*, intimated man's need to "'*rentrer en soi-meme*' and consult his inner light."[15] Sudhir Hazareesingh observed that "Masons in France worshiped their own divinity, the 'Great Architect of the Universe,' who was typically represented in luminous form. Illuminist doctrine was a spiritual creed that asserted the unity of all natural elements and preached a moral resurgence which would eventually lead to man's reintegration into primal Being."[16]

Inherent also in Des Sources's refutation were nascent emanations of a Pan-African consciousness and anti-capitalist sentiments that would emerge later among several Caribbean, African, and African American scholars and activists who elaborated upon these concepts. His was a notion worthy of Martin Bernal's *Black Athena* and men who took pride in their black heritage.[17] Moreover, these early activists and scholars adopted the adjective "Burnleyan" and the phrase "Burnleyan school" to capture the racist and backward content of Burnley's behavior and rhetoric. Both the phrase and the adjective reflected the contempt they wished to convey about Burnley, his rule, and the power he once had over them. Fired by a new sense of confidence, they signified that they had joined the liberation struggle of oppressed peoples that was taking place in the Americas at the time.

CHAPTER 44

The Island of Babel

The present year set in darkly on those who have to earn their bread by the sweat of their brows. But the reduced rate of wages is partly accounted for by the extraordinary fall in the price of sugar, the embarrassed condition of the majority of the planters. But the home Government and our Local government are also to blame. They overcrowded the labor-market, and their purpose in doing so we have already stated.

—"The Past and Present State and the Prospects of Trinidad," *Trinidadian*, 1850

DURING 1850, DARK clouds hovered over the nation. Although the ex-slaves acknowledged that Britain did "a work meet for repentance" and gave "a monstrous largesse, to boot, to their quondam oppressors" (*TR*, "The Past and the Present State and the Prospects of Trinidad," January 16, 1850), they really believed that they should have received the monetary rewards that their proprietors got when they were freed. This initial injustice was exasperated by the introduction of new immigrants whose employment cut into the minimal progress the ex-slaves had made after slavery ended. Not satisfied with this historic injustice, the local legislature continued a costly immigration scheme that was ruinous to both "the colonial treasury and to the pockets and prospects of the people." Such oppressive measures, they argued "consisted in the wish to bolster the interest of the former slaveholders—to enrich them or secure them against supposed loss at the expense of the people, and at the expense of justice in the bargain" (*TR*, January 16, 1850).

The formerly enslaved paid dearly for this scheme. The *Trinidadian* reported that the wages of the laborers were a little above the starving point, and those of the artisans were seriously reduced. "They are often ill-paid. We believe that wages were never lower, and labor more abundant than at the close of the past year [1849]." It concluded: "The present year set in darkly on those who have to earn their bread by the sweat of their brows." To them, the future of the island looked "gloomy and threatening indeed. The events that it embosoms throw before them dismally dark shadows" (*TR*, "The Past and Present State and the Prospects of Trinidad," January 16, 1850).

In May, the Legislative Council requested that the governor bring to the immediate consideration of the secretary of state for the colonies "the pressing necessity of bringing into the Island, at the public expense, *at least* 1,000 Coolies during next year (1851), and of the like number during the year 1852" (*TR*, January 16, 1850). This recommendation led Des Sources to observe that "another extensive scheme of Immigration engrosses the attention and talents of the Honorable Gentlemen, and will, again, we doubt not, signalize their genius" (*TR*, May 8, 1850). Considerations were also being made to introduce more Chinese and captured Africans[1] into the colony to join those from Madeira and North America.

Burnley suggested that a "poll tax" be levied against the subjects to defray the cost of bringing these immigrants to the island. This measure was intended "to rid the city of its useless drifting population, inert capital, and the country's lost means of production" (*TR*, "Dans la séance due Conseil Legislatif," November 9, 1850). Supporters of the poll tax felt that it would push the unemployed to look for work in the farming sector while the opponents of the tax argued it would "hit people whom difficult circumstances have ruined, and who are no less respectable for it. It would be a new wreck added to the general misery." The *Trinidadian* opined: "Sirs Burnley and Philip are therefore not very generous, and above all, not very far-sighted" (*TR*, November 9, 1850).

Troubled by the implications of this measure, and speaking on behalf of "the black middle class" and "the less affluent mass of 'emancipated' Negroes,"[2] Des Sources asked "whether it would be honorable on their [legislators'] part to attempt any further taxation of the people, . . . when the whole community, with one voice, has solemnly proclaimed to the whole world that they are UNFIT to govern the country?" Besides placing much hardship on the working people, Des Sources described this proposal as "taxation without representation," which he saw as "similar to the act of the highwayman who lives on crime. Let not the gentlemen of the Council of Government, if they have yet a particle of decency, think of taxing the people, as long as they are unrepresented" (*TR*, May 8, 1850).

Although the council agreed to bring two thousand Indians to the island for the years 1851 and 1852, Burnley's presented a more ambitious proposal. He wanted to secure a resolution that called for "a *perpetual yearly influx* of one thousand Hindoos" (*TR*, May 18, 1850). This demand for more Indians was in addition to the twenty thousand laborers that had been brought to the island since 1843; to a country whose population was merely about sixty thousand. Given this frenzy for laborers, the *Trinidadian* feared the island would become "the magnet of Emigration; and the inhabitants of the Earth, from the frosty wilds of Siberia to the volcanic mountains of Tierra del Fuego, will soon hasten to contribute to the prosperity of the West Indian Paradise. We hope, however, that its name will not be changed into that of the ISLAND OF BABEL" (*TR*, May 18, 1850).

The planters were not concerned about the welfare of the workers, nor developing a "free and independent peasantry." They were more concerned with providing fuel for their plantations (using men as industrial power) than victuals for their workers. Des Sources complained that while large sums of monies were being spent to subsidize the planters, little was being devoted to local needs. He argued that when the inhabitants petitioned for a reduction of taxes, the legislators turned away "with disgust from the 'sturdy beggars,' and crush such applications in their hands with noble indignation." While, on one hand, the legislators were oppressing the community with taxation, they were "giving away lavishly with the other [hand] for certain purposes, and refusing assistance where charity could be reasonably practiced, and relief is an obligation." He asked, "Is it not time to be rid of this rusty machinery, and to have in its stead one unencumbered with the Burnleyan doting spirit?" (*TR*, June 8, 1850). To them, the adjective "Burnleyan" had become synonymous with the callousness of their oppressors.

On June 15, the *Trinidadian* returned to the topic of immigration and the large sums of monies the Colonial Treasury was squandering on procuring immigrants. It called on the government to reconsider their "narrow and self-ish policy of considering laborers as mere sugar-making tools, and not as men as anxious to better their condition as their employers. We expressed a hope that our legislators would, at least, become sensible of the extravagance of such measures, and take proper steps to make immigration truly beneficial to the Island, and such only as sane men would think of doing" (*TR*, June 15, 1850).

Needless to say, the laboring class and their spokespeople were not inclined to accept the arguments of the planters and of government (one and the same thing) that "the system of immigration has kept up the cultivation of the stable products of the island, and has hitherto, preserved it from ruin." They countered that if one considered the £80,000 and upwards of the money that had been provided for the importation of labor, the taxes imposed by the treasury for such purposes, the amount of vice and immorality that the importation of immigrants incurred, the expenses of the quarterly prosecutions of criminal offenses by immigrants or those in which they were implicated, and the monies spent to upkeep the colonial hospital and a pauper asylum "that a heavy balance would be found against immigration and such as it can never pay" (*TR*, June 15, 1850). By August of that year the attorney general announced that he had received instructions to bring an ordinance to the council in which £1,000,000 would be provided for the purpose of introducing more immigrants into the colony. The attorney general informed the council that he had endeavored to draft the ordinance "in as concise a manner possible, and to suit Mr. Burnley" (*TR*, "Legislative Council," August 3, 1850).

This is not to say that the laboring class was entirely against immigration. They felt that the financial burdens such immigration imposed upon them should be shared by all its citizens. If their rulers were "truly interested in the welfare of the country," they would have remembered that sugar and cocoa planters, merchants, or others contributed to the funds in the treasury. Since "the expenses of immigration are defrayed by the same Treasury, its benefits ought to be opened to all, and not only to the planter" (*TR*, August 3, 1850). To the extent the planters were committed to the progress of the island, it is to that degree they should have been committed to serving the interests of all the people in the colony. It is clear that the more indentured Indians the ruling authorities brought to the island the more the plantation owners could keep down the price of labor and thereby make the industry more profitable to themselves.

The workers did not stay silent in the face of this onslaught. They were not afraid to link their demands for better working conditions with a desire to have greater political control of the state. These demands, combined with a rising sense of racial consciousness and a protonationalist identity, was influenced by the developments related to plantation slavery in the American South of the United States.[3] Des Sources also objected to the incendiary remarks made by William Arrindell, attorney general of Guyana, against the demands of the reform petitions of the Guyanese working people. He contended that Arrindell's sentiments were in sync with those of Warner, Burnley, and others of that ilk who were carrying on the same merciless struggle against the Trinidad working people. He disparaged "the aberrations and prejudices which, in too many instances, contract or disorder the understanding and render the mind incapable of calm and rational deliberation." Their cries of alarm reminded him of similar "angry and disloyal declamations" resounded from every quarter in the West Indies when Great Britain "announced the approaching freedom of the thousands of sufferers in them [the West Indies] kept in cruel bondage; which, however, proved illusive [sic], and but the echo of distempered imaginations" (TR, June 1, 1850). He assured Arrindell and Burnley that their fear of blacks sharing political power with them was overblown, even though blacks, 92 percent of the population, outnumbered whites who were 8 percent of the population. He called for an end to the reckless debate between whites and blacks and urged each group to cease struggling for superiority.

As the society developed, it became necessary to integrate these workers into the economic life of the country. As more wage workers entered into the workforce, there became a greater need to strengthen the banking system. When the West India Bank of an earlier period failed, the Colonial Bank was established on May 15, 1837, to facilitate the smoother transition from an economy based primarily on allowances to the workers to one based on wages. Moreover, "the compensation claims paid to planters when the slaves were emancipated . . . increased the flow of money into the colonies,"[4] which made it more important to establish an efficient banking arrangement. C. A. Calvert, secretary of the Court of Directors of the Colonial Bank in London, warned William Rennie, manager of the Trinidad branch of the bank, "It will be necessary in the first instance to divest yourself of the idea of supplying what are called 'the wants of the community' or of completely filling the void occasioned by the fall of the West India Bank."[5]

On June 1, 1850, the Legislative Council met to consider the introduction of smaller coins to facilitate transactions of "the lower orders" in the economy. The larger coins, the stampee or black dog and the quarter franc pieces, were not adequate to the needs of the transactions of the poorer class. Taking into account their increased participation in the labor market, the government sought to accommodate this growing economic activity by introducing smaller coins (currency) to pay their salaries and facilitate their market transactions. By issuing smaller coins, the coppers, they could increase the demand for commodities that formed the basket of goods of the poor thereby controlling the rise in prices of these commodities.[6]

Initially, Burnley thought it would be unwarrantable and impudent on the part of the bank to force these coins on the public. He saw it as just another way to cut into his wealth. He contended, "the corporation had no other object in view than to sweep away our Mexican dollars, as they had gone down with the doubloons and other gold pieces, as to monopolize the currency of the island." Rennie, an unofficial member of the Legislative Council, disagreed. He encouraged throwing "into circulation a description of coins which in the other British colonies were much valued, and had always answered the wants of the laboring population" (*TR*, June 3, 1850). Burnley remained fearful of the proposition. He believed that it would have harmful consequences on his segment of the community. The resolution was disallowed.

On August 1, sixteen years after the emancipation of the enslaved, Burnley came around to seeing the desirability of introducing the copper coin into the economy, provided the treasury would accept it and be untroubled by its use. Rennie assured the council that the copper "would create confidence, allay the alarm in the community, and the petty shopkeeper would not hesitate to take it" (*TR*, "Legislative Council," August 3, 1850). The attorney general, like the chief justice, was skeptical about the introduction of the copper coin into the economy. He argued somewhat circumlocutiously: "It was with copper as with water, if you open one large sluice and two smaller ones, the water will naturally go to the larger opening." Burnley described the attorney general's comment as being "meaningless and useless." He argued: "It is not more natural that the water in a vessel should run out of the big hole at which it entered, so there would never be any copper in the Treasury" (*TR*, August 3, 1850). The board adjourned after Burnley's contribution.

Slowly but surely, the legislators warmed up to the proposition. The banking needs of the inhabitants demanded it. On August 24, Burnley brought up the issue again when he introduced a resolution to limit the circulation of silver on the island to the sum of forty shillings. It was a face-saving compromise. It was necessary for the central bank to stabilize things since various currencies were floating around in the economy. Still mindful of his class interest, Burnley was prepared to offer concessions to the poorer members of the society. He argued that the "copper coins now introduced were quite small enough to enable the lower classes to obtain the most minute requisite, and would be the smallest article of consumption which the smallest appetite could think necessary. . . . It only remained to do something to prevent any practical inconvenience in the higher classes, and that is to be done by limiting the circulation of British silver" (*TR*, "Silver Currency," August 24, 1850). Supporting Burnley's position, Rennie argued that in an agricultural society such as Trinidad, "British silver has been admitted to be admirably adapted to the payment of wages, aided by copper. As it is not as exportable a coin as the dollar, it will save a fluctuation in the exchange" (*TR*, August 24, 1850).

The adoption of this policy brought the poorer classes into the economy and, to that degree, acknowledged their importance within the economic life of the community. It also thrust the island into a new phase of commercial life in which proper banking practices became a necessary prerequisite for its further growth and development. Strict instructions were sent from England to ensure that these practices were followed. Even the venerable Burnley had to recognize the growing importance of the former slaves within the society. Burnley was losing his hold on the island's economics as well as its politics. Perhaps the *Trinidadian* was not too far off the mark when on June 6 it intoned that the reign of this "grey-headed tyrant" (*TR*, June 6, 1850) was coming to an end.

CHAPTER 45

Fading Glory

Capital is thus the governing power over labor and its products. The capitalist [read slave master] possesses this power, not on account of his personal or human qualities, but inasmuch as he is an owner of capital. His power is the purchasing power of his capital which nothing can withstand.

—Karl Marx, *Economic & Philosophic Manuscripts of 1844*

B Y THE MIDDLE of 1850, Burnley had become one of the most despised capitalists (he once described himself thus) in the country. His erstwhile friends, Lord Harris and Charles Warner, derided him publicly, even as Des Sources continued to express his public indignation against him. On November 9, 1850, Des Sources declared that Burnley could "think strongly [and] express himself clearly; but his heart is not at home. What current or quondam slaveholder was ever blessed with a heart? If such a man there be, we would embrace him and call him brother. But Mr. Burnley is not that man. No! His legislative sayings and doings are a violence done to justice, and an outrage against Christianity and humanity. Without doing him any wrong, we may style him a glib-tongued, smooth-faced, cold-blooded tyrant, who cares nothing for the sufferings of his fellows, provided his own coffers are being filled" (*TR*, November 10, 1849).

This was a harsh judgment, but the working people had become resentful of Burnley's actions as the officials were feeling less intimidated by his power. Such an attitude was not helped by Burnley's insistence that the solution to the colony's labor problems lay in bringing more immigrants, particularly East Indians, into the colony. This anger was not diminished by a report in the *Barbados Liberal* that in Trinidad that year, the sugar and cocoa crops, the principal staples of the colony, seem "to be abundant, notwithstanding the clamor of the Burnley-Warner school on the habitual idleness of the laboring population, and the pretended dread of ruin, economical and moral, unless Government permits the reintroduction of slavery under the guise of promoting industry, etc" (*TR*, January 12, 1850). Apart from the introduction of more Indians, Burnley also proposed buying Africans on the coast of Africa and bringing them to the island as laborers.

By this point the criticism against the importation of Indian immigrants to the island had begun to spill outside of the bounds of the colony and was being described by the Anti-Slavery Society as a new form of slavery. In October, John Scoble, the secretary of the Anti-Slavery Society, accused the attorney general and the governor of having a personal interest in bringing Indians to the island and taking "advantage of their ignorance and helplessness, . . . to pass laws of a complicated character, the practical operation of which is to reduce them to a servile condition but little removed from slavery." Lord Harris took this charge personally. He assured Earl Grey that the immigration ordinance "was passed on the 9th April. I was married on the 16th April. By my marriage I am in no way directly or indirectly interested in plantation property and am only so far connected with those who are, that Lady Harris's brother-in-law is the proprietor of some estates."[1] Lord Harris had married Sarah, daughter of George Cummins, archdeacon of Port of Spain. She died on March 6, 1853.

Lord Harris conceded that immigration was a costly affair, that it was badly managed initially, and that the Indians suffered greatly when they first arrived on the island. However, he remained convinced that both the Africans and the Indians were better off in Trinidad than they were in their countries of origin. He also conceded that his immigration policies created discontent on the island. He blamed the disaffection that arose among the formerly enslaved population as being "aroused and confirmed amongst an ignorant and half civilized population by carefully disseminating amongst them the notion that they are ill-used, tyrannized over, and oppressed. . . . by leading them to suppose that they are obliged to work solely for the benefit of the planter, that planter being a white man, by holding out to them the hope that under other circumstances and under another Government they would be differently and far better treated; by making them believe that the only desire and wish of the present Government, and ultimately of the British Government is to oppress and degrade them."[2]

According to Lord Harris, those notions of discontent were being propagated by the *Trinidadian*, which he called "a disgrace to any community." He depicted the newspaper as being "indifferent, or worse, in religion; impure in morals; revolutionary in politics; socially licentious and libelous and malignant in tone and unscrupulous in attacks on character; generally incorrect, frequently false in its statements of facts; and endeavoring by every means in its power to foster disloyalty and sedition, and to foment and increase animosities of class, of caste, and of color."[3] However, the *Trinidadian's* greater sin was feeding the *Anti-Slavery Reporter* and other such publications with reports that Lord Harris deemed to be dubious about what was taking place on the island. Lord Harris was convinced that the *Trinidadian* was depicting Trinidad in a bad light and that was not good for the image of the colony.

Even as the Anti-Slavery Society was attacking Lord Harris, Burnley too was being subjected to humiliation at home. On September 17, a meeting of the Legislative Council became heated when its members debated a government proposal to increase the salaries of its officials. Burnley did not believe that the government should be spending more on salaries when the colony was in an economic downturn. He described the proposal as "shameless politics" and held them up to ridicule for "proposing an increase in the salaries of employees while the public misery is at its height and while in England they are on the eve of undermining this costly list of sinecurists and monstrous salaries" (*TR*, "Legislative Council," September 18, 1850).

Taking umbrage at Burnley's remarks, Warner responded: "Do you not know that by accepting the post of Councilor, you were committing to support all the views of the Government, *good or bad!*" (*TR*, September 18, 1850). At this rude, insulting remark "addressed to old men of whom a few are very honorable, Mr. Burnley answered only weakly. While remaining within the bounds of strict parliamentary etiquette, he was able otherwise to recall to the Attorney General feelings of his own dignity, at least to those of the most crude respectability." At the end of the debate, Burnley was able to salvage some of this dignity. The *Trinidadian* reported that Warner, "in spite of his habitual volubility, was pitifully beaten by Mr. Burnley" (*TR*, September 18, 1850). However, this exchange indicated the further erosion of Burnley's standing and his fading stature among those who admired and socialized with him during the latter part of his life. In fact, Warner was reputed to be one of his closest friends.

The onslaught against Burnley continued through the legislative term. On November 12, Lord Harris delivered "a semi-royal speech" in which he sternly and perhaps rudely censured Burnley, Philip, and Rennie about the "factious motives and unfair and deceptive [manner]" in which they conducted "their opposition to the measures of the Executive" (*SF*, "Legislative Council," November 20, 1850). Burnley, ever the watchdog of the planters' finances, wanted to know how much money the executive had spent on the ward roads which he felt were more important than the royal roads. While the government informed the council how much it spent on the latter, it was not prepared—or did not have—a report on how much money it had spent on the ward roads. He could not understand why the governor would want to censure him for criticizing what he thought was the government's lavish spending on the royal roads. Taking refuge in his rectitude, Burnley argued that "he was not very thin-skinned or susceptible to anything which might be said of him at the Council Board; and honorable members well knew that he rarely, if ever, lost his temper at the Board—indeed, the great fault which his honorable friend, the attorney general, found with him was, that he said hard things in a cool tone; and he always knew when he had made a hard thrust or used an unanswerable argument, by his honorable friend complimenting him on his 'fine speech.' The Board knew that he was not likely to take umbrage at any trifle" (*TR*, November 23, 1850).

Burnley was taken aback by the governor's censure knowing the prestige he enjoyed (or at least thought he enjoyed) within the society. Although he was not inclined to respond to the governor's charges, were he not to do so "it would appear as if he tacitly admitted the justice of the censure." He reminded the council he had the honor of serving as a member of the council for thirty-six years and that "during the whole of that period he had never heard the slightest slur thrown on his character; although the position of members of Council was an invidious one" (*TR*, November 23, 1850). He emphasized:

> I have been appointed a delegate to go to England to protect the interests of the inhabitants of the colony [he should have said the planters of the colony]. Subsequently, I was appointed an agent for the colony—which is a high situation—when the colony found itself in serious circumstances about the emancipation of the slaves. I received a vote of thanks from the Government I had been sent to oppose for the manner in which I conducted my opposition and I did not oppose it tenderly. I brought back from the Colonial Minister to the governor appointed during my absence recommendations to accept my suggestions and appointing me as a fit person to assist him in the government of the colony. I hold a priority in public opinion which I cannot afford to resign, or have depreciated by any report about what I say at the Board. (*TR*, November 23, 1850)

Burnley could have been writing his epitaph. He was very proud of the contributions he had made to the board and to the society. While he appreciated the bold manner in which the governor had "expressed his sentiments for the good of the colony," he really could not abdicate the oppositional role that he had always carried out "with courtesy and respect." As far he was concerned, it was his "bounden duty" to act as the loyal opposition to the government and nothing that the governor's advisers did would deter him from doing so. He would never vote for nor support any government measure which he believed was not in the interest of the colony. In so doing, he was sure that he would "not only gain the respect of the community, but also merit the esteem of His Excellency, the Governor" (*TR*, November 23, 1850). The *San Fernando Gazette* was so pleased with Burnley's performance that it declared: "Had anyone supposed Mr. Burnley capable of making a factious opposition to the measures of government, the honorable gentleman's defense must have completely removed any such impression" (*SF*, November 20, 1850).

The governor, after having rethought his position, admitted that he did not intend "to make any charges against any of the members of council, nor had he any desire to intimidate or prevent opposition whenever the members thought it necessary." In fact, he found that no body of men acted more conscientiously than the members of the board. His message, he said, "was necessary to show that the Government would defend its officers." The attorney general declared his admiration for Burnley, especially the tone in which he conducted his opposition to the governor, but insisted that the governor's message was delivered "in the full exercise of a fair license to complain of what had been said at the Board." He thought "the governor had been bound to complain, [and] could not have done so in a more fair, moderate and temperate manner" (*TR*, November 27, 1850).

The attorney general was hedging his bets. He wanted to support and to please the governor but did not want to offend Burnley. He confessed that Burnley's services "extended beyond the life of the members of the Board; his conduct had always been upright and honest; and he certainly tempered his opposition with such a happy courtesy that even the Governor, whose measure met with his disapprobation, could never complain about his opposition." He continued: "There was no person whose words were listened to with more respect than his honorable friend's. On questions of money or of the Colonial Bank, the public were always certain of success when he espoused their side. All that were true, and therefore gave the greatest possible weight to his observation; and yet his honorable friend could not hesitate to charge the Government with a lavish expenditure" (*TR*, November 27, 1850). Although the attorney general came "vigorously to the rescue of the Governor" (*SF*, November 20, 1850), it was, at best, a lukewarm endorsement of the governor's behavior.

William Rennie, another subject of the governor's vitriol, was also critical of the attorney general's response. In a short "but very effective speech" (*SF*, November 20, 1850), he demolished much of the attorney general's defense of the governor. He did not think the governor's message was "temperate and mild," as the attorney general claimed, nor was it respectful of the position of the unofficial members of government. Although a great deal had been made about Burnley's criticism of the government's "lavish expenditure," he felt the evidence had borne out Burnley's position. Like the other unofficials, he took great umbrage at the governor's "semi-royal speech" from the throne.

Burnley assured the attorney general, the erstwhile defender of the governor, that "he never intended in the slightest degree" to attack the governor personally and was sorry if it were so interpreted. Curmudgeon as he was, he stuck to his guns. He felt compelled to respond to the governor because his was a prepared and formal message rather than flippant, loosely constructed sentiments that emerged in the cut and thrust of legislative debates. He insisted that before any expense was incurred "the subject should have been brought to the Board, and a vote should have been taken for the expenditure; and by these means the Government would have avoided the charge of lavish expenditure" (*TR*, November 27, 1850).

Burnley took his responsibility as de facto leader of the opposition seriously. He insisted that the executive should be made responsible to the people and that he, as a member of the official opposition, had a responsibility to keep the executive in line and to make it responsible for its spending of the people's money. As he said of himself, he was cool, sharp, and even mercurial in his opposition. At times, he was even imperial. His education at Harrow School for Boys and his assumed life-experiences had prepared him for that role. For all of his adult life he had assumed a powerful position in the society. He was accustomed to getting his way. Occasionally the executive had dropped certain aspects of its legislative proposals to please Burnley. But the governor had a public persona to maintain. Burnley's insistence that the expenditure on the royal roads had doubled, a position that Rennie supported, brought the executive into disrepute and this was not acceptable to the governor. He had to bring Burnley to heel.

Even the attorney general who usually deferred to Burnley was forced to show with whom his loyalty lay. He sided with the governor, although, as Angelo Bissessarsingh suggested, Warner was retained permanently on Burnley's payroll and "personally represented the sugar barons' interests when and where it suited him."[4] Since the governor was his boss, his better self-interest demanded that he demonstrate his loyalty to the governor. It was not difficult for Warner, a particularly dishonest man, to switch his loyalties. Burnley's rule was coming to an end, and he was getting along in age. Six weeks after this debate, Burnley would be dead. For the next twenty-six years, Warner would go on to rule the island, ruthlessly and untouched, until Sir Arthur Gordon, governor of the island, unceremoniously removed him from his post as attorney general in 1870.

CHAPTER 46

Cessation

Fortunately, most fortunately, when under the stifling breath of that doctrine [of the Burnley school] Trinidad was perishing, Lord Harris came to
the rescue. . . . Gentlemen; it is my firm conviction that much of our troubles have had their origin in the fatal policy of William Hardin Burnley.

—Philip Rostant, "The Great Reform Meeting," 1888

PERHAPS IT WAS symbolic that Burnley ended his political reign in Trinidad
by clashing with Lord Harris, the last governor with whom he worked as he
did with Sir Ralph Woodford, the governor who appointed him to the colonial
council in 1813. It was a part of that necessarily ambivalent relationship that he
enjoyed with the governors of the island. Wednesday, November 20, the day
after the debate on the road ordinance, Lord Harris and Burnley clashed once
more when the board resumed its debate on the second reading of the proposal
to establish an inland postal service.

The proposal, an elaborate and forward-looking one, called for the establishment of twenty-two post offices throughout the island. No post office was
established in Tacarigua where Burnley resided. Burnley protested against
these arrangements as he had done previously. He thought that the monies
allocated for the inland post office, if used, would be detrimental to the finances
of the country. While he was prepared to support any reasonable measure that
was designed to benefit the country, he perceived "a certain danger in this one,
which should cause the Board to deliberate more carefully before passing it"

(*TR*, "Legislative Council," December 4, 1850). Still smarting under the governor's rebuke of the previous day, he reminded the board that the governor "had Napoleonized himself" by saying "moi je suis l'état" [I am the state]." Burnley continued "Everything depends on the Governor, and we cannot always be sure of having a Governor who will be one day general road maker, and the next day general mail contractor; and if not, what would we do then? What! Cast off the connexion with the Imperial Post Office, and do what?" (*TR*, December 4, 1850). The colony's connection to Britain remained the only security for the smooth running of things on the island.

Burnley, always reluctant to try anything new especially if it resulted in the colony having to spend additional monies, preferred to retain the informal method of mail distribution that was controlled by the Imperial Post Office. He was not impressed when the attorney general informed him that the Imperial Post Office would continue to deliver the letters for a fixed period and then hand over "to the local government the duty of receiving and delivering all letters coming into the colony, merely maintaining an agent to receive and deliver Mail bags." He believed that a majority of the inhabitants did not want such a system and those who clamored most for it "would be the first to turn on the Government and blame them for any additional trifling expense they might be put to for the measure." He signaled his intention to vote against what he called "an unwise and encumbered measure" (*TR*, December 4, 1850).

Dr. Philip, the unofficial member of Council from the San Fernando area, thought the bill would be beneficial to his constituents. He did not agree with Burnley's objections. His experience had taught him that Burnley "liked to throw cold water on every new measure" even though this measure would be "the very means by which his honorable friend would get that information weekly which he complains so much of not getting" (*TR*, December 4, 1850). Only Burnley and William Rennie voted against the bill. Burnley, however, stood by his word. On December 24, when Lord Harris forwarded the ordinance to Lord Grey, the secretary of state for the colonies, he included "Burnley's protest" against what Burnley called an "unjust, capricious and absurd" ordinance. Lord Harris also included Charles Warner's report to Lord Grey.

Burnley was dead set against the establishment of a post office in that he felt it would obstruct the retention of cheap labor (transferring agricultural workers to the police force); it would exacerbate the problem of squatting; and it would stymie measures to prevent vagrancy on the island. He also believed that the establishment of a post office would be too costly to the colony. (The colony had to subsidize the project by £600 annually.) Ultimately, it would tax the rich who lived in Port of Spain in favor of the poorer classes who lived in the out-lying districts. Six hundred pounds, he suggested, was an enormous financial burden for the colony to sustain, the amount "being equivalent to £500,000 in Great Britain, taking the population, in round numbers, to 30 million and ours [in Trinidad] being 60,000."[1]

After a long lament about the need to cultivate virtuous Christian citizens, Burnley ends his litany with the hope that the clergyman impresses "on their youthful mind that 'honesty is the best policy' when the results of unpunished thefts are every day spread out before their eyes proves to them that one suc-cessful act of plunder is productive of more wealth than months of honest toil."[2] Such a statement led one to wonder if that was the same person who, in his early years, was accused of robbing the widow and orphan's fund and exploiting his slaves. Even near the end of his days, Burnley could see nothing dishonor-able in his slaveholding practices. Burnley could make his crude observation about the formerly enslaved only because he possessed the purchasing power of his capital.

Burnley's final objections to the inland postal service revolved around his feeling that the inhabitants did not desire the measure ("it is solely an exper-iment emanating from the Colonial Government") nor were there any public meetings or petitions by the inhabitants calling for the establishment of such a service. The governor conceded that although no general call was made by the community for its input, "the inhabitants of the colony had been aware that the question has been under consideration for some time and consequently that it was unnecessary to move [that is, to consult the inhabitants] in the matter."[3]

This debate on the inland post office was Burnley's last input into the affairs of the island. On December 29, without any warning, Burnley passed away in Port of Spain at the home of Philip Bernard. His death surprised everyone. He had shown no signs or ill health nor was he slackening down in terms of the pace of his work. In the end he simply ceased to be. In death, the *Trinidadian* emphasized the positive aspects of his life. It wrote:

> Mr. W. H. Burnley died on Saturday, in his 71st year. Mr. Burnley occupied a prominent place among the political men of this island, and the great influence afforded him by his position in society marks with an indelible fingerprint the various unsuccessful phases of our legislation. We will not judge the private indi-vidual here; although each person who dies leaves to society a legacy of good or evil and thus belongs to the press. We will be quiet in front of his grave.
>
> The censorship on the political life of Mr. Burnley has a *vast* field of criticism, but his last acts must in part disarm this censorship. Mr. Burnley, in the last words

of his political career, had adopted an attitude to the Council which gained him numerous supporters. (*TR*, January 1, 1851)

Although Des Sources and others were critical of Burnley's wealth and power while he lived, at his death they seemed to fear the vacuum his absence would create. Des Sources asked rhetorically: "Who will take the political legacy of Mr. Burnley?" and bemoaned: "Today the Council does not contain one independent member, not a man there who can have the courage of his opinion. Mr. Rennie sometimes assisted Mr. Burnley, and his opinion was over and over very energetically expressed, but what is the position of Mr. Rennie in this colony?" Although Rennie fought energetically against the government's excesses, he did not have the wealth or social standing to effect changes or organize similar opposition against government measures that Burnley had possessed. In other words, while Burnley was independently wealthy; Rennie was not. Des Sources closed on a gloomy note. "The future," he said, "will tell if Mr. Burnley has buried in his grave the shadow of our absurd Council's opposition" (*TR*, January 1, 1851).

The obituary notice in the *Port of Spain Gazette* recorded Burnley's long services to the colony and described him as "an accomplished and polished gentleman, of commanding intellect, varied and accurate information, energy of mind, and decision of character." Norman Lamont, his biographer, noted that Burnley was "hot-tempered, . . . a difficult master to serve, . . . [who] brooked no authority, consequently [the reason why he disparaged] the Governors until their departure" (*OG*, 17). He also believed that Burnley had made an important contribution to the colony.

Burnley's business continued as usual after his death. On January 1, 1851, the same day the announcement of his death appeared in the *Trinidadian*, Hume, Bernard and Company, controlled by Burnley's nephew, placed a notice in the *Trinidad Royal Gazette* informing the public that although Burnley had died, his company was still open for business. The company did not miss a beat. The notice was dated Port of Spain, December 31, 1850. It was almost as though nothing of any real significance had happened within his family. Burnley's death, it seemed, was an interruption in their otherwise busy commercial lives, or perhaps, that's just how business was conducted in that part of the world. A similar notice, announcing the continuation of business, was repeated in the *Trinidad Royal Gazette* on January 8, 1851.

On January 8, 1851, Lord Harris sent a terse, matter-of-fact letter to Earl Grey. It read: "I have with much regret to inform Your Lordship of the death of Mr.

Burnley, the Senior Unofficial member of the Legislative Council of this colony. Mr. Burnley had been for 36 years a member of the Council and his loss will be severely felt."⁴ On February 1, at the first meeting of the Legislative Council after Burnley's death, Lord Harris expressed "deep sorrow and regret" for the loss of Mr. Burnley which "would be felt throughout the colony, but more particularly at the Board" (*TR*, February 5, 1851). Those who were close to him, he said, would miss his "agreeable conversation, great intelligence and polished manners." All the members of the council, he said, will miss his "extraordinary energy of mind which he continued to display to the last." They would also miss "the sagacity of his remarks, the playfulness of his wit, the fluency of his speech and, above all, the courteous urbanity never forgotten in political hostility, with which he used to enliven the debates of the Council." He ended his tribute by saying: "Having his prudence, his talents and his conduct, obtained for himself a high commercial and political position in this colony in early life, he maintained it in full vigor to a great old age, and still appeared full of life and energy, when he was suddenly struck down by the mysterious hand of death" (*PG*, "Council of Government," February 4, 1851).

Rennie, Burnley's close friend, described Burnley's death as "a great and severe public calamity" for the colony. He observed that Burnley devoted his entire life "zealously and uncompromisingly advocating what he considered to be her [Trinidad's] best interest." He reiterated that Burnley served the colony for over thirty-six years. During that period, he was "the leading and most distinguished unofficial member of the Board; his entire conduct marked by the most unflinching independence, integrity and ability, and, up to his sudden death, with the greatest activity and perseverance" (*PG*, "Council of Government," February 4, 1851). He concluded his tribute sorrowfully: "At this moment, when the voice of lamentation was so loudly heard, it could be no trifling loss which had occasioned it" (*TR*, February 5, 1851).

The vacancy on the council that resulted from Burnley's death occasioned misgivings. When it was revealed that the governor offered the vacant seat to John Losh, the *Trinidadian* reminded its readers of Burnley's critique of the present council. "He said that the Council had fallen into such disrepute that it was with difficulty any person of independent spirit could be got to accept a seat at the Board. How then will this vacancy be filled up?" On February 6, when the governor informed the council that Losh would fill the vacant seat that was occasioned by Burnley's death, the *Trinidadian* immediately characterized Losh as having "modeled his conduct at the Board on that of the late Mr. Burnley, whose Legislative Euriale he was."⁵ The *Trinidadian* reminded him about the remarks he had made at the public meeting for self-government in April 1850, when he described the government as "weak and incompetent, and little adapted to the colony. There can be no doubt of this and no one will attempt to deny that a reform is absolutely necessary" (*TR*, February 8, 1851). They hoped that Losh would remember his words and not be intimidated by executive power.

In 1863, thirteen years after his death, the *Trinidad Colonist*, in a touch of nostalgia, protested against "probably the most despotic government which ever existed in this or any other British colony." Bemoaning the absence of leaders such as James Kavanah, the owner of several estates in Trinidad and a former mayor of Port of Spain, Burnley, and Losh, the editor asked rhetorically: "What have become of our representative men?" to which it responded: "They were giants in those days, now the men who should be foremost are mere pigmies" (*TC*, September 18, 1863).

Philip Rostant, the editor of *Public Opinion*, turned out to be Burnley's harshest critic. He argued that when Lord Harris arrived, Trinidad was perishing under "the stifling breath" of the doctrines of the "Burnley School." It was at that point that Burnley realized that the policy that he had ruthlessly carried out for all those years had encountered an enemy with whom he would have to grapple. Faced with Lord Harris's determination, his whole empire would have crumbled into dust if he did not modify the harshness to which he had subjected the people. According to Rostant:

> [Burnley] was then an old man, a very old man, most feeble in body, but with his powerful intellect unimpaired. He understood the task of combatting Lord Harris with all the ardor of youth. He combed over statistics and poured over dispatches and state papers. He put his whole soul in the work, but alas, the enfeebled organism did not respond to the impetuous call of an indomitable will. The brain collapsed under the heavy pressure it was asked to bear, and one morning the brave old gentleman was found lying senseless in his room. He had been struck with paralysis during the night, never recovered, and died the same day.
>
> Gentlemen, it is my firm conviction that much of our troubles have their origin in the fatal policy of William Hardin Burnley; but who that knew him could fail to admire the exquisite *gentilhommerie*—there is no English word to express it—of that remarkable man, to bow low in involuntary homage before the mighty spirit which animated that frail body. (*PO*, "The Great Reform: Monster Meeting in the Savanna," January 18, 1887)

Jose Bodu was a bit more balanced in his judgment. He acknowledged that Burnley, as leader of the plantocracy, took "energetic steps" to protect and to support measures that were beneficial to his fellow planters who "regarded him as benefactor to the country." He was not sympathetic to the views of the laboring classes of the society. In fact, "he made strenuous exertions for the advancement of views which were not accepted by an important section of the community."[6] This was putting the case against Burnley in a charitable light. It was 1890, forty years after Burnley's death and things had mellowed somewhat.

Burnley was a colossus of his time. Never sick a day in his life, he was always on the go. To the last, he participated in the business of his country. On December 24, 1850, Lord Harris sent his protest to Earl Grey, the secretary of state for the colonies. On December 29, Burnley ceased to be; a light gone out without a warning. There he was, and then he was no more. Thomas Carlyle says of Homer's epic, *The Odyssey*, "It is like a Bas-relief sculpture: it does not conclude, but merely ceases."[7] Something about this sentiment was analogous to Burnley's life. In the end, he just ceased to be.

CHAPTER 47

RESURGAM

He served the Colony well, particularly in the difficult and anxious years after the ending of apprenticeship. I hope that the Society [Historical Society of Trinidad and Tobago] will keep his memory green, and perhaps number his grave among monuments worthy of preservation.

—Norman Lamont, *Burnley of Orange Grove*, 1947

BURNLEY LIVED A remarkable life. He was a natural leader. In spite of his racism and his authoritarianism, he commanded the admiration of his antagonists. A hard worker, he was in the best of health. He participated in the Legislative Council debate on December 9, the last sitting of its 1850 calendar, protesting to the last the exorbitant cost of fixing the roads. On December 24, Lord Harris sent Burnley's protest against the inland postal services to Earl Grey, the secretary of state. On December 29, Burnley ceased to be; a light had gone out without warning.

Now that Burnley was gone, the time had come to disburse his large fortune. He had become the richest man on the island and certainly one of the richest men in the world. It was left to William (Willie) Hume, who had become very close with his uncle, to break the news of Burnley's death to Burnley's wife Charlotte. On January 17, 1851, writing from St. Thomas, he urged her to hurry to Glasgow, Scotland, to prevent her deceased husband's estates from being swallowed up by her son William's bankruptcy. But then he added: "You will not be surprised to hear what additional troubles *that worthless woman,*

297

Augusta, has caused me!" *(OG*, 19). Was it that Charlotte had known all along what he had known, that Augusta was her husband's paramour, which is why she returned to Trinidad reluctantly and fled as quickly as she could from that palatial mansion in Orange Grove?

Willie's urgent warning to this mother was neither a useless nor exaggerated concern. On February 15, C. A. Calvert, secretary of Colonial Bank at 15 Bishopgate in London, wrote to William Rennie, manager of the Trinidad branch and a friend of Burnley, to inform him that he (or certainly the bank) had heard of the "sudden death of Burnley" and also to inform him (something that Rennie undoubtedly knew) that Burnley "has left considerable property to be divided between his widow and his two sons, the older of whom [William Frederick] was one of the firm of Eccles Burnley & Co., of Glasgow.[1] Should the trustees of that estate be able to make good on a claim to Mr. W. F. Burnley's portion of his father's property, it will be a wonderful on the dividend but it must be expected that every attempt will be made to avoid such a circumstance and nothing must be left unturned for that purpose. This sort of affair is so uncertain in its results that it would be premature at present to found any expectations upon it."[2]

On March 1, 1851, Calvert wrote another letter to Rennie regarding the £38,000 that Eccles, Burnley and Co., William Frederick Burnley's bankrupt company, owed the bank. By then Colonial Bank had done more research on the late William Hardin Burnley's property with a view to retrieving some of the money it had lost through the bankruptcy of William Frederick Burnley's company. It sent the following report to Rennie:

> Eccles Burnley & Co: We learn from Glasgow that all hope of finding a later will by the late Mr. Burnley than the one dated in 1837 is now abandoned by his family who has opened a negotiation with the Trustee for a Settlement. The Trustee agent in Trinidad has sent home [meaning England] a statement of the late Mr. Burnley's affairs to the following effect, viz:

American Funds	£75,000
British Funds	£25,000
Mortgages in the West Indies	£70,000
Estates	£90,000
Total	£260,000

> The family has, however, produced a very different statement. They arrived to the full account, the investment in America funds but say there is nothing in the British and that the value of the mortgages and estate is small. The gross estates only about £108,000. They strike off besides a third of this estate which say belongs to Mr_____ to whom Mr. Burnley had presented _____ but of which he has no evidence. The widow also put in a claim to one half the estate. The Trustee has not

yet obtained full information of legal advice as to this claim but he considers the valuation by the family as quite inadequate.

It seems petty clear that the estate of Eccles Burnley & Co., will derive something by the death of W. Burnley, Sr., but to what amount it is difficult to say at present and as the rankings about to about £400.000 it will require a pretty large sum to make any sensible increase in the dividend. Every 1/- require £20,000.[3]

By March 15, the Burnley family furnished the trustee with a statement on Burnley's property, particularly with regard to the value of his Trinidad estates and William Burnley's share of his father's property. Calvert, who was keeping a close eye on things, reported: "We understand the Trustee objects to the valuation of the Trinidad properties and that he has sent out a case for the opinion of your [meaning Trinidad's] attorney general, and is also consulting Special Counsel in London as to the widow's claim of one half of the entire property.... The Trustee's Agent in Trinidad sent home [to London] a statement estimating Mr. Burnley's property at [£400,000]. This is a very different amount to that stated by the family."[4]

Having valued the property at £400,000, Colonial Bank hoped it would extract more money from what William Frederick would have derived from his father's property. Royal Bank of Canada, to whom William Frederick was also indebted (he was also in bankruptcy in Scotland), also hoped to benefit from the monies his father had bequeathed to him. Calvert noted that Royal Bank of Scotland "will doubtless take good care that the estates recover all that can possibly be got."[5]

By mid-May Colonial Bank could not determine how much they could squeeze out of William Frederick's proceeds from his father's property. On May 16, Calvert wrote to Rennie: "It appears pretty certain that Eccles Burnley & Co estate must benefit by it [that is, his father's estate], but to what extent depends principally upon what is finally settled as regards valuations and Mrs. Burnley, the widow's claim. We do not suppose that Mr _____ claim to be one third of the sugar estates will be admitted, as a body of creditors are not likely to be raking anything they are not compelled to do."[6] Late in life, much to his chagrin, William Hardin had learned that his son was a bad businessman. When William Sr. refused to assist him, little did he know that his son's bad business decisions would imperil the fortune he had left him when he died.

Burnley made out his will on December 4, 1837. It was probated in London on June 2, 1851.[7] On June 15, Joseph Hume wrote to his mother from his diplomatic post in Madrid to say: "Have you heard what Miss Farquhar is doing? Old Johnston has not answered my letter yet about *that viper!* We may thank her for having made my father centre his affections in America, and thus leave his heirs to fight with the law for his inheritance" (*OG*, 19). By then everyone in Burnley's family knew that Augusta was Burnley's mistress for whom he had made adequate provisions in his will. As she lingered at her tranquil cottage in Blackheath, England, Charlotte knew that she was not Burnley's only love.

All told, he was worth £244,171, with £94,269 mostly in American securities. He left his son William Frederick, William Eccles Jr., Joseph Burnley Hume, and William Brackenbridge, solicitor, as the executors of his will. Second, he left his wife an annuity of £1,200 plus "all the household furniture, plates, wines, carriages and carriage horses of which I may be possessed." The rest of the estate was shared among his sons, his nieces and nephews, and Augusta and her family. He gave each of his nieces and nephews, the children of Joseph and Maria Hume, the sum of £500 sterling. To Mary Augusta Farquhar, daughter of James Farquhar, "an annuity of that yearly sum of one thousand dollars to be paid to her own separate use on her own personal receipt so that in the event of her marriage it shall not be at the subject of the disposal or subject to the debts, engagements or control of any husband."[8] He also left smaller sums to William Burnley Farquhar and his sister Elizabeth Curson Farquhar.

Next, he gave his first son, William, "the one half equal parts of all the residue of my estates real and personal after the payment of one half of the above mentioned annuities."[9] Since his second son, Joseph, was only about sixteen years old when the will was written, he was to be paid an annual sum of £200 until he reached the age of 25. "As soon as he shall have attained the age of thirty years that there be paid to him a clear annuity or yearly sum of one thousand pounds sterling to be also paid half yearly in advance and of his attaining the age last mentioned I give and devise to my said son Joseph Hume Burnley and his heirs so much of the said trust states and of the accumulations thereof as might then remain unapplied to the payment of the annuities above given to them."[10] Prior to his death, Burnley gave William Burnley Hume, his nephew "one third of the whole landed proper in Trinidad, and that of the live-and-dead stock thereon" (*OG*, 18).

William Hume's closeness to his uncle, William Hardin Burnley, created considerable animosity between William Frederick and his cousin, William Hume. In 1854 William Frederick was ordered to pay William Hume £15,000 for the third of the estate that William Hume inherited from William Sr.[11] This inheritance made Hume an influential man in Trinidad. Subsequently, William Frederick appointed his brother-in-law, William Eccles, as his Trinidad attorney.

Together, they built the "Coolie Orphan Home" in 1857. It was later renamed St. Mary's Children's Home.

Thirteen days after Burnley's estate was probated, Joseph wrote to his mother from his diplomatic post in Madrid to complain about his father's paramour once again: "Have you heard what Miss Farquhar is doing? Old Johnson has not answered my letter yet about that viper! We may thank her for having made my father center his affections in America, and thus leave his heirs to fight with the law for his inheritance" (*OG*, 19).

Burnley was not alone in this regard. This bequeathal of monies and property to the colored mistresses and the offspring of these unions was an age-old problem in Trinidad. Even as the whites built "higher and higher barriers around themselves to keep these [black people] as far as possible away from them and to retain the political power in their hands,"[12] the white men could not stay away from the charms of black women. Governor Ralph Woodford, a person highly respected by Burnley, described the danger these relations posed as early as the 1820s. He wrote:

> Several instances have lately occurred of very considerable bequests made by white persons to their natural colored children, and from the very great extent of illicit connection in the colony, which in a few years may tend to throw a great preponderance on the side of that description of persons already too numerous, I am induced to represent the matter to Your Lordship to suggest the propriety of restraining by an Order in Council the inhabitants of this colony from bequeathing by will more than a certain proportion of property to their natural colored children and that the same may be paid to them in money only.
>
> Many of the foreign settlers in the colony who have survived the remembrance of their European connections have substituted illicit ones and have lately bequeathed their property to their natural colored children, to the exclusion of their brothers and sisters; it happens that this property is of the most valuable that the island contains and the respectable part of the white population are threatened with a gradual increase of the colored, arising from sources that degrade both the one and the other, while they perpetuate the seeds of mutual hatred and contempt.[13]

On Sunday, June 15, 1851, a spring day that felt more like a cold November day, as Charlotte hunkered down in her Blackheath cottage in Greater London, she may not have shared in Governor Woodford's fear about the degeneration of white men in the West Indies who entered into "illicit" relations with black women. The only thing she knew for sure was that she was not Burnley's only love and that Augusta, a feisty woman, was laying claim to her husband's inheritance.

On January 8, 1851, when Lord Harris wrote to Earl Grey to announce the
death of Burnley, he recommended that Hume be appointed to fill the vacancy
occasioned by Burnley's death. On March 15, the Colonial Office informed Lord
Harris that the queen had appointed Hume to fill the vacancy created by his
uncle's death. In April of that year, Hume was named as an unofficial member of
the Legislative Council, making it the first time in British Parliamentary history
that a father served in the British Parliament while his son served as an unofficial member of the Legislative Council in one of its colonies. This appointment
signified the continuation of Burnley's reign, by proxy, on the island of Trinidad.

J. G. Cotton Minchin, one of Harrow's noblest sons, noted that one of the
"salient features of Harrow" was its "directing through her sons the fortunes
of Empire."[14] Such a spirit allowed Englishmen at home and abroad "to look
upon his kith and kin across the ocean no longer as Colonists, but as heirs ... of
England's deathless fame."[15] Burnley was performing that function in Trinidad.
Burnley might have been thinking of Harrow as he breathed his last;[16] he might
have heard his fellow Harrovians singing in unity:

> So once again your glasses drain,
> And may we long continue
> From Harrow School to rise and rule
> By heart and brain and sinew,
> And as the roll of Harrow's scroll
> Page after page is written,
> May Harrow give the names that live
> In Great and Greater Britain![17]

Burnley left his mark on Trinidad and the West Indies. He was certainly one
of the Caribbean's most prominent political figures while he lived. In fact, he
became such an eminent figure on the island of Trinidad that Donald Wood
described him as "a founding father of British Trinidad."[18] By and through his
achievement he may have fulfilled one of the grandest goals of his alma mater,
which suggested that in serving in Trinidad, he was serving in the cause of
creating a "Greater Britain." He remained a titanic force in promoting his and
British interests in the Caribbean.

Burnley's remains were placed in a massive mausoleum at the northwestern
corner of Lapeyrouse Cemetery, Port of Spain. Today it stands neglected and
alone, his name barely visible on the inner wall of the cemetery at the back of
Colville Street and Tragrette Road. At the head of what remains of the mausoleum, engraved in bold letters, is the motto RESURGAM which, translated into

English, means, "I shall rise again" or "I shall live again." Beneath that motto is the following inscription:

> Sacred to the memory of the Hon. William Hardin Burnley
> who departed this life, 29 December 1850.
> Aged 70 years.

The Latin motto RESURGAM carries with it the sentiments, "I should be resurrected from the dead," as all Christians believe. As I looked at that engraving on a very hot day of May 2016, I couldn't help but think that even after fifty years of tyrannical rule on the island, even after he served in the Legislative Council until a few days before he died, William Hardin Burnley felt he would never leave the island or perhaps, as the masons in France, he believed in his own divinity. Like François Mitterrand, the French president, Burnley may have wanted to assert to his fellow Trinidadians: "I believe in the forces of the spirit, and I will not leave you."[19]

Today his name is but a faint echo in Trinidad and Tobago's national memory. Maybe the time has come to look upon the impact he had in shaping the history of the region and the part he played in the transatlantic slave system. In the words of Norman Lamont, one hopes that the nation finds the courage to "number his grave among [its] monuments worthy of preservation" (*OG*, 18). Who knows, one day he may rise again in all of his power and glory and, perhaps, even in his shame, demanding that we give him the attention that he deserves?

Notes

PROLOGUE: BURNLEY AT ORANGE GROVE

1. Although Trinidad and Tobago were separate political units during Burnley's life, in this text I sometimes use today's name even when I speak exclusively about Trinidad.

2. Donald Wood, *Trinidad in Transition: The Years after Slavery* (Oxford: Oxford University Press, 1986), 126.

3. William D. Rubinstein, *Who Were the Rich? A Biographical Dictionary of British Wealth-holders, Volume One, 1809–1839* (London: The Social Affairs Unit, 2009).

4. These are the estates for which Burnley was awarded compensation by the Compensation Board. Norman Lamont claims that Burnley's will revealed that he also owned Endeavor, Phoenix Park, Petersfield, and Esperanza; and that he possessed shares in Forres Park, Bonaventure, Concord, Barataria, and Nelson estates.

5. Bridget Brereton, "History, Heritage and Green Spaces," *Trinidad Express*, January 2, 2014.

6. This information is taken from my grandfather's notebook. All of my family information is taken from this source.

7. Emma Dicken, *Our Burnley Ancestors and Allied Families* (New York: The Hobson Book Press, 1946), 45.

8. Ibid., 49.

9. Count Cavour, the founder of modern Italy, and C. H. J. Hayes describes Senior as "the economist par excellence" and the "final flower of the classical school" respectively. Quoted in S. Leon Levy, *Nassau W. Senior, 1790–1864: Critical Essayist, Classical Economist and Adviser of Governments* (Boston: Bruce Humphries, 1943), 15.

10. John W. Vandercook, *Black Majesty* (New York: Harper & Brothers, 1828), 28. When one reads *Black Majesty* one understands why Burnley was so afraid of the nocturnal activities of the Africans (*PG*, February 3, 1849).

11. Christopher Hitchens, *Thomas Jefferson: Author of America* (New York: Harper Perennial, 2009), 30.

12. For an examination of Jefferson's racist positions and a frank elaboration of his relationship with Sally Hemmings, his black mistress, see E. M. Halliday, *Understanding Thomas Jefferson* (New York: Perennial, 2002).

13. Between 1932 and 1946 the Historical Society of Trinidad and Tobago published several interesting articles on important sites, events, and persons associated with the Caribbean. Norman Lamont's "Burnley of Orange Grove" was one of those lectures. British scholars and colonial civil servants undertook most of this research. In 1941 the society published Sir Alfred Claud Hollis's *A Brief History of Trinidad Under the Spanish Crown*, with the assistance of the government printer. Hollis was the governor of Trinidad from 1930 to 1936. At the end of the 1930s, ITCA (the Imperial College of Tropical Agriculture and forerunner of the University

of the West Indies, St. Augustine) agreed to house the society's collection at its library. Gertrude Carmichael, author of *The History of the West Indian Islands of Trinidad and Tobago* (1961), was appointed as the college librarian "responsible for cataloguing and organizing the material." In 1950 Eric Williams, Oxford-trained scholar, chief minister and premier of the island (1956–1962), and prime minister (1962–1981), became the chairman of the society. As distinct from emphasizing accounts of Europeans in the West Indies, Williams emphasized the contributions of West Indians in the making of their own history. (Kelvin Jarvis, "The Historical Society of Trinidad and Tobago, 1932–1954," *Caribbean Quarterly* 44, no. 3/4 (September/December 1998): 91–104.

14. Richard Franklin Kane, "The Sociology and Politics of Fernando Henrique Cardoso" (master's thesis, Illinois State University, 2004), 30.

15. Christopher Caldwell, "No Sense of History without a Good Biography," *Financial Times*, May 12, 2012.

16. Selwyn Ryan, *Eric Williams: The Myth and the Man* (Jamaica: University of the West Indies Press, 2009).

CHAPTER 1: BURNLEY'S EMERGENCE

1. Alfred Claud Hollis, *A Brief History of Trinidad Under the Spanish Crown* (Port of Spain: government printer, 1941), 92. This book was published with the assistance of the Trinidad government.

2. Ibid., 93.

3. Ibid., 91.

4. Lionel Mordant Fraser, *History of Trinidad, 1781–1839*, vol. 1 (Port of Spain: Government Printing Office, 1891), 102.

5. Hollis, *Brief History of Trinidad*, 98.

6. Jean-Baptiste Philippe, *Free Mulatto* (1824; repr. Wellesley, MA: Calaloux Publications, 1996), 8.

7. John Lamont, the great uncle of Norman Lamont, came to Trinidad from Scotland in 1802. He acquired his first estate in 1809. By 1825 he was "proprietor of two estates and continued to operate as an attorney who supervised estates for other Scots." When he died in 1850 he had acquired wealth "that would have propelled him into the ranks of the super-wealthy in Scotland had he returned." Stephen Mullen, "John Lamont of Benmore: A Highland Planter Who Died 'in harness' in Trinidad," *Northern Scotland* 9 (2018): 44–46. See "A Trinidad Plantation," Norman Lamont, *Problems of Trinidad* (Port of Spain: Yuille's Printerie, 1933), 224–33.

8. The language in Smithson's will is rather colorful. It reads: "Whereas I have a lawful right to the third part of five negroes in HARDIN BURNLEY SENIOR's possession in Hanover County which negroes he has had in his possession ever since the yeare 1757 as well as I now Remember and I have never received any satisfaction from them as yet I do therefore and appointe that of my Executors shall think fitt upon advising with able lawyer think fitt to Seu his Executors and if they recover any money from Mr. Burnley or his Executors I do hereby will and appointe the same be equally Divided among all my children that are then living. Rulon N. Smithson" (Lune Co., VA Wills 3:187).

9. Emma Dicken, *Our Burnley Ancestors and Allied Families* (New York: The Hobson Book Press, 1946), 25.

10. Ibid.

11. David Gange, *The Victorians* (London: Oneworld, 2016), 73.

12. Andrea Wulf, *Invention of Nature: Alexander von Humboldt's New World* (London: John Murray, 2015), 163.

13. Dicken, *Our Burnley Ancestors*, 26–27.

14. See Peyton Randolph, *Reports on Cases Argued and Determined in the Courts of Appeals of Virginia, Volume 1* (Richmond: Peter Cotton, 1823), 108–13.

CHAPTER 2: BURNLEY'S SCHOOLING

1. The poverty of Charles Dickens's family forced him to leave school to work in a blacking factory. His father was placed in a debtor's prison. *Oliver Twist*, a bitter invective against the English Poor Laws of 1834, examines the distorted version of the Victorian's emphasis on the virtues of hard work. In the highly stratified English system, the aristocrat (the highest class) did not have to work with their hands for a living whereas the poor were made the subject of hatred and cruelty.

2. Thomas Hughes, *Tom Brown's Schooldays* (1857; repr. Oxford: Oxford University Press, 2008), 26–27.

3. Richard Brown, "Educating the middle-classes, 1800–1870," *Looking at History*, February 2, 2011, http://richardjohnbr.blogspot.com/2011/02/educating-middle-classes-1800–1870.html.

4. Although the school was initially for poor students, or "free scholars" as they were called, things had changed considerably when Burnley got there. In 1780 only eight inhabitants sent their sons to Harrow and by 1816 there were only three free scholars. When the school was built in 1615, Harrow on the Hill was a strong farming community. As late as 1960 there were still about sixty families on the Hill. The boys from the community preferred to rear their sheep and make their hay rather than devote themselves to the acquisition of "useless knowledge." See Edmund W. Howson and George Townsend Warner, eds., *Harrow School* (London: Edward Arnold, 1898), 35.

5. For a list of the families who owned homes in Harrow on the Hill that were used as boarding houses, see chap. 5, in Howson and Warner, *Harrow School*.

6. Christopher Tyerman, *A History of Harrow School, 1324–1991* (Oxford: Oxford University Press, 2000), 153.

7. E. D. Laborde, *Harrow School: Yesterday and Today* (London: Winchester, 1948), 32.

8. J. G. Cotton Minchin, *Old Harrow Days* (London: Methuen, 1898), 3.

9. David Turner, *The Old Boys: The Decline and Rise of the Public School* (New Haven: Yale University Press, 2015), 3.

10. For a description of Harrow's "Academic Curriculum," see Dale Vargas, *The Timeline History of Harrow School: 1572 to the Present* (Harrow: Worth Press, 2010), 106–11.

11. Minchin, *Old Harrow Days*, 11.

12. Howson and Warner, *Harrow School*, 32.

13. Minchin, *Old Harrow Days*, 29.

14. Tyerman, *History of Harrow School*, 155.

15. Minchin, *Old Harrow Days*, 150.

16. Turner, *Old Boys*, 40.

17. Vargas, *Timeline History of Harrow School*, cover description.

18. Tyerman, *History of Harrow School*, 148.

19. Turner, *Old Boys*, 58.

20. Ibid., 152.

21. W. T. J. Gun, comp. and ed., *The Harrow School Register, 1571–1800* (London: Longmans, Green and Company, 1934), xxix.

22. Howson and Warner, *Harrow School*, 34.

23. George Orwell, *Why I Write* (London: Penguin, 1984), 58.

24. Andrew Sanders, introduction to Thomas Hughes, *Tom Brown's Schooldays*, ix.

CHAPTER 3: BURNLEY'S ENTRANCE INTO TRINIDAD

1. Anne Hall Williams, conversation with the author, Harrow-on-the-Hill, August 9 and 12, 2016.

2. W. T. J. Gun, comp. and ed., *The Harrow School Register, 1571–1800* (London: Longmans, Green and Company, 1934).

3. "Protectors of Slaves' Reports" *Anti-Slavery Reporter* iv, no. 14 (August 1831).

4. "Abridged details of services rendered to this island since its conquest by Mr. St. Hilaire Begorrat, exclusive of those mentioned in the petition" (CO 95/134, 1841).

5. Trinidad Slave Register 1813, Plantation Slaves, CO T71/501.

6. Anthony Cooke, "An Elite Resisted: Glasgow West India Merchants, 1783–1877," *Journal of Scottish Historical Studies* 32, no. 2 (November 2012): 158. Almost every respectable English gentleman had a woman of African descent (or a mulatto as they sometimes called them) as his housekeeper/mistress. Picton had four children with Rosette Smith, while his successor, Thomas Hislop, had three children with another woman of African descent. As one Englishman residing in Trinidad wrote to his friend, George Cumberland, in England: "Gentlemen here to be fashionable must have handsome housekeepers which are generally Mulattoes or mestes but some prefer still deeper shades of the sun and these ladies are entitled to every privilege of the house except a seat at Table; it is considered a degradation to a white person to sit down in public with a colour' one." Quoted in James Epstein, *Scandal of Colonial Rule: Power and Subversion in the British Atlantic during the Age of Revolution* (Cambridge: Cambridge University Press, 2012), 145.

7. William Eccles Jr. was the son of James Eccles.

8. "'The Passion of the World': Conflict and Society in the Caribbean," online exhibition, Kings College, London, 2015, http://www.kingscollections.org/exhibitions/specialcollections/caribbean/internationalrivalry/trinidad.

9. For a discussion of Picton's trial and its impact on shaping the early political and literary discourses of the island, see Selwyn R. Cudjoe, *Beyond Boundaries: The Intellectual Tradition of Trinidad and Tobago in the Nineteenth Century* (Wellesley: Calaloux, 2003), chap. 1.

10. Epstein, *Scandal of Colonial Rule*, 24.

11. Ibid, 89.

12. Lewis Grant to Viscount Goderich, CO 295/93, 1832.

13. Gertrude Carmichael, *The History of the West Indian Islands of Trinidad and Tobago* (London: Alvin Redman, 1961), 247.

14. Carl Campbell, *Cedulants and Capitulants: The Politics of the Coloured Opposition in the Slave Society of Trinidad, 1783–1838* (Port of Spain: Paria Publishing, 1992), 154. Gallagher, the first printer in Trinidad under British rule, published the first newspaper in Trinidad, the *Trinidad Courant*, in 1807. Other reports suggest that he began to publish the *Trinidad Weekly Courant* as early as 1796. After he was thrown out of Trinidad, he took his printing press to Venezuela where he published *La Gazeta de Caracas* (*The Caracas Gazette*). On October 24, 1808, he published the first newspaper in Venezuela.

15. Roderick Cave, "Early Printing and the Book Trade in the West Indies," *The Library Quarterly* 48, no. 2 (April 1978): 187.

16. Fraser notes that as early as 1810 Burnley had established himself in the society "where in after years he was destined to play a very leading part" (*HT*).

CHAPTER 4: THE COMING OF RALPH WOODFORD

1. Eric Williams, *History of the People of Trinidad and Tobago* (Port of Spain: PNM, 1962), 73.

2. Ronald K. Huch and Paul R. Ziegler, *Joseph Hume: The People's M.P.* (Philadelphia: American Philosophical Society, 1985), vii. Although Hume held a seat in the House of Commons, he was not considered "holding an office" in the British sense of the term. According to Huch, "an office would require an appointment by the Prime Minister," which Hume never received (Ronald Huch, communication with the author, January 10, 2010).

3. Huch and Ziegler, *Joseph Hume*, 3.

4. Thomas Piketty, *Capital in the Twenty-First Century* (Cambridge: The Belknap Press of Harvard University, 2014), 5.

5. David Weatherall, *David Ricardo: A Biography* (The Hague: Martinus Nijhoff, 1976), 180.

6. Valerie E. Chancellor, *The Political Life of Joseph Hume, 1777–1855* (Stratford-on-Avon, Warwickshire: Bloomfield and Son, 1986), 25.

7. Huch and Ziegler, *Joseph Hume*, 13. Huch and Zieler got Burnley's first name wrong (they called him Joseph) and Maria's first name wrong (they called her Mary). George Dames Burtchael records their marriage as 1818 (*Genealogical Memoirs of the Members of Parliament* [Dublin: Sealy, Bryers, and Walker, 1888]) whereas John Aiken records their marriage as 1815 (*Monthly Magazine and British Register* 40, part 2 [1815], 273).

8. Huch and Ziegler, *Joseph Hume*, 13.

9. Weatherall, *David Ricardo*, 181.

10. See Joseph Burnley Hume, *Joseph Hume: A Memorial* (London: John W. Parker, 1855).

11. Chancellor, *Political Life of Joseph Hume*, 6.

12. Gertrude Carmichael, *The History of the West Indian Islands of Trinidad and Tobago* (London: Alvin Redman, 1961), 106.

13. Margaret Williamson, "'The Mirror-Shield of Knowledge': Classicizing the West Indies," in *Classics and Imperialism in the British Empire* (Oxford: Oxford University Press, 2010), 82.

14. The motion was put forth on July 25, 1822 (*H*, 133).

15. "Commission of Inquiry," July 25, 1822.

16. Edmund Burke, *The Speeches of the Right Honorable Edmund Burke in the House of Commons; and in Westminster Hall* (London: Longman, Hurst, Rees, Orne, and Brown, 1816), 311–12.

17. "Commission of Inquiry," *British Hansard*, July 25, 1822. I have changed the speech in this citation, originally reported in the past tense, to the present tense.

18. Ibid.

19. Chancellor, *Political Life of Joseph Hume*, 33.

20. For a discussion of Hume's role in the debate for the compensation of slave owners, see Nicholas Draper, *The Price of Emancipation* (Cambridge: Cambridge University Press, 2010), 110, 111, 158.

21. Jean-Baptiste Philippe, *Free Mulatto* (1824; repr. Wellesley, MA: Calaloux Publications, 1996), 259.

CHAPTER 5: OPPOSITION TO EMANCIPATION FROM TACARIGUA

1. "Minutes of Evidence Taken by the Sub-Committee of the Agricultural and Immigration Society," *Papers Relative to the Affairs of Trinidad*, 1841, 94. The Trinidad Slave Register 1813, Plantation Slaves, lists the plantation Orange Grove as being owned by Edward Barry and Ralph McClintock as manager. It consisted of having 136 slaves, of which more than half (84) were of African origin. See CO T71/501, 176.

2. L. A. A. de Verteuil, *Trinidad: Its Geography, Natural Resources, Administration, Present Condition, and Prospects* (London: Chassell, 1884), 39.

3. Edward Batson, conversation with the author, September 15, 2016. Edward was the son of Frederick Batson, the last general manager of Orange Grove or the Trinidad Sugar Estates. The Gordon family lived in the servant's quarters of this mansion from around 1930 to 1948; they were asked to vacate the building when his father died in 1948 (interview with Horace Gordon, January 25, 2014).

4. See Frederick Douglass, *Narrative of the Life of Frederick Douglass: An American Slave* (Boston: Anti-Slavery Office, 1845).

5. Charles Buxton, *Memoirs of Sir Thomas Fowell Buxton*, 5th ed. (London: John Murray, 1852), 113.

6. House of Commons Debate, May 15, 1823, vol. 9.

7. Buxton, *Memoirs of Sir Thomas Fowell Buxton*, 115.
8. Wikipedia, "Henry Bathurst, 3rd Earl Bathurst," last modified March, 7, 2018, 8:40, https://en.wikipedia.org/wiki/Henry_Bathurst,_3rd_Earl_Bathurst.
9. William H. Burnley, *Opinions on Slavery and Emancipation in 1828* (London: James Ridgway, Piccadilly, 1833), 32–34. The content of these letters is taken from Burnley's contribution to the Board of Council.
10. Ibid., 36–37.
11. Letter to His Excellency Sir Ralph Woodford, Tacarigua, August 18, 1823; Burnley, *Opinions on Slavery*, 4.
12. For the three articles with which members took exception and the resolution that the governor submitted to Lord Bathurst, see *History of Trinidad*, vol. 2 (*H*).

CHAPTER 6: TOWARD PLANTER CONTROL OF THE COLONY

1. Charles Buxton, *Memoirs of Sir Thomas Fowell Buxton*, 5th ed. (London: John Murray, 1852), 127–28.
2. William Law Mathieson, *British Slavery and Its Abolition, 1823–1838* (London: Longmans, Green, 1926), 148–49.
3. "Protectors of Slaves' Report," *Anti-Slavery Reporter* 4, no. 14 (August 1831), 82.
4. H. C. Pitts, *100 Years Together: A Brief History of Trinidad from 1797 to 1897* (Port of Spain: Trinidad Publishing Company, 1948), 23.
5. C. L. R. James, *The Life of Captain Cipriani: An Account of British Government in the West Indies* (Durham: Duke University Press, 2014), 47.
6. Woodford to Lord Bathurst, CO 295/61, 1824.
7. This letter, sent on May 1, 1824, was signed by Burnley, James Cadett, Robert Neilson, and Benjamin Roberts. See CO 295/61, 1824.
8. CO 295/61, 1824.
9. "To His Excellency, Sir Ralph Woodford," May 14, 1824, CO 295/61, 1824.
10. Frederic Hammet to James Cadett," May 15, 1824. CO 295/61, 1824.
11. James Cadett to Frederic Hammet," May 15, 1824. CO 295/61, 1824.
12. Hammet to Cadett, May 18, 1824. CO 295/61, 1824.
13. CO 295/61, 1824.
14. Mathieson, *British Slavery*, 149–50.
15. Ibid., 150.
16. Minutes of His Majesty's council, October 7, 1824, CO 295/65, 1824.
17. Ibid.
18. Quoted in Mathieson, *British Slavery*, 174.
19. Ibid.
20. Minutes of His Majesty's council, November 4, 1824, CO 295/65, 1824.
21. Woodford to Bathurst, December 7, 1824.
22. Woodford to Bathurst, CO 295/66, 1825.

CHAPTER 7: LIFE ON THE PLANTATION

1. Although the official document, *Trinidad Negroes*, is presumed to be a full transcript of the hearings, it left out the testimony of five witnesses: Reverend William Le Goff; George Fitzwilliams; Henry Gloster; Samuel Ely; and Robert Neilson. For a complete listing of persons who testified at the hearings, see CO 295/66, 1825.
2. Carl C. Campbell, *Cedulants and Capitulants* (Port of Spain: Paria, 1992), 253.
3. Howard W. Odum, defines "practical sociology" and "sociological" writings as useful materials for the study of what constitutes "scientific sociology" but do "not conform to the more accurate definition of sociology as the scientific study of human society in which authentic

methods of study by sociologists are utilized, nevertheless they reflect a popular sociology comprehending the teachings, writings, philosophies, and action programs that connote social inquiry, social interpretation, social reform, social welfare, social work, and other applied social work disciplines." Howard W. Odum, *American Sociology: The Story of Sociology in the United States through 1950* (New York: Longmans, Green, 1951), 384.

4. See extract from the Blue Book of 1833, CO 295/97.

5. Adam Hochschild, *Bury the Chains: Prophets and Rebels in the Fight to Free an Empire's Slaves* (London: Pan Books, 2006), 17.

6. Kim Severson, "Finding a Lost Strain of Rice, and Clues to Slave Cooking," *New York Times*, February 13, 2018.

7. Ibid.

8. The intensive period of slavery began in 1783 when the population of Trinidad was approximately 3,000 persons of which 2,000 were aboriginal Indians and 310 were enslaved persons. The story of Cudjoe, who was born in 1765, is instructive. Cudjoe, a slave of sixty years, had been with his master all his life. In 1824 when he was manumitted he still owed his master $100. According to his master, "The first 14 years of his life he could render little or no service to his master, and was a yearly expense to him of 25 dollars from which I debit Cudjoe 350 dollars. . . . I credit Cudjoe his labour from 14 years to 40, 26 years, 5 days in a week at 8 dollars per month ($2,496); 10 years labour from 40 to 50 at 4 dollars per month ($480); 10 years labor 50 to 60 at 2 dollars per month ($140)" for a total of $3,116. According to the master, it cost him $3,156 to maintain Cudjoe for the sixty years he spent with him, which meant, according to his calculations, that Cudjoe still owed him $40. To make matters worse, the master ended his accounting in the following manner: "Cudjoe's wife has been the same expense as her husband and from sexual weakness could only perform 2/3rds of the labour that was done by her husband. Consequently she would have been indebted to her master more than one thousand dollars after sixty years of service." This means that Cudjoe and his wife were enslaved from 1774 to 1824. *TG*, August 14, 1824.

9. Nicholas Draper notes: "Despite the strenuous efforts to bring labor to British Guiana . . . and Trinidad, the [slave] registers show that in the new colonies [that is, Guyana and Trinidad] the enslaved populations declined between 1817 and 1833. Morality rates were exceptionally high in these territories. Being valuable did not protect the enslaved people." "The Rise of a New Planter Class? Some Countercurrents from British Guiana and Trinidad, 1807–33," *Atlantic Studies* 9, no. 1 (March 2012): 68–69.

10. James Epstein, *Scandal of Colonial Rule: Power and Subversion in the British Atlantic during the Age of Revolution* (Cambridge: Cambridge University Press, 2012), 236.

11. Eric Williams, *Capitalism and Slavery* (1944; repr. Chapel Hill: University of North Carolina Press, 1994), 6.

12. The word "combosse" or *combasse* is still used in Trinidad to describe one of the two women in a relationship with the same man. Nurah-Rosalie Cordner, a Trinidad professional, notes that in her family, the word "combus," as in "like ahy is yuh combus" was/is used in "women's circles by an older woman to a girl who was being fresh or rude." The word was also used "when the tone and/or volume of a response to a girl child volunteered some gossip which was considered to be too big/grown for the child." Nurah-Rosalie Cordner, conversation with the author, May 18, 2016. Ferdie Ferreira and Anthony County confirmed the use of this word in contemporary Trinidadian language, conversations with the author, July 26, 2014.

13. Basil Matthews, *Crisis of the West Indian Family* (Westport, CT: Greenwood, 1971), 20. In spite of its Eurocentric and Roman Catholic bias, this book offers an interesting reading of slave life in Trinidad.

14. W. E. B. Du Bois, *The Philadelphia Negro* (1899; repr. New York: Kraus-Thomson, 1975), 67.

15. Ibid., 72.

16. James Hamilton to Lewis Grant, CO 295/93, 1833. See Selwyn R. Cudjoe, ed., *Narratives of Amerindians in Trinidad and Tobago; or, Becoming Trinbagonian* (Wellesley: Calaloux, 2016), 37–41.

17. The *coartado* referred to the practice in which a slave agrees with his master as to the price he must pay for his manumission. After he has paid any part of the price, he cannot be transferred by his master to any other owner.

18. CO 295/66, 1825.

19. Ibid.

20. Ibid.

21. Du Bois, *Philadelphia Negro*, iii, 30. *The Philadelphia Negro* was not the first study on the social conditions of Africans in the United States. Du Bois points out that three other studies were undertaken in 1837, 1847, and 1856. Necessarily, the studies can be described as examples of "practical sociology." Du Bois's study sought "to cull judiciously from all these sources and others, and to add to them specially collected data for the years 1896 and 1897."

22. Herbert Atheker, "New Introduction to *The Philadelphia Negro*," in Du Bois, *Philadelphia Negro*.

CHAPTER 8: BURNLEY'S ASCENDANCY

1. William Law Mathieson, *British Slavery and Its Abolition, 1823–1838* (London: Longmans, Green, 1926), 27–28.

2. Luke O'Sullivan and Catherine Fuller, eds., *The Correspondence of Jeremy Bentham, Volume 12: July 1824 to June 1828* (Oxford: Claredon Press, 2006), 221.

3. Adams was a dear friend of Bentham whom he visited from one to three times a week between 1815 and 1817 while he was the U.S. Ambassador to Great Britain. Adams was selected to be U.S. Ambassador by James Madison, president of the United States, who was a close friend of the Burnleys of Virginia. (See Stephen Conway, ed., *The Correspondence of Jeremy Bentham, Volume 9: January 1817 to June 1820* [Oxford: Clarendon Press, 1869].)

4. O'Sullivan and Fuller, eds., *Correspondence of Jeremy Bentham, Volume 12*, 224. A note in this text says that both of these letters were sent together. See Conway, ed., *Correspondence of Jeremy Bentham, Volume 9*.

5. Mathieson, *British Slavery*, 180.

6. See Bridget Brereton *A History of Modern Trinidad, 1783–1962* (Oxford: Heinemann, 1981), 78.

7. CO 295/81, 1829.

8. See Hammett's letter that appeared in the *Port of Spain Gazette*, August 8, 1829.

9. CO 295/81, 1829.

10. Ibid.

CHAPTER 9: DECLARATION OF INDEPENDENCE

1. CO 295/83, 1829.

2. William Law Mathieson, *British Slavery and Its Abolition, 1823–1838* (London: Longmans, Green, 1926), 195–96.

3. This committee consisted of Francis Peschier, William Burnley, Joseph Peschier, Henry Murray, St. Hilaire Begorrat, Edward Jackson, Robert Busche, James Porter, Henry Scott, John Black, Josiah Bobbins, L. Lapeyrouse, George Reich, John Lamont, H. Huggins, John Boissiere, Bob Gray, P. D. Sonper, L. Brown, George Farfan, George Blaire, and Bick Joell, of whom five were to be governors. They shall also "have the powers of nominating a sub-committee for any of the purposes of their appointment—and in the event of the death, or resignation of any of the members that the committee shall appoint others in their place" CO 295/90, 1831. John Boissiere was the great-granduncle of Eric Williams, the first prime minister of Trinidad and Tobago, who Williams quotes approvingly in *The History of the People of Trinidad and Tobago*. See Michael Rogers Pocork, *Out of the Shadows of the Past: The "Great House" of Champs Elysées, Trinidad, and the Families Who Lived There, 1780–1932* (Port of Spain: Paria, 1993) for an examination of this family connection.

4. CO 295/90, 1831.

5. Ibid.

6. CO 295/91, 1831.

7. Quoted in Mathieson, *British Slavery*, 205

8. Ibid.

9. CO 295/90, 1831.

10. Letter from Bryanstone Square, London, CO 295/91, 1831.

11. Ibid.

12. CO 295/90, 1831 (italics in the original).

13. Joseph Marryat was the father of the Joseph Marryat who Burnley and his committee appointed as the agent of the colony in 1829.

14. CO 295/90, 1831.

15. CO 295/92, 1832. Andre Llanos, a native of Venezuela, was an "advocate" [lawyer] since 1804, of the Royal Audiencia. He came to Trinidad in 1813 and held various positions on the island including being a member of council in 1823.

16. CO 295/92, 1832.

CHAPTER 10: BRIGHTER HORIZONS

1. See Eric Williams, "Massa Day Done," chap. 5, in Selwyn R. Cudjoe, ed., *Eric E. Williams Speaks: Essays on Colonialism and Independence* (Wellesley: Calaloux, 2006), 237–64.

2. CO 295/92, 1832.

3. Ibid.

4. Ibid.

5. Ibid.

6. Ibid.

7. Ibid.

8. Ibid.

9. Ibid.

10. James Pope-Hennessy, *West Indian Summer: A Retrospect* (London: B. T. Batsford, 1943), 88.

11. During those days, Trinidad was so forested that the major means of transportation on the island, particularly during the rainy season, was the river and the sea.

12. Adam Hochschild, *Bury the Chains: Prophets and Rebels in the Fight to Free an Empire's Slaves* (London: Pan, 2006), 23.

13. CO 295/92, 1832.

CHAPTER 11: MONSTROUS UNNATURAL RESULTS

1. For example, see his letter of December 1, 1832, to Viscount Goderich in which he asks to be favored with a response so that he could "communicate upon the subject with my constituents in that country" (CO 295/96, 1832).

2. CO 295/92, 1832.

3. Ibid.

4. Ibid.

5. Ibid.

6. Ibid.

7. Ibid.

8. Ibid.

9. See Joseph Marryat to Lord Goderich, October 30, 1832, CO 295/96, 1832.

10. Ibid.

11. CO 295/92, 1832.

12. Quoted in Adam Hochschild, *Bury the Chains: Prophets and Rebels in the Fight to Free an Empire's Slaves* (London: Pan, 2006), 344.

CHAPTER 12: OPINIONS ON SLAVERY AND EMANCIPATION

1. Mathieson, *British Slavery and Its Abolition, 1823–1838* (London: Longmans, Green, 1926), 223.
2. Charles Buxton, *Memoirs of Thomas Fowell Buxton*, 5th ed. (London: John Murray, 1852), 221.
3. Ibid., 233.
4. Mathieson, *British Slavery and Its Abolition*, 223.
5. Buxton, *Memoirs of Thomas Fowell Buxton*, 219–20.
6. Ibid., 220 (italics in the original).
7. Ibid., 221.
8. See James Anthony Froude, *The English in the West Indies: Or the Bow of Ulysses* (New York: C. Scribner's Son, 1900). See also J. J. Thomas's refutation of Froude's views in *Froudacity: West Indian Fables Explained* (1890; repr. London: New Beacon, 1969).
9. The arguments Burnley made against apprenticeship, particularly as it related to the power of the master to punish his slave, were analogous to those he made against the first attempts by the Colonial Office to ameliorate slavery in 1823. See his letter of August 18, 1823, that he sent to Governor Woodford (*OS*, 1–9).
10. Buxton, *Memoirs of Sir Thomas Fowell Buxton*, 273.
11. Ibid., 279.
12. Mathieson, *British Slavery and Its Abolition*, 242
13. See Selwyn R. Cudjoe, *Movement of the People*: Essays on Independence (Ithaca, NY: Calaloux, 1983), 97–120.
14. Mathieson, *British Slavery and Its Abolition*, 243.

CHAPTER 13: THE POLITICS OF COMPENSATION

1. Nicholas Draper, communication with the author, October 27, 2012.
2. CO 295/100, 1833.
3. See Nicholas Draper, *The Price of Emancipation*: Slave-Ownership, Compensation and British Society at the End of Slavery (Cambridge: Cambridge University Press, 2010), 128.
4. Burnley to Stanley, CO 295/100, 1833.
5. Ibid.
6. Ibid.
7. Burnley to Shaw-Lefevre, CO 295/100, 1833.
8. Burnley to Stanley, CO 295/100, 1833.
9. Ibid.
10. Burnley to Shaw-Lefevre, CO 295/100, 1833.
11. Ibid.
12. Ibid.
13. Ibid.
14. Hill to Stanley, CO 295/101, 1834.

CHAPTER 14: THE NEW SOCIETY

1. CO 295/100, 1833.
2. Roderick A. McDonald, ed., *Between Slavery and Freedom: Special Magistrate John Anderson's Journal of St. Vincent during the Apprenticeship* (Philadelphia: University of Pennsylvania Press, 2001), 31.
3. CO 295/100, 1833.
4. Ibid.
5. Ibid.
6. CO 295/105, 1834.

7. Burnley may have had a point here since the personalities at the Colonial Office changed so much during that period.

8. CO 295/105, 1834.

9. The language is taken from Andy Martin, *The Boxer and the Goalkeeper: Sartre vs. Camus* (London: Simon & Schuster, 2012), 222.

10. CO 295/105, 1834.

11. Ibid.

12. Martin, *Boxer and the Goalkeeper*, 42.

13. CO 295/105, 1834.

14. Ibid.

15. Richard S. Reddie, *Abolition!: The Struggle to Abolish Slavery in the British Colonies* (Oxford: Lion, 2007), 207.

16. Jean-Paul Sartre, preface to Fantz Fanon, *The Wretched of the Earth*, trans. Richard Philcox (New York: Grove Press, 2004), lviii.

17. Reddie, *Abolition!*, 224.

CHAPTER 15: PREPARING FOR EMANCIPATION

1. CO 295/105, 1834.

2. Ibid.

3. Ibid.

4. Ibid.

5. Between 1833 and April 1835, there were eight secretaries and undersecretaries of state. In one year, from April 1834 to April 1835, there were three secretaries and three undersecretaries of state which led Robert Montgomery Martin to conclude: "The names will sufficiently indicate the fluctuations of counsel that must prevail in the Colonial Office during this period." *The Colonial Magazine and Commercial-Maritime Journal* 1, p. 80.

6. CO 295/105, 1834.

7. Ibid.

8. Ibid.

9. Ibid.

10. Although Burnley lived most of his adult life in Trinidad and was fighting Britain to gain more advantages for himself and the planters, he also identified, or certainly was identified, as British and referred to Britain as "home" as when Joseph Marrayat wrote to George Grey with regard to the vacancy on the council occasioned "by the return home of Mr. Burnley." CO 205/109, 1835.

11. CO 295/105, 1834.

12. See Edward Jackson to Secretary Stanley, April 8, 1834, in CO 295/105, 1834.

13. Ibid.

14. Russell Ellice was the chairman of the East India Company of which Burnley's father was a director. He was also one of the first directors of the British American Land Company and a director of the first New Zealand Company of which Edward Gibbon Wakefield was a director. He was the brother of Edward Ellice, a member of Parliament for Coventry from 1818 to 1826 and again from 1830 to 1836, secretary to the Treasury from 1830 to 1832, and secretary of War from 1832 to 1834. These two brothers, both of whom were slave owners, were Burnley's personal friends. On April 30, 1829, Edward wrote to Burnley to keep him informed on West Indian affairs in London. "Letter Book, 1828–29, 1930–1831," National Library of Scotland. Burnley, it should be noted, was in touch with all of the leading players in Great Britain.

15. These resolutions are listed in Burnley's record of the meeting. See CO 295/105, 1834.

16. Ibid.

17. The delegation's rationale for such an action reads as follows: "That without previous apprenticeship, until they were accustomed to the climate and had acquired a proper knowledge of cultivation, they could never be secure in the enjoyment of health or subsistence. That being by this mode distributed in small numbers on settled estates, in the midst of a society

of Creole Negroes, they would soon acquire civilized habits and European tongues—but left unrestricted, they would naturally herd together forming an African community in the center of the present population, preserving forever their own barbarous usages and languages. That if many planters were anxious to procure their services at present, it proves only the great deficiency of labor in the colony." CO 295/105, 1834.

18. Ibid.

19. Governor Hill to the Commandants of the Quarters, Government House, July 12, 1834, CO 295/102, 1834.

CHAPTER 16: BURNLEY'S VIEWS ON APPRENTICESHIP

1. Steven Marcus, *Engels, Manchester and the Working Class* (New York: W. W. Norton, 1985), 45.

2. Studholme Hodgson, *Truths from the West Indies* (London: William Ball, 1838), 317.

3. Young Anderson to Mr. Beldam, 1835.

4. CO 295/103, 1834.

5. Trinidad Slave Register 1813, Plantation Slaves, CO T71/501, 139.

6. Senior was one of the most distinguished economists of his time. His advice was sought by senior cabinet ministers and his name was frequently mentioned in parliamentary debates. Joseph Hume, the veteran parliamentary leader, on one occasion acknowledged in the House of Commons that he "was proud to call Senior his friend, and to say he concurred in his chief opinions." S. Leon Levy, *Nassau W. Senior: The Prophet of Modern Capitalism* (Boston: Bruce Humphries, 1943), 16.

7. Special Archives, University of Bristol. I wish to thank Shantelle George for unearthing this bit of correspondence.

8. Ibid.

9. See Levy, *Nassau W. Senior*, 232–33.

10. Special Archives, University of Bristol.

11. Ibid.

12. Alexis de Tocqueville, *Oeuvres Completes, Tome VI, Correspondance Anglaise, Correspondance et Conversations D'Alexis de Tocqueville et Nassau William Senior* (Paris: Gillimard, 1991), 72.

13. Special Archives, University of Bristol. Antigua decided to grant freedom to all its slaves immediately, a bold measure at the time.

14. From a note from my friend Paget Henry (author of *Peripheral Capitalism and Underdevelopment in Antigua*, 1985), January 14, 2017.

15. CO 295/102, 1834.

16. CO 295/106, 1835.

17. Ibid.

18. In general, when the apprentices worked more than ten or twelve hours or when they had some spare time by finishing their tasks early, "they are paid in cash, rum, provision or merchandize at the rate of three bitts per diem, the bitt being the tenth part of a dollar or about 5 1/4 sterling" (Young Anderson to Mr. Beldam).

19. Ibid.

CHAPTER 17: APPRENTICESHIP

1. In a letter to Lord Glenelg, Burnley stated the objective of his visit to these territories in a slightly more nuanced way. Its sole purpose, he said, was to observe and to consider "the state and efficiency of the laboring population in these various places, under different aspects of slavery and freedom; to enable me to form a more correct opinion as to the probable results of the measures now in progress in the British colonies" (Burnley to Glenelg, CO 295/109, 1835).

2. Ibid., 148. Gladstone corresponded with Burnley (at least intermittently) from about 1833 to 1839. In April 1836, three months before the hearings of the Select Committee, Gladstone made

references in his diaries to a letter he wrote to Burnley. See William E. Gladstone, *The Gladstone Diaries, 1833–1839*, vol. 2 (Oxford: Oxford University Press, 1968), 20, 40, 234, 389.

3. This defaming article appeared in the *Antigua Weekly Register* and was published subsequently in the *Port of Spain Gazette*. I wish to thank Stephen Mullen for sending this article to me.

4. CO 295/109, 1835.

5. See "The Blue Books," 1835. English colonial officials referred to Africans liberated from slave vessels during the era of abolition as "liberated Africans." Once liberated, they could be enlisted in the Royal Navy or the West India Regiment, or indentured in British colonies such as Sierra Leone or the Caribbean. It is estimated that fifty-two thousand liberated Africans were sent to the British Caribbean between 1807 and 1867, the majority of them between 1834 and 1838. I thank Shantelle George for this note.

6. CO 295/109, 1835.

7. Ibid.

8. The slave trade was abolished in 1807. Thereafter, any vessel that was seized "illegally carrying slaves were taken as prize, the master was fined and the slaves became forfeited to the Crown." This meant that they became government slaves and many were apprenticed or enlisted into the Royal Navy or the army, especially the West Indian Regiments and the Royal African Corps." Many of these liberated Africans were sent to West Indian colonies, particularly Trinidad and Guyana, which needed laborers. See Guy Grannum, *Tracing Your Caribbean Ancestors: A National Archives Guide*, rev. 3rd ed. (London: Bloomsbury, 2012), 42–44.

9. Rosanne Marion Adderley, *New Negroes from Africa: Slave Trade Abolition and Free African Settlement in the Nineteenth-Century Caribbean* (Bloomington: Indiana University Press, 2006), 68.

10. CO 295/106, 1835.

11. Adderley, *New Negroes from Africa*, 68.

12. CO 295/106, 1835.

13. Ibid.

14. Ibid.

15. Ibid.

16. Ibid. On October 7, 1835, Hill reported to Lord Glenelg on his distribution of the 262 captured Africans that were sent from Cuba in the *Siete Hermanas*, the last of the liberated Africans to be sent to Trinidad. Hill made an equitable distribution of these Africans giving out the male Africans to twenty-two estates. He allocated no more than six Africans to each estate, a number quite different from Jackson and Burnley's proposal. He was at pains to note to Lord Glenelg that "this firm (Grey Losh and Company in which Mr. Burnley is the chief partner) made applications to have Africans for forty-two estates upon the arrival of this shipment. From his extensive connection with the property of this colony, I placed this lot (of six in his Couva estate and twelve in two lots of six) . . . with his firm." Jackson received six Africans for his Golden Grove estate in Arouca. In an effort to demonstrate his fairness, Hill gave St. Luce Philip, a colored planter and physician of South Naparima, a lot of six Africans. Hill says: "Dr. Philip is a benevolent colored gentleman in the first medical practice, much esteemed for his acquirements and good character. He was educated at Edinburgh where he married into a respectable family. He is a valuable friend for the useful influence he exerts amongst the colored classes." Governor Hill also used his wife, Lady Hill, to assist him in placing fifty-four females under twelve years of age in the homes of "respectable individuals" primarily around Port of Spain. CO 295/108, 1835.

17. CO 295/106, 1835.

18. CO 295/109, 1835.

19. Ibid.

20. Burnley to Grey, December 26, 1835, CO 295/109, 1835.

21. M. C. M. Simpson, ed., *Correspondence and Conversations of Alexis de Tocqueville with Nassau William Senior from 1834 to 1859*, vol. 1 (London: Henry S. King, 1872), 14.

22. Ibid., 15.

23. Alexis de Tocqueville, *Democracy in America*, trans. Henry Reeve (New York: Barnes and Noble, 2003), xxiv.

CHAPTER 18: THE VIRTUES OF LAND POSSESSION

1. Edward Wakefield, an Englishman of extraordinary energy and ability, made a name for himself in England during that period for his colonialization scheme and his ability to marry the use of wastelands in the new British territories of Western Australia, New Zealand, and Canada and the scarcity of laborers that these territories experienced.
2. Paul Bloomfield, *Edward Gibbon Wakefield: Builder of the British Commonwealth* (London: Longmans, Green, 1961), 100.
3. The "sufficient price" was the leitmotiv of Wakefield's theory on British colonialism. The first lands in Australia, New Zealand, and Canada were sold on these principles. For a definition of the term, "sufficient price," see Bloomfield, *Edward Gibbon Wakefield*.
4. Burnley to Glenelg, CO 295/109, 1835.
5. CO 295/109, 1835.
6. Nassau William Senior and Charles Chadwick, *Report from His Majesty's Commissioners for Inquiring into the Administration and Practical Operation of the Poor Laws* (London: B. Fellowes, 1834), 181.
7. Ibid, 192.
8. CO 295/109, 1835.
9. Ibid.
10. Ibid.
11. Ibid.
12. Ibid.
13. Ibid.
14. Ibid.
15. Ibid.
16. Ibid.
17. Ibid.
18. Ibid.

CHAPTER 19: AN ARTFUL ENEMY

1. CO 295/109, 1835.
2. Ibid.
3. CO 295/110, 1836.
4. CO 295/109, 1836.
5. CO 295/110, 1836.
6. The offending sentence, referring to a charge that Burnley made against Rothery, reads as follows: "Mr Burnley knew this when he framed this charge. He may perhaps be able to reconcile his conduct upon this occasion with his notions of honor and honesty, but Your Lordship may probably regard it as an unworthy and artful attempt to deceive you and to defame the character of an absent man." CO 295/113, 1836.
7. Ibid.
8. Ibid.
9. Ibid.
10. Ibid.
11. Ibid.
12. Ibid.
13. Ibid.
14. Ibid.
15. The term "invaluing" could be read as devaluing or that of making something "valueless or

without value." See C. T. Onions, ed., *The Shorter Oxford English Dictionary on Historical Principles*, vol. 1 (Oxford: Clarendon Press, 1973), 1106.

16. CO 295/110, 1836.

17. CO 295/113, 1836.

18. Ibid.

19. Ibid.

20. Scotland to Sir George Grey, CO 295/113, 1836.

21. Ibid.

22. George Orwell, *Politics and the English Language* (London: Penguin, 2013), 15.

CHAPTER 20: CHANGING FORTUNES

1. Robert Gildea, *Children of the Revolution: The French, 1799–1914* (London: Penguin, 2009), 80.

2. Stephen Mullen, *It Wisnae Us: The Truth About Glasgow and Slavery* (Edinburgh: The Royal Incorporation of Architects in Scotland, 2009), 66.

3. See Parliamentary papers, 1833, *Evidence upon oath touching The Condition and Treatment of the Negro Population of the British West Indian Colonies, Taken before a Select Committee of the House of Lords*, Part I: Island of Jamaica. Taken Before a Select Committee of the House of Lords, Session 1832.

4. Anthony Cooke, "An Elite Revisited: Glasgow West India Merchants, 1783–1877," *Journal of Scottish Historical Studies* 32, no. 2 (November 2012): 132. Cooke says: "Marriage was often a way of cementing one's role in a business partnership or forging a new one, 'a mechanism for reinforcing business networks and partnerships.'" Robert and James Eccles were born in Ireland, which is more reason why they would want to integrate their families into the ruling elite of Glasgow.

5. CO 295/112, 1836.

6. Ibid.

7. CO 295/126, 1839.

8. Professor Bridget Brereton takes exception to this position. She claims that Cyrus Prudhomme David was "blacker" than Philip because the latter was a "light-complexioned man of mixed European and African descent" as opposed to David who was a "dark-skinned person of mainly or entirely African descent" ("How Do We Interpret the Term 'Black'? *Trinidad Express*, July 26, 2013). See also Bridget Brereton, "Cyrus Prudhomme: The Black Legislator," *Trinidad Express*, July 17, 2013; Selwyn R. Cudjoe, "St. Luce Philip: The First Black T&T Legislator," *Trinidad Express*, July 25, 2013; and Selwyn R. Cudjoe, "The Blackness of Black or, How Black is Really Black?" http://trinicenter.com/Cudjoe/2013/0608.htm.

9. CO 295/126, 1839.

10. Ibid.

11. John Metivier, "St. Mary's," unpublished.

12. See CO 295/118, 1837; A. G. Spearman to James Stephen.

13. House of Lords debate, December 11, 1837, vol. 39, 941.

14. The reports were as follows: *Report on Negro Education: Negro Education, Jamaica*, October 19, 1837; *Negro Education, Windward & Leeward Islands*, April 14, 1838; and *Negro Education, British Guiana and Trinidad*, August 14, 1838.

15. C. J. Latrobe, *Negro Education, British Guiana and Trinidad*, copy of a report from C. J. Latrobe, Esq., to Lord Glenelg, on Negro Education in British Guiana and Trinidad, London, August 14, 1838, 1.

16. Ibid., 20. Captain Span was the owner of Paradise and Cane Farm sugar plantations in the quarter of Arouca.

17. Evidence given by J. H. Hamilton, Anglican clergyman of the Church of England, "Minutes of Evidence Taken by the Sub-Committee of the Agricultural and Immigration Society," *Papers Relative to the Affairs of Trinidad*, 1841, 71.

18. George Padmore, whose birth name was Malcolm Nurse, changed his name when he arrived

in New York in the 1920s. It was a pseudonym he used to disguise his involvement with the Communist Party while he was in New York.

19. E. L. Joseph, *History of Trinidad* (London: Henry James Mills, 1838), 264.
20. Ibid., 271.

CHAPTER 21: BURNLEY'S IMMIGRATION INITIATIVES

1. CO 295/125, 1839.
2. Ibid.
3. Julie Winch, *Philadelphia's Black Elite: Activism, Accommodation, and the Struggle for Autonomy, 1787–1848* (Philadelphia: Temple University Press, 2002), 50
4. Ibid., 55.
5. Ibid., 63.
6. Donald Wood, *Trinidad in Transition* (Oxford: Oxford University Press, 1986), 49.
7. Ibid., 239.
8. Ibid., 48.

CHAPTER 22: THE ROAD TO PROSPERITY

1. Quoted in Madhavi Kale, *Fragments of Empire: Capital, Slavery, and Indentured Labor in the British Caribbean* (Philadelphia: University of Pennsylvania Press, 1998), 13 (italics added). See also John Scoble, *Hill Coolies: A Brief Exposure of the Deplorable Condition of the Hill Coolies in British Guiana and Mauritius* (London: Harvey and Darton, 1840), 4. Gladstone lived in England. He never visited the Caribbean.
2. Guppy notes that the mortgages the mortgagees held "were Spanish hypothecations, not affording amply security as modern mortgages [that was in 1888], but affording great latitude to dishonest borrowers. The credit merchants appropriated the compensation money for the slaves in part payment for the money due them and were anxious to realize the whole" (Scoble, *Hill Coolies*, 4).
3. CO 295/129, 1839.
4. MacLeod to Lord Stanley, CO 295/144, 1844.
5. CO 295/129, 1839.
6. CO 295/127, 1839.
7. Ibid.
8. Ibid.
9. A note appended to the letter that Governor Mein sent to the Marquis of Normanby.
10. CO 295/127, 1839.
11. See CO 295/126, 1839.
12. Ibid.
13. CO 295/128, 1839.
14. CO 295/127, 1839.

CHAPTER 23: BURNLEY'S CHANGING RACIAL RHETORIC

1. Burnley to Lord Russell, CO 295/127, 1839. This letter was published as "Mr. Burnley's Letter to Lord John Russell" in the *Anti-Slavery Reporter*, no. 8 (April 22, 1840).
2. Julie Winch, *Philadelphia's Black Elite: Activism, Accommodation, and the Struggle for Autonomy, 1787–1848* (Philadelphia: Temple University Press, 1988), 63.
3. Lord Stanley to Charles Marryat, CO 295/138, 1842.
4. Burnley to Lord Russell, CO 295/127, 1839.
5. Madhavi Kale, *Fragments of Empire: Capital, Slavery, and Indian Indentured Labor in the British Caribbean* (Philadelphia: University of Pennsylvania Press, 1998), 44.
6. William Burnley, *Description of the Island of Trinidad and the Advantages to be Derived from Emigration to That Colony* (New York: James Van Norden, 1839), 4.

7. Ibid., 5.

8. Burnley to Lord Russell, CO 295/127, 1839.

9. Winch, *Philadelphia's Black Elite*, 64.

10. Ibid., 65.

11. Burnley to Lord Russell, CO 295/132, 1840.

12. CO 295/127, 1839.

13. See Burnley's letter of January 8, 1840, to Lord Russell on the prospects of planting cotton and tobacco in the West Indies that appeared in *Guiana Chronicle* on May 4, 1840. In 1897, *Timehri*, a journal of the Agricultural and Commercial Society of British Guiana that was edited by James Rodway, republished this letter. *Timehri: The Royal Journal of the Agricultural and Commercial Society of British Guiana* xl (1897): 65–74.

14. CO 295/127, 1839.

15. Ibid.

16. Samuel Ringgold Ward, *Autobiography of a Fugitive Negro* (1855; repr. New York: Arno Press and the New York Times, 1968), 51.

17. Ronald K. Burke, *Samuel Ringgold Ward: Christian Abolitionist* (New York: Garland Publishing, 1995), 6.

18. Kenny Reilly, "Anti-Slavery Movements in British North America and the Transnational Life of 'Obedient Servant' Samuel Ringgold Ward," *Mount Royal Undergraduate Humanities Review* 4 (2017): 58.

CHAPTER 24: A CONTINUING REQUEST FOR LABOR

1. Burnley to Vernon Smith, CO 295/132, 1840.

2. Ibid.

3. Ibid.

4. Le Merchant to Stephen, CO 295/132, 1840.

5. Burnley, "Petition against the Equalization of Duties on British and Foreign Sugars," CO 295/132, 1840.

6. Ibid.

7. Ibid.

8. MacLeod to Lord Russell, CO 295/130, 1840.

9. Ibid.

10. Lord Russell to MacLeod, CO 295/130, 1840.

CHAPTER 25: VISITING FAMILY IN VIRGINIA

1. Prior to the introduction of the steamship, the average time it took to travel between New York and Liverpool was twenty-two days, and the return journey took as long as thirty-four days. During severe winters the westward journey could take as long as forty-eight days. See C. R. Vernon Gibbs, *Passenger Liners of the Western Ocean; A Record of the North Atlantic Steam and Motor Passenger Vessels from 1838 to the Present Day* (London: Staples Press, 1952), 25. In 1819 the SS *Savannah*, a hybrid steam and sailing ship, crossed the Atlantic from Georgia to Liverpool without passengers; whereas the Dutch vessel, the *Curacao*, "was the first steamship to carry passengers between the Old World and the New," (ibid., 26). On July 4, 1840, the sailing of *Britannia*, Cunard's first steamer, marked the inauguration of "the first regular timetabled passenger service across the Atlantic" (Ian Thomson, "Carrying on Cruising: 175 Years of Cunard," *FT Weekend*, August 1, 2015). It took fourteen days to cross the Atlantic. For an account of the *Savannah's* crossing the Atlantic, see John Laurence Busch, *Steam Coffin: Captain Moses Rogers and the Steamship* Savannah *Break the Barrier* (New Canaan, CT: Hodos Historia, 2010).

2. Gibbs, *Passenger Liners of the Western Ocean*, 30. Charles Dickens traveled on the *Britannia* in January 1842. Despite of calling his cabin an "utterly impracticable, thoroughly hopeless,

and profoundly preposterous box," he traveled once more on another Cunard steamship from Liverpool to Boston via Halifax in 1844 (Thomson, "Carrying on Cruising").

3. C. R. Vernon Gibbs, *Passenger Liners*, 31.

4. Burnley to Lord Russell, CO 295/132, June 19, 1840.

5. Ibid.

6. Burnley to Lord Russell, CO 295/132, June 19, 1840, 8.

7. Emma Dicken, *Our Burnley Ancestors and Allied Families* (New York: The Hobson Book Press, 1946), 45.

8. Ibid., 49.

9. "To James Madison from Hardin Burnley, 15 December 1787," Founders Online, National Archives (http://founders.arcives.gov/documents/Madison/01-10-02-0205-09). See also Robert A. Rutland and Charles F. Hobson, eds., *The Papers of James Madison, vol. 10, 27 May 1787–2 March 1788* (Chicago, University of Chicago Press, 1977).

10. Kurt T. Lash, "The Lost History of the Ninth Amendment (I): The Lost Original Meaning," Loyola Law School (Los Angeles) Public Law and Legal Theory, Research Paper No. 2004-5, February 2004, 42.

11. National Governors Association, 2015, https://www.nga.org.

12. James Madison, the fourth president of the United States (1809–1817), is recognized as the father of the U.S. Constitution. He drafted the Constitution and was a champion of the U.S. Bill of Rights. Together with John Jay, he produced *The Federalist Papers* in 1788. As Thomas Jefferson's secretary of state (1801–1809), he supervised the Louisiana Purchase (1804), which essentially doubled the size of the United States. He led the nation into the War of 1812, which resulted in many enslaved Americans being sent to Trinidad to form what is now called "Company Villages."

13. Dicken, *Our Burnley Ancestors*, 53–54.

14. "Papers Relative to the Affairs of Trinidad," 65, CO 295/134, 1841. Although this and other papers relative to hearings of the subcommittee first appeared in 1841, they were later included in William Burnley's *Present Condition of Trinidad, as Exhibited by the Evidence Taken by the Agricultural and Immigration Society of the Colony* (Port of Spain: Teacher & Company, 1842). For purposes of convenience all references regarding the hearings are taken from the latter work and are cited in this text as *O*.

15. CO 295/134, 1841.

CHAPTER 26: BURNLEY AND THE QUESTION OF FREE LABOR

1. Henry James Ross, *Thoughts on the Objectionable System for Labor from Wages in the West India Colonies* (1842; repr. Kingston: Ian Randle, 2005), 70.

2. Woodville K. Marshall, the introduction to Ross, *Thoughts on the Objectionable System*, 25.

3. Ross, *Thoughts on Objectionable System*, 106.

4. Ibid., 108.

CHAPTER 27: THE EVIL OF SQUATTING

1. Colonial Land and Emigration Office, November 30, 1841, CO 295/135, 1841.

2. James Stephen, "Note attached to the Colonial Land & Emigration Office Report," November 30, 1841, CO 295/135, 1841.

3. MacLeod to Lord Stanley, CO 295/134, 1841.

4. See the Colonial Land & Emigration Office Report, December 3, 1841, CO 295/135, 1841.

5. James Stephen, "Notes Appended to the Colonial Land & Emigration Report," December 3, 1841, CO 295/135, 1841.

6. Ibid.

7. Ibid.

8. *Observations* was described in several ways. It was called a book, a pamphlet, and a brochure. In this chapter, I refer to it in all of those ways, mostly as the reviews described them.

9. Woodville K. Marshall, introduction to Henry James Ross, *Thoughts on the Objectionable System of Labour for Wages in the West India Colonies* (1842; repr. Kingston: Ian Randle, 2005), 23.

10. F. C. Bowen was the principal editor of the *Port of Spain Gazette*.

CHAPTER 28: POLICING THE NEGROES

1. The members of the committee were as follows: Lord Stanley, Mr. Pakington, Viscount Howick, Mr. Godson, Sir Earley Wilmot, Mr. Charles Howard, Sir Charles Douglas, Mr. Vernon Smith, Mr. Emerson Tennent, Mr. Grantley Berkeley, Mr. Hawes, Mr. Bankes, Mr. Villiers Stuart, Mr. Barclay, and Viscount Chelsea. Burnley was asked to testify before this committee, which he did.

2. Frederick H. Smith, *Caribbean Rum: A Social and Economic History* (Gainesville: University Press of Florida, 2005), 118.

3. E. L. Joseph, *History of Trinidad* (London: Henry James Mills, 1838), 90.

CHAPTER 29: WAGING WAR AGAINST AFRICANS

1. Burnley had great respect for Warner. One observer noted that his melodious accents "were more worthy of the admiration of the British House of Parliament, than of the Legislative Council of Trinidad. L. B. Tronchin, "Charles Wm. Warner and His Times," *PO*, September 28, 1888.

CHAPTER 30: DOMESTIC MATTERS

1. Karina Williamson, "Mrs Carmichael: A Scotswoman in the West Indies, 1820–1826," *International Journal of Scottish Literature* no. 4 (Spring/Summer, 2008).

2. James Pope-Hennessy, *West Indian Summer: A Retrospective* (London: B. T. Batsford, 1943), 83.

3. Mrs. [A. C.] Carmichael, *Domestic Manners and Social Condition of White, Coloured, and Negro Population of the West Indies, Vol. 2* (London: Whittaker, Treacher, 1833), 304.

4. *The Trinidad Almanac and Public Register for the Year 1827* (Port of Spain: J. Holman, 1827), 20.

5. John Metivier, "St. Mary's," unpublished.

6. L. A. A. de Verteuil, *Trinidad: Geography, Natural Resources, Administration, Present Condition, and Prospects* (1856; repr. London: Cassell, 1884), x.

7. Ibid., 69.

8. "A Letter from a Colored Man," CO 295/155, 1846. See "The Case of Alexander Fitzjames" in Nemata Amelia Blyden, *West Indians in West Africa, 1808–1880* (Rochester, NY: University of Rochester Press, 2000), for a description of Fitzjames's life.

9. Ibid.

10. Lord Stanley to MacLeod, CO 295/150, 1846.

CHAPTER 31: LAND OCCUPATION

1. C. L. R. James, *A History of Pan African Revolt* (Oakland, CA: PM Press, 2012), 60–61

2. Lord Harris to Earl Grey, CO 295/156, 1847.

3. As a result of the governor's meeting of June 12, a commission consisting of the attorney general, the solicitor general, Burnley, John Losh, and Henry Scott, was appointed to come up with a final policy on the land occupation question. Its charge was "to examine into, and determine the validity of the claims of any occupant on Crown Lands who has not obtained a grant of the same, and who will have to shew, whether he claims through a permission of a Commandant—or other public officer—or by length of possession—or in what other way he

considers himself entitled to such lands. . . . No claim, where possession has been taken after 1st of August 1838, will be received" (*PG*, July 21, 1843).

4. Charles Warner, the solicitor general, explained that the then chief justice protested against the trespass ordinance that was passed in 1838 because he thought it was unnecessary "as the aggrieved party might bring his action at law, and secondly, it would prevent friends visiting the laborers" In other words, the proprietors could have used such a law to harass the laborers and their friends (*PG*, November 3, 1843).

5. On July 26, 1844, Governor MacLeod appointed Robert Guppy to proceed to Sierra Leone to find out why so few Africans had immigrated to Trinidad. Guppy reported that Africans distrusted the white man who had treated them cruelly. Many of them were unwilling to leave their country and their chiefs. Although Sierra Leone failed to supply Trinidad with workers, according to *Public Opinion*, Guppy's "Report and advice had a great share in promoting the introduction of coolies from India." See Robert Guppy, "Report on the State of Emigration to Trinidad," October 30, 1844, CO 295/144; and Robert Guppy, *PO*, October 18, 1887, respectively.

6. C. B. Franklin, *After Many Years: A Memoir* (Port of Spain: Franklin's Electric Printery, 1910), 42.

7. David McDermott Hughes, "'Paradise without Labour': How Oil Missed Its Utopian Moment," https://rucore.libraries.rutgers.edu/rutgers-lib/37808/, 10.

CHAPTER 32: THE NEW ORDER OF THINGS

1. John Scoble, *Hill Coolies: A Brief Exposure of the Deplorable Condition of the Hill Coolies in British Guiana and Mauritius* (London: Harvey and Darton, 1840), 4.

2. Scoble notes: "It was stated also . . . that the Whitby found difficulty in inducing natives to go [to Guyana and Mauritius], and that force was required to accomplish this object . . . it was subsequently discovered that the trade of kidnapping Coolies had been extensively carried on, and that prison depots had been established in the villages near Calcutta for the security of the wretched creatures, where they were most infamously treated, and guarded with the utmost jealousy and care, to prevent escape, until the Mauritian and Demerara slavers were ready for their reception" (ibid., 7–8). Scoble analogized the kidnapping of the Indians as being "second only to atrocity to those connected with the African slave-trade" (ibid., 25).

3. Between 1833 and 1917, 238,000 and 145,000 Indians were introduced into Guyana and Trinidad respectively; between 1854 and 1883, 39,000 Indians were introduced into Guadeloupe; and between 1853 and 1924, 56,000 Indians were introduced into Dutch Guiana. See Eric Williams, *Capitalism and Slavery* (1944; repr. Chapel Hill: University of North Carolina Press, 1994), 28.

4. MacLeod to Lord Stanley, CO 295/146, 1845.

5. The last stanza of the poem reads as follows: "Then a health to him—the gallant chief—who leaves our sorrowing shore. / Long, long shall live the memory of him we all deplore [*sic*]; / And the name we thus accord him shall descend to other days, / When mute shall be the voices now commingling in his praise: / Yes—our children of his fame shall be as jealous and as proud, / And pledge 'the good Sir Henry' the gallant, good MacLeod." *PG*, April 21, 1846.

6. Horatio Nelson Huggins, *Hiroona: An Historical Romance in Poetic Form*, ed. Desha Amelia Osborne (Kingston, Jamaica: University of the West Indies Press, 2015), 319.

7. Paula Burnett, ed., *The Penguin Book of Caribbean Verse in English* (Harmondsworth, UK: Penguin, 1986), 1. See also Selwyn R. Cudjoe, *Beyond Boundaries: The Intellectual Tradition of Trinidad and Tobago in the Nineteenth Century* (Wellesley: Calaloux, 2003), 290–95.

8. "Construction of Railways in the Colonies, Trinidad," *Accounts and Papers of the House of Commons: Railways* 63 (1847): 21.

9. Veront M. Satchel and Cezket Sampson, "The Rise and Fall of Railways in Jamaica, 1845–1975," *The Journal of Transport History* 24, no. 1 (March 2003): 1–21.

10. "Construction of Railways in the Colonies," 23.

11. Ibid., 25.

12. Nicholas Draper, communication with the author, February 24, 2017.

CHAPTER 33: THE GREAT RAILWAY DEBATE

1. Simon Jenkins, *A Short History of England* (London: Profile Books, 2011), 199.
2. Karl Marx, "The Future Results of British Rule in India," *New-York Daily Tribune*, August 8, 1853.
3. See a description of Warner's ascendancy to power in Donald Wood, *Trinidad in Transition: The Years after Slavery* (Oxford: Oxford University Press, 1986), 180–81.
4. "Construction of Railway in the Colonies, Trinidad," *Accounts and Papers of the House of Commons: Railways*, vol. 63, 1847, 22.
5. What is remarkable about this exchange was the learned acquaintance that Burnley, Warner, and the other officials had about the work of the leading political economists of the day. In December 15, 1846, in combating Burnley's "monstrous proposal . . . that by increasing the present taxes upon the necessaries of life, we shall make labor cheaper and more plentiful," the editor of the *Port of Spain Gazette* turned to Adam Smith's *Wealth of Nations* to respond to Burnley. He said: "We have no doubt the honorable gentlemen [on the tariff committee set up by the Legislative Council] have, one and all, at some period of their lives, perused so celebrated a work as the *Wealth of Nations*." The editor then quoted several passages from *Wealth of Nations* to support his argument. In his contribution to the railway debate, it was only natural that Burnley would draw on Smith, Ricardo (his brother-in-law's best friend), and Say to support his arguments.

CHAPTER 34: TOWARD MODERNITY

1. Eric Williams, *Capitalism and Slavery* (1944; repr. Chapel Hill: University of North Carolina Press, 1994), 4.
2. This line was adapted from John Milton's *L'Allegro*. The pertinent verse reads as follows: "There let Hynen oft appear / In saffron robe, with taper clear, / And pomp, and feast, and revelry, / With mask, and antique pageantry; / Such sights as youthful poets dream / On summer eves by haunted stream." I am thankful to William Cain, my colleague at Wellesley College, for locating these lines of poetry.
3. "Construction of Railways in the Colonies, Trinidad," *Accounts and Papers of the House of Commons: Railways*, vol. 63, 1847, 21.
4. Ibid.
5. Henry Scott to Messr. Amory, Sewell & Moores, February 19, 1848, CO 295/165, 1848.
6. Ibid.
7. Donald Wood, *Trinidad in Transition* (Oxford: Oxford University Press, 1986), 180
8. *London Globe*, March 20, 1847, reproduced in *PG*, May 7, 1847.
9. Williams, *Capitalism and Slavery*, 90.

CHAPTER 35: THE AGONY OF DESPAIR

1. William A. Green, *British Slave Emancipation: The Sugar Colonies and the Great Experiment 1830–1865* (Oxford: Clarendon Press, 1976), 229.
2. Ibid., 236.
3. Ibid., 238, 240.
4. Harris to Earl Grey, October 21, 1847, CO 295/158, 1847.
5. Green, *British Slave Emancipation*, 245.
6. Harris to Earl Grey, February 21, 1848, CO 295/160, 1848.
7. Harris to Earl Grey, CO 295/161, 1848.
8. Margaret D. Rouse-Jones, *The Colonial Bank Correspondence, 1837–1885* (1848; repr. Newton, Port of Spain: Paria, 1986), 20.
9. Harris to Earl Grey, CO 295/162, 1848.

10. Rouse-Jones, *Colonial Bank Correspondence*, 5.

11. Losh to Harris, CO 295/164, 1848.

CHAPTER 36: BURNLEY'S CALLOUSNESS

1. Unless stated otherwise, all of Burnley's remarks in this chapter are taken from this report citing his comments during the debate.

2. See Will Hutton, "Cecil Rhodes was a racist, but you really can't readily expunge him from History," *Guardian*, December 20, 2015.

3. On the night of March 20, 1804, when Bonaparte ordered the murder of the Duke d'Enghien, a likely Bourbon pretender, Talleyrand is reported to have said, "C'etait pluqu'um crime, c'etait un faute." (It was worse than a crime; it was a blunder.) Charles Butler, *Reminiscences of Charles Butler* (London: John Murray, 1824), 161. The notion here is that in matters of state, a mistake is worse than a crime. Many historians view this incident as a bloody stain on Napoleon's character. In Burnley's thinking, one should err on the side of strength and harshness rather than on the side of "mistaken legislation" that could have serious consequences for future generations.

4. Cecil Jenkins, *A Brief History of France* (London: Running Press, 2011), 121

5. CO 295/162, 1848.

6. Ibid.

7. In May 1848, George Numa Des Sources, a black man who had emigrated from Santo Domingo to Trinidad in 1804, established the *Trinidadian* to refute the lies that were being spread about black people and to stand up against the oppression they were undergoing at the hands of the state. He became a veritable thorn in the side of the local government.

CHAPTER 37: THE VOICE OF THE PEOPLE

1. Michael Toussaint, "George Numa Dessources, The Numancians, and the Attempt to Form a Colony in Eastern Venezuela, circa 1850–1854," in Heather Cateau and Rita Pemberton, eds., *Beyond Tradition*: Reinterpreting the Caribbean Historical Experience (Kingston, Jamaica: Ian Randle, 2006), 205. Some scholars also spell Des Sources's name "Dessources."

2. Following Benedict Anderson incisive analysis of the mode of nation formation, Elleke Boehmer writes: "The process of national self-making in story and symbol is often called *imagining the nation*. What this phrase implies is that the nation as we know it is a thing of social artifice—a symbolic formation rather than a natural essence. It exists in so far as the people who make up the nation have it in mind, or experience it as citizens, soldiers, readers of newspapers, students, and so on." Elleke Boehmer, *Colonial and Postcolonial Literature* (Oxford: Oxford University Press, 1995), 185.

3. Toussaint, "George Numa Dessources," 200.

4. Douglass delivered these speeches at Canandaigua, New York, on August 1, 1847 and 1857; Poughkeepsie, New York, August 2, 1858; and Geneva, New York, August 1, 1860.

5. John W. Blassingame, *The Frederick Douglass Papers*, vol. 3 (New Haven: Yale University Press, 1985), 190.

6. John W. Blassingame, *The Frederick Douglass Papers*, vol. 2 (New Haven: Yale University Press, 1982), 69.

7. Ibid., 84.

8. Blassingame, *Frederick Douglass Papers*, vol. 3, 188–89. In his speech Douglass noted: "All civilized men at least, have looked with wonder and admiration upon the great deed of justice and humanity which has made the first of August illustrious among the days of the year. But to no people on the globe, leaving out the emancipated men and women of the West Indies themselves, does this day address itself with so much force and significance, as to the people of the United States (189).

9. John Stauffer, *Giants: The Parallel Lives of Frederick Douglass and Abraham Lincoln* (New York: Twelve, 2008), 72.

10. See John Blassingame's introduction to *Narrative of the Life of Frederick Douglass* (New Haven: Yale University Press, 2001), xxiii.
11. The serialization of Douglass's *Narrative* began on July 10 and concluded on November 6, 1850.
12. Nathan Irvin Huggins, *Slave and Citizen: The Life of Frederick Douglass* (Boston: Little, Brown and Company, 1980), 21.
13. Maxwell Philip, *Emmanuel Appadocca; or, Blighted Life: A Tale of the Boucaneers* (1854; repr. Amherst: University of Massachusetts Press, 1997), 6.

CHAPTER 38: BURNLEY'S DECLINING SIGNIFICANCE

1. Harris to Lord Grey, CO 295/166, 1849.
2. Ibid., February 9, 1849.
3. Harris to Lord Grey, CO 295/166, 1849.
4. Harris to Earl Grey, CO 295/166, 1849. For the new conditions under which East Indians were to be recruited to the island, see also the resolution passed by the Legislative Council of Trinidad on November 13, 1848 (CO 295/166, 1849). John Scoble, the secretary of the Anti-Slavery Society, vigorously opposed these new regulations. He described these sanctions, which unhappily received the blessings of the Home Government, as a "new attempt at coercion with deeper regret than surprise; and deplore the counsels, as they foresee the pernicious effects which must result from it." John Scoble to Earl Grey, January 23, 1849, CO 295/160, 1849.
5. Harris to Earl Grey, CO 295/168, 1849.
6. Harris to Earl Grey, CO 295/167, 1849.
7. Ibid.
8. William Curtis to Earl Grey, CO 295/169, 1849.
9. Anthony de Verteuil, *Sir Louis de Verteuil: His Life and Times, Trinidad, 1800–1900* (Port of Spain, Trinidad: Columbus Publishers, 1973), 40–41.

CHAPTER 39: LIVING LIKE A LORD

1. Frederick Douglass, *My Bondage and My Freedom* (New Haven: Yale University Press, 2014), 302.
2. "John Candler's Visit to Trinidad," *Caribbean Studies* 4, no. 3 (October 1964): 66.
3. Ibid., 70.
4. For an analysis of the impact of Carlyle's essay on the discussion of race and class in the United States of America and the Caribbean, see Robert J. Scholnick, "Emancipation and the Atlantic Triangle: John Bigelow's *Jamaica in 1850*," introduction to John Bigelow's *Jamaica in 1850, or, the Effects of Sixteen Years of Freedom on a Slave Colony* (Champaign: University of Illinois Press, 2006).
5. Proposed branch offices were to be set up at Diego Martin, Chaguanas, Couva, Point-a-Pierre, Oropouche, La Brea, Cedros, San Fernando, Savanna Grande, Alley's Creek, St. Juan, St Joseph, Arouca, and Arima.

CHAPTER 40: THE LABORERS' REBELLION

1. Anti-Slavery Society, *Negro Apprenticeship in the British Colonies* (London: 1837), 4.
2. Studholme Hodgson, *Truths from the West Indies* (London: William Ball, 1838), 322.
3. Ibid.
4. "December Criminal Sessions," December 14, 1849, CO 295/170, 1850.
5. Warner's Opening remarks to the Jury, "December Criminal Sessions," December 14, 1849, CO 295/170, 1850.
6. Ibid.
7. I refer to this upheaval as a rebellion, a case that I have made in another context ("The 1849 Hair Rebellion," unpublished).
8. Harris to Earl Grey, October 6, 1849, CO 295/168, 1949.

9. This discrepancy between native-born Trinidadians and foreign-born outsiders in the police force persisted until 1903 when the Water Riots broke out. Of the 611 members of the police force then, only sixty-five were natives of Trinidad. More than half of the police force (340) were natives of Barbados. Of the three Indo-Trinidadians in the police force, only one was born in Trinidad. The two others were born in Guyana. In 1903, as in 1849, most of the police sergeants and other high-ranking police officers were recruited from the Irish constabulary. As late as 1920, the entrance exam used in the Trinidad police force was based on the Royal Irish Academy.

10. "December Criminal Sessions," December 21, 1849, CO 295/170, 1850.

CHAPTER 41: BURNLEY CONFRONTED

1. Margaret Mann, *The Letters of Margaret Mann*, ed. Danielle Delon (Port of Spain, Trinidad: National Museum and Art Gallery of Trinidad and Tobago, 2008), 374.

2. Ibid., 375–76.

3. Guiseppi to Johnson, CO 295/168, 1849.

4. Jeremy D. Popkin notes: "The Piquet movement, as the peasant revolt in the south [of Haiti] were called, showed that democratic ideas had taken root among the population, but the response of Haiti's post-revolutionary elites demonstrated that they were unwilling to take any steps in the new direction of democracy. By 1847, Haiti had fallen under the rule of a black general, Faustin Soulouque, who crowned himself emperor in 1848 and instituted the most ruthless dictatorship the country had known since its independence." *A Concise History of the Haitian Revolution* (Oxford: Wiley-Blackwell, 2012), 157.

5. The Jacobins were the most radical members of the French Revolution. They were responsible for overthrowing the Girondists in 1793. For a discussion of the revolutionary ideas that shaped the French Revolution, see Jonathan Israel, *Revolutionary Ideas: An Intellectual History of the French Revolution from "The Rights of Man" to Robespierre* (Princeton, NJ: Princeton University Press, 2015).

6. Gerry Besson, communication with the author, April 13, 2018.

CHAPTER 42: REVOLUTIONARY IDEAS

1. Jean-Pierre Boyer served with President Alexandre Petion and Henri Christophe after they killed Jean-Jacques Dessalines in 1806. He served again with Petion against Christophe. After the two leaders died, he unified the country in 1821 but fled the country in 1843 after a rebellion against his rule.

2. Quoted in Sandra M. Gustafson, *Imagining Deliberative Democracy in the Early American Republic* (Chicago: University of Chicago Press, 2011), 55–56.

3. Umberto Eco, *Inventing the Enemy: And Other Occasional Writings*, trans. Richard Dixon (London: Vintage, 2013), 17

4. Katherine Prior, "George Francis Robert Harris," *Oxford Dictionary of National Biographies* (Oxford: Oxford University Press, 2004).

5. Lord Harris to Early Grey, November 12, 1849, CO 295/168, 1849.

6. Lord Harris to Earl Grey, November 10, 1849, CO 295/168, 1849.

7. Fyodor Dostoevsky, *Crime and Punishment*, trans. Michael R. Katz (New York: Liveright Publishing Corporation, 2018), 570.

8. See Jean Fagan Yellin, introduction to Harriet Beecher Stowe, *Uncle Tom's Cabin* (Oxford: Oxford University Press, 1998), xvii.

9. The term "brutifies" or "brutifier" in French is defined as follows: "to make like a brute; or to make senseless or unfeeling, stupid or unfeeling." Douglass used the term "brute," or the capacity of slavery to transform a person into a brute, or a beast, several times in his *Narrative*. The word "brutifies" was used frequently in literature by writers such as Michel de Montaigne, Emile Zora, and Harriet Martineau, who wrote a historical romance about Toussaint L'Ouverture, *The Hour and the Man* (1841) ("Signifying Toussaint: Wordsworth and Martineau,"

European Romantic Review, 22, no. 3 [June 2011]: 335). Harriet Beecher Stowe, drawing on Douglass's work, says of an advertisement of George Harris's capture: "The Lord made 'em men, and it's a hard squeeze getting 'em down into beasts," *Uncle Tom's Cabin*, 112.

10. In her illuminating work, *Imagining Deliberative Democracy in the Early American Republic*, Sandra M. Gustafson observed that "oratory is the pre-eminent genre of republicanism, and many of the major formulations of modern republican thought were initially presented in orations like these [Bolivar, Lafayette, and Webster] which were later circulated in letters, newspaper accounts, and pamphlets, reaching national and international audiences" (284).

11. Robert Gildea, *Children of the Revolution: The French, 1799–1914* (London: Penguin, 2009), 7–8.

12. See Nemata Amelia Blyden, *West Indian in West Africa, 1808–1880: The African Disapora in Reverse* (Rochester: University of Rochester Press, 2000). Fitzjames, a man of mixed heritage (described himself as "colored man of African and European descent"), was a law student at Middle Temple. He was called to the English bar in 1847.

CHAPTER 43: A NEW CONSCIOUSNESS

1. See, for example, Gustave Louis Savary's response to Charles Warner, whom he felt had treated him in a demeaning way: "Recollect that I am your equal. So far as I am individually concerned, I could well afford to treat your words with the contempt they so well deserve. As for you, I look upon you as a dangerous and false man. . . . You smack, Sir, a little of the absolutism of Russia. A ten years residence in *England* taught me to abhor everything like oppression, a twelve years residence here, since my return, has not made me your sycophant, nor the base and degrading wretch—a spy—who worms the secrets from the bosom of his unsuspecting friend. The events which occurred here on the first of October last still haunt your fevered brain." Gustave Savary, "To the Honorary Charles Warner," *TR*, November 13 1849.

2. John Stauffer, *Giants: The Parallel Lives of Frederick Douglass and Abraham Lincoln* (New York: Twelve, 2008), xiii.

3. Acts 17:26 (King James Version).

4. J. J. Thomas, a Trinidad linguist of the nineteenth century, claims in *The Theory and Practice of Creole Grammar* (1869; repr. London: New Beacon, 1969) that the Creole spoken by the Trinidad native was mixture of French and African words.

5. Francine de Plessix Gray, introduction to Alexandre Dumas, *The Man in the Iron Mask*, trans. Joachim Neugroscell (London: Penguin, 2003), xii.

6. Tom Reiss, *The Black Count: Glory, Revolution, Betrayal and the Real Count of Monte Cristo* (London: Vantage, 2013), 248–49.

7. Ibid., 325.

8. Albert Camus, *The Rebel: An Essay of Man in Revolt*, trans. Anthony Bowen (New York: Vintage, 1991), 17.

9. Jean Fagan Yellin, introduction to Harriet Beecher Stowe, *Uncle Tom's Cabin* (Oxford: Oxford University Press, 1998), xii.

10. Frederick Douglass, *Narrative of the Life of Frederick Douglass: An American Slave* (Boston: Anti-Slavery Office, 1845), 54.

11. See Susan Buck-Morss, *Hegel, Haiti, and Universal History* (Pittsburgh: University of Pittsburgh Press, 2009), 61.

12. Jacey Fortin, "James H. Cone, a Founder of Black Liberation Theology, Dies at 79," *New York Times*, April 29, 2018.

13. See James Cone, *Black Theology and Black Power* (New York: Seabury Press, 1969), 6–7.

14. Camus, *The Rebel*, 22 (italics added).

15. Sudhir Hazareesingh, *How the French Think: An Affectionate Portrait of an Intellectual People* (UK: Penguin, 2015), 80.

16. Ibid., 58.

17. See Martin Bernal, *Black Athena: The Afroasiatic Roots of Classical Civilization, The Fabrication of Ancient Greece, 1785–1985*, vol. 1. (New Brunswick: Rutgers University Press, 1987).

CHAPTER 44: THE ISLAND OF BABEL

1. "After the British abolished slavery in 1807, the term captured Africans referred to enslaved Africans on foreign slave ships that were intercepted by the British Navy. They were then liberated and sent to Sierra Leone, St. Helena or the British Caribbean." Shantelle George, communication with the author, July 30, 2016.
2. Michael Toussaint, "Afro-West Indians in Search of the Spanish Main" (PhD diss., University of the West Indies, St. Augustine, Trinidad, 1999), 174.
3. Ibid., 162. Toussaint also argues that the 1850s saw a rise in "Afro-consciousness" among Trinidadians and a greater "awareness of their identity as British West Indian subjects."
4. Margaret D. Rouse-Jones, *The Colonial Correspondence, 1837–1885* (Newton, Port of Spain: Paria, 1986), 1.
5. Ibid., February 16, 1848, C/1848/4.
6. I suppose this is where the term "coppers" came into the Trinidad vocabulary to describe its currency; as the older folks used to say, "I only have a few coppers."

CHAPTER 45: FADING GLORY

1. Lord Harris to Earl Grey, CO 295/171, 1850.
2. Lord Harris to Earl Grey, CO 295/173, 1851.
3. Ibid.
4. Angelo Bissessarsingh, "Charles William Warner, CB," https//www.geni.com/people/Charles William Warner-CB/6000000002497436676. Sebastian Ventour explained, "A retainer is a fee a client pays to a lawyer to secure his or her services" (communication with the author, July 13, 2016).

CHAPTER 46: CESSATION

1. Protest against "An Ordinance for the Establishment of an Inland Post and Rates of Postage for the Colony," CO 295/171, 1850.
2. Ibid.
3. Ibid.
4. Lord Harris to Earl Grey, CO 295/173, 1851.
5. In Greek mythology Eurayle was depicted as one of the two immortal Gorgans. They had heads with snake scales, long teeth like pigs' tusks, bronze hands, and golden wings and were so ugly that they turned anyone who looked at them into stone. By calling Losh "Euriale," Des Sources, the author of the article, suggests that since Burnley was tough, Losh's job, as Burnley's "Euriale" was to scare people into doing what Burnley wanted (somewhat analogous to Donald Trump sending in enforcers if one did not agree to his terms) (Mary Lefkowitz, communication with the author, July 30, 2016). The remarkable thing about this exchange was the casual way in which the newspaper used this bit of Greek mythology in its commentary, the understanding being that readers would readily recognize what was meant.
6. Jose M. Bodu, *Trinidadiana* (Port of Spain: A. C. Blondel, 1890), 14.
7. Thomas Carlyle, *The French Revolution: A History* (London: Continuum, 2010), 193.

CHAPTER 47: RESURGAM

1. Eccles, Burnley and Co., a mercantile company whose concerns "were carried on by subscribers in Glasgow under the firm Robert Eccles & Company and in Greenock under George James Eccles were dissolved by mutual consent. . . . Sequestration of the company or copartnership carrying on business as merchants in Glasgow under the firms of Eccles Burnley & Co., and James and Eccles & Co., and in Greenock, as under the firm of George James Eccles, and as a company, and of John Roland, William Frederick Burnley, and Andrew Eccles, all

merchants in Glasgow and George James Eccles in Greenock, as partners thereof and as individuals" (Centre for the Study of the Legacies of British Slave-ownership, University College of London). In August 1848 when Losh, Spiers and Company went under, Roland intervened with William Rennie, to set aside to the bankruptcy of the company but was unsuccessful. See John Roland to C. A. Calvert, quoted in Margaret D. Rouse-Jones, *The Colonial Bank Correspondence, 1837–1885* (Newton, Port of Spain: Paria, 1986), August 16, 1848, C/1848/18.

2. Rouse-Jones, *The Colonial Bank Correspondence,* February 15,1851, C/1851/5.

3. Rouse-Jones, *Colonial Bank Correspondence,* March 1, 1851, C/1851/6.

4. Rouse-Jones, *Colonial Bank Correspondence,* March 15, 1851, C/1851/18.

5. Ibid.

6. Rouse-Jones, *Colonial Bank Correspondence,* May 16, 1851, C/1851/11.

7. "North American Wills Registered in London, 1611–1857: Burnley, William Hardin late of Trinidad and one of HM Council there but then of NYC" (PROB 11/2133).

8. "The Will of William Hardin Burnley, Esquire." *North American Wills Registered in London, 1611–1857,* PROB 11/2133. Peter Wilson Coldham, Genealogical Society, Baltimore, Maryland 2007, 15.

9. Ibid.

10. "The Will of William Hardin Burnley, Esquire."

11. See "Minute of Agreement Between William Frederick Burnley, merchant in Glasgow, on the one part, and William Burnley Hume of Trinidad, on the other part," Registrar General Office, Scotland, July 2, 1854. I am indebted to Gerard Besson for sending me this document.

12. Carlton Robert Ottley, *Slavery Days in Trinidad: A Social History of the Island from 1797–1838* (Diego Martin, Trinidad: C. R. Ottley, 1974), 64.

13. Ibid., 63.

14. J. G. Cotton Minchin, *Old Harrow Days* (London: Methuen, 1898), 190.

15. Ibid., 191.

16. Lord Palmerston, Burnley's fellow Harrovian, is reported to have loved Harrow to the last. In paying tribute to Lord Palmerston's love of Harrow, Minchin says of him: "*Dulces moriens reminiscitur Argos* [As he dies, he remembers his beloved Argos]" (Virgil).

17. Eaton Fanning, "Stet Fortuna Domus." "When Raleigh Rose a Gentleman's A-Bowling," Harrow Association, www.harrowassociation.com document.

18. Donald Wood, *Trinidad in Transition* (Oxford: Oxford University Press, 1986), 126.

19. Sudhir Hazareesingh, *How the French Think: An Affectionate Portrait of an Intellectual People* (New York: Basic Books, 2015), 54.

Index

SELWYN R. CUDJOE was born in Tacarigua, Trinidad, West Indies, where he received his early education. He attended Fordham University, Columbia University, and Cornell University, where he received his doctoral degree. He has taught at Fordham, Cornell, Ohio, and Harvard universities and Wellesley College, where he is a professor of Africana studies. He has held two distinguished chairs at Wellesley: the Margaret E. Deffenbaugh and LeRoy T. Carlson Professor in Comparative Literature and the Marion Butler McLean Professor in the History of Ideas. He has received several awards from National Endowment for the Humanities and the American Council of Learned Societies and is the author of *V. S. Naipaul: A Materialist Reading, Beyond Boundaries: The Intellectual Tradition of Trinidad and Tobago in the Nineteenth Century,* and *Caribbean Visionary: A. R. F. Webber and the Making of the Guyanese Nation.* He has also written for the *New York Times, Washington Post, New Left Review, Trinidad Express,* and other publications.